*Seventh Edition*

# MILSTEAD'S
# HEALTH POLICY
# *and* POLITICS
## A NURSE'S GUIDE

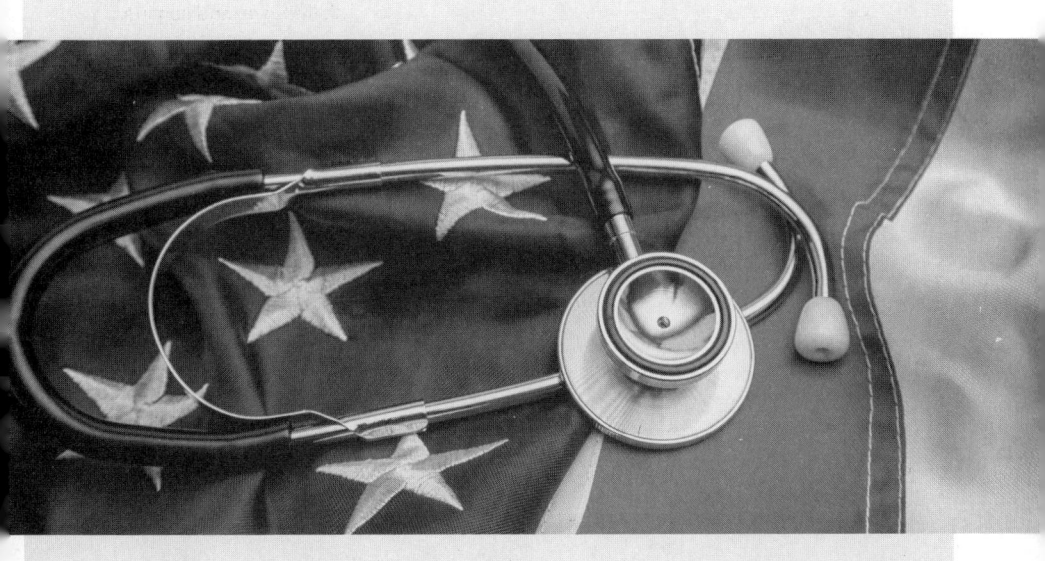

*Seventh Edition*

# MILSTEAD'S
# HEALTH POLICY
# *and* POLITICS
## A NURSE'S GUIDE

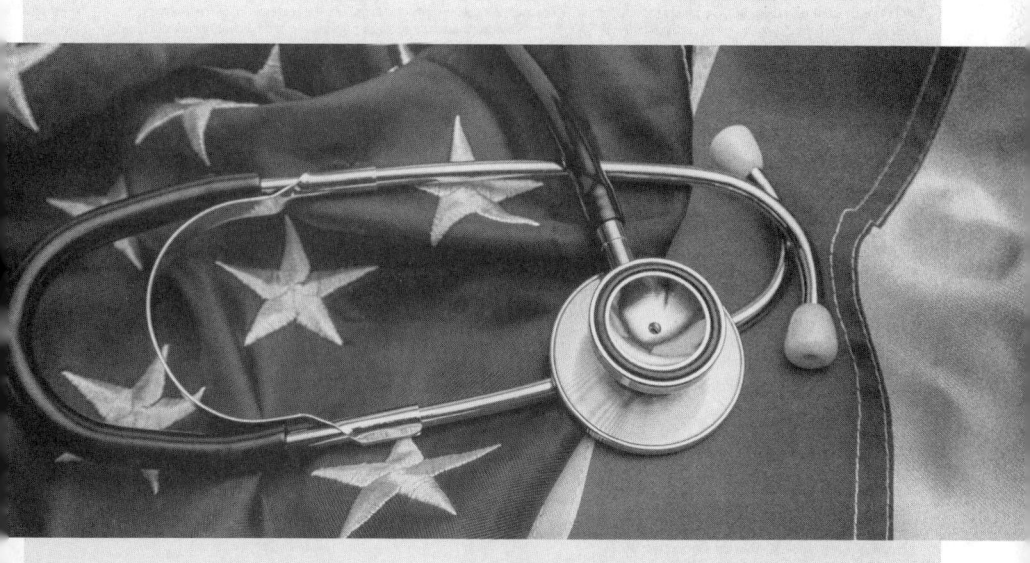

**NANCY M. SHORT, DrPH,
MBA, RN, FAAN**

Associate Professor Emerita
School of Nursing
Duke University
Durham, North Carolina

JONES & BARTLETT
LEARNING

World Headquarters
Jones & Bartlett Learning
25 Mall Road, Suite 600
Burlington, MA 01803
978-443-5000
info@jblearning.com
www.jblearning.com

Jones & Bartlett Learning books and products are available through most bookstores and online booksellers. To contact Jones & Bartlett Learning directly, call 800-832-0034, fax 978-443-8000, or visit our website, www.jblearning.com.

Substantial discounts on bulk quantities of Jones & Bartlett Learning publications are available to corporations, professional associations, and other qualified organizations. For details and specific discount information, contact the special sales department at Jones & Bartlett Learning via the above contact information or send an email to specialsales@jblearning.com.

Copyright © 2022 by Jones & Bartlett Learning, LLC, an Ascend Learning Company

All rights reserved. No part of the material protected by this copyright may be reproduced or utilized in any form, electronic or mechanical, including photocopying, recording, or by any information storage and retrieval system, without written permission from the copyright owner.

The content, statements, views, and opinions herein are the sole expression of the respective authors and not that of Jones & Bartlett Learning, LLC. Reference herein to any specific commercial product, process, or service by trade name, trademark, manufacturer, or otherwise does not constitute or imply its endorsement or recommendation by Jones & Bartlett Learning, LLC and such reference shall not be used for advertising or product endorsement purposes. All trademarks displayed are the trademarks of the parties noted herein. *Milstead's Health Policy and Politics: A Nurse's Guide, Seventh Edition* is an independent publication and has not been authorized, sponsored, or otherwise approved by the owners of the trademarks or service marks referenced in this product.

There may be images in this book that feature models; these models do not necessarily endorse, represent, or participate in the activities represented in the images. Any screenshots in this product are for educational and instructive purposes only. Any individuals and scenarios featured in the case studies throughout this product may be real or fictitious but are used for instructional purposes only.

The authors, editor, and publisher have made every effort to provide accurate information. However, they are not responsible for errors, omissions, or for any outcomes related to the use of the contents of this book and take no responsibility for the use of the products and procedures described. Treatments and side effects described in this book may not be applicable to all people; likewise, some people may require a dose or experience a side effect that is not described herein. Drugs and medical devices are discussed that may have limited availability controlled by the Food and Drug Administration (FDA) for use only in a research study or clinical trial. Research, clinical practice, and government regulations often change the accepted standard in this field. When consideration is being given to use of any drug in the clinical setting, the healthcare provider or reader is responsible for determining FDA status of the drug, reading the package insert, and reviewing prescribing information for the most up-to-date recommendations on dose, precautions, and contraindications, and determining the appropriate usage for the product. This is especially important in the case of drugs that are new or seldom used.

24604-9

**Production Credits**
VP, Product: Marisa Urbano
Director of Product Management: Matthew Kane
Product Manager: Tina Chen
Manager, Content Strategy: Carolyn Pershouse
Content Strategist: Paula-Yuan Gregory
Project Specialist: Erin Bosco
Digital Project Specialist: Rachel DiMaggio
Senior Marketing Manager: Jennifer Scherzay
Product Fulfillment Manager: Wendy Kilborn
Composition: S4Carlisle Publishing Services
Cover Design: Kristin E. Parker
Text Design: Kristin E. Parker
Senior Media Development Editor: Troy Liston
Rights Specialist: Maria Leon Maimone
Cover Image (Title Page, Part Opener, Chapter Opener):
 © Rclassenlayouts/iStock/Getty Images Plus/Getty Images.
Printing and Binding: LSC Communications

**Library of Congress Cataloging-in-Publication Data**
Names: Short, Nancy M. (Nancy Munn), author.
Title: Milstead's health policy and politics : a nurse's guide / author, Nancy M. Short.
Other titles: Health policy and politics (Milstead)
Description: Seventh edition. | Burlington, Massachusetts : Jones & Bartlett Learning, [2022] | Preceded by Health policy and politics : a nurse's guide / [edited by] Jeri A. Milstead, Nancy Munn Short. Sixth edition. [2019]. | Includes bibliographical references and index.
Identifiers: LCCN 2021014691 | ISBN 9781284228519 (paperback)
Subjects: MESH: Legislation, Nursing | Health Policy | Politics | Nurse's Role | United States
Classification: LCC RA425 | NLM WY 33 AA1 | DDC 362.17/3--dc23
LC record available at https://lccn.loc.gov/2021014691

6048
Printed in the United States of America
25 24 23 22 21    10 9 8 7 6 5 4 3 2 1

# Contents

List of Exemplars ........................................................ x
Preface ................................................................ xi
Letter from the Founding Editor ................................. xiii
Contributors ......................................................... xv
Reviewers ........................................................... xxiii

**CHAPTER 1 Informing Public Policy:
An Important Role for Registered Nurses ................... 1**
*Nancy M. Short*

Introduction ............................................................ 2
The Politics of Clinical Practice ..................................... 2
Policy Instruments .................................................... 4
Policy as a Process ................................................... 8
Public Policy, Political Determinants of Health,
 and Clinical Practice ............................................... 9
Why You Are the Right Person to Influence Health Policy ......... 13
Practice and Policy .................................................. 17
Organizational Involvement ....................................... 18
Taking Action ........................................................ 19
A Professional Nursing Workforce ................................ 19
Innovation in Health Care: Reform or Incrementalism? ........... 20
Developing a More Sophisticated Political Role for Nurses ........ 22
Working With the Political System ................................ 22
Conclusion ........................................................... 23

**CHAPTER 2 News Literacy ................................... 27**
*Cindy Vanek*

Introduction ......................................................... 28
Bias Within the Media ............................................. 28
How Do We Detect Bias? .......................................... 35
Personal and Cognitive Biases .................................... 37

Bias Within Health Care ........................................ 40
Strategies to Minimize Bias .................................... 44
Nursing's Obligation to Impact Bias Within Health Policy
    Development or Reform...................................... 45
Conclusion ..................................................... 49

## CHAPTER 3  Problem Identification and Agenda Setting: What Rises to a Policymaker's Attention? ........ 57
*Rick Mayes and Kenneth R. White*

Introduction ................................................... 58
Overview of Models and Dimensions .............................. 63
The Kingdon Model .............................................. 64
Importance of Contextual Dimensions............................. 67
Target Populations and Issue Characteristics ................... 68
Advocacy Coalition Framework.................................... 68
Path Dependency................................................. 68
Punctuated Equilibrium ......................................... 69
Litigation...................................................... 71
Conclusion ..................................................... 71

## CHAPTER 4  Policy Analysis and Design..................... 77
*AnnMarie L. Walton*

Introduction ................................................... 78
The Policy Design Process ...................................... 82
Research Informing the Policy Process........................... 83
Public Opinion Informing the Policy Process..................... 86
The Design Issue ............................................... 87
Policy Instruments (Government Tools)........................... 89
Behavioral Dimensions .......................................... 92
Conclusion ..................................................... 93

## CHAPTER 5  Policy Enactment: Legislation and Politics... 97
*Amy L. Anderson*
*With acknowledgment to the many contributions of Dr. Janice Lanier*

Introduction ................................................... 98
Structure of Government: Federal, State, and Local.............. 99
The Executive Branch ........................................... 99
The Legislative Branch ........................................ 102
The Judicial Branch............................................ 102
The Legislative Process........................................ 106

Funding Legislation: Winning a Seat at the Table . . . . . . . . . . . . . . . 108
Power: Who Has It? You Want It!. . . . . . . . . . . . . . . . . . . . . . . . . . . . . 108
Political Strategy . . . . . . . . . . . . . . . . . . . . . . . . . . . . . . . . . . . . . . . . . 114
Nurses Engaged in Legislative Policy Change . . . . . . . . . . . . . . . . . 115
Conclusion . . . . . . . . . . . . . . . . . . . . . . . . . . . . . . . . . . . . . . . . . . . . . . 116

## CHAPTER 6  Policy Implementation: Avoiding Policy Failure . . . . . . . . . . . . . . . . . . . . . . . . . . . . . . . . . . . . 121
*Leslie Sharpe*

Introduction . . . . . . . . . . . . . . . . . . . . . . . . . . . . . . . . . . . . . . . . . . . . . 122
Federal and State Policy Implementation 101. . . . . . . . . . . . . . . . . . 124
Conceptual Framework. . . . . . . . . . . . . . . . . . . . . . . . . . . . . . . . . . . . 126
Policy Implementation Research Versus
   Implementation Science . . . . . . . . . . . . . . . . . . . . . . . . . . . . . . . . 131
Power: What Is Needed to Get Policy Implemented? . . . . . . . . . . . . 132
Involving Nurses in Implementation. . . . . . . . . . . . . . . . . . . . . . . . . 135
Conclusion . . . . . . . . . . . . . . . . . . . . . . . . . . . . . . . . . . . . . . . . . . . . . . 135

## CHAPTER 7  Government Response: Regulation . . . . . . . . . . 147
*Julia L. George and Catherine Moore*

Introduction . . . . . . . . . . . . . . . . . . . . . . . . . . . . . . . . . . . . . . . . . . . . . 148
Health Professions Regulation and Licensing. . . . . . . . . . . . . . . . . 149
Regulation Versus Legislation . . . . . . . . . . . . . . . . . . . . . . . . . . . . . . 154
The Federal Regulatory Process. . . . . . . . . . . . . . . . . . . . . . . . . . . . 165
Conclusion . . . . . . . . . . . . . . . . . . . . . . . . . . . . . . . . . . . . . . . . . . . . . . 172

## CHAPTER 8  Health Policy and Social Program Evaluation . . . . . . . . . . . . . . . . . . . . . . . . . . . . . . . . . . . . . . . 177
*Anne Derouin*

Introduction . . . . . . . . . . . . . . . . . . . . . . . . . . . . . . . . . . . . . . . . . . . . . 178
Evaluation Processes . . . . . . . . . . . . . . . . . . . . . . . . . . . . . . . . . . . . . 180
Challenges to Effective Policy and Program Evaluation . . . . . . . . . 185
Conclusion . . . . . . . . . . . . . . . . . . . . . . . . . . . . . . . . . . . . . . . . . . . . . . 191

## CHAPTER 9  The Influence of Patient Health Data on Health Policy . . . . . . . . . . . . . . . . . . . . . . . . . . . . . . . . . . . . . 197
*Toni Hebda*

Introduction . . . . . . . . . . . . . . . . . . . . . . . . . . . . . . . . . . . . . . . . . . . . . 198
Data and Electronic Resources: Their Relationship
   to Health Care. . . . . . . . . . . . . . . . . . . . . . . . . . . . . . . . . . . . . . . . . 201

viii  Contents

Big Data: Its Significance for Healthcare Delivery and Policy . . . . . 201
The Relationship Between Evidence-Informed Practice
 and Big Data. . . . . . . . . . . . . . . . . . . . . . . . . . . . . . . . . . . . . . . . . . 211
Initiatives That Support Big Data . . . . . . . . . . . . . . . . . . . . . . . . . . . 211
Implications for RNs, APRNs, and
 Other Healthcare Professionals . . . . . . . . . . . . . . . . . . . . . . . . . 212
Conclusion . . . . . . . . . . . . . . . . . . . . . . . . . . . . . . . . . . . . . . . . . . . . . 217

## CHAPTER 10  Financing Health Care . . . . . . . . . . . . . . . . . . . . . . . . 227
*Nancy M. Short*

Introduction . . . . . . . . . . . . . . . . . . . . . . . . . . . . . . . . . . . . . . . . . . . . 229
Opportunity Costs and Normal Goods . . . . . . . . . . . . . . . . . . . . . . . 230
Does More Spending Buy Us Better Health?. . . . . . . . . . . . . . . . . . 231
Health Insurance . . . . . . . . . . . . . . . . . . . . . . . . . . . . . . . . . . . . . . . 232
The Individual Mandate and Penalties . . . . . . . . . . . . . . . . . . . . . . 238
Healthcare Entitlement Programs. . . . . . . . . . . . . . . . . . . . . . . . . . 239
Provider Payment Models. . . . . . . . . . . . . . . . . . . . . . . . . . . . . . . . . 243
Hospitals and Outpatient Reimbursement. . . . . . . . . . . . . . . . . . . . 245
Access to Care . . . . . . . . . . . . . . . . . . . . . . . . . . . . . . . . . . . . . . . . . 247
Disparities . . . . . . . . . . . . . . . . . . . . . . . . . . . . . . . . . . . . . . . . . . . . 250
Information Asymmetry in Health Care . . . . . . . . . . . . . . . . . . . . . . 251
Comparative Effectiveness Research
 and Quality-Adjusted Life-Years . . . . . . . . . . . . . . . . . . . . . . . . . 253
Bending the Healthcare Cost Curve Downward . . . . . . . . . . . . . . . 254
Policies to Watch . . . . . . . . . . . . . . . . . . . . . . . . . . . . . . . . . . . . . . . 255
Conclusion . . . . . . . . . . . . . . . . . . . . . . . . . . . . . . . . . . . . . . . . . . . . 257

## CHAPTER 11  The Impact of Nurse Influence on Global Health Policy . . . . . . . . . . . . . . . . . . . . . . . . . . . . . . . 263
*Jeri A. Milstead*

Introduction . . . . . . . . . . . . . . . . . . . . . . . . . . . . . . . . . . . . . . . . . . . 264
International Organizations. . . . . . . . . . . . . . . . . . . . . . . . . . . . . . . 265
Globalization, Immigration, and Migration. . . . . . . . . . . . . . . . . . . 267
Conclusion . . . . . . . . . . . . . . . . . . . . . . . . . . . . . . . . . . . . . . . . . . . . 271
Policy Exemplars Around the World. . . . . . . . . . . . . . . . . . . . . . . . . 274
Chapter Discussion and Summary Activity . . . . . . . . . . . . . . . . . . . 291

**CHAPTER 12  An Insider's Guide to Engaging in Policy Activities** .........................................**293**

*Nancy M. Short and Jeri A. Milstead*

Introduction ............................................... 293
Creating a Fact Sheet ....................................... 293
Contacting Your Legislators ................................. 294
What to Expect When You Visit Your Policymaker ............... 296
Preparing to Testify ........................................ 297
Participating in Public Comment Periods
  (Influencing Rule Making) ................................ 299
How to Write an Op-Ed ...................................... 301
Twitter as a Tool to Influence Policy and Politics................. 302
Growing From a Novice to an Expert in Policy and Politics ....... 306
Wielding Parliamentary Procedures to Influence Policy.......... 308
Money and Politics......................................... 310
For Serious Thought ....................................... 312
Recommended E-Subscriptions............................. 312
Influential Organizations Affecting Health Policy ............... 313

**Index** ............................................................ **315**

# List of Exemplars

**EXEMPLAR 11-1 The Impact of Nurses in the Policy Process in Italy**.........................................274
Alessandro Stievano, PhD, MSoc, MEd, FAAN, FFNMRCSI

**EXEMPLAR 11-2 Panama: Persistence Pays When You Have a Goal** ........................................277
Lydia Gordón de Isaacs PhD, MSN, BSN, RN

**EXEMPLAR 11-3 Empowering Women in Rural Villages in Rwanda: A Sustainable Model**.................278
Harriet A. Fields, EdD, RN

**EXEMPLAR 11-4 Nurse Involvement in Policy Decisions Affects Public Health in Croatia**...............282
Andreja Šajnić, MSN RN

**EXEMPLAR 11-5 Nurse Influence in Policy Decisions in Portugal** .........................................286
Miguel Padilha, PhD, RN, CRRN, PI-Tech4EduSim/CINTESIS

**EXEMPLAR 11-6 Continuing Nursing Education in Albania: Evolution and Future Prospects for Health Policy** ............................................288
Ippolito Notarnicola, PhD, RN

# Preface

This is a contributed text for healthcare professionals who are interested in expanding the depth of their knowledge about public health policy and in becoming more sophisticated in their involvement in the political and policy processes. The scope of the content covers the whole process of making public policy within broad categories of problem identification and agenda setting, policy analysis, strategy and policy development/design, policy adoption/enactment, and implementation of policy and evaluation of the programs spawned by policy. The primary focus is at the federal and state levels, although the reader can adapt concepts to the global or local level. Content is focused on the importance of three aspects of engagement for nurses and other health professionals: health policy advocacy, health policy analysis, and health policy research.

## Why a Seventh Edition?

With this seventh edition, we celebrate 22 years of serving instructors, students, health professionals and others both here in the United States and abroad. The *Seventh Edition* has an addition to the title: it is now **Milstead's** *Health Policy and Politics* in recognition of the founding editor of this widely used textbook, Dr. Jeri A. Milstead.

This edition introduces new authors with fresh perspectives—all of whom have a significant experiential basis for their health policy expertise. I heartily welcome Dr. Amy Anderson, Ms. Julie George, Dr. Rick Mayes, Dr. Catherine Moore, Dr. Cynthia Vanek, Dr. Annmarie Walton, and Dr. Kenneth White and delight in those who have continued as authors over the years: Dr. Leslie Sharpe, Dr. Anne Derouin, and, of course, Dr. Milstead.

New to this edition:

- A full chapter on discerning bias in resources and references as well as news and information literacy.
- New illustrations and a consistent layout to clarify key terms and ideas and to stimulate discussion via case studies.
- Sentinel references are now indicated by shading to help students comprehend the past and the trajectory of political science theories and research.

Example of shading of sentinel references:

> **References**
> AARP Public Policy Institute. (2021). *The future of nursing: Campaign for action.* Center to Champion Nursing. https://campaignforaction.org/about/leadership-staff/the-rwjf-and-aarp-partnership/.
> Aiken, L. H., Clarke, S. R., Cheung, R. B., Sloane, D. M., & Silber, J. H. (2003). Educational levels of hospital nurses and surgical patient mortality. *Journal of the American Medical Association, 290*(12), 1617–1623.
> Aiken, L. H., Cimotti, J. P., Sloane, D. M., Smith, H. L., Flynn, L., & Neff, D. E. (2012). Effects of nurse staffing and nursing education on patient deaths in hospitals with different work environments. *Medical Care, 49*(12), 1047–1053.
> Aiken, L. H., Sloane, D. M., Bruyneel, L., Van den Heede, K., Griffiths, P., Busse, R., Diomidous, M., Kinnunen, J., Kózka, M., Lesaffre, E., McHugh, M. D., Moreno-Casbas, M. T., Rafferty, A. M., Schwendimann, R., Scott, P. A., Tishelman, C., van Achterberg, T., & Sermeus, W. for the RN4CAST consortium. (2014). Nurse staffing and education and hospital mortality in nine European countries: A retrospective observational study. *Lancet, 383*(9931), 1824–1830.
> Brannon, V. (2018). Statutory interpretation: Theories, tools and trends. Congressional Research Service Report 45153. https://crsreports.congress.gov/product/pdf/R/R45153
> Centers for Disease Control and Prevention. (2020). Overview of CDC's policy process. U.S. Department of Health and Human Services. https://www.cdc.gov/policy/analysis/process/docs/cdcpolicyprocess.pdf

- Discussions of the concept of power and structural racism are new in this edition.
- A guide on how to use Twitter to influence health policy and politics.
- Significantly revised and updated chapters: Chapter 6, "Policy Implementation: Avoiding Policy Failure"; Chapter 7, "Government Response: Regulation," and Chapter 11, "The Impact of Nurse Influence on Global Health Policy."
- Includes updates and discussion of the 2020 elections.
- Answers for chapter discussion questions and case studies are available for instructors within the Navigate digital course materials from Jones & Bartlett Learning.

The sequence of the chapters is presented in a linear fashion, in accord with the Centers for Disease Control and Prevention's policy process model. However, readers will note immediately that the policy process in practice is not linear. The "stages" of policymaking do not just overlap, they often are inseparable. In the real world, policy problems and policy solutions frequently emerge together, rather than one after another. In defending their work, members of Congress love to repeat a quotation often (wrongfully) attributed to Otto von Bismarck: "If you like laws and sausages, you should never watch either one being made." In other words, the legislative process, though messy and sometimes unappetizing, can produce healthy, wholesome results. For health professionals who champion evidence-based decision making, political processes that lead to health policies can be a real challenge to understand.

# Letter from the Founding Editor

Perhaps you are wondering about the change in the title of the *Seventh Edition* of this book. The change is part of my succession planning. This book grew out of several coincidences (do you believe in coincidence?). When I moved in 1985 from my home state of Ohio to South Carolina to teach at Clemson University, I knew I would have to obtain a doctoral degree. At that time, there were only four PhD in nursing programs in the U.S. South, and with none in South Carolina; I had to choose a related field. Part of my former position included the role of lobbyist, and I found the whole experience fascinating. Working with legislators, lobbyists, and government officials opened my eyes to a whole new approach to nursing, although there was little focus in this area in nursing education at the time. I was fortunate to be less than 2 hours away from the University of Georgia that, at that time, had one of the top 10 programs in political science in the United States. By the time I graduated, Hilary Clinton was working to create a healthcare system at the national level and both health care and policy were at the top of the governmental agenda.

About this time, I discovered four other nurses with master's degrees in nursing who had earned PhDs in political science, and our dissertation research had been conducted on five different components of the policy process. A book was born. This theory-based, research-based textbook on health policy and nursing was the first of its kind in the profession and set a high standard for those that followed. There were very few resources for nurses at the time, and the book took root.

Over the years, authors retired or dropped off and we were fortunate to maintain our standard with new and seasoned experts and excellent writers from across the country. The original research became examples for case studies, and the political theory continued to provide a solid base for nursing practice. We moved through many editions, and the book has been sold in more than 20 countries (and on six of the seven continents!) and has become a standard in many nurse educational programs. It has been my pleasure to work with intelligent, committed, well-educated nurses and other professionals throughout the years who have shared their knowledge, expertise, and skills with readers. Their impact on the profession, on the policy process, and on the health of the nation has been awe-inspiring. They have led the way to an awakening within nursing of the power we wield and the importance of our participation beyond the bedside.

After five editions, I realized I needed to think about future versions and the leadership needed to continue the work. I canvassed the contributing authors about their interest in working with me in succession planning. Dr. Nancy Short

xiii

responded, and we arranged a face-to-face meeting. We spent a whole day getting to know each other personally, sharing our thoughts about what we wanted for the book: to educate, inspire, and motivate readers, especially graduate students and to make the connection between nurse practice, policy decisions, and politics, or the art of influence. We talked about content gaps we wanted to fill or enhance. We discussed ideas about how to keep the book alive for readers, such as including more case studies and interactive activities.

I valued Nancy's public health background and her education and experience in economics and finance and decided she would bring an expanded view to the focus of the book; she was a "good fit." We agreed that we would be co-editors and senior authors on the *Sixth Edition* and that Nancy would be the sole editor/author on the *Seventh Edition*. After 22 years of a successful textbook, the publisher decided to title the *Seventh Edition*, edited by Short, as **Milstead's Health Policy and Politics: A Nurses Guide**. I was delighted and very humbled.

I want to thank the publisher, Jones & Bartlett Learning, for their unstinting expertise and guidance. Their advice and support and the excellence of their staff have contributed immensely to the high standard of excellence, readability, and content integrity of this book. And we kept them happy by meeting their deadlines!

As always, I will put in a "plug" for the greatest group of cheerleaders anyone could ask for—my family. My four children and spouses: Kerrin (the late George) Biddle, Kevin Milstead and Gregg Peace, Joan and Nick Russell, and Sara and Steve Lott; my three grandchildren and spouses (well, George just got engaged): Sunny and Heath Nethers, George Biddle and Lindsay Lachowsky, and Matt and Cynthia Lott; and two great-grandchildren Colton and Gunner Lott. My siblings: Mary Lorane Davis, Dr. Lynne Boylan, Joe (Shirley) Boylan, and the late Jack (Nete) and Mike (Sandy) Boylan are just the best. I love you all dearly. My husband, Glenn, died at age 42 but always thought I could do anything and my late-in-life fiancé, Ed Salser, brought light into my life for three whole years. I wake up every morning and say, "I'm the luckiest woman I know."

So, *Health Policy and Politics* will continue to educate readers about the whole U.S. policy process from agenda setting to government response (usually legislation and regulation) to policy/program design, implementation, and evaluation. The book offers opportunities for research on different aspects of the policy process. We hope to excite readers and point out places in this fluid, nonlinear, "messy" process of decision-making where they can become involved actively, whether at the local, state, national, or global level. Nurses' voices must be heard—we are the largest component of the healthcare workforce globally and consistently are the most trusted among a wide range of professionals. There are so many occasions where nurse expertise can identify problems, critically think through the issues, and recommend solutions. Access to health care, health disparities, equity, discrimination and lack of diversity, cost, quality, professional scope of practice—all are issues in which nurses have a vested interest. Nurses will learn how to move from being novices to becoming more sophisticated spokespersons and patient advocates for nursing and health issues. We will continue and enhance Nightingale's legacy.

—*Jeri A. Milstead*

# Contributors

**Amy Anderson**, DNP, FAAN, is an Assistant Professor in the Harris College of Nursing and Health Sciences and an Assistant Professor and Health Policy & Advocacy Lead for the School of Medicine at Texas Christian University. Dr. Anderson is a Visiting Fellow at The Heritage Foundation in Washington, D.C. and a former International Council of Nurses Global Nurse Leadership Institute Policy Program Fellow.

With an exceptional nursing career spanning 25 years, Dr. Anderson is respected as a policy fellow, thought leader, and educator. Dr. Anderson's policy contributions include providing consultation, presentations, and workshops for the AARP Future of Nursing Campaign and the American Association of Nurse Practitioners. Her signatures include a conservative case for full practice authority, Title VIII funding, and healthcare workforce legislation. One of her most notable accomplishments was shifting the strategy and messaging in West Virginia to advance HB4334.

Dr. Anderson recently served as expert counsel for the National Coronavirus Recovery Commission on COVID-19. Dr. Anderson was an inaugural member of the Global Think Tank Townhall convened by the Think Tanks & Civil Societies Program of the Lauder Institute at University of Pennsylvania working on global policy solutions to the pandemic crisis. Her op-eds have been featured on Fox Business, The Daily Signal, Real Clear Health, *The Washington Times*, and *Tribune* line.

Dr. Anderson holds a BSN and MSN from Abilene Christian University and a Doctor of Nursing Practice from Texas Tech University Health Sciences Center. She is a fellow in the American Academy of Nursing.

**Anne Derouin**, DNP, APRN, CPNP, FAANP, is a Clinical Professor, Duke University School of Nursing. She also holds an appointment in the Division of Community and Family Medicine at Duke. She currently serves as Assistant Dean for the MSN Program. Prior to her role as Assistant Dean, she was Lead Faculty for the PNP-Primary Care/MSN program at Duke University School of Nursing. A full-time faculty member since 2011, she is a dual-certified pediatric nurse practitioner with more than 30 years' experience in pediatric nursing. She has strong ties to the Duke and Durham communities and has completed clinical service and research projects in Africa and Central America. She received her BSN in 1989 from the University of Michigan, master's degree in nursing in 2000 and a Doctor of Nursing Practice in 2010, both from Duke University.

Dr. Derouin is on the Executive Advisory Board for the Duke–Johnson & Johnson Leadership Training program and has served as a coaching circle mentor to Duke–J&J fellows since 2013. Dr. Derouin serves as the North Carolina Advocacy Chair for the National Association of Pediatric Nurse Practitioners (NAPNAP) and currently sits on the Executive Board of Directors. Considered an adolescent clinical expert, she is active in the Society of Adolescent Health and Medicine (SAHM), the American Academy of Nurse Practitioners (AANP), and is the co-chair for the Adolescent Special Interest Group of NAPNAP. She has participated in pediatric, school-based health and advanced nursing practice advocacy efforts at the state and federal levels and has been selected for advocacy fellowships for several professional organizations, including the School-based Health Alliance (formally National Assembly of School-based Health Centers), Nurse in Washington Internship (NIWI), Shot@Life (World Health Organization's global vaccine efforts), and as a Faculty Policy Intensive Fellow for the American Association of Colleges of Nursing (AACN).

**Julia L. George**, MSN, RN, FRE, has spent much of her nursing career in nursing regulation. She has 25 years of experience with the North Carolina Board of Nursing (NCBON) and has served as the Chief Executive Officer of NCBON since 2008. She holds a master's degree in nursing from the University of North Carolina at Chapel Hill and is a fellow in the National Council of State Boards of Nursing (NCSBN) Institute of Regulatory Excellence. Ms. George has been actively involved at both the national and international levels of nursing regulation. She served for 13 years on the Board of Directors for NCSBN and served as president of NCSBN from 2018–2020. Ms. George is also the recipient of the prestigious R. Louise McManus Award, given by NCSBN for individual leadership in regulatory excellence. During her terms as President-Elect and President of NCSBN, she served as a member of the International Nurse Regulatory Collaborative (INRC). The INRC is a group of nine international nurse regulators seeking to identify commonalities, promote research and influence policy to protect the public's health, safety, and welfare around the world.

Ms. George is known for her innovation in nursing regulation. She was instrumental in moving to a philosophy of "Just Culture," both in North Carolina and throughout the country. She has made numerous presentations throughout the country related to Just Culture in healthcare regulation. Ms. George has frequently served as a source of education and information for the North Carolina General Assembly in matters of health policy related to nursing.

**Toni Hebda**, PhD, MSIS, RN-BC, CNE, is Professor of Nursing at Chamberlain College MSN online program and co-author of *The Handbook of Informatics for Nurses and Healthcare Professionals*, now in its sixth edition. She has presented internationally and nationally on nursing informatics, and has practiced as a staff nurse and nursing instructor, in addition to her work in information services. She is nationally certified in nursing informatics through the American Nurses Credentialing Center. Dr. Hebda is a member of the American Medical Informatics Association, the American Nurses Association, Sigma Theta Tau

International, the American Nursing Informatics Association, and the Healthcare Information and Management Systems Society.

Dr. Hebda earned a PhD, MSIS, and MNEd from the University of Pittsburgh, a BSN from Duquesne University, and a diploma from Washington (PA) Hospital School of Nursing. The focus of her doctoral program was on higher education. Her dissertation examined the use of computer-assisted instruction among baccalaureate programs.

**Rick Mayes**, PhD, is a Professor of Public Policy in the University of Richmond's Department of Political Science and chair of the Health Studies program. He is also a Professor of Nursing at the University of Virginia. He earned his PhD at the University of Virginia in 2000 and a National Institute of Mental Health postdoctoral traineeship at the U.C. Berkeley School of Public Health in 2002. From 1992–1993, he worked on Medicaid policy in the White House for George H. W. Bush, and thereafter on health insurance and Medicare policy at the AARP during the Clinton administration's healthcare reform effort of 1993–1994. He is a graduate of the University of Richmond (BA, 1991), and he has taught international public policy and global health on Semester at Sea.

His writings have appeared in numerous prominent newspapers and journals, and he is the author of several books, including *Universal Coverage: The Elusive Quest for National Health Insurance* (2005, University of Michigan Press), co-author of *Medicare Prospective Payment and the Shaping of U.S. Health Care* (2008, Johns Hopkins University Press) with Robert Berenson, MD, and co-author of *Medicating Children: ADHD and Pediatric Mental Health* (2009, Harvard University Press) with fellow University of Richmond professors Catherine Bagwell and Jennifer Erkulwater.

His most enjoyable and rewarding professional experiences have involved taking groups of University of Richmond students to Peru, the Dominican Republic, Appalachia, and Acadia National Park in Maine on healthcare research and community service trips. His classes are popular and his teaching has been recognized with several awards. In 2013, students elected him to give the university's "Last Lecture."

**Jeri A. Milstead**, PhD, RN, NEA-BC, FAAN, is senior nurse consultant for public policy, leadership, and education. Dr. Milstead is Professor and Dean Emerita, University of Toledo College of Nursing, where she served for 10 years, was director of graduate programs at Duquesne University for 3 years, and a faculty member at Clemson University for 10 years. She is the founding editor and senior author of *Health Policy and Politics: A Nurse's Guide* that is sold in 22 countries (and on 6 of 7 continents) and the *Handbook of Nursing Leadership: Creative Skills for a Culture of Safety*. She has invited chapters in four other current nursing textbooks, has published in national and international journals, and was editor-in-chief of *The International Nurse* from 1995 to 2006 when the publication was retired. Dr. Milstead was a policy advisor in the Washington, DC office of Sen. Daniel K. Inouye (D-HI), was president of the State Board of Nursing for South Carolina, and held leadership positions in the State Nurses Associations in Ohio, Pennsylvania, and South Carolina. She is a fellow of the

American Academy of Nursing and a member of ANA/ONA and Sigma Theta Tau International. She is board-certified as a Nurse Executive-Advanced by the American Nurses Credentialing Commission.

Dr. Milstead has been honored with the Mildred E. Newton Distinguished Educator award (OSU College of Nursing Alumni Society) and the Cornelius Leadership Congress award (the ONA's "most prestigious" award). She has been recognized as a "Local Nursing Legend" by the Medial Heritage Center at OSU and has been inducted into the Ohio Senior Citizen's Hall of Fame and the Washington Court House (Ohio) School System Academic Hall of Fame. She was named a "Transformer of Nursing and Health Care" (Ohio State University College of Nursing Alumni Association) and as a "Pioneer" in distance education and a career achievement (University of Toledo). She has also received a Creative Teaching award (Duquesne University) and two political activism awards. From 2005 through 2008, she was appointed to the Toledo–Lucas County Port Authority, where she chaired the port committee and was a member of a trade delegation to China. She has conducted research or consultation in The Netherlands, Jordan, Nicaragua, and Cuba.

Dr. Milstead holds a PhD in Political Science with majors in public policy and comparative politics from the University of Georgia, an MS and BS, cum laude, in nursing from The Ohio State University, and a diploma from Mt. Carmel Hospital School of Nursing where she is a Distinguished Alumna and current member of the Board of Trustees.

**Catherine Moore**, PhD, MSN, BSN, RN, is a regulatory consultant and legislative liaison with the North Carolina Board of Nursing (NCBON). A chief function of Dr. Moore's role with the NCBON is to provide consultative and educational services to members of the North Carolina General Assembly, nurses, occupational regulators, healthcare education and practice communities, and the public. A recent example of this work is the 2019 legislation which included provisions to update the North Carolina Nursing Practice Act. Dr. Moore serves as co-chair for the NCBON research committee, which focuses on conducting research to enhance public protection. She is also a current participant in the National Council of State Boards of Nursing International Center for Regulatory Scholarship.

Dr. Moore has 18 years of nursing experience with a clinical background in neonatal intensive care. Prior to her role with the NCBON, she served on the North Carolina Nurses Association's staff leadership team as the Director of Nursing Practice and Education—a role that enhanced her skills in interprofessional collaboration and the development and facilitation of liaison relationships. Dr. Moore is a strong proponent of healthcare policies that promote access to care and the safe delivery of nursing services. She has published and presented on policies that impact utilization of nurses in the delivery of health care. Her dissertation research, which explored how stakeholders for nurse practitioner full practice authority determine the appropriate time to pursue legislative changes to nurse practitioner scope of practice regulations, was awarded the Sigma Theta Tau Gamma Zeta Chapter PhD Award for Excellence. Dr. Moore's professional interests include nursing regulation, nursing workforce, healthcare safety, healthcare policy, and interprofessional collaboration.

**Leslie Sharpe**, DNP, FNP-BC, is a Clinical Assistant Professor at University of North Carolina-Chapel Hill (UNC-CH) School of Nursing and Lead Faculty of the FNP Program. She served as the lead provider and manager of Sylvan Community Health Center in North Carolina. Dr. Sharpe facilitated the opening and ongoing growth of this school-based community health center with the goal of increasing access to health care. She educates nurse practitioners and nurses about actively engaging in advocacy efforts related to health policy and improving the health of North Carolinians. As chairperson of the NC Nurses Association's NP Council Executive Committee from 2011–2014, she represented nurse practitioners at state legislative political events and educated legislators and other stakeholders in health care about advanced practice registered nurse issues. She currently serves as the NP PAC co-treasurer. One of her passions is serving as a mentor for NPs in the legislative and advocacy arena; as such, she facilitates a "leadership circle" of local APRNs in the NC Research Triangle. Dr. Sharpe completed her DNP at Duke University.

**Nancy Munn Short**, DrPH, MBA, RN, FAAN, is Associate Professor, Emerita at Duke University School of Nursing in Durham, North Carolina, where she was on the faculty from 2003 to 2020, when she retired. From 2002 to 2006 she served as an Assistant Dean at the school. Dr. Short received the School of Nursing's Distinguished Teaching Award in 2010 and the Outstanding DNP Faculty award in 2017, 2016, 2015, 2013, 2011, and 2010 (the DNP program began in 2009) for her courses on health policy, comparative international health systems, transformational leadership, and health economics. In 2009, she was recognized as an Arnold J. Kaluzny Distinguished Alumnus by the UNC-CH Gillings School of Global Public Health. Dr. Short completed a postdoctoral fellowship as a Robert Wood Johnson Foundation Health Policy Fellow from 2004 to 2007. As a part of this fellowship, in 2005, she served as a Health Legislative Aide for U.S. Senate Majority Leader, Bill Frist. With Darlene Curley, she served as co-chair of a AACN Think Tank charged with making recommendations to the board regarding improving health policy education for nurses.

Dr. Short is nationally known as an advocate for public health. She has provided consultation to the UNC Public Health Management Academy, the UNC Institute for Public Health on international issues related to distance learning, and the Johnson & Johnson Nurse Leadership Program at Duke.

She served as a member of the Durham County (North Carolina) Board of Health. In 2014, she completed a 2-year tenure on the Board of Directors of the National Association of Local Boards of Health, where she specialized in the development of performance standards for the approximately 3,000 boards of health in the United States. Under the auspices of the U.S. Department of State, she delivered leadership and quality management training to a bicommunal (Turkish and Greek) program for nurses in Cyprus.

Dr. Short earned a Doctor of Public Health degree with a major in health policy and administration at the University of North Carolina's Gillings School of Global Public Health and a Master of Business Administration and a Bachelor of Science in Nursing from Duke University.

**Cindy Vanek**, DNP, RN, CNAA, decided she was going to do something in the field of medicine/nursing at the age of 9 after her father experienced a prolonged illness. That decision has culminated in 42 years dedicated to the profession of nursing. Dr. Vanek earned her Bachelor and Master of Science degrees in Nursing from the University of Rochester. She began her nursing career at the University's Strong Memorial Hospital in the field of pediatric nursing and led an effort to open Strong's Pediatric Intensive Care Unit, the first PICU in upstate New York, then and now part of the Golisano Children's Hospital at the University.

In search of warmer weather, Dr. Vanek and her family moved to Florida in 1980 where she became the Chief Nursing Officer for Good Samaritan Medical Center in 1984 and, in 1997, she led a process for her hospital to sign an affiliation agreement with a leading medical center in eastern United States. The medical center chosen for that affiliation was Duke University Medical Center and led to the creation of the Helen and Harry Gray Cancer Institute at Good Samaritan Medical Center in West Palm Beach, Florida. This also commenced a 24-year relationship exemplifying dedication to excellence in nursing practice and quality patient care between Dr. Vanek and the Duke Health System.

In 1999, Dr. Vanek became a Consulting Associate faculty member for Duke University's School of Nursing (DUSON). Within that appointment, Cindy helped DUSON's distance-learning students find quality clinical placements and mentors in West Palm Beach, and later in Vero Beach, Florida. Key to her role as faculty, were monthly trips to Duke that were primarily focused on aspects of cancer services that were needed in West Palm Beach. Those services included a Patient Support Program partnering cancer survivors with recently diagnosed patients, the first cancer research clinical trials program in West Palm Beach, a cancer genetics screening program, and an education program for oncology nurses to expand their knowledge and skills preparing them to sit for the oncology nursing certification exam. During this time, Dr. Vanek watched her two sons graduate from Duke University, served on the Board of Overseers for the Duke Cancer Institute and the Board of Advisors for Duke's School of Nursing, and developed an ardent love of Duke basketball.

In 2005, Indian River Medical Center recruited Dr. Vanek to Vero Beach, Florida, as Vice President, Chief Nurse Executive, and later as Senior Vice President/Chief Operating Officer. While there, Dr. Vanek led two Duke affiliations, one with the Duke Heart Center and another with Duke's Cancer Institute. It was also during this time that Dr. Vanek's desire to teach leadership skills to others grew and she enrolled in the Doctor of Nursing Practice program concentrating on Executive Leadership at American Sentinel University. She graduated summa cum laude and received her DNP degree in December of 2013. Her interest in and experience with health policy developed during these years as she advocated for health services within her healthcare system, community, and state. Dr. Vanek teaches leadership courses for Duke University's School of Nursing and Southern New Hampshire University.

**AnnMarie Lee Walton**, PhD, MPH, RN, OCN, CHES, FAAN, is a tenure-track Assistant Professor at the Duke University School of Nursing, in Durham, North

Carolina, where she teaches health policy and population health courses. In this role, she educates future nurse leaders to value and apply their expertise in quality, safety, and the patient experience, to consider social contributors to health, and encourages them to lead improvements in health and health care in our country. Prior to becoming a faculty member, Dr. Walton worked for 13 years in inpatient hematology/oncology in roles from Clinical Nurse I through Clinical Nurse IV and co-created the first nurse manager job share in the state of North Carolina. Dr. Walton's program of research centers on understanding and minimizing occupational exposure to carcinogens. She has been a leader in developing, advocating for, and implementing a North Carolina state law focused on safer hazardous drug handling. As a result of that work, and activities with the North Carolina Future of Nursing State Action Coalition, Dr. Walton was named a Breakthrough Leader in Nursing by the Future of Nursing Campaign for Action in 2014 and honored as the Oncology Nursing Society Health Policy and Advocacy Award winner in 2016. She became a fellow in the American Academy of Nursing in 2020. Dr. Walton feels passionately about nurses understanding and then bringing their expertise in quality, safety, and the patient experience to serve on boards and commissions and has done some avocational research on nurses' engagement on boards, commissions, and in elected positions. She was a co-chair for the sustainability workgroup of the National Nurses on Boards Coalition and cofounded the North Carolina Nurses Association's Nurses on Boards 2020 Council. She frequently speaks to local and regional audiences about board service. Dr. Walton earned her PhD in nursing from the University of Utah, a postdoctoral fellowship, MPH, and BSN from the University of North Carolina at Chapel Hill, and a BS from the University of Maryland College Park.

**Kenneth R. White**, PhD, AGACNP, ACHPN, FACHE, FAAN, is the UVA Health Professor of Nursing Emeritus at the University of Virginia School of Nursing. He is also Sentara Healthcare Professor of Health Administration, Emeritus, and Charles P. Cardwell, Jr. Professor, Emeritus, at Virginia Commonwealth University (VCU). Dr. White is also visiting professor at the Luiss Guido Carli University in Rome, Italy.

Dr. White received a PhD in health services organization and research from VCU, an MPH in health administration from the University of Oklahoma, and an MS in nursing from VCU and a post-master's acute care nurse practitioner certificate from the University of Virginia. He has more than 40 years of experience in healthcare organizations in clinical, administrative, governance, academic, and consulting capacities. Dr. White is a registered nurse, an adult-gerontology acute care nurse practitioner, a certified palliative care nurse practitioner, and a fellow and former member of the Board of Governors of the American College of Healthcare Executives and a fellow of the American Academy of Nursing. He is also a member of the board of the American Academy of Nursing and served a 4-year term as President-Elect (2019–2021) and President (2021–2023).

He is author of five editions of *The Well-Managed Healthcare Organization, Thinking Forward: Six Strategies for Highly Successful Organizations,* and *Reaching Excellence in Healthcare Management; Take Charge of Your Healthcare Management*

*Career: 50 Lessons That Drive Success; Boost Your Nursing Leadership Career: 50 Lessons That Drive Success*; and a contributing author to the books *Human Resources in Healthcare: Managing for Success, Managerial Ethics in Healthcare: A New Perspective*, and *Evidence-Based Management in Healthcare* (all published by Health Administration Press). Dr. White is also a contributing author to the books *Advances in Health Care Organization Theory* (Jossey-Bass), *Peri-Anesthesia Nursing: A Critical Care Approach* (Saunders), *On the Edge: Nursing in the Age of Complexity* (Plexus), and *Introduction to Health Services* (Delmar).

Dr. White has received American College of Healthcare Executive's James A. Hamilton Award (2012), Exemplary Service Award (2011), Distinguished Service Award (2009), Edgar C. Hayhow Award (2006), and two Regent's Awards (1999 and 2010). He has also received the Virginia Nurses Association award for Virginia's Outstanding Nurse (1999), the VCU President's Award for Multicultural Enrichment, and numerous teaching awards. He is the founding chair of ACHE's LGBTQ Forum. In 2019, Dr. White received ACHE's Gold Medal Award, its highest award for contributions to leadership in health care.

# Reviewers

Barbara Blozen, EdD, MA, RN, BC, CNL

Joseph F. Burkhard, DNSc, CRNA

Eileen K. Fry-Bowers, PhD, JD, RN, CPNP, FAAN

Oscar Daniel Lee, PhD, APRN-CNS, CNE

Joy Moss, MSN, RN

Kereen Mullenbach, MSN, MBA, PhD, RN

Gladeen Roberts-Margraf, RN, PhD, FACHE, NEA-BC

Celeste Shawler, PhD, PMHCNS-BC (Professor Emeritus)

Catherine Stiller, PhD, RN, CNE

Jean M. Truman, DNP, RN, CNE

Lisa Young, DNP, APN, FNP-BC

# CHAPTER 1

# Informing Public Policy: An Important Role for Registered Nurses

Nancy M. Short

## KEY TERMS

**Advanced practice registered nurse (APRN):** A registered nurse with an advanced degree in nursing, certified by a nationally recognized professional organization. The four types of APRNs are nurse practitioner (NP), clinical nurse specialist (CNS), certified nurse-midwife (CNM), and certified registered nurse anesthetist (CRNA).

**Canons:** Rules of thumb, or guidelines, typically used by courts to interpret and rule on disagreements between policy and public law.

**Healthcare provider professionals (HCPs):** Registered nurses, advanced practice registered nurses, physicians, pharmacists, dentists, psychologists, occupational and physical therapists, dieticians, social workers, and physician assistants, and others who are licensed or authorized by a state or territory to provide health care.

**Policy:** A consciously chosen course of action: a law, regulation, rule, procedure, administrative action, incentive, or voluntary practice of governments and other institutions.

**Policy process:** A process that involves problem identification, agenda setting, policy design, government/organizational response, budgeting, implementation, and evaluation of the policy.

**Political determinants of health (PDoH):** Political forces, ideologies, processes, and decisions that determine the health of individuals and populations.

**Political power:** Political and social sciences refer to executive, legislative and judicial powers. For our purposes, common types of governmental powers exerted on health professionals and health programs are coercive power, blocking power, and purchasing power, which influence what nurses can and cannot do as well as the environments in which nurses work.

**Politics:** The process of influencing the allocation of scarce resources.

**Public policy:** A program, law, regulation, or other legal mandate provided by governmental agents; also includes actual legal documents, such as opinions, directives, and briefs, that record government decisions.

**Rules and regulations:** Instructions authorized by specific legislation detailing the actions to be taken to implement that legislation. They are developed by government agencies, often with the assistance of experts such as registered nurses.
**Statutes:** Written laws passed by a legislative body. They may be enacted by both federal and state governments and must adhere to the rules set in the U.S. Constitution. They differ from common law in that common law (also known as case law) is based on prior court decisions.
**System:** Spelled with a capital "S," the U.S. healthcare delivery and finance system (usage specific to this text).
**system:** Spelled with a lowercase "s," a group of hospitals and/or clinics that form a large healthcare delivery organization (usage specific to this text).

# Introduction

In March 2020 the nursing profession was thrust into the national and global spotlight as the nature of "essential workers" gained momentum and meaning amid the COVID-19 pandemic (see **Figure 1-1**). Ironically, long before the emergence of the novel human coronavirus, 2020 had been designated as "The Year of the Nurse and Midwife" by the World Health Organization to honor Florence Nightingale's 200th birthday. The severity of the pandemic propelled nurses into high visibility as they invented new ways to use ventilating equipment, led public health efforts, found ways to preserve personal protective equipment (PPE), identified improvements in patient treatments (e.g., turning patients prone), and provided astounding examples of compassionate care day after day in the face of danger. Largely because of the 24-hour news cycle and social media, today nursing has momentum and a platform unlike any other time in its history. But is this really the case? Nurses have thought "Now is our time!" at other important moments in history.

# The Politics of Clinical Practice

Looking back to the 2010 Institute of Medicine[1] (IOM) report, *The Future of Nursing: Advancing Health, Leading Change*, nursing seemed positioned to gain more authority (or at least shed some "supervision"). The report examined how nurses' roles, responsibilities, and education should change to meet the needs of an aging, increasingly diverse population and to respond to a complex, evolving healthcare system. In response to the IOM report, the Robert Wood Johnson Foundation (RWJF) and the American Association for Retired People (AARP) launched a joint *Campaign for Action* that was soon translated into state-level activities (AARP Public Policy Institute, 2021). The *Campaign for Action* was crafted as a prescription for nurses to facilitate the nation's shift

---

[1] Important to note: The name of the Institute of Medicine was changed to the National Academy of Medicine in 2016.

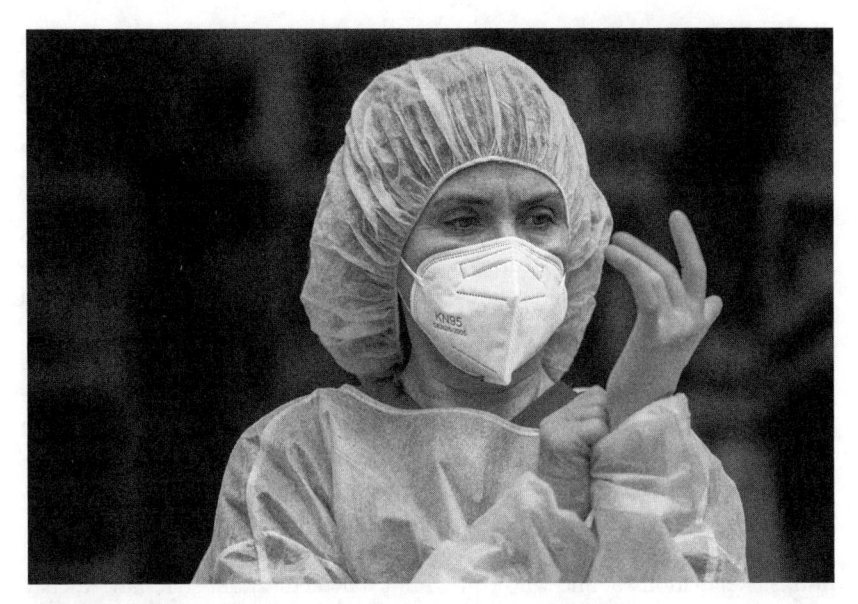

**Figure 1-1** Health policy and politics determines who gets personal protective equipment.
© Juanmonino/E+/Getty Images

from hospital-based services to a system focused on prevention and wellness in the community: nursing's time had arrived. It was a strong push that influenced nursing education and practice for a decade. The IOM report coupled with other evidence spurred changes in policy and practice, and in many ways positioned the profession to take advantage of its magnified voice in 2020.

A 10-year follow-up report card featuring two national nurse leaders, Drs. Sue Hassmiller and Mary Dickow, discussed significant gains in the nursing profession, including a dramatic increase in the number of registered nurses (RNs) with bachelor's degrees; the removal of many barriers to nurse practitioner (NP) practice in many states and the Veteran's Administration system; improvements in the percentage of minority students entering nursing, along with an emphasis on improving diversity and inclusivity; and success in placing more RNs on healthcare governance boards (Stringer, 2019).

This progress has spurred the RWJF to fund a second study focused on the future of nursing. This time the focus is on the nurse's role in addressing the social determinants of health and health equity. Dr. Hassmiller, who served as the National Academy of Medicine Senior Scholar in Residence and Adviser to the President on Nursing from 2019 to 2021, was tapped to lead the study. The RWJR report will be completed and distributed in 2021.

Nursing practice—that is, what we are allowed to do, required to perform, or prohibited from engaging in—is determined by **public policy**. Thus, nursing practice is a highly political activity. Policy is the end result of the process used to discover the best solution to an identified social problem. Politics is the process of this discovery—the dickering about values, ideology, and costs.

This text is framed around the **policy process** and is best read by progressing from beginning to end. Nurses and other **healthcare provider professionals (HCPs)** are ideally positioned to participate in the policy arena because of their history, education, practice, and organizational involvement. In this chapter, *policy* is an overarching term used to define both an entity and a process. The purpose of public policy is to direct problems to the government's attention and to secure the government's response. Not all health and healthcare issues require a government response: some are best resolved by volunteers, philanthropy, or professional organizations. In this text we will explore what rises to the level of public policy.

The definition of *public policy* is important because it clarifies common misconceptions about what constitutes policy. In this text, the terms *public policy* and *policy* are used interchangeably. The process of creating policy can be focused on many areas, most of which are interwoven. For example, environmental policy deals with determinants of health such as hazardous materials, particulate matter in the air or water, and safety standards in the workplace. Education policies are more than tangentially related to health—just ask school nurses. Regulations define who can administer medication; state laws dictate which type of sex education can be taught. Defense policy is related to health policy when developing, investigating, or testing biological and chemical weapons. There is a growing awareness of the need for a health-in-all-policies approach to strategic thinking about policy.

Health policy directly addresses health problems and is the specific focus of this text. In general, **policy** is a consciously chosen course of action: a law, regulation, rule, procedure, administrative action, incentive, or voluntary practice of governments and other institutions. By comparison, **politics** is the process of influencing the allocation of scarce resources. See **Table 1-1** for an explanation of the ideology and priorities of the five major political parties in the United States.

## Policy Instruments

Official government policies reflect the beliefs and values of elected Members, the administration in power, and the will of the American people. Laws (or **statutes**) are one type of policy instrument that serve as legal directives for public and private behavior. Laws are made at the international, federal, state, and local levels and are considered the principal source in guiding conduct. Lawmaking usually is the purview of the legislative branch of government in the United States, although presidential vetoes, executive orders, and judicial interpretations of laws also have the force of law.

Policy instruments at the level of national governance include, but are not limited to, the following:

- *Bills*: A bill is proposed legislation under consideration by a legislative body (i.e., the U.S. Senate or the House of Representatives).
- *Act*: An act is legislation that has passed both houses of Congress and has been either approved by the president or has passed Congress over his veto, thus becoming law. Also known as a *statute*.

## Table 1-1  Political Parties in the United States and Their Ideological Perspectives

| Democratic | Republican | Libertarian | Green | Constitution |
|---|---|---|---|---|
| ■ Raise incomes and restore economic security for the middle class.<br>■ Create good-paying jobs.<br>■ Fight for economic freedom and against inequality.<br>■ End systemic racism.<br>■ Guarantee civil rights (especially for vulnerable groups).<br>■ Protect voting rights.<br>■ Secure environmental justice.<br>■ Ensure the health and safety of all Americans. | ■ Preserve the U.S. Constitution.<br>■ Require a balanced budget for the federal government.<br>■ Repeal and replace the Affordable Care Act.<br>■ Maintain a strong military.<br>■ Make America energy independent.<br>■ Secure U.S. borders.<br>■ Promote hard work to end poverty.<br>■ Promote family.<br>■ Promote religious liberty. | ■ Protect civil liberties.<br>■ Encourage noninterventionism.<br>■ Promote laissez-faire capitalism.<br>■ Abolish the welfare state.<br>■ Keep government to a minimum.<br>■ Ensure that the role of government is to protect the rights of every individual, including the rights to life, liberty, and property. | ■ Ensure protection of the environment.<br>■ Promote nonviolence and antiwar positions.<br>■ Decentralize wealth and power to promote social justice.<br>■ Encourage grassroots democracy.<br>■ Promote feminism and gender equity.<br>■ Encourage respect for diversity and promote LGBT rights.<br>■ Focus on community-based economics.<br>■ Promote personal and global responsibility.<br>■ Encourage a future focus and sustainability.<br>■ Acknowledge ecological wisdom. | ■ Restore honesty, integrity, and accountability to government.<br>■ Limit the federal government only to those roles outlined in the U.S. Constitution; the best government is local government.<br>■ Restore "true capitalist" principles to U.S. economic policies. |

© Matt Trommer/Shutterstock.  © Hafakot/Shutterstock.

- *Executive orders*: An executive order is an instruction issued by the president that is used to direct the actions of the executive branch and has the effect of law. Executive orders are given numbers and are abbreviated as EO.###. Executive orders may amend earlier orders.
- *Presidential directive*: A presidential directive is a specific type of executive order that states the executive branch's national security policy and carries the force and effect of law that states requirements for the actions of the executive branch.
- *Rules and regulations*: **Rules and regulations** are the guidelines or instructions for doing something correctly and are the principles that govern the conduct or behavior of a person or organization. The primary difference between a rule and a regulation is that a rule is not legally binding, whereas a regulation is. These two terms are often erroneously used as synonyms.
- *Resolution*: A resolution is a form of legislative measure introduced and potentially acted upon by only one congressional chamber and is used for the regulation of business only within the chamber of origin. Depending on the chamber of origin, they begin with a designation of either H.Res. or S.Res.
- *U.S. Code*: All federal laws passed by the U.S. Congress are codified (included) into the U.S. Code for reference. The U.S. Code is divided by subject area into 50 sections called *titles*. Each title is then divided into chapters, subchapters, parts, sections, paragraphs, and clauses. U.S. Code references are written as follows:

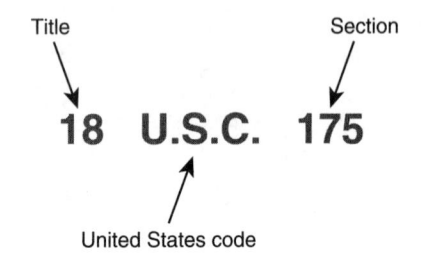

Title → 18 **U.S.C.** 175 ← Section
↑
United States code

Additional commonly used terms, such as *position statement, resolution, goal, objective, program, procedure, law,* and *regulation,* are not really interchangeable with the word *policy*. Rather, they are the formal expressions of policy decisions.

Several tools can be used to help determine the meaning of an ambiguous statute or to recognize the multiple plausible interpretations of a statute. These tools fall into the following four categories: (1) the text of the statute, (2) legal interpretations of the statute, (3) the context and structure of the statute, and (4) the purpose of the statute. Because laws are formatted and written in "legislative language," they are often difficult to read or understand. **Table 1-2** describes two commonly used **canons** of public law.

The agency assigned to interpret a particular law may have difficulty interpreting the law due to the speed with which some laws are passed and the nature of legislative language. Sometimes the interpretation of a law is legally challenged in the court system. Judicial interpretation of public law occurs in four ways: (1) through the court's interpretation of the meaning of broadly written laws that are vague regarding details; (2) by the court determining how some laws are applied, that is, by resolving questions or settling controversies; or (3) by the court interpreting the Constitution and declaring a law unconstitutional, thereby nullifying the entire statute; and (4) by the court resolving conflicts between states and the federal government (Brannon, 2018). Judicial decisions about statutes are generally the final word on statutory meaning and will determine how a law is carried out—at least, unless Congress acts to amend the law. The legitimacy of any particular statutory interpretation is often judged by how well it carries out the will of the legislative body that generated it. For example, aspects of the Affordable Care Act (ACA) have been challenged many times in the judicial branch. Three of these challenges have been heard by the U.S. Supreme Court.

**Table 1-2** Functions of Commonly Used Canons of Legislation Language

| Terminology | Function Served |
| --- | --- |
| **And** versus **or** | "And" typically signifies a list, meaning that each condition in the list must be satisfied, whereas "or" typically signifies a disjunctive list, meaning that satisfying any one condition in the list is sufficient. |
| **May** versus **shall** | "Shall" indicates that a certain behavior is mandated by the statute, whereas "may" grants discretion to the agency charged with implementing the law. |

**Spotlight:** The Patient Protection and Affordable Care Act of 2010 in the U.S. Supreme Court

***National Federation of Independent Business v. Sebelius (Sec. of HHS)* (2012).** In its 2012 ruling, the Court upheld the constitutionality of the ACA's individual mandate, which required most people to maintain a minimum level of health insurance coverage to begin in 2014. However, the Court found that the ACA's Medicaid expansion mandate was unconstitutionally coercive of states, and held that this issue was fully remedied by limiting the enforcement authority of the Health and Human Services Secretary. The ruling left the ACA's Medicaid expansion intact in the law, but the practical effect of the Court's decision made Medicaid expansion optional for individual states.

***King et al. v. Burwell (Sec. of HHS)* (2014).** David King did not want to buy health insurance. The 64-year-old Vietnam veteran worked as a limo driver and made $39,000 a year, and if it weren't for the subsidies (in the form of tax credits) afforded him by the ACA, King would not be able to, or have to, buy health insurance. King and three others filed a lawsuit against the government arguing that subsidies were supposed to be only for those purchasing health care through state-run health exchanges, not the federal one. The case focused on four words: "established by the State." Thirty-four states had

*(continues)*

opted against establishing exchanges under the Affordable Care Act, instead allowing residents to purchase health care through HealthCare.gov, the federal marketplace. The plaintiffs' suit argued that subsidies/tax credits were only for people purchasing health care on exchanges "established by the State." Although the legislative language of the ACA pertaining to the tax credits only referred to the exchanges established by the states, the Internal Revenue Service created a regulation that made the tax credits available to those enrolled in plans through federal as well as state exchanges.

The Court held that Congress did not delegate the authority to determine whether the tax credits are available through both state-created and federally created exchanges to the Internal Revenue Service, but the language of the statute clearly indicates that Congress intended the tax credits to be available through both types of exchanges. When the plain language of the section in question is considered in the context of the statute as a whole, it is evident that the federally created exchanges are not meaningfully different from those created by the states, and therefore federally created exchanges are not excluded from the language referring to exchanges created by the states (Oyez, 2014).

*California v. Texas* (2020). In 2018 the Republican-controlled Congress enacted an amendment to the ACA that set the penalty for not buying health insurance at zero. Texas and several other states and individuals filed a lawsuit challenging the individual mandate to purchase insurance, arguing that because the penalty was zero, it could no longer be characterized as a tax, and was therefore unconstitutional. California and several other states joined the lawsuit to defend the individual mandate. Arguments were heard in November 2020, and the decision is expected to be released in summer 2021. Questions to be answered include: (1) Is the individual mandate of the ACA, which now has a penalty of zero for not buying health insurance, now unconstitutional? (2) If the individual mandate is unconstitutional, is it severable from the remainder of the ACA? The result of this case may overturn the ACA, in effect repealing it (Oyez, 2020).

## Policy as a Process

For the purposes of understanding just what policy is, it is best to think in terms of policy as a process. Policymaking comprises six processes that are conducted within the context of stakeholder engagement and education (see **Figure 1-2**):

1. Problem identification and agenda setting
2. Policy analysis
3. Policy design
4. Policy enactment
5. Policy implementation
6. Evaluation of policy outcomes

This text discusses the six steps of the policy process. Note that the steps in the policy process are not necessarily sequential or logical. For example, the definition of a problem, which usually occurs in the agenda-setting phase, may change during fact-finding and debate. Program design may be altered significantly during implementation. Evaluation of a policy or program (often considered the last phase of the process) may propel onto the national agenda

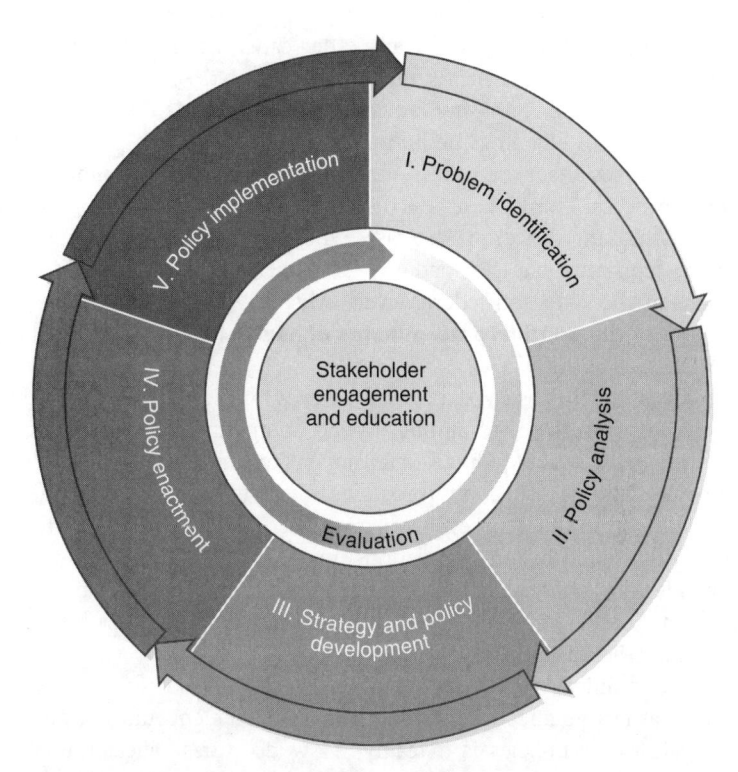

**Figure 1-2** The policy process.
Centers for Disease Control and Prevention. (2012). Overview of CDC's Policy Process. Atlanta, GA: Centers for Disease Control and Prevention, U.S. Department of Health and Human Services. Retrieved from https://www.cdc.gov/policy/analysis/process/

(often considered the first phase of the process) a problem that differs from the originally identified issue. For the purpose of organizing one's thoughts and conceptualizing the policy process, we will examine the policy process from a linear perspective in this text, but it is important to recognize that this path is not always strictly followed.

Opportunities for health professionals' input throughout the policy process are unlimited. Nurses are articulate experts who can address both the rational shaping of policy and the emotional aspects of the process. Nurses cannot afford to limit their actions to monitoring bills; they must seize the initiative and use their considerable collective and individual influence to ensure the health, welfare, and protection of the public and healthcare professionals.

# Public Policy, Political Determinants of Health, and Clinical Practice

In our basic education as nurses and HCPs, we learned about the social determinants of health (SDoH) as the root causes of good or bad health. But what are the drivers of the SDoH? In general, the drivers of the SDoH are political decisions; therefore, the causes of health and of disease/illness are driven as much by policy and politics as by any other cause. These political determinants of health do not get nearly the attention they deserve from the health professions. Yet, there is nothing radical in acknowledging the part played by political choices in affecting the nation's health; indeed, the premise of this text is that nurses affect the health of populations through their influence on the policy process. Think of areas as disparate as vaccines, air quality, seat belt safety, and smoking cessation—all cases where the public's health was better off for the legislative choices made by lawmakers, political appointees, and politicians at the state and federal levels (Mishori, 2019). See **Figure 1-3** for a depiction of the **political determinants of health (PDoH)** as envisioned by Ranit Mishori (2019).

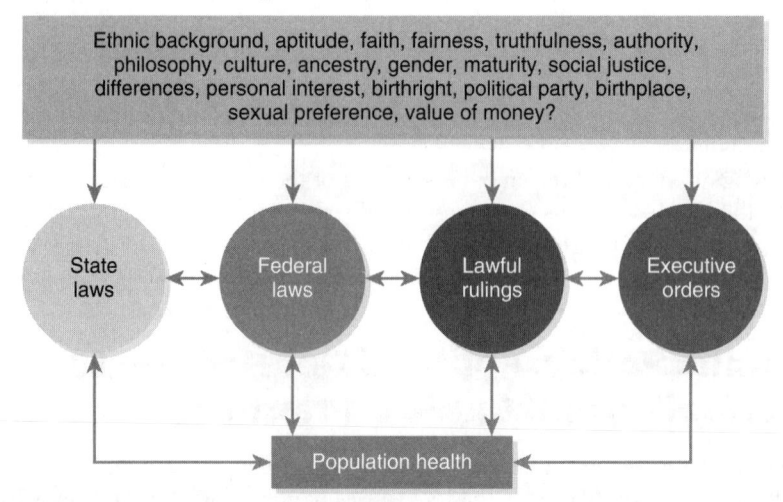

Health is largely based on political choices, and politics is a continuous struggle for resources/power among myriad competing interests. Looking at health through the lens of political determinants means analyzing how different power constellations, institutions, processes, interests, and ideological positions affect health within different levels of governance. Health is political: health is unevenly distributed in our populations, many social determinants of health are dependent on political action, and health is a critical dimension of human rights, even though there is no "right" to health care guaranteed within the U.S. Constitution (Kickbusch, 2015).

"Lack of political will" is often cited as the main reason for failing to deal with political factors affecting health. How do nurses encourage a culture in which health-in-all-policies is a reality? How do nurses affect the political will of our nation? Nurses can engage in health policy analysis, health policy advocacy, and health policy research (often referred to as health services research). Sometimes it is difficult to discern any difference between advocacy

**The political determinants of health**

Ethnic background, aptitude, faith, fairness, truthfulness, authority, philosophy, culture, ancestry, gender, maturity, social justice, differences, personal interest, birthright, political party, birthplace, sexual preference, value of money?

State laws ↔ Federal laws ↔ Lawful rulings ↔ Executive orders

Population health

**Figure 1-3** The political determinants of health.
Data from Mishori, R. (2019). The social determinants of health? Time to focus on the political determinants of health!. *Medical care*, 57(7), 491-493.

and analysis. This text will help you distinguish among advocacy, analysis, and research in health policy.

Legislation, along with rules and regulations, are the upstream causes that affect most aspects of our health, with the list being too exhaustive to include here. For example, downstream effects of reproductive health laws, such as the content of sex education in public schools, influence teen pregnancy as well as infant and maternal mortality rates; natural disaster planning and preparation results in downstream health effects of who lives and dies during a catastrophic event; the apportionment of parks and recreational spaces provides or disallows safe play spaces for children; the chemicals included in our water systems prevent dental caries or poison us; corporate oversight results in clean air or polluted air; a declaration of war determines what is spent on the military versus on schools and clinics; and so on. At this point, you may be wondering if there is anything related to health and health systems that is not affected by politics and policy. In a 2015 editorial in the *British Medical Journal*, Kickbusch wrote, "Health is a political choice and politics is a continuous struggle for power among competing interests." So why aren't these determinants of health taught broadly in health professionals' education? The main challenge for creating the field of "political epidemiology" lies in creating opportunities, either by design or in the analysis, to identify causal effects of political variables on population health. As stated by Mackenbach (2014):

> Overcoming this challenge will require ingenuity, as well as some stealing from other disciplines (such as comparative political science). Combining quantitative approaches, such as econometric techniques for evaluating natural experiments, with qualitative studies to reconstruct the causal pathways leading all the way from upstream politics to downstream health, is also likely to be useful. (p. 2)

Most of us have been educated and acculturated to believe that an individual's health is largely the result of personal choices and behaviors; however, during the COVID-19 pandemic we saw that government planning, preparation, funding, and policies had a huge effect on the health of individuals and populations, with some nations faring much better than others. **Case Study 1-1** provides the opportunity to further delve into the direct relationship between health policy and clinical practice.

## CASE STUDY 1-1: Legislation to Address Health Professional License Portability During a Public Health Emergency: It's All in the Details!

Regulating the practice of nursing (and other health professions) is accomplished at the state level. In the early days of the COVID-19 pandemic, patients turned to telehealth to continue receiving care from the safety of their homes. At the same time, states that were being hardest hit by the virus were beginning to experience provider shortages, especially nurses, forcing hospitals and health systems to seek assistance from professionals from other states. In August 2020, bills were introduced in Congress that were aimed at improving access to care through provider mobility and interstate telehealth by allowing providers to practice anywhere in the country with one state license—with some critical exceptions.

"The Nurse Licensure Compact (NLC) and other interstate compacts allow providers in many states to quickly relocate or reach patients using telehealth. However, the response during the COVID-19 pandemic was slow in states that had not already joined compacts, a complication that was at least partially due to lack of health provider license portability. In response to the growing COVID-19 crisis, governors across the country issued executive orders waiving state licensing requirements for healthcare providers, allowing providers to deliver in-person and telehealth services outside of their states of licensure in order to improve patient access to care. However, many stakeholders argued that these changes were happening too slowly and were inconsistent from state to state, complicating telehealth responses to patients from out of state. A number of healthcare advocates began to urge the federal government to intervene and pre-empt state licensing laws, allowing providers to practice across state lines as long as they had one state license. However, as many discovered for the first time, the federal government does not currently possess the legal authority to do so" (NCSBN, August 21, 2020).

In response to this problem, Members of Congress introduced a number of bills that would temporarily allow providers to practice across state lines when a Public Health Emergency has been declared:

- *Equal Access to Care Act (S.3993)*: This bill was introduced in the U.S. Senate on June 17, 2020, to allow healthcare providers to deliver telehealth services in any U.S. jurisdiction with only one license. If this bill had become law, it would have legally pre-empted the Nurse Licensure Compact and other compacts with regard to the location of care during telehealth interactions. The National Council of State Boards of Nursing (NCSBN) opposed the bill.
- *Temporary Reciprocity to Ensure Access to Treatment (TREAT) Act (S.421)*. The TREAT Act was introduced in the Senate on August 4, 2020. A companion bill (H.R.8283) was introduced in the House of Representatives on September 17, 2020. These bills provided for the temporary licensing authority for healthcare professionals to practice in-person or via telehealth anywhere in the United States with a license in good standing in only one jurisdiction during a period where both a Public Health Emergency has been declared by the secretary of Health and Human Services (HHS) and a national emergency has been declared by the president. The temporary licensing would remain in effect for up to 180 days after the emergency period concluded. When practicing telehealth, healthcare professionals would be required to follow the practice laws and regulations in their jurisdiction of licensure, not the jurisdiction where the patient is located.

    Unlike the Equal Access to Care Act, the TREAT Act addressed concerns related to state-based licensure, discipline, and the NLC through the addition of three critical provisions in Section 4 of the bill:
    - *Subsection (f): Investigative and Disciplinary Authority.* This provision would allow jurisdictions to investigate and take disciplinary action against a provider by preventing them from practicing in their jurisdiction, and then require such as preclusion to be reported to the licensing authority in the provider's state of licensure.

- *Subsection (g): Multiple Jurisdiction Licensure.* This provision would require a provider to follow the practice laws and regulations in the jurisdiction where the patient is located if the provider holds a license in that jurisdiction, alleviating legal confusion about which license would apply in these situations.
- *Subsection (h): Interstate Licensure Compacts.* This provision would exempt providers who hold a multistate license or privilege to practice in multiple jurisdictions through an interstate compact from being subject to this bill.

The inclusion of these provisions better preserves state-based public protection regulatory models and addressed federal legislation's inherent legal conflicts with the NLC and other compacts. In response to the provisions included, the NCSBN remained neutral on the TREAT legislation.

This case study reminds us of the need for constant vigilance to ensure that nursing avoids the unintended consequences of well-intended public policies.

# Why You Are the Right Person to Influence Health Policy

When we think of **political power**, we may think of how people, governments, and powerful groups may compel us to do things or even to think a certain way. This sort of power is known as *coercive power*. Coercive power is typically exercised by parents over children. It is also exercised by laws such as those establishing a minimum drinking age for purchasing alcohol or tobacco products or permitting underage marriage only with the consent of a parent or guardian. The second type of power important for nurses to understand is *blocking power*. This type of power has also been referred to as *negative decision power*. Blocking power is used to prevent issues from rising to legislative attention either by limiting an issue from getting on the agenda or by relegating it to a low priority on the agenda. Impeding or limiting policy and social choices has been studied much less than coercion. Examples of blocking power include the political gridlock we typically see around the annual federal budget process based on the use of congressional rules to create a stalemate and control of information flow. Google has been said to be the world's largest censor by blocking access to millions of websites (Epstein, 2016). A third type of power affecting health programs and systems is *purchasing power*. The best example of this in the healthcare arena is the purchasing power of the federal Medicare program, which determines reimbursement rates for healthcare providers.

Influence and power may also be gained from the strategic use of social media or from the 24-hour news cycle (**Figure 1-4**). The COVID-19 pandemic catapulted nurses and other essential workers into the limelight, providing the nursing profession with a voice that is not usually available.

Nursing's education requirements, communication skills, rich history, leadership, and trade association involvement, as well as our practice venues, uniquely qualify nurses to influence thought leaders and policymakers. Nursing and nurses have an ongoing impact on health and social policies.

**14** Chapter 1 Informing Public Policy

**Figure 1-4** Frontline nurses catapulted into the 24-hour news cycle in 2020.
Tom Stiglich at Creators.com.

**Figure 1-5** illustrates some aspects of nurses' impact on the health and well-being of populations.

Advanced studies build on education and experience and broaden the arena in which nurses work to a systems perspective, including both regional health **systems** and the overall U.S. **System** of healthcare delivery and finance. Nurses not only are well prepared to provide direct care to persons and families, but also act as change agents in the work environments in which they practice and the states/nations where they reside.

Nurses have developed theories to explain and predict phenomena they encounter in the course of providing care. In their practice, nurses also incorporate theory from other disciplines such as psychology, anthropology, education, biomedical science, and information technology. Integration of all this information reflects the complexity of nursing care and its provision within an extremely convoluted healthcare System. Nurses understand that partnerships are valued over competition, and that the old rules of business that rewarded power and ownership have given way to accountability and shared risk.

Communication skills are integral to the education of nurses, who often must interpret complex medical situations and terms into common, understandable, pragmatic language. Nurse education programs have formalized a greater focus on communications than is present in any other professional education program. From baccalaureate curricula through all upper levels of nurse education, major segments of nursing courses focus on individual communications and group processes. Skills include active listening, reflection, clarification,

| | |
|---|---|
| 1852 | **Florence Nightingale** used statistics to advocate for improved education for nurses, sanitation, and equality. |
| 1861 | **Clarissa "Clara" Barton** was a hospital nurse in the American Civil War. She founded the American Red Cross. |
| 1879 | **Mary Mahoney** was the first African American nurse in the United States and a major advocate for equal opportunities for minorities. |
| 1903 | North Carolina creates first Board of Nursing in the nation and licenses the first registered nurse. |
| 1906 | **Lillian D. Wald**, nurse, humanitarian, and author, made many contributions to human rights and was the founder of American Community Nursing. She helped found the NAACP. |
| 1909 | The University of Minnesota bestows the first bachelor's degree in nursing. |
| 1916 | **Margaret Higgins Sanger** was an American birth control activist, sex educator, writer, and nurse. Sanger popularized the term "birth control" and opened the first birth control clinic in the United States (later evolved into Planned Parenthood). |
| 1925 | The Frontier Nursing Service was established in Kentucky with advanced practice nurses (midwives). |
| 1955 | **RADM Jessie M. Scott, DSc**, served as assistant surgeon general in the U.S. Public Health Service; led the Division of Nursing for 15 years; and provided testimony before Congress on the need for better nursing training that led to the 1964 Nurse Training Act, the first major legislation to provide federal support for nurse education during peacetime. |
| 1966 | The nurse practitioner (NP) role is created by **Henry Silver, MD**, and **Loretta Ford, RN**. |
| 1967 | **Luther Christman, PhD**, became the first male dean of a School of Nursing (at Vanderbilt University). Earlier in his career, he had been refused admission to the U.S. Army Nurse Corps because of his gender. He was the founder of the American Association for Men in Nursing, as well as a founder of the National Student Nurses Association. |
| 1971 | Idaho statutorily recognizes advanced practice nursing. |
| 1978 | **Faye Wattleton, CNM**, was elected president of the Planned Parenthood Federation of America—the first African American and youngest person ever to hold that office. She was the first African American woman honored by the Congressional Black Caucus. |
| 1987 | **Ada S. Hinshaw, PhD**, became the first permanent leader at the National Institute of Nursing Research at the National Institutes of Health. |
| 1989 | **Geraldine "Polly" Bednash, PhD**, headed the American Association of Colleges of Nursing's legislative and regulatory advocacy programs as director of government affairs. She became CEO of AACN in 1989 and coauthored AACN's landmark study of the financial costs to students and clinical agencies of baccalaureate and graduate nursing education. |
| 1992 | **Eddie Bernice Johnson, BSN**, was the first nurse elected to the U.S. Congress (D-TX), where she was a strong voice for African Americans and pro-nursing policies. |

**Figure 1-5** Prominent nurses who have influenced policy. *(continues)*

| | |
|---|---|
| 1996 | **Beverly Malone, PhD**, was elected president of the American Nurses Association; President Clinton appointed her to the Advisory Commission on Consumer Protection and Quality in the Health Care Industry and to the post of deputy assistant secretary for health within the Department of Health and Human Services. |
| 1998 | **Lois G. Capps, BSN**, was a U.S. Representative from California from 1998–2017, where she founded the Congressional Nursing Caucus. |
| 2001 | **Major General Irene Trowell-Harris, EdD, RN, USAF (Ret.)**, served as director of the Department of Veterans Affairs, Center for Women Veterans. She was instrumental in establishing fellowship for military nurses in the office of Senator Daniel K. Inouye (D-HI). |
| 2009 | **Mary Wakefield, PhD**, became the first nurse appointed as director of the Health Resources and Services Administration. In 2015, she became the acting deputy secretary for the Department of Health and Human Services. She also served as chief of staff for U.S. Senators Quentin Burdick (D-ND) and Kent Conrad (D-ND). |
| 2010 | **Mary D. Naylor, PhD**, was included as a member of the Medicare Payment Advisory Commission, which influences health policy, and she also holds memberships on the RAND Health Board and the National Quality Forum Board of Directors, as well as serving as past-chair of the board of the Long-Term Quality Alliance. |
| 2011 | **LTG Patricia Horoho, MSN, RN**, became the first female and nurse to command the U.S. Army's Medical Command and serve as the surgeon general of a military department over the 239-year history of the Department of Defense. She was honored by Time Life Publications for her actions at the Pentagon on September 11, 2001. |
| 2013 | **Marilyn Tavenner, MHA, RN**, became the first nurse confirmed as administrator of the Centers for Medicare and Medicaid Services, serving during the rollout of the Affordable Care Act of 2010. |
| 2013 | **Joanne Disch, PhD**, became an influential voice for health policy as chair of the national board of directors for the American Association of Retired Persons and the American Academy of Nursing. |
| 2019 | **Ernest Grant, PhD**, became the first male elected as the American Nurses Association's president, championing the plight of immigrants and refugees to the United States. |
| 2020 | **Sheila P. Burke, MSN**, chaired Baker Donelson's influential Government Relations and Public Policy Group, following a distinguished career in government. In 1995, she was elected secretary of the Senate, the chief administrative officer of the U.S. Senate. She served from 2000 to 2007 as a member of the Medicare Payment Advisory Commission. She worked for 19 years on Capitol Hill on the staff of the Senate Majority Leader Bob Dole. She then served as the deputy secretary and chief operating officer of the Smithsonian Institution. |

**Figure 1-5** Continued.

assertiveness, role playing, and other techniques that build nurse competence levels. These same skills are useful when talking with policymakers.

Nursing care is not only a form of altruism, it also incorporates intentional action (or inaction) that focuses on a person or group with actual or potential health problems. The education of nurses puts them in the position of discovering and acknowledging health problems and health system problems that may demand intervention by public policymakers. For these reasons, accrediting agencies require policy content within nurse education programs.

## Practice and Policy

Evidence and theory provide the foundation for nursing as a practice profession. Nurses stand tall in their multiple roles—provider of care, educator, administrator, consultant, researcher, political activist, and policymaker. In their daily practice, nurses spot healthcare problems that may need government intervention, although not all problems nurses and their patients face in the healthcare System are amenable to solutions by government. Corporations, philanthropy, or collective action by individuals may best solve some problems. Most nurses are employees (as are most physicians today) and must navigate the organizations in which they work. By being attuned to systems issues, nurses have developed the ability to direct questions and identify solutions. This ability is reflected in the relationships that nurses can develop with policymakers.

Nurses bring the power of numbers when they enter the policy arena. According to a 2018 report from the National Council of State Boards of Nursing (NCSBN), there were 4,096,607 registered nurses (RNs) and 920,655 licensed practical nurses/licensed vocational nurses (LPN/LVNs) in the United States as of October 2019 (NCSBN, 2020). Collectively, nurses represent the largest group of healthcare workers in the nation.

Nurses have many personal stories that illustrate health problems and patients' responses to them. These stories have a powerful effect when a nurse brings an issue to the attention of policymakers. Anecdotes often make a problem more understandable at a personal level, and nurses are credible storytellers. By applying evidence to a specific patient situation, nurses may also bring research to legislators in ways that can be understood and can have a positive effect.

Nurses live in neighborhoods where health problems often surface and can often rally friends to publicize a local issue. Nurses are constituents of electoral districts and can make contacts with policymakers in their districts. Nurses vote. It is not unusual for a nurse to become the point person for a policymaker who is seeking information about healthcare issues. A nurse does not have to be knowledgeable about every health problem, but a nurse often has knowledge of a specific patient population as well as a vast network of colleagues and resources to tap into when a policymaker seeks facts. The practice of nursing prepares the practitioner to work in the policy arena. Note that the public policy process depicted in Figure 1-2 involves the application of a decision-making model in the public sector.

All facets of nursing practice and patient care are highly regulated by political bodies. State boards of nursing and other professional regulatory boards exert much influence in interpreting the statutes that govern nursing. Scope of practice is legislated by elected members but then defined in the rules and regulations by boards. Because each state and jurisdiction defines the practice of nursing differently, nursing scope of practice varies widely across the specific states. A fear expressed by many boards is that their decisions may interfere with Federal Trade Commission (FTC) rules that restrict monopoly practices. In 2014, the FTC published a policy paper addressing the regulation of the **advanced practice registered nurse (APRN)** that includes five key findings with important implications for policymakers:

1. APRNs provide care that is safe and effective.
2. Physicians' mandatory supervision of and collaboration with advanced nurse practice is not justified by any concern for patient health or safety.
3. Supervision and collaborative agreements required by statute or regulation lead to increased costs, decreased quality of care, fewer innovative practices, and reduced access to services.
4. APRNs collaborate effectively with all healthcare professionals without inflexible rules and laws.
5. APRN practice is "good for competition and consumers" ("FTC Policy Paper," 2014, p. 11).

Professional nurses who are knowledgeable about the regulatory process can more readily spot opportunities to contribute or intervene prior to final rule making.

## Organizational Involvement

Professional organizations bring their influence to the policy process in ways that a single person may not. There are myriad nurse-focused organizations, including those in specialty areas, education-related organizations, and leadership-related organizations. For example, the American Nurses Association, the National League for Nursing, and Sigma Theta Tau International state a commitment to advancing health and health care in the United States and/or on a global scale, as noted in their mission statements and goals, and offer nurses opportunities to develop personal leadership skills. The Oncology Nurses Society, the American Association of Critical Care Nurses, the American Association of Nurse Anesthetists, the Emergency Nurses Association, and many other specialty organizations focus on policies specific to certain patient populations and provide continuing education. Participating on committees within trade associations provides opportunities to learn about the organization, its mission, and its outreach efforts in more depth.

Professional associations afford their members experiences to become knowledgeable about issues pertinent to the organization or the profession. These groups can expand a nurse's perspective toward a broader view of health and professional issues, such as at the state, national, or global level. This kind of change in viewpoint often encourages a member's foray into the process of public policy. Some nurses are experienced in their political activity. They serve as chairs of legislative committees for professional organizations, work as campaign managers for elected officials, or present testimony at congressional, state, or local hearings; a few have run for office or hold office.

Political activism is a major expectation of most professional organizations. Many organizations employ professional lobbyists who carry those organizations' issues and concerns forward to policymakers. These sophisticated activists are skilled in the process of getting the attention of government and obtaining a response. Nurses also have an opportunity to voice their own opinions and provide information from their own practices through active participation in organizations. This give-and-take builds knowledge and confidence when nurses help legislators and others interpret issues.

## Taking Action

Nurses cannot afford to limit their actions in relation to policy. Instead, nurses need to share their unique perspectives with bureaucrats, agency staff, legislators, and others in public service regarding what nurses do, what nurses and their patients need, and how their cost-effectiveness has long-term impacts on health care in the United States.

Many nurses are embracing the whole range of options available in the various parts of the policy process. They are seizing opportunities to engage in ongoing, meaningful dialogues with those who represent the districts and states and those who administer public programs. Nurses are becoming indispensable sources of information for elected and appointed officials, and they are demonstrating leadership by becoming those officials and by participating with others in planning and decision making. By working with colleagues in other health professions, nurses often succeed in moving an issue forward owing to their well-recognized credibility and the relatively fewer barriers they must overcome.

## A Professional Nursing Workforce

Nurses can bring research and creativity to efforts geared toward solving public policy issues such as high drug prices, patient readmission rates, deployment of screening tools, and the most efficacious use of RN and APRNs. Aiken and colleagues have reported repeatedly that hospitals with higher proportions of baccalaureate-prepared nurses demonstrate decreased patient morbidity and mortality (Aiken et al., 2003, 2012, 2014; Van den Heede et al., 2009; Wiltse-Nicely, Sloane, & Aiken, 2013; You et al., 2013). Aiken's research includes studies in the United States and in nine European countries. Although the NCSBN has stated that it is not ready to support legislation or regulation that requires a bachelor of science in nursing (BSN) as the entry level into practice as a registered nurse, the marketplace is moving in a different direction (**Figure 1-6**). Many healthcare agencies limit new hires to those with a BSN and have policies that require RNs with associate's degrees or diplomas to complete a BSN within 5 years of employment. Academic institutions have expanded or created RN-to-BSN programs in response to the demand from the accrediting agency for Magnet status, the American Nurses Credentialing Center.

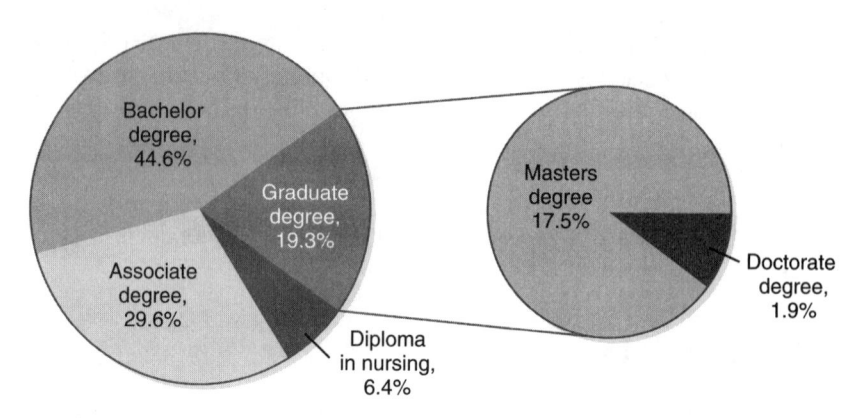

**Figure 1-6** Highest nursing and nursing-related educational attainment.

U.S. Department of Health and Human Services, Health Resources and Services Administration, National Center for Health Workforce Analysis. 2019. Brief Summary Results from the 2018 National Sample Survey of Registered Nurses, Rockville, Maryland.

---

**Spotlight:** Title VIII of the Affordable Care Act: Community Living Assistance Services and Supports (CLASS) Act

The CLASS Act was intended to allow Americans who are or who become disabled to receive a $50 daily payment to put toward assisted living. The amount was to be spent on home health care, adult daycare, and other services to allow those with disabilities to stay in their homes when possible. The amount could also go toward care provided by assisted living facilities, nursing homes, and group homes. The program was intended to be self-funded and would have reduced the deficit by $70.2 billion over 10 years by allowing people to remain employed and stay out of nursing homes and hospitals. The CLASS Act entered into force on January 1, 2011, but by October 1 it was determined to be unworkable. It could not compete with private-sector plans that offered better benefits.

---

# Innovation in Health Care: Reform or Incrementalism?

Starting with the Truman administration in the 1940s, every U.S. president's administration has struggled to reform the healthcare system to meet the needs of all U.S. residents. President Barack Obama declared early in his administration that a major priority would be health care for all, and in 2010 the Patient Protection and Affordable Care Act (commonly known as the ACA and "Obamacare") was established. More than a decade later, some aspects of the ACA continue to be controversial. The ACA includes 10 legislative titles; some of the titles were found to be unworkable or unsustainable during the implementation phase. The ACA is an example of sweeping reform, and its passage into law was a political feat. Most changes in health policy are incremental rather than sweeping.

During the 115th and 116th Congresses, the Trump administration, together with a Republican majority in the Senate, took steps to weaken the ACA, including the following:

- Eliminating of the mandate that all Americans purchase health insurance (Supreme Court case).
- Sharply reducing support for marketing the state-level health insurance exchanges as well as for the exchange navigators who could help guide those who need this insurance.
- Reducing the number of days of the annual enrollment period by one-half.
- Reneging on financial commitments to health insurers (the ACA provided for various subsidies to insurance companies to reduce their risks of losing money if they participated on the exchanges).
- Expanding access to cheaper insurance coverage that does not meet the quality standards for health insurance required by the ACA. (The ACA was originally intended to bolster the quality of health insurance through such measures as requiring insurers in the individual and small-group markets to cover 10 essential benefits, guaranteeing coverage of those with preexisting conditions at premium rates similar to heathier enrollees, and reducing risks of medical bankruptcy by prohibiting insurers from imposing certain spending caps on health care for an enrollee).

These and other actions to reduce the effectiveness and scope of the ACA did not require full legislative repeal. Instead, there has been a chipping away and erosion of the ACA's intended reforms to improve the U.S. healthcare System, reduce costs, and improve access to care for millions of Americans.

The 2020 elections did not provide a clear mandate to either a conservative or liberal point of view regarding the future of healthcare legislation. President Biden will need to work with a slim Democratic majority in the 117th Congress to amend, strengthen, and improve the ACA—or replace it. Former Senate Majority Leader Mitch McConnell, reelected in 2020 to his seventh 6-year term, will lead the Republican minority to possibly obstruct and delay much of the Biden administration's agenda (as he promised to do during the Obama administration). No party has a clear pathway to the super-majority (two-thirds of the Senate) needed to control specific types of votes. Based on recent history, the election cycle may return the congressional majority to the Republicans in 2022.

Divided government allows more points of view to be considered when designing policies; however, it can also cripple a government's ability to get anything done. As this text goes to press, Biden's cabinet appointments as well as other advisory positions are unknown; hopefully, nurses will be included. One of Biden's first actions as president-elect was to create a White House Coronavirus Task Force; the original appointees did not include any nurses.

Nurses must speak out as articulate, knowledgeable, caring professionals who contribute to the whole health agenda and who advocate for their patients and the community. All healthcare professions have expanded the boundaries of practice from their beginnings. Practice inevitably reflects societal needs and conditions; homeostasis is not an option if the provision of health care is to be relevant.

> **Spotlight:** Voting in the Senate
>
> Most issues in the Senate are decided by a simple majority vote: one-half plus one of the senators voting, assuming the presence of a quorum. For instance, if all 100 senators vote, the winning margin is at least 51. Under Senate precedents, a tie vote on a bill defeats it. Some super-majority votes (also known as extraordinary majority) are explicitly specified in the Constitution; implicitly, they also exist in authority granted in Article I, Section 5, which says, "Each chamber may determine the Rules of Its Proceedings." Under this constitutional power, the Senate has imposed on itself a number of additional super-majority requirements. These include invoking cloture, suspending the rules, postponing treaty consideration indefinitely, making a bill a special order (antiquated), and waiving the Congressional Budget Act of 1974, Senate Rule XXVIII, Senate Rule XLIV, and the Statutory Pay-As-You-Go Act of 2010 (also known as "pay-go").
>
> What is cloture? A three-fifths vote of all senators (60 of 100) is required to invoke cloture—the closure of debate—on most bills. However, a two-thirds vote of the senators present and voting is required to invoke cloture on measures or motions to amend Senate rules. Once cloture has been invoked, the 30 hours of debate available during postcloture consideration may be extended by a three-fifths vote of all senators duly chosen and sworn.

# Developing a More Sophisticated Political Role for Nurses

Nurses who are serious about political activity realize that the key to establishing contacts with legislators and agency directors is to forge ongoing relationships with elected and appointed officials and their staffs. By developing credibility with those active in the political process and demonstrating integrity and moral purpose as client advocates, nurses are becoming players in the complex process of policymaking.

Nurses have learned that by using nursing knowledge and skill, they can gain the confidence of government actors. Personal stories drawn from professional nurses' experience anchor conversations with legislators and their staffs, creating an important emotional link that can influence policy design. Nurses' vast network of clinical experts produces nurses in direct care who provide persuasive, articulate arguments with people "on the Hill" (i.e., U.S. congressional Members and senators who work on Capitol Hill).

# Working With the Political System

Many professional nurses and APRNs develop contacts with legislators, appointed officials, and their staffs. Groups that offer nurse interaction include the U.S. House Nursing Caucus and the Senate Nursing Caucus (membership shifts with the election cycle). Members hold briefings on nurse workforce planning, patient and nurse safety issues, vaccinations, school health, reauthorization of legislation (e.g., the Emergency Medical System Act, the Ryan White Act), preparedness for bioterrorism, and other relevant and pertinent issues and concerns.

Nurses must stay alert to issues and be assertive in bringing problems to the attention of policymakers. It is important to bring success stories to legislators and officials—they need to hear what good nurses do and how well they practice. Sharing positive information will keep the image of nurses positioned within an affirmative and constructive picture.

## Conclusion

Healthcare professionals must have expert knowledge and skills in change management, conflict resolution, active listening, assertiveness, communication, negotiation, and group processes to function appropriately in the policy arena. Professional autonomy and collaborative interdependence are possible within a political system in which consumers can choose access to quality health care that is provided by competent practitioners at a reasonable cost. Professional nurses have a strong, persistent voice in designing such a healthcare system for today and for the future.

The policy process is much broader and more comprehensive than the legislative process. Although individual components can be identified for analytical study, the policy process is fluid, nonlinear, and dynamic. There are many opportunities for nurses in advanced practice to participate throughout the policy process. The question is not *whether* nurses should become involved in the political system, but *to what extent*. Across the policy arena, nurses must be involved with every aspect of this process. By knowing all the components and issues that must be addressed in each phase, the nurse in advanced practice will find many opportunities for providing expert advice. APRNs can use the policy process, individual components, and models as a framework to analyze issues and participate in alternative solutions.

## Chapter Discussion Points

1. What is the number (or designation) of your voting district? Obtain your voting record from the board of elections and describe your citizenship in regard to voting in elections.
2. Identify a health- or healthcare-related problem you have encountered in your community or in practice (e.g., "My patients all have dental problems and have no means of paying for dental care"). Discuss how the diagram of the policy process (Figure 1-2) can help inform how you approach finding a solution to this problem. Reflect on which level of government might address this problem and why. Identify the stakeholders in this issue.
3. Read fact-based (not opinion) books or journalistic articles or listen to podcasts about the changing paradigm in healthcare delivery and payment systems. Suggestions for reading include *Priced Out* (2019) by Uwe Reinhardt,

**Chapter 1** Informing Public Policy

*Being Mortal* (2014) by Atul Gawande, articles/blog postings in *The Atlantic* and *Health Affairs*, and *Which Country Has the Best Health Care* (2020) by Ezekiel Emanuel.
   a. List three questions you have after reading this material.
   b. List three new ideas you have gained.
   c. Commit to three actions that you will take as a result of being informed by this material.
4. Consider a thesis, graduate project, or dissertation on a specific topic (e.g., clinical problems, healthcare issues). Use the policy process as a framework.
5. Use a search engine to explore a policy related to a health or healthcare topic such as Supplemental Nutrition Assistance Program (SNAP) benefits, the nursing workforce, or the National Practitioner Database (NPDB). Which government agencies are responsible for developing the policy? For enforcing the policy? How has the policy changed over time? What are the consequences of not complying with the policy? What is needed to change the policy?
6. Identify nurses and healthcare professionals who are elected officials at the local, state, or national level. Follow them on Twitter and Facebook to determine how they became policy experts, what their objectives are, and to what extent they use their clinical knowledge in their official capacities. Ask the officials if they tapped into nurses' groups during their campaigns. If so, what did the nurses and HCPs contribute?
7. Watch a health- or healthcare-related hearing in the U.S. House of Representatives or the Senate. These are accessible online at www.congress.gov. The House Energy and Commerce Committee and the Senate Health, Education, Labor, and Pensions Committee are good choices. Discuss three things you learned from the hearing. Was there testimony by nurses or other clinicians? Would nursing/HCP testimony be valuable at this hearing? How are witnesses chosen? What topics could you testify about (think of the patient population you work with)?
8. Discover how to get notifications (and agendas) of upcoming health-related committees in your state government. Who are the chairs of these committees?

# CASE STUDY 1-2: The Addiction Epidemic

You are an acute care nurse practitioner who works in an urban emergency room (ER). You see many people who come to the ER who have overdosed on heroin. Emergency medical services (EMS) personnel may administer a drug that might reverse the overdose such as naloxone (Narcan). You may see three overdoses during each 12-hour shift; some of these patients are admitted to the hospital, and others are sent home with a consultation for psychiatric follow-up. You are becoming hardened to the issue and have begun to question what you can do to address this epidemic.

## Case Study Discussion Questions
1. You hear that the state health director is convening a task force. List four actions you can take to be invited to participate in this task force.
2. Which other healthcare professionals should be included on the task force?
3. Which state agencies and regulatory boards could add value to the discussion?
4. Which information/experience could the APRN use to lead a discussion about widespread addiction?
5. Identify three issues that might be brought up at a meeting that could derail a focus on public safety. Which tactics can the nurse use to bring the discussion back to the issue of safety?

## References

AARP Public Policy Institute. (2021). *The future of nursing: Campaign for action.* Center to Champion Nursing. https://campaignforaction.org/about/leadership-staff/the-rwjf-and-aarp-partnership/.

Aiken, L. H., Clarke, S. R., Cheung, R. B., Sloane, D. M., & Silber, J. H. (2003). Educational levels of hospital nurses and surgical patient mortality. *Journal of the American Medical Association,* 290(12), 1617–1623.

Aiken, L. H., Cimotti, J. P., Sloane, D. M., Smith, H. L., Flynn, L., & Neff, D. E. (2012). Effects of nurse staffing and nursing education on patient deaths in hospitals with different work environments. *Medical Care,* 49(12), 1047–1053.

Aiken, L. H., Sloane, D. M., Bruyneel, L., Van den Heede, K., Griffiths, P., Busse, R., Diomidous, M., Kinnunen, J., Kózka, M., Lesaffre, E., McHugh, M. D., Moreno-Casbas, M. T., Rafferty, A. M., Schwendimann, R., Scott, P. A., Tishelman, C., van Achterberg, T., & Sermeus, W. for the RN4CAST consortium. (2014). Nurse staffing and education and hospital mortality in nine European countries: A retrospective observational study. *Lancet,* 383(9931), 1824–1830.

Brannon, V. (2018). Statutory interpretation: Theories, tools and trends. Congressional Research Service Report 45153. https://crsreports.congress.gov/product/pdf/R/R45153

Centers for Disease Control and Prevention. (2020). Overview of CDC's policy process. U.S. Department of Health and Human Services. https://www.cdc.gov/policy/analysis/process/docs/cdcpolicyprocess.pdf

Epstein, R. (2016, June 22). How did Google become the Internet's censor and master manipulator, blocking access to millions of websites? *U.S. New and World Report.* https://www.usnews.com/opinion/articles/2016-06-22/google-is-the-worlds-biggest-censor-and-its-power-must-be-regulated

FTC policy paper examines competition and the regulation of APRNs. (2014). *American Nurse,* 46(3), 11.

Institute of Medicine. (2010). *The future of nursing: Leading change, advancing health.* National Academies Press.

Kickbusch, I. (2015). The political determinants of health—10 years on. *British Medical Journal,* 2015;350:h81.

Mackenbach, J. P. (2014). Political determinants of health. *European Journal of Public Health,* 24(1), 2.

Mishori, R. (2019). The social determinants of health? Time to focus on the political determinants of health. *Medical Care,* 57(7), 491–493.

National Council of State Boards of Nursing. (2020, August 21). *Policy briefing: Members of Congress introduce legislation to address health professional license portability during a public health emergency.* https://www.ncsbn.org/14954.htm

National Council of State Boards of Nursing. (2020). NCSBN's environmental scan: A portrait of nursing and healthcare in 2020 and beyond. *Journal of Nursing Regulation,* 10(4), S1–S36.

Oyez. (2014). *King v. Burwell.* https://www.oyez.org/cases/2014/14-114

Oyez. (2020). *California v. Texas.* https://www.oyez.org/cases/2020/19-840

Patient Protection and Affordable Care Act of 2010. (2010). Pub. L. No. 111-148, 124 Stat. 119.

Stringer, H. (2019, July 1). *IOM Future of Nursing report card: Progress after 10 years with Sue Hassmiller and Mary Dickow*. Nurse.com blog. https://www.nurse.com/blog/2019/07/01/iom-future-of-nursing-report-card-progress-after-10-years/

U.S. Department of Health and Human Services, Health Resources and Services Administration, National Center for Health Workforce Analysis. (2019). *Brief summary results from the 2018 National Sample Survey of Registered Nurses*. Author.

Van den Heede, K., Lesaffre, E., Diya, L., Vleugels, A., Clarke, S. P., Aiken, L. H., & Sermeus, W. (2009). The relationship between inpatient cardiac surgery mortality and nurse numbers and educational level: Analysis of administrative data. *International Journal of Nursing Studies, 46,* 796–803.

Wiltse-Nicely, K. L., Sloane, D. M., & Aiken, L. H. (2013, June). Lower mortality for abdominal aorta aneurysm repair in high volume hospitals contingent on nurse staffing. *Health Systems Research, 48*(3), 972–991.

You, L.-M., Aiken, L. H., Sloane, D. M., Liu, K., He, G-P, Hu, Y., . . . Sermeus, W. (2013). Hospital nursing, care quality, and patient satisfaction: Cross-sectional survey of nurses and patients in hospitals in China and Europe. *International Journal of Nursing Studies, 50*(2), 154–161.

# CHAPTER 2

# News Literacy

Cindy Vanek

## KEY TERMS

**Belief system:** A group or set of principles that, together, become the basis of a philosophy.

**Bias:** An attitude of mind that predisposes one to favor something.

  **Gatekeeping bias:** Omission of news stories that do not adhere to the individual's predispositions.

  **Ideological bias:** Shaping information to mirror an opinion or belief.

  **Media bias:** The slanting of information about a news event or the selection of events or stories to be reported in a manner that aligns with a given belief system.

  **Personal and cognitive bias:** An error in thinking that impacts decisions or judgments of an individual.

  **Political bias:** The altering of information to make a political position more attractive to individuals.

**Facts:** Things that are is known or proven to be true.

**Ideology:** The opinions, values, and beliefs of either an individual or a group.

**Information environment:** The aggregate of individuals, organizations, or systems that collect, process, or disseminate information used for decision making.

**Infotainment:** Information presented as news in a style that is intended to be entertaining.

**Journalism:** The collection and editing of news for presentation through the media with the functions of informing, educating, guiding, or entertaining.

**Journalist:** A person who writes for newspapers, magazines, or news websites or prepares news for video broadcast.

**Media:** Communication channels through which news, entertainment, education, data, or promotional messages are disseminated. Includes every form of broadcasting and narrowcasting, including newspapers, magazines, TV, radio, billboards, direct mail, telephone, fax, and Internet.

**Media literacy:** The process of understanding and using the mass media in an assertive and nonpassive way. Includes having an informed and critical understanding of the nature of the media, the techniques used, and the impact of those techniques.

**Personal values:** A person's principles or standards of behavior; one's judgment of what is important in life.

**Societal values:** A set of moral principles defined by the dynamics, institutions, traditions, and cultural beliefs of a society that act as implicit guidelines to orient individuals and corporations to conduct themselves properly within the social system.
**Value:** The regard that something is held to deserve; the importance, worth, or usefulness of something.

# Introduction

Most of us believe that we are not biased; we believe that we can read, hear, and consider both sides of an argument, find the facts, and come to a reasonable conclusion. But is this really the case? This chapter suggests that everyone is biased. Developing bias is the result of having opinions, values, and beliefs—it is a result of living. We are, in fact, taught to have opinions, values, and beliefs, and as we age, these concepts will morph and change, but they will remain. Opinions are valuable because they make us think. A **value** is a concept that we consider to be important; values may be **personal values** or **societal values**. They give us standards to live by. Beliefs are thoughts or statements that individuals hold to be true regardless of whether they can be seen or felt or proven. **Bias** develops from these opinions, values, and beliefs. It is unavoidable. We must recognize that we are not, nor can we make ourselves, a blank page. How we deal with and use our biases is what matters. How we react to others whom we know have biases is what matters. As nurses, we need to accept our biases and use them to improve our lives, the lives of our patients and their families, our communities, and our profession.

This chapter will discuss the various types of bias and how bias can be detected within the media, within professional articles, within research, and within everyday conversations. Types of **personal and cognitive bias** will be described. The dangers of bias will be presented, with aids provided to identify bias within organizations and to verify **facts**. The importance of self-reflection and strategies to minimize bias will be discussed with regard to the engagement of the nursing profession in health policy development and reform.

# Bias Within the Media

**Media**, according to the Cambridge Dictionary (2020), includes newspapers, magazines, TV, radio, billboards, direct mail, telephone, fax, and Internet writings. It is available to all who choose to access a given medium. Within media, one will find news or journalistic reporting of an event or events; commentary, which is an explanatory series of notes or comments; and **infotainment**, which is a presentation of information in a manner that is meant to be entertaining. As journalists add commentary or blend information and entertainment, bias often is introduced. Dramatic elements often are added to factual material, resulting in what is often called *soft news*. The types of elements added, and the bias they convey, can change how an individual will interpret the information.

For example, a news report from a sporting event may state, "The Yankees defeated the Mets Saturday with a final score of 10 to 3." Adding commentary to the information might result in a statement that says, "The well-coached Yankees defeated a clumsy-looking Mets team Saturday with a final score of 10-3." If the journalist wants to entertain their audience or reader while presenting the information, they might report the final score while describing or adding multiple pictures of errors made by the Mets team that would make the audience laugh.

Common types of bias within the media include political bias and ideological bias. **Political bias** occurs when a story or news event is altered to make a political position more attractive to the listeners or readers. **Ideological bias** occurs when information is shaped to mirror an opinion, belief, or cause the media outlet supports. Some media outlets will either support or attack a candidate or political party based on their political bias. A media outlet might also criticize the need for a community service or healthcare policy based on its ideological bias. Bias within the media happens when a journalist slants information about a news event to align with a given **belief system**. Colloquial terms for media bias include *false news* or *fake news*. Media bias can be the result of multiple factors, including who owns the media outlet, its sources of income, and the ideology of both those working within the organization and those who make up its audience (University of Michigan, 2014).

**Media bias** can also stretch the truth to the point that it becomes a lie. Stories can be crafted to influence; they can also be crafted to deceive or misinform the reader or audience. Consider two opposing political candidates who want to convince the American public that they have a better answer for improving the country's healthcare system, specifically the cost of prescription drugs. It is reported in the news that the incumbent candidate stated, "I have reduced the average cost of prescription drugs for Americans from $1,200 per person to less than $750 per person per year." Another news outlet reports that the challenger stated, "Prescription drug costs for an American citizen currently averages $1,200 per year. We must reduce this cost for all Americans." However, the incumbent has provided false information in an effort to win votes. In the media, the incumbent's statement is called false news after a **journalist** or organization fact-checks the information and determines that the latest research shows that the average cost of prescription drugs per person is and remains $1,200 per year. They report the incumbent's statement as a lie, and they will suggest that it was stated to win political favor. Do we believe the incumbent, the challenger, or do we recognize our doubt and research the facts on our own? Given the many ways a story can be slanted to emphasize a point or to gain the approval of the audience, the reader/listener needs to be able to discern truth from fiction.

Understanding that media bias is often difficult to recognize, how do we look for and identify it? How do we develop **media literacy**? According to the University of Michigan (2014), "The most common ways bias manifests itself in the news are through word choice, omissions, the limiting of debate, framing of the story, and a biased selection and use of sources."

When reading or listening to reports about news events, we must be sensitive to the words being used. We must try to determine if key words are being manipulated so that they are expressing a belief or opinion. Information can be manipulated by simple editing or rearranging words, lost content, staged pictures or video, computer generated material, or algorithm driven 'deep-fake' images, voices, or even movements that are very realistic and misleading. Journalists in a newsroom may be misled by a deceptive caption or story accompanying a picture; the picture is real but the caption twists the reality. A witness who does not fully understand a scene playing out in front of them may provide a false narrative to a real video. For example, a short film clip of a man being dragged by an angry an Arab group circulated on the Internet shortly after the attack on the American Embassy in Benghazi, Libya, with a story claiming that it depicted the U.S. ambassador. The photo went viral on Facebook and led many Americans to believe that Ambassador Stevens was tortured, castrated, and killed by this mob. The real situation was quite different: the picture had been posted to the Internet years before the 2012 incident. The gruesome photo is of an Argentine soldier in 2004 that appeared in a story by Spanish newspaper HYPERLINK "https://www.diariodeleon.es/" Diario de León about Argentinian military torture. Real photo. False narrative. (AP, 2019). Similarly, our interpretations of information can be influenced if the information we receive is purposely limited. This often happens when the issue involves a crime or national security. We must consider what sources are used when news is reported and how those sources are used.

News details can be framed to reflect conflict, consensus, or reactions. The details of an event can also be organized to demonstrate a wrong that has occurred. Reporting is supposed to answer the questions of who, what, where, when, and how. What we must understand is that our interpretation of the information can be influenced by how that information is framed.

When information is framed from a political perspective, an understanding of the political spectrum is necessary. The terms *left wing* and *right wing* became popular in the 18th century during the French Revolution. During this time, those who sat to the left of the presiding officer of the French National Assembly supported the revolution and opposed the old regime. They wanted radical change. Those who sat to the right of the presiding officer supported maintaining traditional society, and voila, the concept of left versus right was born (*Left Wing vs. Right Wing*, n.d.). Political theorists now support the idea of a spectrum of political ideology ranging from liberal (left) to conservative (right). One theory, the Horseshoe Theory, depicted in **Figure 2-1**, suggests that the continuum from the political left to the political right bends such that the extreme ends of the continuum are closer to each other; that is, they are not that different from one another.

Proponents of the Horseshoe Theory point to similarities between the far left and the far right—both are concerned with getting and holding power, both seek to organize groups, and both can become fanatical in the belief that they are correct. However, critics suggest that the Horseshoe Theory is a simplistic way to consider political ideologies and, more often, an individual will lean to the left on one matter and to the right on another. We move right or left, or we change position on the horseshoe, based on our personal **ideology** and values. Wherever one may fall on the political spectrum, the need to identify bias

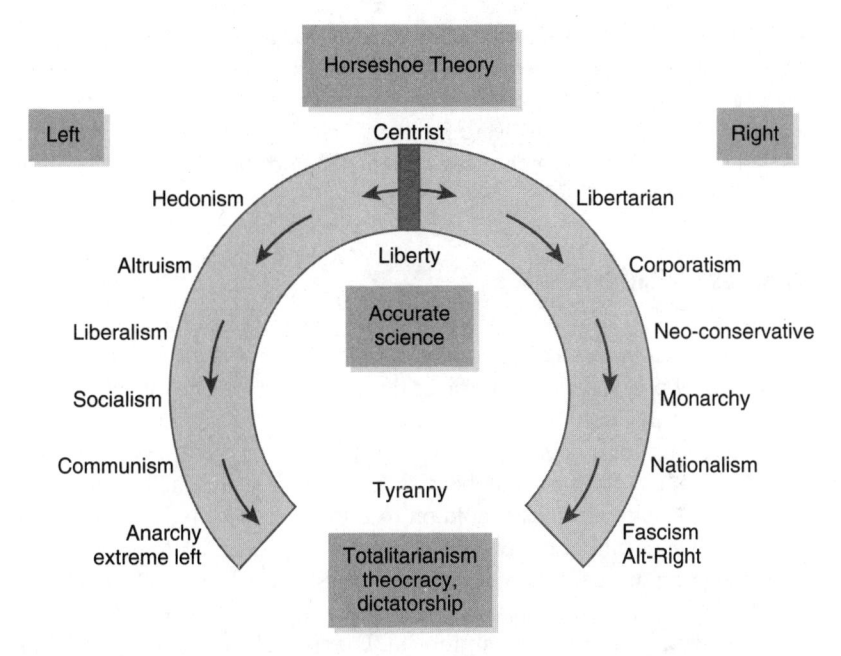

**Figure 2-1** Political ideology.

remains. Though there are many types of bias, the seven types discussed in the following sections are some of the ones most commonly mentioned.

## Liberal Bias

The term *liberal bias* is often used when an individual or organization supports liberal or progressive policies. From a political perspective, liberal policies are those that alleviate social ills and protect civil liberties and human rights; they emphasize the need for government to solve problems in the belief that the role of government is to ensure that no one goes without or is in need. Liberal policies are policies that are considered socially progressive (Lexico, 2020a, para. 1). *Progressivism* is defined as "support for or advocacy of social reform" (Lexico, 2020d, para. 1). Progressivism pushes government to be more responsive to economic and social demands. Workplace safety regulations, limits on working hours, workers' compensation programs, and child labor restrictions all resulted from progressive movements in U.S. history. Liberalism is associated with the political left.

An example of liberal bias is a media outlet focusing primarily on social issues while pushing for government interventions to correct them. Liberal bias, as with all types of bias, dismisses opposing views. However, the liberal policies promoted by certain political parties are not based solely on the party's desire to erase social injustices: their popularity often depends on the position and strength of those who have or yearn to have political power. The history of the struggle between liberalism and conservatism is a fascinating study of influence and manipulation that began in the 1950s. After Democrat Franklin

Roosevelt's New Deal was enacted in 1933, conservatives became more verbal about the dangers of liberalism. The struggle between the two groups at times became a battlefield as liberals pushed for government solutions to social ills. During the 1960s, as the Medicare program was proposed and approved, the so-called "battle lines" became more entrenched and have remained so until today (Walsh, 2018).

## Conservative Bias

We cannot have a discussion of liberal bias without balancing it with a discussion of conservative bias. In a political context, *conservatism* is defined as "the holding of political views that favor free enterprise, private ownership and socially traditional ideas; commitment to traditional values and ideas with opposition to change or innovation" (Lexico, 2020c, para. 1). Thus, conservatives will seek data that affirm existing beliefs. For example, investors follow a conservative philosophy when they hold on to prior views or forecasts and refuse to acknowledge new information.

Considering this definition, conservative bias would be an action that uses tactics to support a conservative mindset or that emphasizes perceived issues with a conservative approach to a problem. For example, imagine yourself in a room with someone who tends to lean toward conservative thinking. You walk into the room and express a few seemingly legitimate concerns with liberal thinking about an issue. Your listener nods in agreement, smiles, leans toward you, offers his hand to shake, and says excitedly, "You are so right!" Several days later, you meet this individual again and offer evidence to question conservative approaches to a different problem. Now, your listener shakes his head in disagreement, he distances himself from you, puts his hands in his pockets, and says, "How can you say that. You are so wrong!"

In 2014, two faculty from the Stanford Graduate School of Business conducted a study of conservative bias among American politicians (Broockman & Skovron, 2017). They surveyed politicians throughout the country to obtain their perceptions about their constituents' opinions on nine issues: abolishing federal welfare, same-sex marriage, universal health care, abortion, banning of assault rifles, background checks for gun purchase, amnesty for undocumented immigrants who have paid taxes for 2 years or more, allowing questioning of suspected undocumented immigrants, and religious exemptions for birth control and other health services coverage. They found that "politicians of both parties dramatically overestimate their constituents' support for conservative policies. We also show Republicans overestimate constituency conservatism especially and that this partisan difference may arise from differences in politicians' information environments. Our findings suggest a novel way democratic representation may fail; politicians can systematically misperceive what their constituents want" (Broockman & Skovron, 2017, p. 1). Brookman and Skovron (2017) suggest that if citizens want to change this misperception, the **information environment** surrounding politicians must change or politicians will "get nominated, elected, and reelected without knowing what their constituents want" (p. 38).

## Libertarian Bias

*Libertarianism* is "the political philosophy that advocates only minimal state intervention in the free market and the private lives of citizens" (Lexico, 2020e, para. 1). Those who adhere to a libertarian point of view would argue that activities such as drug use and prostitution, because they harm only the participants, should be legal. Libertarianism is associated with the political right. In the United States, the Cato Institute is a think tank devoted to libertarian ideology.

## Mainstream Media Bias

Mainstream media bias is bias found within a form of the media that influences large numbers of people (*Cambridge Dictionary*, 2020). It results when information that is printed, stated, or televised by a few large news media outlets becomes information that is printed, stated, or televised by other outlets. Conversely, if it is known that these large media outlets will not print or televise information because it is offensive, that information will not be shown by others. This phenomenon began in the 19th century when most newspapers were explicitly linked to a political party and the economic interests of its publisher. As historian Chilton Williamson writes of this period, "The presentation of facts simply as facts, editors and writers reasoned, cannot accomplish the exalted goal of saving civilization" (Thornton, 2013). The citizenry was the imaginary jury that needed to be convinced and papers were the means used by politicians to convince them. Toward the end of the 19th century, a circulation war developed between the Hearst and Pulitzer newspapers. Editors and publishers of smaller outlets were supported by, or their paper was owned by, one or the other large publishing house, resulting in published stories similar to those published by the "better" and bigger papers.

Has this practice continued? According to Thornton (2013),

> This rampant partisanship that characterized newspapers for most of their existence may strike us as deplorable, but it functioned much in the same way that James Madison in Federalist 10 wanted political institutions to work. Just as in government, partisan media factions would balance and limit opposing factions, thus protecting the freedom of the citizenry as a whole by limiting the scope of any one faction's power and influence (para. 8).

It was not until the 1960s that the press's partisanship came under serious scrutiny. First, **journalism** became a profession certified by a university degree rather than a trade, and the perspectives of journalists expanded. The idea that the press should not report facts but should mold public opinion was no longer accepted. Second, the rise of television led to a decline in the number of newspapers. The three television networks and the big metropolitan papers became the desired sources for information. The 1980s brought a rise in talk radio, cable news shows, and the Internet, challenging the mainstream media for the public's ear. Today, media outlets are instantly held accountable in ways that were unthinkable just a few decades ago. Partisan spin on news still exists, but mainstream bias or the tendency to report what others are reporting has lessened significantly.

## Corporate Bias

Corporate bias occurs when information is influenced based on the opinions, beliefs, and values of a corporation's owners (Quora, 2018). Because media outlets are businesses, they must make money to pay expenses. Most do so via advertisements. Media outlets with large numbers of viewers or readers are more desirable to advertisers. Viewers will go to those media outlets that provide the information that they want to see and/or hear. The owner of the media outlet wants more viewers, which will attract more advertisements, and so on. Corporate bias is the impact that money has on the media. Corporate bias is all around us. If you click on the homepage of any news source, there will be substantive stories, but there will also be stories about celebrities, scandals, cute animals, human interest stories, etc. Note that the media is often aware of their corporate bias. When Stephen Colbert took over for David Letterman on *The Late Show*, he was aware that people wanted to talk about the newly elected president, Donald Trump. This piece of infotainment served multiple purposes: (1) it showed viewers what Donald Trump was up to, (2) it provided entertainment, and (3) it poked fun at itself and its viewers.

*Corporatism* has been defined as the cooptation of interest groups into governmental decision-making and the formalization of their role, because they have become too important to ignore. Alternatively, it has also been interpreted as the suborning of dissident elements and their conversion into agents of control for a powerful state, such as in Fascist Italy in World War II.

## Activist or Cause Bias

Activists of a given cause often state that the media or the scientific community is biased against their cause because the field is too specialized. They will offer anecdotal stories to support their theories and beliefs. They believe that the media chooses not to cover their cause due to the media's own bias. They will offer examples of sources and publications that they consider to be the best sources available on the specified subject. Statements from other publications will be discarded as those having a cause or activist bias. This action will be defended with statements that the opposing publications were written by individuals unable to understand the issue or too biased to fairly present the facts. An example of this type of bias is information published that relates to the antivaccination cause.

## Gatekeeping Bias

**Gatekeeping bias** refers to the belief that journalists consciously choose what news stories to report based on their ideological bias. Do journalists fail to report news stories that do not adhere to their preconceived beliefs? If so, that practice could, if pervasive, have an impact on what people perceive to be significant issues. Topics that are focused on in the news tend to drive or at least contribute to political agendas. As noted by Hassell, Hobein, and Miles (2020), "Identifying gatekeeping bias in news coverage, however, has proven to be incredibly difficult. In part, this is because identifying the full population of news from which journalists could select stories is difficult" (p. 1).

How do journalists respond to a potential news story? How do they choose what they write or speak about? Hassell et al. (2020) conducted a study to determine whether ideology skews story choice among journalists. A large survey was designed to test for ideological bias and the tendency of a journalist to gatekeep—that is, to report only those stories that agreed with the journalist's ideology. Each journalist was given potential news stories available within their media market and asked to choose which stories they would cover. In addition, data from election returns and Twitter data about journalist networks were examined to determine the journalists' ideology and compare that to news stories chosen by the journalists. Out of 1,511 completed surveys, 78.23% journalists identified as Democrat and 21.77% identified as Republican. When queried about ideological leanings, 78.03% self-reported that they were liberal and 21.97% self-reported that they were conservative. Results showed that even though the responding journalists identified predominantly as liberals and Democrats, they did not exhibit liberal media bias in what they chose to cover (Hassell et al., 2020).

## How Do We Detect Bias?

In today's environment of information overload, we are constantly reading. We read for enjoyment, for information, and for work or school. We read emails, texts, news banners, and news summaries that show up on our smartphones. How do we detect bias in what we see or read? Many of us watch for bias in the news, but does it also occur within the professional literature or within the research performed? Can we identify bias during a friendly conversation—both our own and that of others? Let us begin with a discussion of whether bias exists, and how personal bias functions.

### Bias Within the News and Media

Many of us get our news from our computers, and many traditional newspapers are struggling to survive. Television continues to be the most common source for news. Consider the following findings reported by Mitchell (2018) from studies conducted by the Pew Research Center for Journalism and Media.

Data from a 2016 study showed:

- 47% of Americans preferred to watch the news, 34% preferred to read the news, and 19% preferred to listen to the news.
- 44% of Americans preferred receiving news from the TV, while 34% preferred receiving news from the web, 14% preferred listening to news on the radio, and 7% preferred print.
- Nearly all adults got at least some news digitally.

**36** **Chapter 2** News Literacy

Data from a subsequent 2018 study showed:

- A drop of 5% for those who preferred watching the news on television and an 8% increase in those who preferred online news outlets.
- 76% of Americans aged 18 to 49 preferred to read the news on the web, whereas 43% of Americans 50 and older preferred to read the news on the web.
- The gap between those who stated they got news online versus those who accessed news via television dropped from 10% to 6%, with television remaining the leading choice.

How do we detect bias in each of these media, and does the bias differ based on the particular medium? Can we listen to or read news and separate the facts from the commentary, political bias, and information added for entertainment purposes? The lines between commentary and news have become blurred. Turner (2017) suggests that the advent of 24/7 news sources resulted in the need to add commentators to fill time. Today, politicians, lawyers, and other professionals provide commentary in the same manner that former football players provide commentary during a game. We can identify a statement like "The quarterback just threw a bad pass that couldn't be caught" as commentary for an "incomplete pass." We need to do the same when watching, reading, or listening to news (**Figure 2-2**).

In 2017, a Gallup poll found that 62% of Americans believe political bias exists in the reporting of news. At that time, the majority (64%) believed the Democratic Party was favored and a minority (22%) believed the Republican Party was favored (Brown, 2017). In 2018, a Gallup/Knight survey found that 45% of Americans believed there was "a great deal" of political bias in news

**Figure 2-2** Being aware of political bias.
www.CartoonStock.com

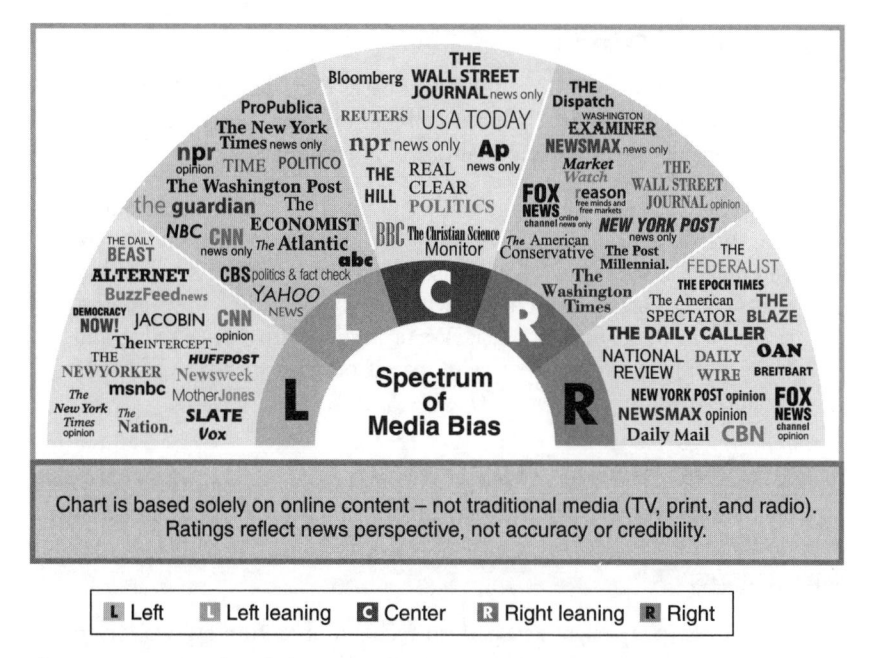

**Figure 2-3** Media bias chart.

coverage. These findings reflect a sharp increase from polls measuring the same question; a 1989 poll reported that 25% believed there was a great deal of political bias in the news, whereas by 2012 that number had increased to 37% (Jones & Ritter, 2018).

Several organizations develop and publish media bias ratings. One such organization, AllSides, offers a media bias chart that categorizes various online media outlets on a spectrum from left to right (**Figure 2-3**).

These studies have hopefully convinced you (if you were not already convinced) that bias will be found in our news sources. To complicate matters, as we read externally biased news sources, we add the following into the mix:

- *Our own political beliefs and ideas.* We will slant our understanding of a statement or description of an event based on our beliefs and ideas, often without realizing it.
- *Our opinion of the worth of the vehicle used for the information.* We tend to assume that information is based on fact because we consider the source or reference to be scientific or respected within the field.
- Our own lenses of personal and cognitive biases.

## Personal and Cognitive Biases

We use a number of different personal and cognitive biases to interpret the events and people around us. Here we describe some of the more common personal and cognitive biases.

## Anchoring Bias

Anchoring bias occurs when an individual bases their view of something based on preexisting information. The preexisting information "anchors" the person's opinion. Consider the following example of anchoring bias:

> If I were to ask you where you think Apple's stock will be in 3 months, how would you approach it? Many people would first say, "Okay, where's the stock today?" Then, based on where the stock is today, they will make an assumption about where it is going to be in 3 months. That is a form of anchoring bias. We're starting with a price today, and we're building our sense of value based on that anchor. (Corporate Finance Institute, n.d., para. 2)

## Cognitive Bias of Apophenia

Apophenia is a type of cognitive bias that occurs due to an unmotivated recognition of patterns. According to Buetow (2018), this type of bias is common among nurses:

> Nurses routinely engage in pattern recognition and interpretation in qualitative research and clinical practice. However, they risk spontaneously perceiving patterns among things that are not meaningfully related. Although all people are prone to this cognitive bias of "apophenia," nurses may be at increased risk because they commonly produce or at least use qualitative research that can be highly interpretive. (p. 1)

## Attribution Bias

Attribution bias comes into play when a person decides that an occurrence was caused by an individual characteristic of a person or was the result of a specific situation or circumstance (Cridland, 2013). Attribution bias causes a person not to consider the bigger picture. We become angry or frustrated when we judge another person to be responsible for an event, but then become less upset when we appreciate that external circumstances are responsible. For example, we become annoyed at how slow the person in the passing lane is driving only to discover that the road narrows to one lane ahead and that the driver had no choice but to slow down.

## Confirmation Bias

Confirmation bias happens when someone wants something to be true and they end up believing it to be true. Confirmation bias occurs as a direct result of a desire for one's beliefs to be true. Confirmation bias stops us from gathering more information once we have convinced ourselves that what we wanted to believe happened did happen (Heshmat, 2015). Examples include the arrogant thinking of a narcissist who believes that their interpretation of an event is the true interpretation or the individual with an obsessive-compulsive disorder who believes that everything is dirty.

## Framing

Imagine that there are three people, Susan, Maria, and Janelle, sitting in a room deciding what to do with their Saturday afternoon. Susan asks if they should all go to a museum. The last time Maria went to a museum she was fascinated by the exhibits and quickly responds saying, "Yes, let's go!" Janelle, however, says, "You two go ahead, I need to get some work done but I'll meet you for dinner." As the friends continue to talk, they discover that Janelle, the friend who had work to do, had visited a museum in the past year and felt the exhibits were poorly done. Both Maria and Janelle responded to the question based upon a previous experience; that is, each of them *framed* their decision based on the positive or negative connotation going to the museum generated for each. The *Framing Effect* occurs when an individual decides upon an option based on whether the options presented stimulate positive or negative connotations or feelings. We can influence others by setting a positive context or frame. As nurses we know that how information is presented can greatly influence how a patient responds. Oftentimes, how we frame a problem can influence if and how soon it is solved (Association for Psychological Science, 2016).

## Halo Effect and Horns Effect

Why are attractive people perceived to be smarter, funnier, or more likeable then less attractive people? The *Halo Effect* is a cognitive bias that influences our impression of someone based on how we feel about their character; that is, perceptions of one trait can carry over to others (Cherry, 2020). The *Horns Effect* works in a similar fashion but with negative impressions. The halo effect was initially described in 1920 when Edward Thorndike asked commanding officers to describe characteristics of their soldiers. Thorndike wanted to know if the rating of one characteristic influenced how others were rated—the answer was a resounding "yes." This cognitive bias (and its negative counterpart) has been a recognized influencer of our perceptions for at least 100 years.

## Self-Serving Bias

*Self-serving bias* has been defined as "People's tendency to attribute positive events to their own character but attribute negative events to external factors" (Boyles, 2013, para. 1). Self-serving bias occurs in all types of situations, and across all ages, genders, and cultures. It can change over time due to experiences or emotional factors. Western and Eastern cultures tend to prize different characteristics; these cultural attitudes can influence the collective bias of a community. Although it can bolster one's self-esteem, it can also lead to conflict and adverse relationships (Herndon, 2018). Consider the student who does well on an exam and decides the result is because he studied hard and understood the material well. His friend, however, did not do so well and explains that the result was because the instructor's teaching methods were poor. Both are using self-serving bias to explain the results.

## Status Quo Bias

Status quo bias develops from an innate belief that something is better if left alone; that is, that doing nothing is better than the disruption of change (Rius, 2019). Status quo bias is equivalent to loss aversion or a need to stay in control. Dean et al. (2017) suggest that this type of thinking is more likely when an individual is overwhelmed by choices. In nursing practice, status quo bias may have a lot to do with the staff's resistance to change even though the evidence shows that the change will enhance patient safety. It might also explain patient resistance to a change in therapies despite the evidence presented. Recommended lifestyle changes may be ignored because the patient perceives the status quo to be better or at least adequate. We must recognize that individuals, be they nurses or patients, consider the status quo to be safe because it has worked in the past. It makes the less risky decision appear to be the easier decision.

# Bias Within Health Care

We have discussed the types of bias found within the media as well as several ways our personal or cognitive biases can influence our thinking and decision making. Now let us consider if bias is also found in health care.

## Bias Within Healthcare Provider Groups

A recent study by Burgess et al. (2019) examined completed questionnaires from 3,756 medical students in their first and fourth years of study representing 49 medical schools to determine their political ideology and whether their ideology impacted care. Of the incoming medical students, 47.7% were identified as liberal, 33.3% as moderate, and 19.0% as conservative. The researchers noted that a more conservative ideology was found among fourth-year students, with "more explicit attitudes toward stigmatized groups, lower internal motivation to control racial prejudice, lower levels of trait empathy and empathy toward patients, and lower levels of patient-centered attitudes" (Burgess et al., 2019, p. 114). How can that type of ideological bias be avoided?

The authors make several recommendations regarding physician education, including increasing diversity among students, ensuring the success of individuals from marginalized populations, and further research to better understand the most effective interventions for reducing bias among medical students as well as all health professionals. They also note that, although their findings were more negative among more conservative students, politically conservative providers "may bring other valuable qualities to health care [and we need to] tap into positive attributes associated with political conservatism, such as conscientiousness, and moral values that are endorsed more strongly by conservatives, such as loyalty, self-control, and duty toward upholding the social norms of their group" (Burgess et al., 2019, p. 133). These findings can certainly not be generalized to all provider groups, but we can ask the same questions. If the same questionnaire were used with nursing students, what would the results tells us, and how could we use those results to diminish dangerous forms of bias and promote patient-centered care?

## Bias Within Health Literature

Those of us working in health care or health-related fields gather information from many types of written sources. Most of us think of literature as being fiction or nonfiction, poetry or prose. Literature is a form of human expression (Rexroth, 2019), and it can be written or presented orally. Scholarly literature is literature that "is written by researchers who are experts in their field" (Rutgers, 2020). Popular literature is written by journalists, employed by the organization for which they write, who "cover news and current events in a field, write profiles of people, places, or events, and express political opinions" (Rutgers, 2020). Trade and professional literature covers news within an identified field, reporting on research, opinions, trends, or events occurring within that field. Gray literature is also an important source of information and primarily refers to unpublished research, such as research reports, government reports, evaluations, theses, dissertations, webcasts, poster sessions, presentations, etc. The Fourth International Conference on Gray Literature defines *gray literature* as "That which is produced on all levels of government, academics, business and industry in print and electronic formats, but which is not controlled by commercial publishers" (California State University, 2020, para 2). Can we find bias in all of these types of literature? Again, the answer is "yes."

*Publication bias* refers to the tendency in scientific reporting whereby authors are more likely to submit, and journals are more likely to publish, pieces with results that would be considered positive (Joober et al., 2012). All authors have a bias, and researchers hope that their study results support their hypotheses. Some write in support of that bias; others try to be more balanced in their writing.

Publications can publish scholarly articles, and they can publish propaganda. We call this the *free press,* and it is derived from the Bill of Rights within the First Amendment to the U.S. Constitution, which states, "Congress shall make no law respecting an establishment of religion, or prohibiting the free exercise thereof; or abridging the freedom of speech, or of the press; or the right of the people peaceable to assemble, and to petition the Government for a redress of grievances" (U.S. Const. amend. I).

When reading professional articles, we can try to assess their level of bias by considering where the publication may fall on a liberal–conservative continuum, but this is oriented more toward news publications and media outlets, not as much for healthcare publications. We can, however, ask ourselves several questions as we read an article:

- *Is the information accurate?* Think critically about what the article is saying. Read more on the topic.
- *Do I doubt this information?* Investigate your doubts. Search for answers and use your best judgment.
- *Is this a peer-reviewed article?*
- *When was the article published?* Has new information or evidence been published since that date?

How can we trust the professional scientific information that is published? One method is to ensure that the information we are reading and are about to act upon has been peer reviewed. In the scholarly community, peer review is considered the most valid form of research evaluation because it ensures the following:

- *Evaluation.* Most journals engage in a process of peer review to ensure that the highest-quality articles are selected for publication.
- *Integrity.* Peer reviewers are independent of the journal publication and the research that has been conducted. Thus, peer review protects the integrity of the publishing process and the scholarly record.
- *Quality.* Peer reviewers offer revisions and ask questions in order to improve the quality of the research article and to prompt the author to consider new insights with regard to their research methods and the results that they have compiled. The peer review process gives authors access to the opinions of experts in the field who can provide support and insight (SAGE Publishing, 2020).

If an article has been peer reviewed, then you should have confidence that the material presented has been reviewed and accepted by experts in the field prior to its publication.

## Bias Within Research

Nurses are taught to rely on evidence. According to Jyothi (2012), evidence-based practice (EBP) is:

> a conscientious, explicit and judicious use of current best evidence with clinical expertise, and patient values to make decisions about the care of patients. It's the process of shared decision-making between practitioners, patient and significant others, based on research evidence, the patient's experiences and preferences, clinical expertise, and other robust sources of information. (p. 82)

Ultimately, EBP requires us to apply evidence from research to our practice. Evidence drives improvement initiatives and the standardization of healthcare practices and policies (Bower & Nemec, 2017). The Agency for Healthcare Research and Quality (2018) states that "evidence-based research provides the basis for sound clinical proactive guidelines and recommendations" (para. 1). Without question, EBP has become a cornerstone of health care. However, if we are to base our clinical decisions on research, how can we be certain that the research is not influenced by bias? The answer is, we cannot be certain.

Bias can occur within any stage of the research process. Researchers can introduce bias at any point from the design of the study and sampling to the collection and analysis of data. It is not a matter of whether bias is present:

> Unfortunately, bias is unavoidable. Biases are the inclinations, tendencies or opinions of researchers that may skew the results of their work. Because all experiments are designed and carried out by humans, they all contain at least some potential for bias. Solving for this variable, therefore, is crucial in obtaining reliable data. (*How Psychology Addresses Research Bias,* 2018, para. 1)

Understanding this enables us to critically review the scientific literature. When making clinical decisions, there often is no time to consider concepts such as error rates, statistical powers, inter-rater reliability, or data integrity. How then can we decide which evidence to incorporate into the process of care? The answer lies in our ability to recognize faults within scientific claims and our ability to think critically about the research that generated the evidence.

## Finding the Faults Within Scientific Claims

When we read a scientific study, what should we look for? Most of us will read an article or news report about a study with a slight (and healthy) dose of skepticism regarding the science. For example, many of us will question the results of a study if the statistical analysis of the data is not shared. We may decide to move on, but was the problem one of bad science or bad reporting of the science? **Figure 2-4** offers 12 points to consider when separating the "good" science from the "bad" science.

## Bias Within Professional Conversations

Nurses often find themselves in conversations with other providers and healthcare professionals. Those discussions will impact their practice. As discussed,

The Red Flags of Bad Science
(pseudoscience, quackery, scams)

**G** et past the clickbait.
- anecdotes
- testimonials
- ancient wisdom
- headlines: "recently found in nature"

**L** ook for crazy claims.
- conspiracy theories
- Cure-alls
- miracles – just because you don't know how it works doesn't make it magic

**A** nalyze sources
- is a celebrity doctor, Nobel winner, appealing to authority rather than evidence?
- "buy my book, videos, subscription" – my results are unpublished elsewhere
- testimonials
- "natural/organic"

**D** etermine outside expert opinions
- be skeptical – check references
- avoid misinterpretations of events
- are expert's statements/findings taken out of context

**Figure 2-4** A guide to spotting bad science.
Compound Interest 2015.

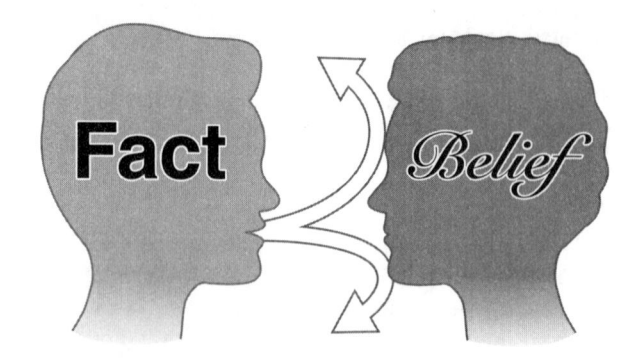

**Figure 2-5** What motivates these authors?

earlier in this chapter, we all have cognitive and personal biases. How do we determine which opinions and statements are reasonable or factual?

Asking yourself questions and critically thinking about the content of the conversation helps (**Figure 2-5**). What facts were included in the discussion? What facts were missing? Do I need more information? Is the argument logical? What point of view was expressed? What is my point of view? Identifying bias is not always easy. It may *not* come in the form of a blatantly prejudicial statement. It is *not* always irrational. The best defense against bias is to appreciate its existence, identify it, check the facts, and try to minimize it when making clinical decisions.

## Strategies to Minimize Bias

Recognizing bias in health care is important because it can lead to disparities in care. If we are unaware of bias, we are blind to the dangers it may create. Unintentional bias is especially difficult to manage; it can happen unknowingly despite an individual's best intentions. What can we do to eliminate it? Bucknor-Ferron and Zagaja (2016) suggest five strategies to minimize unintentional or unconscious bias:

1. *Personal awareness.* Having personal awareness is "the process of looking inward to recognize beliefs and values that can lead to unconscious bias" (p. 61). Awareness helps us to diminish the impact these beliefs and values may have on patient interactions. Awareness helps us to recognize the attitudes and behaviors that are acceptable, and those that are unacceptable.
2. *Acknowledgment.* Acknowledging that a bias exists allows one to accept accountability and responsibility to remove that bias. Removing bias helps nursing as a profession to foster the behaviors that enhance the nurse–patient relationship.
3. *Empathy.* Healthcare professionals must be able to empathize with patients and their circumstances to understand how they are feeling. Buckow-Ferron and Zagaja (2016) state that "Nurses can develop empathy by making a conscious effort to understand the patient's situation, become fully immersed in the patient point of view, and get a sense of what it's like to be walking in the patient's shoes" (p. 61). A common example

occurs when we care for a patient who presents with health problems caused by high-risk behaviors such as smoking or abuse of drugs or alcohol. Our feelings about this behavior can easily become a barrier to care by negatively impacting how we interact with the patient. We must recognize these feelings to develop practice behaviors that will mitigate these feelings.
4. *Advocacy*. Nurses frequently take on the role of patient advocate by helping patients navigate through the complex healthcare system, helping them to express their concerns and/or questions and educating them so they can make informed decisions and participate in their care. Advocating for patients requires nurses to put the patient's beliefs and feelings ahead of their own; at times it will require the nurse to allow the patient's biases to influence decisions while silencing their own.
5. *Education*. Raising awareness to the bias that exists within health care requires education. Formal discussions regarding patient-centered care and equality of care help to enhance a healthcare professional's sensitivity to internal and external biases. Strengthening the knowledge base of all providers by focusing on evidence, creating an atmosphere of acceptance and inclusion, and being transparent will diminish the dangers of bias.

# Nursing's Obligation to Impact Bias Within Health Policy Development or Reform

## Reflection

How many times have we been told to "reflect" on something by a parent, teacher, friend, or mentor? The process begins early in life when, as a child, we are given a "time out" to reflect upon what we did (and that we apparently should not have done) or what we could have done better. We are asked to reflect quietly, in writing, or in a conversation. Why? It is how we learn; it is how we grow. It helps us to understand an event or experience. It helps us learn from our mistakes and appreciate our achievements as we develop our personal belief system. Reflection allows us to see our values and feelings at work. If we like what we see, we can try to repeat that action; if we are not pleased with what we see, we can try to change it.

In health care, reflection can help us to understand why we do things the way we do. Regardless of our specialty, reflection helps us to critique our professional practice to determine how we can make it better. Having colleagues and mentors available to help us supports the process as we make judgments and decisions.

Self-reflection is also an important skill that nurses must use as they strive to improve health care. Nurses who take on advanced practice roles quickly find that public policy impacts what the scope of their practice will be. They also quickly learn that practice possibilities are impacted by politics and the political atmosphere they find themselves in. Suddenly, nurses realize that what they can do professionally is not only based upon science and evidence and education, it is based upon political decisions made by a body of predominantly non-nurses. They realize they may need to change those political decisions to change or enhance their practice.

## Know Your Political Identity

Successfully managing health policy change requires identifying the bias that exists within the policy. It also requires understanding one's own political identity. Recognizing liberalism, conservatism, progressivism, and libertarianism, within the policies that govern our practice and within ourselves, is necessary during health policy analysis and change initiatives.

Understanding these philosophies will help nurses politick for the changes they see as necessary to ensuring health and wellness for those they serve. Understanding these philosophies will also help them identify the biases that influence policy and lawmakers' reactions to recommendations related to health policy. Nurses are taught to follow the evidence. They can present scientific evidence that proves that a policy needs to change and get no reaction because the political philosophy of the group or the individual's ideological bias overshadows the evidence. Appreciating that political and ideological bias exists will help nurses decide which government official or group might support the change they believe is needed and when the timing for change is right.

## Check Your Facts

Fact-checking has become a necessary endeavor, especially with respect to political claims. How often do we say, "That can't be right!" and then scramble to check a fact. Where do we look for the answer? Should we post the question on Facebook or should we go to Google and ask the question? Someday we may be able to access an automated site that will perform computational fact-checking to distinguish between checkable and uncheckable statements. Today, fact-checking is performed by humans and, as we have learned, humans are biased. During the 2012 presidential campaign, Mitt Romney's pollster, Neil Newhouse, said, "Fact-checkers come to this with their own sets of thoughts and beliefs and you know what? We are not going let our campaign be dictated by fact-checkers" (Robertson et al., 2020, p. 218).

Can we separate the bias from the fact, the truth from the belief? Fortunately, a number of organizations and resources are available to help us do so. A recent study by Robertson, Mourao, and Thorson (2020) reported in the *International Journal of Press/Politics* investigated audience relationships with fact-checking through a survey fielded after the election of former president Trump in 2016. Their key findings were as follows:

- The establishment of dedicated fact-checking organizations is a recent phenomenon driven by outlets such a PolitiFact and FactCheck.org.
- Following the U.S. example, this form of journalism has spread worldwide, with operations being established in South America, Africa, and Europe.

- The fact-checking movement has been criticized by both academia and the public.
- Although fact-checking sites describe themselves as neutral, they are viewed as political by audiences.
- The influence that fact-checking has on the media is limited.
- Liberals are more likely than conservatives to share their content.
- Fact-checks are shared in a biased way.

Fact-checking was designed to be objective; "In the eyes of audiences, however, fact-checkers are perceived as partisan actors in a divided media system" (p. 234).

How then do we know which fact-checking sites can be trusted? The following fact-checking sources are generally recognized as being nonpartisan:

- *PolitiFact*: PolitiFact is an independent fact-checking website supported by the Poynter Institute.
- *FactCheck.org*: FactCheck.org is a fact-checking project developed by the Annenberg Public Policy Center of the University of Pennsylvania.
- *Lead Stories*: The Lead Stories FactChecker is a web-based fact-checking platform supported by the RAND Corporation.
- *Science Feedback*: Science Feedback is a nonprofit that offers two online fact-checkers, one on climate and one on health.
- *AP Fact Check*: The Associated Press developed this fact-checker to support accountability in journalism around the globe.
- *"Fact Checker"*: The *Washington Post* offers a weekly blog that fact-checks issues of national importance.
- *Snopes.com*: Snopes is the oldest and largest fact-checking site on the Internet.
- *PunditFact*: This site is dedicated to checking the accuracy of claims by pundits, columnists, bloggers, political analysts, the hosts and guests of talk shows, and other members of the media.
(Media Bias Fact Check, 2020)

Although fact-checking can help, misinformation, lies, and omission of critical information will continue to make it into the news we receive. Bill Adair, a professor of journalism and public policy at Duke University's Sanford School of Public Policy, once stated something we all need to remember. When asked about the best way to identify and navigate misinformation (during the COVID-19 pandemic) he stated,

> There's always the tendency to pick the extremes. As journalists we focus on the fight over the mask rather than the 97% of people who are complying with masks. It is not news when dog bites man. It is news when the man bites the dog. But I think we have to put things into perspective for people and make sure they understand when we are talking about the outliers. What has changed in the digital age is that the outliers, the fringe, has a megaphone it never had before. (Ferreri, 2020, para. 25)

## Find an Influential Organization That Can Help

As nurses and other health professionals work to create or change health policy, they can often find an organization whose goals align with their own. State and national organizations such as the American Nurses Association and its affiliated state nursing associations have access to the expertise and funding needed to accomplish some of nursing's goals, especially those related to the scope of nursing practice. Most nurses are familiar with these organizations. They are not as familiar with organizations such as think tanks that can help them navigate the political quagmire that stands between them and health or healthcare policy change. The Cambridge Dictionary defines the term *think tank* as "a group of experts brought together, usually by a government, to develop ideas on a particular subject and to make suggestions for action" (Cambridge Dictionary, 2020c, para. 1). The United States has around 2,000 think tanks—nearly a third of the world's total (The Best Schools, 2020). American think tanks are constantly researching solutions for the world's problems and then arguing, advocating, and lobbying for policy changes at the local, state, and federal levels. The following are some of the more influential think tanks in the U.S. political landscape:

- *Urban Institute.* The mission of the Urban Institute is to "open minds, shape decisions, and offer solutions through economic and social policy research" (Urban Institute, n.d., para. 1). This organization looks for opportunities to use its research in support of change. The Urban Institute claims to be a nonpartisan organization that does not take positions on hot-button current political issues. However, the organization is known as a liberal or left-leaning think tank because its researchers often come to conclusions that call for policies that advance the progressive agenda.
- *Commonwealth Fund.* The Commonwealth Fund promotes a high-performing healthcare system and advocates for low-income families, the uninsured, minorities, young children, and the elderly. It has a liberal bias. Do not confuse it with the Commonwealth Foundation (which focuses on issues in Pennsylvania).
- *Kaiser Family Foundation (KFF).* The KFF focuses on major healthcare issues in the United States and, to a lesser extent, the world. Over the years, it has become a must-read for healthcare devotees and a quality nonpartisan source for up-to-date and accurate information on health policy.
- *American Enterprise Institute (AEI).* The AEI seeks limited government, private enterprise, individual liberty and responsibility, vigilant and effective defense and foreign policies, political accountability, and open debate. The AEI has become the most prominent think tank associated with neoconservatism, a variant of conservatism that is more moderate, and has succeeded in placing its members in influential government positions.
- *Brookings Institution.* One of the oldest think tanks in the United States, the mission at Brookings is "to conduct in-depth research that leads to new ideas for solving problems facing society at the local, national and global level" (Brookings Institution, n.d., para. 1). The *Washington Post* (2009) has described Brookings as centrist and liberal. The *Los Angeles Times* (2008)

has described Brookings as liberal-leaning and centrist. Briefings and other documents from Brookings are often quoted.
- *Cato Institute.* The Cato Institute is also a public policy research organization "dedicated to the principles of individual liberty, limited government, free markets, and peace. Its scholars and analysts conduct independent, nonpartisan research on a wide range of policy issues" (Cato Institute, n.d., para. 1). The organization accepts no funding from government entities; 80% of its funding is received through tax-deductible contributions from individuals.
- *Heritage Foundation.* The mission of the Heritage Foundation is to "formulate and promote conservative public policies based on the principles of free enterprise, limited government, individual freedom, traditional American values, and a strong national defense" (Heritage Foundation, 2020, para. 2). The goals of the organization are threefold: to provide timely accurate research on key policy issues, to effectively market their findings to primary audiences, and to pursue conservative policies to help Americans build a better life.

Organizations, when used to support the need to change a given policy or to support a new policy, can be powerful allies. Finding those with similar goals is part of the process for change. Using their resources, their research, and their expertise is an important action to consider. Whether we as nurses are passionate about clean water, school lunch programs, improving access to care, or practicing to the full scope of our license, much can be accomplished by influencing health and healthcare policy. In 2016, there were approximately 2.86 million registered nurses in the United States (Statistica, 2019). Certainly, we have different interests and, yes, we have different biases, especially about what is needed most. However, we can find others with similar interests and we can put our biases to work, for us and for those we serve. Identifying organizations with similar interests can help us open the doors that need to be opened.

# Conclusion

Bias is alive and well. It is an unavoidable addition to our thinking processes. Primary types of bias include political bias that alters information based upon a political position, ideological bias that shapes information to mirror an opinion or belief, and personal or cognitive biases that shape information based on personal experiences and desires. Bias appears in the media, within professional articles, within research, within organizations, and within everyday conversations. Bias exists within health care. Political parties develop campaign agendas that include healthcare issues; political debates argue proposals that can range from offering Medicare coverage to all citizens and retaining and improving the Affordable Care Act ("Obamacare") to repealing the Affordable Care Act and allowing private insurers to decide policies related to coverage. Ideological bias is heard when abortion, the right to die, and other moral issues are debated. Personal and cognitive bias is heard when a provider's experience is used to identify what they believe to be a wrong within health care.

Nurses have an obligation to get involved with change when they believe a healthcare practice or lack of practice creates an adverse situation for a group of individuals. Nurses need to become more comfortable using their voices to improve health care for all and to address circumstances that negatively impact health. Before raising our voices, we need to reflect upon the need we see, sorting out the science from the bias, to know our personal biases and political identities, to know the facts that relate to a given healthcare policy or health determinant, and to look for others who can support our goals. We need to navigate fake news and find a way to deal with misinformation that can impact health and health care. Then, our obligation is to speak up to impact health and healthcare policies, whether it is at the practice, organizational, local, state, national, or even global level.

## Chapter Discussion Points

1. Define *bias*. List three examples of political bias influencing public health policy.
2. List three types of media bias.
3. Describe methods that can be used to identify bias with professional healthcare publications, research, and conversations.
4. Give a healthcare policy example of what an individual would advocate for if they tended to politically lean toward:
    a. Conservatism
    b. Progressivism
    c. Libertarianism
5. What steps would you take to influence bias within healthcare policy development or reform?
6. How can professional nurses become engaged in healthcare advocacy so that bias does not lead to healthcare disparities?

## CASE STUDY 2-1: Meeting a Community Public Health Need

### Background
On March 23, 2010, the Patient Protection and Affordable Care Act (ACA) was enacted. Most people think that this act was limited to offering health insurance options for millions of Americans who were uninsured. However, the ACA also impacted many other areas of health care by including important requirements for patient safety and quality as well as for organizations that operated one or more hospitals. Within Section 501(c)(3) of the ACA, hospital organizations must meet specific requirements to become or remain tax exempt. These requirements, listed in Section 501(r)(3-6) of the act, included the requirement for a Community Health Needs Assessment, or CHNA (IRS, 2019b).

The ACA's rules spell out a need for a CHNA to be completed at least once every 3 years. A hospital organization is also required to "adopt an implementation strategy to meet the community health needs identified through the CHNA" (IRS, 2019a, para. 3). The CHNA also requires input from persons within the community who have "special knowledge of or expertise in public health" (IRS, 2019a, para. 4). The finished document is to be made available to the public, and the authorized body of the hospital must adopt or formally approve the implementation strategy. There are many more requirements for this document, and it has become a major organizational undertaking to ensure that it is developed correctly, meets the intent of the ACA's requirements, and is implemented. Because many individuals from various backgrounds are involved, the introduction of bias is inevitable.

## Addressing an Identified Need

The case study describes a need identified by a nonprofit health system for its defined community. The health system documented a newborn mortality rate that was twice the national average and identified this as a need to be addressed. Further analysis revealed that the organization had two neonatologists on staff and a nursery area but no designated Level II or III Neonatal Intensive Care Services (NICU). A lack of perinatology services for high-risk pregnant women within the community was documented. In addition, the demographics of pregnant women included a subset of those who did not receive consistent prenatal care. Private obstetricians would not accept noninsured patients and would refer their high-risk patients to private perinatologists who were located either 34 or 70 miles away and were affiliated with a hospital that included a Level III NICU. Women who did not have the means or insurance to establish themselves with these private perinatologists would present to the hospital in labor and deliver their newborn. Often, shortly after delivering, they would be told that their newborn was being transferred to a Level III NICU. The statistical outcome of this situation was a newborn/neonatal mortality rate that was two times the national rate.

The CHNA describing this need was presented to the health system's board of directors. The board designated the issue to be a priority and requested a proposal to address it. To develop this proposal, a task force of individuals from various organizations and backgrounds was assembled. They worked on several corrective action plans but could not agree on one. The board intervened, primarily because 3 months had passed, and suggested that the task force present the top two plans. The plans are described as follows.

## Plan A

Plan A included the following:

- The organization would employ three obstetricians to ensure prenatal care for all members of the community.
- The organization would contract with a perinatologist to develop a perinatal clinic to be offered one to two times per week to provide specialty care for all high-risk pregnant patients.
- The organization would renovate space to accommodate both services and acquire the necessary supplies and equipment inclusive of an ultrasound device that could perform Level II ultrasounds.
- A transfer agreement with a facility that provided a team to retrieve and transport a high-risk pregnant patient or a high-risk newborn would be arranged.
- Private obstetricians within the community would be financially supported for care provided to uninsured or underinsured patients.
- A community drive would be held to raise funds to support the program's startup capital costs.

## Plan B
Plan B included the following:

- A formal transfer agreement would be arranged with two facilities that had the capability to care for both high-risk pregnant women and high-risk newborns. This would hopefully ensure that the capacity would be available when needed.
- Transport services would be offered by a private charitable organization within the community for high-risk patients who needed to see a perinatologist located outside of the community.
- The hospital would complete the process to apply for state designation as a Level II NICU. If approved, necessary space would be renovated, and equipment purchased. Nursing staff would receive additional training to care for infants requiring this level of care.
- Two additional obstetricians would be recruited to the community as private practitioners.
- The hospital would undertake recruitment of a perinatologist to the community as a private practitioner.

## Case Study Discussion Questions

1. Which plan would you advocate for, and why? What is driving your decision? Can you identify the types of personal cognitive biases at work within your decision?
2. Many on the board would not discuss the pros and cons of each plan without knowing the projected cost for each. Estimated budgets of expenses and revenue were presented. Start-up capital costs were considered a nonfactor because philanthropy was available to cover those expenses. Projected ongoing costs and revenue for Plan A suggested that the program would operate at a loss of approximately $300,000 per year. Plan B was projected to financially operate at a near break-even level based upon predicted annual income.

    Does this change your choice of plans and, if so, why? Are your biases regarding your choice of plan strengthened or weakened by this information?
3. The majority of the health system's board members are retired corporate executives. The community leadership is Republican. What ideological and/or political biases would you expect to underlie the board's discussion and decision?
4. The community has its own newspaper that tends to recognize and praise community organizations that help those in need of services. Which plan would you expect the newspaper to promote? What type of media bias would underlie this choice?
5. This community also has a Healthcare Taxing District that voters had mandated several years prior to this discussion and decision. Party affiliation for registered voters within the county is 43% Republican, 34% Democrat, and 23% Independent or not known. The Healthcare Taxing District's mandate is to support health and healthcare services for those in need. Funds are raised based upon a property tax millage rate and total approximately $20 million annually. The hospital receives approximately $11 million per year for services rendered to indigent patients and the remaining $9 million is allocated to various nonprofit community organizations that focus on health and/or health care. The board of the Taxing District are elected by the public; two of seven members have a healthcare background and four of seven are registered Republicans. What biases do you think might influence this group's reaction to the two plans?
6. If you were tasked with presenting the two plans, what steps would you take to minimize the impact of bias on the final decision?

## Outcome
Ultimately, the hospital's board of directors approved Plan A. Physicians were recruited, and within approximately 1 year the program was operational. During this year of preparation, a presentation was made to the Healthcare Taxing District Board and they approved a request for an additional $300,000 per year to fund the program. Within 3 years the neonatal mortality rate had decreased to the national average. Three years later (6 years after opening) the Healthcare Taxing District withdrew funding, and 2 years after that decision, the hospital was sold to a for-profit healthcare system and the program was dismantled.

## References

Agency for Healthcare Research and Quality. (2018). *Clinical guidelines and recommendations.* https://www.ahrq.gov/prevention/guidelines/index.html

Association for Psychological Science. (2016). *How language 'framing' influences decision-making.* https://www.psychologicalscience.org/publications/observer/obsonline/how-language-influences-decision-making.html

Bower, E. J., & Nemec, R. (2017). Origins of evidence-based practice and what it means for nurses. *International Journal of Childbirth Education, 32*(2), 14–18.

Boyles, A. (2013). *The self-serving bias: Definition, research, and antidotes.* https://www.psychologytoday.com/us/blog/in-practice/201301/the-self-serving-bias-definition-research-and-antidotes

Broockman, D., & Skovron, C. (2018). Bias in perceptions of public opinion among political elites. *American Political Science Review, 112*(3), 542–563. https://doi.org/10.1017/S0003055418000011

Brown, L. (2017). *Poll: 62 percent of Americans see partisan bias in media.* https://townhall.com/tipsheet/laurettabrown/2017/04/05/poll-62-percent-of-americans-see-partisan-bias-in-media-n2309415

Brookings Institution. (n.d.). *About us.* https://www.brookings.edu

Bucknor-Ferron, P., & Zagaja, L. (2016). Five strategies to combat unconscious bias. *Nursing, 46*(11), 61–62.

Buetow, S. (2019). Apophenia, unconscious bias and reflexivitiy in nursing qualitative research. *International Journal of Nursing Studies, 89,* 8–13. https://doi.org/10.1016/j.ijnurstu.2018.09.013

Burgess, D. J., Hardeman, R. R., Burke, S. E., Cunningham, B. A., Dovidia, J. F., Nelson, D. B., Perry, S. P., Phelan, S. M., Yeazel, M. W., Herrin, J., & van Ryn, M. (2019). Incoming medical students' political orientation affects outcomes related to care of marginalized groups: Results from the medical student CHANGES study. *Journal of Health Politics, Policy and Law, 44,* 113–146. https://doi.org/10.1215/03616878-7206755

California State University. (2020). *Nursing Grey Literature.* https://libraryguides.fullerton.edu/c.php?g=392484&p=7554644

Cambridge Dictionary. (2020a). *Media.* https://dictionary.cambridge.org/us/dictionary/english/media

Cambridge Dictionary. (2020b). *Mainstream media.* https://dictionary.cambridge.org/dictionary/english/mainstream-media

Cambridge Dictionary. (2020c). *Think Tank.* https://dictionary.cambridge.org/us/dictionary/english/think-tank

CATO Institute. (n.d.). *About Cato.* https://www.cato.org/about

Chemical Safety Facts. (2015). *A rough guide to spotting bad science.* https://www.chemicalsafetyfacts.org/chemistry-context/spotting-bad-science

Cherry, K. (2020). *Why the halo effect influences how we perceive others.* https://www.verywellmind.com/what-is-the-halo-effect-2795906

Corporate Finance Institute. (n.d.). *Anchoring.* https://corporatefinanceinstitute.com/resources/knowledge/trading-investing/anchoring-bias/

Cridland, C. (2013). *Attribution biases—How do you see the world?* https://www.mediate.com/articles/CridlandC3.cfm

Dean, M., Kibris, O., & Masatlioglu, Y. (2017). Limited attention and status quo bias. *Journal of Economic Theory, 169*, 93–127.

Ferreri, E. (2020). *Navigating fake news: How Americans should deal with misinformation online.* https://today.duke.edu/2020/08/navigating-fake-news-how-americans-should-deal-with-misinformation-online

Hassell, H., Holbein, J. B., & Miles, M. R. (2020). *There is no liberal media bias in which news stories political journalists choose to cover.* https://advances.sciencemag.org/content/6/14/eaay9344/tab-pdf

Heritage Foundation. (2020). *About Heritage.* https://www.heritage.org/about-heritage/mission

Herndon, J. (2018). *What is a self-serving bias and what are some examples of it?* https://www.healthline.com/health/self-serving-bias

Heshmet, S. (2015). *What is confirmation bias?* https://www.psychologytoday.com/us/blog/science-choice/201504/what-is-confirmation-bias

*How psychology addresses research bias.* (2018). https://www.brescia.edu/2018/01/research-bias/

Internal Revenue Service. (2019a). *Community health needs assessment for charitable hospital organizations—Section 501(r)(3).* https://www.irs.gov/charities-non-profits/community-health-needs-assessment-for-charitable-hospital-organizations-section-501r3

Internal Revenue Service. (2019b). *Requirements for 501(c)(3) hospitals under the Affordable Care Act—Section 501(r).* https://www.irs.gov/charities-non-profits/charitable-organizations/requirements-for-501c3-hospitals-under-the-affordable-care-act-section-501r

Jones, J. M., & Ritter, Z. (2018). *Americans see more news bias; most can't name neutral source.* https://news.gallup.com/poll/225755/americans-news-bias-name-neutral-source.aspx

Joober, R., Schmitz, N., Annable, L., & Boksa, P. (2012). Publication bias: What are the challenges and can they be overcome? *Journal of Psychiatry & Neuroscience, 37*(3), 149–152. https://doi.org/10.1503/jpn.120065

Jyothi, N. (2012). Evidence-based practice—the future of nursing and the role of the nurse. *International Journal of Nursing Education, 4*(2), 82–84.

Lajka, A. (November 26, 2019). *Photo shows soldier being tortured, not the U.S. ambassador to Libya.* https://apnews.com/article/8216252563

*Left Wing vs. Right Wing.* (n.d.). https://www.diffen.com/difference/Left_Wing_vs_Right_Wing

Lexico. (2020a). *Liberal.* https://www.lexico.com/en/definition/liberal

Lexico. (2020b). *Conservative.* https://www.lexico.com/en/definition/conservative

Lexico. (2020c). *Conservatism.* https://www.lexico.com/definition/conservatism

Lexico. (2020d). *Progressivism.* https://www.lexico.com/definition/progressivism

Lexico. (2020e). *Libertarianism.* https://www.lexico.com/definition/libertarianism

Los Angeles Times. (2008). *"Left Leaning" or "nonpartisan".* https://latimesblogs.latimes.com/readers/2008/05/left-leaning-or.html

Media Bias Fact Check. (2020). *10 Best Fact Checking Websites for 2020.* https://mediabiasfactcheck.com/2020/04/12/the-10-best-fact-checking-websites-for-2020/

Mitchell, A. (2018). *Americans still prefer watching to reading the news—and mostly still through television.* https://www.journalism.org/2018/12/03/americans-still-prefer-watching-to-reading-the-news-and-mostly-still-through-television/

New Jersey Institute of Technology. (2020a). *How to evaluate information sources: Critical thinking.* https://researchguides.njit.edu/c.php?g=671586&p=4727718

New Jersey Institute of Technology. (2020b). *How to evaluate information sources: Identify bias.* https://research guides.njit.edu/evaluate/bias

Quora. (2018). *What is an example of corporate bias?* https://www.quora.com/What-is-an-example-of-corporate-bias

Rexroth, K. (2019). *Literature.* https://www.britannica.com/art/literature

Rius, A. (2019). *What is status quo bias in sales and marketing?* https://corporatevisions.com/status-quo-bias/

Robertson, C. T., Maourao, R. R., & Thorson, E. (2020). Who uses fact-checking sites? The impact of demographics, political antecedents, and media use on fact-checking site awareness, attitudes, and behavior. *International Journal of Press/Politics*, 25(2), 217–237. https://doi.org/10.1177/1940161219898055

Rutgers, The University of New Jersey. (2020). *Popular literature vs. scholarly peer-reviewed literature: What's the difference?* https://www.libraries.rutgers.edu/scholaly_articles

SAGE Publishing. (2020). *Purpose of peer review.* https://us.sagepub.com/en-us/nam/purpose-of-peer-review

Statistica. (2019). *Number of registered nurses in the US from 2001–2016.* https://www.statista.com/statistics/185734/number-of-registered-nurses-in-the-us-since-2001/

The Best Schools. (2020). *The 50 most influential think tanks.* https://thebestschools.org/features/most-influential-think-tanks/

Thornton, B. (2013). *A brief history of media bias.* https://www.hoover.org/research/brief-history-media-bias

Turner, M. (2017). *Commentary vs. journalism: Are journalists biased?* https://www.schooljournalism.org/commentary-vs-journalism-are-journalists-biased/

University of Michigan. (2014). *News bias explored—What form does news bias take?* http://www.umich.edu/~newsbias/manifestations.html

Urban Institute. (n.d.). *About the Urban Institute.* https://www.urban.org/aboutus

Walsh, D. A. (2018). *How the right wing convinces itself that liberals are evil.* https://washingtonmonthly.com/magazine/july-august-2018/how-the-right-wing-convinces-itself-that-liberals-are-evil/

Washington Post. (2009). *In economy speech, Obama offers tax breaks and spending programs.* https://www.washingtonpost,com/up-dyn/content/article/2009/as/08/AR2009120803928.html

# CHAPTER 3

# Problem Identification and Agenda Setting: What Rises to a Policymaker's Attention?

Rick Mayes and Kenneth R. White

## KEY TERMS

**Bounded rationality:** The reality that rationality is limited; that human decision-making is influenced by emotions, fatigue, and a constant lack of full information; and that time is always limited. In short, decision-makers are goal-oriented and adaptive, but because of human cognitive and emotional architecture, they sometimes fail, occasionally in important decisions.

**Contextual dimensions:** Studying issues in the real world, in the circumstances or settings of what is happening at the time.

**Focusing event:** A sudden event or critical episode that catapults a public problem or issue to policymakers' and the general public's attention simultaneously. It is usually shocking, relatively rare, and harmful and/or strongly suggestive of potentially greater harms in the future.

**Iron triangle:** Legislators or their committees, interest groups, and administrative agencies that work together on a policy issue.

**Path dependency:** A phenomenon whereby each step along a policy pathway makes it increasingly difficult to change course thereafter. It describes the dynamic whereby each step in a particular policy direction induces further movement in the same direction—making the costs of exit (change) from a policy path rise over time. In other words, policies at rest tend to stay at rest.

**Policy entrepreneurs:** Elected politicians, leaders of interest groups, or motivated and energetic individuals who use their knowledge of the policymaking process and work with others to promote policy change. They consistently seek to take advantage of focusing events and windows of opportunity to champion their proposals and to get others to focus on addressing a particular public problem. They tend to be willing to pursue a trial-and-error strategy to turn their policy ideas into policy innovations, and hence disrupt the status quo.

**Public policy:** A course of action in response to a public problem; it is whatever governments choose to do or not to do. It involves political decisions for implementing programs to achieve societal goals. It is the outcome of any political struggle over finite resources: who gets what, when they get it, and how they get it.

**Punctuated equilibrium:** Rare moments when bursts of change from the status quo occur in political systems and processes that usually are stable and normally only allow incremental change (if any).

**Streams:** Metaphor used in John Kingdon's classic research on agenda setting that describes the interaction of public problems, policies, and politics that couple and uncouple throughout the process of agenda setting (Kingdon, 1995).

**Window of opportunity:** Limited time frame for action.

# Introduction

Why do some issues receive more government attention than others and some issues never receive any attention at all despite their urgency and importance? Who and what determines which issues policymakers focus on and what options emerge for their consideration? The answers to these questions help explain how political power is exercised and, as a consequence, who gets what, where, and when in our society. The answers also construct a roadmap for how registered nurses (RNs), advanced practice registered nurses (APRNs), and other interprofessional healthcare workers (IPHCWs) can most effectively and efficiently involve themselves in the policymaking process in order to both advance their own interests and to have major public concerns that nurses are experts on be addressed by government officials. Like all allied healthcare professionals, nurses face a number of problems and frustrations in the healthcare sector that *can* be reduced and even eliminated by a course of action adopted or created by policymakers. Ultimately, **public policy** is just problem-solving on a larger, collective scale. So, knowing what problems get policymakers' attention and how options emerge for their review is vitally important. It is important to note that policy is not an intervention per se, but that it leads directly to the development and implementation of interventions (Leeuw et al., 2014).

This chapter emphasizes the agenda-setting aspect of policymaking by using case studies at the local, state, and national levels. Agenda setting is the process of moving a problem to the government's attention so that different solutions can be considered by policymakers. Because nurses work on the front lines of all levels of the health system and in every healthcare setting, they are experts on what causes the majority of medical need. In addition, nursing is also the most respected profession in the United States, and has been for about two decades (Reinhart, 2020). Thus, nurses can and should play a uniquely influential role in advocating for, analyzing, and researching policies that improve the public's health and that address disparities and problems in the healthcare sector (Rasheed et al., 2020).

Fortunately for nurses and other IPHCWs, health issues are particularly appealing to politicians and policymakers. There is broad public consensus that health is an issue that is very important and deserving of attention. Health is not an issue that needs extensive explanation or justification to get on policymakers' agendas. No politician or elected official wants to be perceived as ignoring health issues or as opposing access to health care. As a result, healthcare-related politics tends to focus on "connecting solutions to problems" rather than on debating the existence of problems or the worthiness of a response (Campos & Reich, 2019).

Health is also an issue that drives voting behavior and election outcomes. Most voters care profoundly about such topics as Medicare, their health insurance, pharmaceutical costs, policies on preexisting conditions, copay and out-of-pocket limits on health spending, dependents being able to stay on their parents' health insurance plans until they are 26, access to family planning resources, and more (NPR et al., 2016). Policymakers and elected officials seeking reelection, therefore, have incentives to put health issues on their agenda, to be seen as offering solutions, and to avoid blame for problems or inaction on salient health matters. All these attributes of health policy work in nurses' and other healthcare stakeholders' favor because they make health an issue that is regularly on policymakers' agendas. That's the good news.

The bad news is that policymakers face the same limits on their time and attention that nurses do. Referred to as **bounded rationality** and the *behavioral theory of choice*, goal-oriented policymakers fully intend to rationally address all problems on the agenda universe and the systemic agenda to find the optimal solutions. However, cognitive limits, time constraints, and insufficient or an overwhelming amount (or lack) of information restricts policymakers' ambitions (Simon, 1995). Just as there are only so many patients for whom nurses can be responsible, there are only so many issues, problems, and possible options and responses that policymakers can closely focus on and try to address at any given time on their institutional and decision agendas. Uncertainty abounds, and the next public issue or problem is always beckoning for policymakers' time and attention (Jones, 2002). These limits lead to the more realistic and pragmatic necessity of *satisficing*—a combination of *satisfying* and *sufficing*. In short, policymakers will seek "good enough" responses to any issue that manages to get all the way to their decision agenda. Note that because of these limitations and constraints most policy change is incremental, a phenomenon known as **path dependency** (Pierson, 2000). Occasionally, however, bursts of major change, or **punctuated equilibrium**, will dramatically disrupt the status quo.

The various levels of the political agenda are as follows (**Figure 3-1**; Birkland, 2016):

- *Agenda universe*: All ideas that could possibly be brought up and discussed in a society.
- *Systemic agenda*: All issues that are commonly perceived as meriting public attention within the legitimate jurisdiction of the existing governmental authority.
- *Institutional agenda*: Items that have risen to the attention of a governing body.
- *Decision agenda*: Items about to be acted on by a governing body.

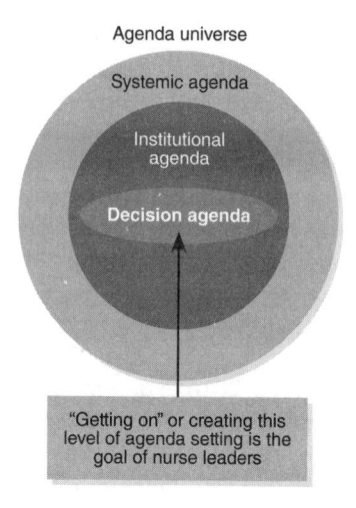

**Figure 3-1** Levels of the political agenda.

## CASE STUDY 3-1: A Local-to-National Example: The CAPABLE Model for Senior Citizens

Policies can be pioneered by nurses in hospitals and health systems just as much as in political and legislative settings. These new health policies can then be replicated across the country through their adoption by national programs like Medicare and Medicaid and multistate hospital and health systems. The Community Aging in Place—Advancing Better Living for Elders (CAPABLE) model illustrates how nurses and interprofessional leaders can create an interdisciplinary care model that addresses the social determinants of health, improves quality outcomes, and reduces total costs and spending. Sarah Szanton, professor of nursing and director of the Center of Innovative Care in Aging at the Johns Hopkins University School of Nursing, codeveloped CAPABLE to reduce disability and promote healthier aging at home (Szanton et al., 2016). The program's aim is to address many senior citizens' inability to take care of their basic needs like preparing meals, going to the bathroom, or dressing themselves. These unmet needs often result in admission to a long-term facility that compromises the individual's dignity and costs them, or taxpayers, thousands of dollars per month (Szanton, n.d.). Interestingly enough and related to the main theme of this chapter, Professor Szanton was a public health lobbyist before she decided to become a nurse.

CAPABLE is a low-cost program that integrates an interprofessional team—consisting of an occupational therapist, a nurse, and a handyman—who work with older adults, especially low-income urban men and women of color. The program began as an occupational therapy model and was called ABLE. Nursing and home repairs were added to the model later, and it became CAPABLE. The program's teams provide support to older adults to enhance their ability to live independently by assessing what matters to them to be able to age in place and then provides limited nursing care, occupational therapy, and home repairs based solely on those goals. Tested in Baltimore, Maryland, in research trials funded by the National Institutes of Health (NIH) and the Centers for Medicare and Medicaid Services (CMS)

Innovation Center, it has since expanded to 32 sites in 13 cities and 17 states throughout the United States from Maine to Texas and Alaska, with several rural sites where the need for elder care is often the most acute (Dassah et al., 2018). In terms of the programmatic results of this nurse-led initiative, CAPABLE's initial cost of approximately $2,825 per elderly participant has been found to result in significant reductions in measures of hospitalizations, emergency department use, and Medicare costs—approximately $10,000 per participant (Ruiz et al., 2017). When it comes to Medicaid spending and health system utilization, CAPABLE has been found to lower the likelihood of inpatient and long-term service use of low-income, elderly Medicaid participants and reduce monthly spending by $867 (Fortinsky & Robison, 2018). The model also improves activities of daily living, reduces fall rates, decreases hospitalizations, and improves patients' reports of high satisfaction with care (Spoelstra et al., 2019).

The CAPABLE model is a good example of nurse-led policy innovation (Sowers, 2016) in the private sector that influences public health outcomes. Most interventions for older people with disabilities have emphasized physical ability, but CAPABLE adds a major contribution—home modifications that restore physical function, given that declines in physical activity often are irreversible (Aliberti & Covinsky, 2019). CAPABLE also addresses the impact of pain, depression, and medication complexity. Spending their days literally on the front lines of healthcare provision and patient need, nurses know the micro-level realities like these as well if not better than any other healthcare professional. And, with almost 5 million registered nurses in the United States, the profession represents 1.5% of the entire U.S. population (National Council of State Boards of Nursing [NCSBN], 2019). Nurses' knowledge and expertise and their numbers provide the profession an opportunity to significantly influence the policy agenda for the betterment of public health. The nursing profession has viable solutions to the most challenging health policy debates because of its unique connection to patients, populations and systems (Miyamoto & Cook, 2019). For these kinds of nurse-crafted solutions to universal problems to gain ground, more and more nurses need "to sit at policy-making tables; form multisector and cross-sector partnerships with leaders from education, transportation, community development, and the environment; and get involved in leadership efforts to take actions to attain these goals, particularly at the local level, where the policy environment is usually more open to positive change" (Hassmiller & Kuehnert, 2020, p. 131).

## CASE STUDY 3-2: A Local-to-Regional-to-State Example: The Incremental Journey to Full Practice Authority for Virginia Nurse Practitioners

Licensing requirements for nurse practitioners vary from state to state—from full practice authority (FPA) in 22 states and the District of Columbia and Guam to reduced or restricted scopes of practice in the remaining states. According to the American Association of Nurse Practitioners (AANP, 2019), full practice authority is "the authorization of nurse practitioners (NPs) to evaluate patients, diagnose, order and interpret diagnostic tests and initiate and manage treatments—including prescribe medications—under the exclusive licensure authority of the state board of nursing." Legislative efforts are ongoing in states without FPA to remove barriers that restrict scope of practice. Nurse practitioners (NPs) often work at a grassroots level to influence legislative changes. Such is the example with incremental change in scope of practice laws for NPs in Virginia (Smith et al., 2020).

In 1975, legislation was passed in Virginia that required licensing for NPs to be governed by the Joint Boards of Nursing and Medicine. Since that time, incremental changes have been legislated, such as required certification for licensing, gradual expansion of prescriptive authority, and updated supervisory language and collaborative practice agreements. In 2016, a bill was introduced to eliminate mandated practice agreements in medically underserved communities. The bill was met with strong resistance from the Medical Society of Virginia, and although it was not passed, it did receive subcommittee approval. Keeping in mind incremental change, House Bill 793 was introduced in 2018, and although it was not an FPA bill, it was the next step in reducing practice barriers. Smith and colleagues (2020, p. 35) state: "Consistent with Kingdon's model, nurses working on this legislation highlighted the potential impact of HB793 on access to care in Virginia (the problem). Approving HB793 would remove access barriers by providing a path for NPs to practice independent of a collaborative agreement (the policy solution)." The Virginia General Assembly passed HB793, but not without controversy and compromise.

HB793 requires NPs to have 5 years of full-time practice (or 5,000 hours) before applying for an autonomous license. This is the longest transition to practice time in the nation and continuation of the oversight of the Joint Boards of Medicine and Nursing (Smith et al., 2020). To reach a compromise, the nurse advocate community accepted the conditions. Although compromise may have seemed undesirable, it is an important feature of the policymaking process (Kingdon, 2011). Progress has been made, but there is more work to be done for FPA.

How did the agenda start at a grassroots level? A goal of the Virginia Council of Nurse Practitioners (VCNP), headquartered in Charlottesville, has been to advocate for FPA. NPs, with the support of VCNP, were active in drafting legislation and searching for a patron in the Virginia legislature who would introduce the bill. It was essential to have the support of a lobbyist and legal advice. Grassroots efforts started with the 12 VCNP regional presidents mobilizing local and regional members to send predrafted emails to their legislators. Members were incentivized, motivated, and celebrated for participating. Each of the regions held a legislative reception to expose legislators to NPs and to learn more about the FPA legislation. It was important to get to "key" legislators, the ones who serve on the health and human services committees. VCNP recruited members to provide testimony during the legislative session.

Note that the U.S. Congress may pass a law that directs an agency to take action on a certain subject and set a schedule for the agency to follow in issuing rules. More often, an agency surveys its area of legal responsibility, and then decides which issues or goals have priority for rulemaking. A few of the many factors that an agency may consider are:

- New technologies or new data on existing issues
- Concerns arising from accidents or various problems affecting society

- Recommendations from congressional committees or federal advisory committees
- Petitions from interest groups, corporations, and members of the public
- Lawsuits filed by interest groups, corporations, states, and members of the public
- Presidential directives
- Requests from other agencies

## Overview of Models and Dimensions

Numerous researchers have developed theories of agenda setting. Many of these theories stress four categories of factors that influence what issues and problems get on policymakers' agendas and frame their set of possible options: actors, ideas, interests, and institutions. *Actors* comprise motivated **policy entrepreneurs**, activists, and other representatives of professional groups and organizations. They are people who care deeply about an issue and seek to draw attention to problems, link them to policy responses, and take advantage of windows of opportunity for change whenever they can (Beland & Katapally, 2018). *Ideas* refer to the power of shared norms and values in getting an issue on the policymakers' agenda. "It's not what you say, it's how you say it" is a common refrain in public opinion surveys and polling, suggesting that how an issue is framed can move it up or down (or off) public officials' agendas (Scheufele & Tewksbury, 2006). *Interests*, such as reelection (political self-preservation), economic benefit, national security, professional advancement, and more, shape the behavior of policymakers and those who work to influence them. An issue is more likely to get on the policy agenda when the interests of interest groups, issue advocates, and policy entrepreneurs align with the ambitions and reelection interests of policymakers (Brolan & Hill, 2016). *Institutions* are the organizational structures, rules, and procedures that are entrenched and shape actors' expectations, preferences, and behaviors (March & Olsen, 2008). Institutions are the settings—the legislatures, boards, executive suites, commissions, and councils—where the actors meet and deliberate over what will be on the agenda and how it will be managed. The **Iron Triangle** Model provides a visual of the bureaucratic agencies, interest groups, and congressional committees working together to advance an agenda and act in their own interests (**Figure 3-2**).

Researchers have also developed models that seek to explain when and how policies change once they have risen to the top of policymakers' agendas. The *punctuated equilibrium model* aims to explain how and why public policies tend toward stability for long periods of time and then be punctuated by brief bursts of radical change from the status quo (Baumgartner & Jones, 1991). The *advocacy coalition model* emphasizes the increased influence that occurs when multiple groups converge to advocate together on behalf of an issue or proposal (Sabatier, 1998). *Path dependency models* contend that once policies are in place, they normally become resistant to significant change (Pierson, 2000).

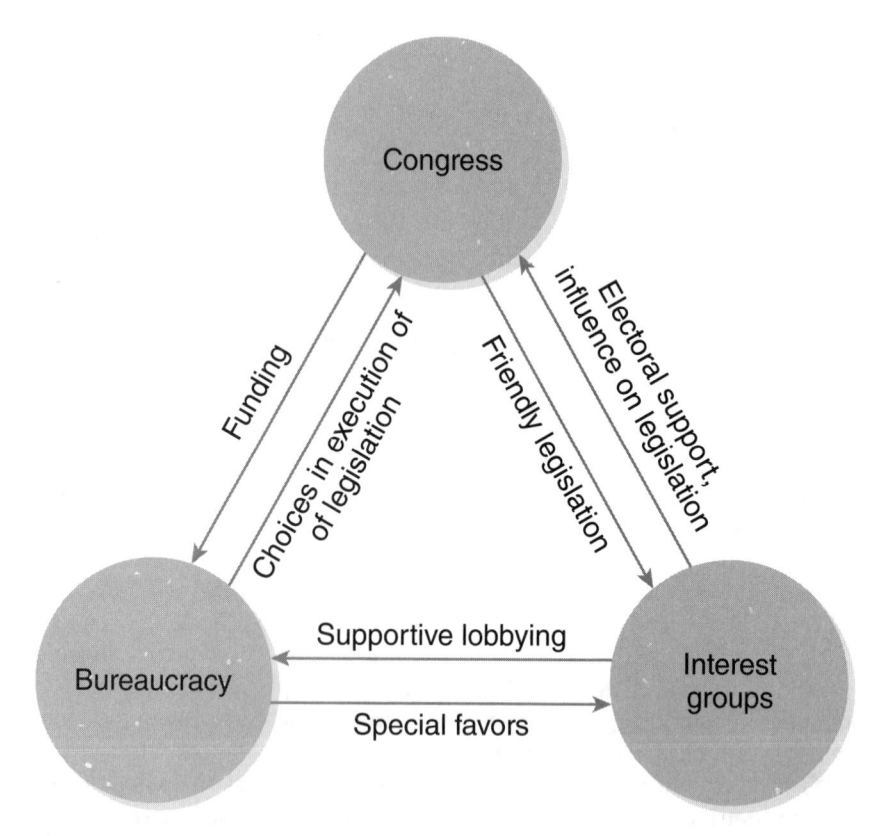

**Figure 3-2** Iron Triangle of politics.

Data from Frank R. Baumgartner and Beth L. Leech. 1998. *Basic Interests: The Importance of Groups in Political Science*. Princeton, NJ: Princeton University Press.

## The Kingdon Model

The most popular analytical model for understanding why and when policy agendas change as they do is the Kingdon model developed by John Kingdon (2011; **Figure 3-3**). In this model, the agenda refers to an array of issues viewed as the "pressing problems of the moment," and alternatives represent the policy options available to solve these problems (Kingdon, 2011). Kingdon used the metaphor of three **streams**—the problem stream, policy stream, and the politics stream—at least two of which need to converge at some point for a policy **window of opportunity** to open for change. The catalyst for these relatively rare windows of opportunity is usually a **focusing event** that punctuates the status quo (or policy equilibrium) that normally exists. Examples of such events include 9/11, Hurricane Katrina, the mortgage crisis and subsequent recession of 2008–2009, Barack Obama's election as the first president of color, COVID-19, the murder of George Floyd, and so on.

Kingdon distinguished between the "essential" and "residual" randomness of these events. For example, elections occur at regular intervals, which produce routine opportunities for windows of opportunity to occur. Even with these

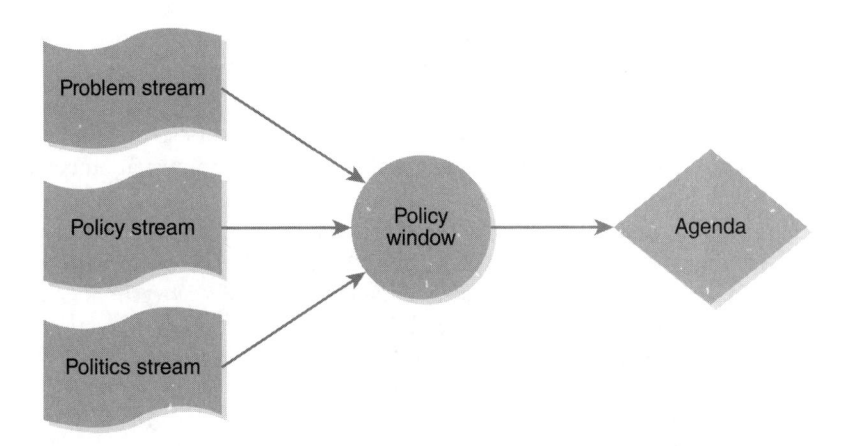

**Figure 3-3** The Kingdon Model.

Data from Herweg et al. Straightening the three streams: Theorising extensions of the multiple streams framework. 2015 European Consortium for Political Research.

routine opportunities for change, though, major departures from the status quo are still relatively rare. Yet there is a residual randomness such that occasionally crises lead to major change, and sometimes elections unexpectedly lead to dramatic changes in political membership and unanticipated electoral winners replace long-standing policymakers. When this happens, windows of opportunity open for the political agenda to change in new and unprecedented ways.

Kingdon's model draws upon the Carnegie School of organizational theory and the works of Herbert Simon, Johan Olsen, James March, and others who emphasized the limits of human cognition. His model is also biological in that there is a naturally incremental nature to policy evolution, where policies best adapted to survive do so over long periods of time but that there are moments when policies experience brief and major bursts of change (Baumgartner, 2016). Inspired by Cohen, March, and Olsen's (1972) garbage-can model of organizational choice, Kingdon's model emphasizes ambiguity and policymakers' time constraints.

In the problem stream, Kingdon distinguishes between conditions, which people may be aware of, and problems, which garner the attention of policymakers and lead them to act. In his model, interest groups and policy entrepreneurs play the biggest roles for pushing issues onto political agendas (Kingdon, 2011). They organize protests, engage in letter-writing campaigns, visit policymakers, and attend public meetings and hearings. They also seek to form coalitions with other interest groups and policy entrepreneurs to try to convince policymakers to have an issue receive more attention and to push forward possible proposals to address them. For example, nurses can work with parent–teacher associations to push for new policies mandating an RN in every school.

In the policy stream, ideas are generated by an informal network of civil servants, interest groups, academics, researchers, and consultants who collaborate together on responses to problems. From the interaction among this loose connection of participants, Kingdon argued, emerges a "policy primeval soup" that contains many policy ideas floating around that combine with one another in various ways (Kingdon, 2011). Ideas gestate over long periods of time, evolve, and are championed by interest groups and policy entrepreneurs who fight to push them higher on policymakers' agendas. They work so that they are ready in the event a crisis occurs or an election produces an unusual outcome and a new policy window opens.

In the *political stream*, changes in the national mood, interest group campaigns, and government makeup can contribute to a window of opportunity opening. Elections of new presidents, congressional leaders, governors, state legislative leaders, mayors, and county leaders, among others, can dramatically reshape the policy agenda (Kingdon, 2011). President Obama and Democrats in Congress worked to protect the ACA from repeal attempts by Republicans in the House and Senate and state Republican politicians from 2010 to 2018. From 2019 to the present, President Trump and Republicans in Congress have worked to try to repeal and replace the ACA, while Democrat politicians have worked to maintain the ACA and expand Medicaid in a number of states.

*Policy entrepreneurs* play a key role in the problem, policy, and political streams (**Figure 3-4**). They are the "squeaky wheel" advocates who constantly seek to collaborate with other advocates and policymakers to address problems and to try to make things better (Mintrom, 2019). Policy entrepreneurs are the "advocates who are willing to invest their resources—time, energy, reputation, money—to promote a position in return for anticipated future gain in the form of material, purposive, or solidary benefits" (Kingdon, 2011, p. 179). They have keen policy and political bargaining skills and persevere in keeping issues in front of policymakers who are often more inclined to listen to experts (Brasil, 2017). For example, in the healthcare arena, policy entrepreneurs have been calling on state officials to expand nurses' scope of practice to meet increased acute access problems of primary care in rural areas (Gregg et al., 2018). Nurses have been found to have far more potential for greater political influence in agenda setting and policy formation than they have realized or achieved (Whitehead, 2003). Yet most nurses probably do not see their lives

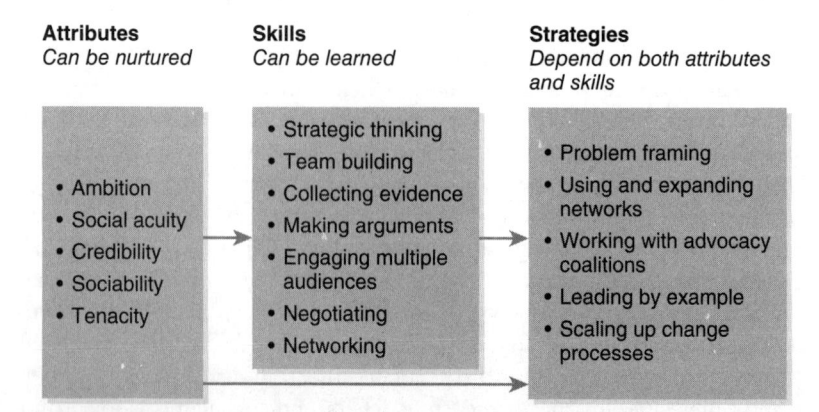

| Attributes<br>Can be nurtured | Skills<br>Can be learned | Strategies<br>Depend on both attributes and skills |
|---|---|---|
| • Ambition<br>• Social acuity<br>• Credibility<br>• Sociability<br>• Tenacity | • Strategic thinking<br>• Team building<br>• Collecting evidence<br>• Making arguments<br>• Engaging multiple audiences<br>• Negotiating<br>• Networking | • Problem framing<br>• Using and expanding networks<br>• Working with advocacy coalitions<br>• Leading by example<br>• Scaling up change processes |

**Figure 3-4** Common attributes, skills, and strategies of policy entrepreneurs.

Mintrom, M. (2019). So you want to be a policy entrepreneur? *Policy Design and Practice, 2*(4), 307-323. https://doi.org/10.1080/25741292.2019.1675989

as full of free time and open space for significantly increased policy advocacy (Monroy, 2020).

## Importance of Contextual Dimensions

Other policy scholars have added to the Kingdon model by emphasizing different **contextual dimensions** or factors in which policies get on the agenda, alternatives are formulated, and policies are put into effect. The first context is *political*. Political power is very fragmented in the United States. The political system includes numerous checks and balances and overlapping jurisdictions that were purposely created to make radical change difficult and rare. The federal government is divided; Congress, the presidency, and the judiciary contend with each other and contest each other's authority. The federal government then contends with 50 state governments that resist being told what to do.

A second context is *economic*. Economics is centered on scarcity. There are never enough resources to meet every need and want. When the economy is struggling, the general public and elected officials are usually focused on "fixing" the economy, and other policy priorities become sidelined. However, healthcare policy is essentially economic policy, because health care accounts for 18% of the U.S. economy and the healthcare sector is the single largest employer that has traditionally added jobs during recessions (thus reducing their severity; Salsberg & Martiniano, 2018).

*Social and cultural values* make up the third context that affects policy agendas. The norms of a society and what is culturally permissible influence what policymakers will consider and pursue in terms of policy change. For example, consider the following question: Is health care a human right? In almost all other high-income countries, access to basic health care is viewed socially and culturally as a human right similar to legal representation and food, shelter, and clothing. Yet this question has not been definitively settled in the United States. Similarly, paying for nursing school in the United States has usually been viewed culturally and socially as an individual responsibility; in other countries, however, the state pays for nursing education because healthcare providers are seen culturally and socially as essential workers (Collins & Hewer, 2020). The difference in whose responsibility it is to pay for nurses' education is fundamentally social and cultural in nature.

A final context that impacts agenda setting and policymaking is the *administrative* context. This context pertains to the practical concerns of who will implement a policy and how will they do so. For example, it is one thing to pass, create, and implement a new national ACA website (healthcare.gov) for individuals to purchase health insurance policies, but it is quite another to actually make it a reality (McIntyre & Song, 2019). Sometimes agenda setting is less about what should be done about a certain problem or need than what *can* be done. The majority of Americans agree that everyone should have access to basic health care, but how this should be achieved and paid for has been the subject of intense debate for decades and continues to this day (Gawande, 2017).

## Target Populations and Issue Characteristics

In addition to emphasizing the role of the political context in agenda setting, Deleon, Schneider, and Ingram (2007) highlight the social construction of target populations (i.e., those groups affected by the policy). They propose that one can best understand agenda setting, alternative formulation, and policy implementation by knowing how elected officials perceive different target populations. Thus, a policy proposal's target population—categorized as the advantaged, contenders, dependents, and deviants—has a profound impact on its likelihood of being seriously considered (Deleon et al., 2007). Their model suggests that pressure to initiate beneficial policies that will aid those groups viewed in a positive light—the "advantaged" and "dependents"—will be seen in a positive light, whereas those groups that are seen negatively—"contenders" and "deviants"—will be targeted by punitive policies (Deleon et al., 2005). For example, in many U.S. states, uninsured children of low-income parents qualify for public health insurance coverage through Medicaid or the Children's Health Insurance Program (CHIP), but their parents will not qualify for Medicaid. Low-income senior citizens, however, normally qualify for Social Security, Medicare, and Medicaid (as dual-eligibles). Age clearly influences the public's and policymakers' perceptions and framing of who is deserving (i.e., "deservedness").

## Advocacy Coalition Framework

The advocacy coalition framework (ACF) is predicated on the idea that interest groups organize in policy communities around a particular policy domain, such as health care. The ACF presumes that most policymaking is so complex that, like the medical field, participants must specialize if they want to influence outcomes. In characterizing policymaking as a gradual process that plays out over many years, the ACF views the beliefs of policy participants as relatively stable. The result is that major policy change is difficult and unusual (Weible & Sabatier, 2007). According to the ACF, the participants include not only the traditional Iron Triangle (Figure 3-2) of elected officials, agency staff, and interest group representatives, but also academics, researchers, and journalists who specialize in that policy domain. In the ACF, agenda setting and policymaking occur within ordinarily stable assumptions of what is normal and feasible and by the dominant path of policymaking that has been in place for a long period of time.

## Path Dependency

A common question surrounding agenda setting has to do with why most policy agendas seem to permit only incremental change when major adjustments are needed for addressing ongoing social problems and unmet public needs. The answer is that agenda setting and policy creation typically occur in a context that is significantly shaped by existing policies. This reality impacts what ideas and proposals can even get on a policy agenda. Policies created at earlier points affect, going forward, how social problems are understood, whether they are defined as matters worthy of public attention and government action, and whether they find a place on the political agenda (Mettler & Sorelle, 2018).

Policies create resources and incentives that influence the formation and activity of social groups and affect processes of "social learning" among the major political actors. Therefore, there is a strong case to be made for studying the feedback patterns between economic and political events and policy responses that unfold over longer periods of time (Pierson, 2000). For example, Jacob Hacker (2002) has shown that the parallel growth of public welfare programs (e.g., Social Security and Medicare) and private welfare (e.g., health insurance) is a classic example of how "private social benefits have 'policy feedback' effects that are not all that different from the policy feedback effects that are created by public social programs" (Hacker, 2002, p. 26) In both instances, "major public policies constitute important rules, influencing the allocation of economic and political resources, modifying the costs and benefits associated with alternative political strategies, and consequently altering ensuing political development" (Hacker, 2002, p. 26).

## Punctuated Equilibrium

In contrast to path dependency's strength as a model that helps explain the mostly gradual, and even static, nature of agenda setting and policy change, punctuated equilibrium theory (PET) focuses on the few exceptions to the rule. Political processes occasionally produce large-scale departures from the past. Most American political institutions were conservatively designed to thwart efforts at radical change and to make mobilizations necessary to overcome existing interests. Borrowing from evolutionary biology, PET posits that massive shifts in public understanding of problems, major crises, and dramatic election outcomes can lead to episodes of rapid change in what gets on policymakers' agendas and what can be passed and implemented (Baumgartner et al., 2018). An idea, such as mandatory vaccination policies and mask wearing during pandemics, can gain attention during a disease outbreak (i.e., measles, COVID-19) that threatens public safety and economic activity in unprecedented ways. These ideas can quickly become unstoppable. Civil war monuments that have stood for decades despite their controversial nature can suddenly be torn down after a violent racist incident. Gay marriage can be illegal for centuries and then very rapidly gain public support and legal protection across numerous states and decisively by the Supreme Court.

## CASE STUDY 3-3: The Patient Protection and Affordable Care Act (ACA): From Clinton's Failure to Obama's Success to Trump's Failure to "Repeal and Replace" the ACA

A classic example of agenda setting, punctuated equilibrium, and path dependency is the Affordable Care Act (ACA). The passage of the ACA in March 2010 was a remarkable policy breakthrough that achieved long-sought expansions of health insurance coverage and strengthened insurance regulations (e.g., forbidding exclusions for preexisting conditions and allowing dependents to stay on their parents' health plans until age 26). The ACA's roots, however, lie in the failed efforts of Democrats' and President Clinton's efforts at comprehensive healthcare reform in 1993–1994.

In both 1992–1993 and 2009–2010, policy windows for health reform opened due to the convergence of problem, policy, and political streams in the form of the national elections of 1992 and 2008 that punctuated long-existing policy equilibriums. In both instances, long-running problems with millions of uninsured Americans collided with the ending of 8 years of Republican control of the White House. This collision created a new and rare political agenda that permitted consideration of major health policy changes (Cammisa & Manuel, 2013).

What limited both Clinton's and Obama's efforts at significant healthcare reform, however, was path dependency. All the institutions, programs (Medicare, Medicaid), policy traditions (employer-provided health insurance), tax legacies (the tax exemption of employer-provided health insurance), and more that have built up over decades constrain and limit the ability to dramatically change the healthcare system. Clinton tried to ignore the resistance of path dependency and failed; Obama and Democrats in Congress in 2009–2010 learned from Clinton's 1993–1994 failure and modified the ACA proposal according to the constraints imposed by path dependency (Oberlander, 2010).

As Paul Starr, Princeton University sociologist and recipient of the Pulitzer Prize for his seminal history of the medical profession in *The Social Transformation of American Medicine* (2017), explains, Obama benefited from a reform consensus that had emerged in the years leading up to Obama's election to the presidency in 2009. The Clinton plan was far more ambitious than Obama's Affordable Care Act, particularly on cost containment. The ACA was also less threatening to the healthcare industry. By 2009, Democrats had coalesced around a path dependency reform model of the Massachusetts strategy—expanding Medicaid, subsidizing private coverage in limited insurance exchanges, and backing it up with a (weak) individual mandate (Starr, 2013). With a more unified Democratic Party and more interest group support than Clinton had in 1993–1994, Obama was able to succeed in getting legislation passed and implemented (Starr, 2017). At the same time, the ACA's impact has been far more limited compared to what Clinton proposed in 1993 because of the limits of path dependency. Not a single Republican voted for the ACA in either house of Congress. Democrats could only pass a more modest, incremental policy of health reform due to the institutional, economic, and political constraints that path dependency imposes in a governmental system that is defined by intense checks and balances and extensive fragmentation of political power (Hacker, 2010).

Ironically, the path dependency limits that Obama faced in successfully passing modest healthcare reform with the ACA also limited President Trump's and Republicans' efforts to "repeal and replace" the ACA during the Trump administration (Hacker & Pierson, 2018). Even their attempts to reduce Medicaid eligibility for low-income individuals failed due to the resiliency inherent in path dependency, where institutions and programs in place for just a few years can survive concerted efforts to destroy them (Rosenbaum, 2018). The ACA's path-dependent survival is a testament "to its particular balance and timing of benefits and costs being shielded long enough by election results and the constitutional separation of powers to have its benefits take root" (Peterson, 2018, p. 605). In this sense, the ACA's resiliency has come to resemble that of Social Security, Medicare, and Medicaid, providing valuable benefits to millions of American beneficiaries and healthcare providers (Peterson, 2020).

## Litigation

Another venue in which organizations and individuals can influence policy agendas and effect change is the legal system. The courts provide a space separate from legislatures, the business world, and health systems where professional nurses and IPHCWs can join lawsuits, initiate legal challenges themselves, and file amicus briefs (statements in support of sides in existing cases). For example, in 2020 the Wisconsin Nurses Association filed an amicus brief with the Wisconsin Supreme Court supporting Wisconsin governor Tony Evers's "Safer at Home Extension" executive order that ordered all individuals in Wisconsin to stay at home or in their place of residence during the COVID-19 outbreak in order to reduce the rate of disease transmission and to keep health providers, including nurses, safer in hospitals that had limited personal protective equipment. The New York State Nurses Association (NYSNA) filed lawsuits against health systems in New York over a lack of personal protective equipment during New York City's devastating COVID-19 outbreak in spring 2020 (United States District Court for the Southern District of New York, NYSNA, 2020).

Another form of legal action that nurses can engage in to impact policy is whistleblowing. Whistleblowing is the public reporting of wrongdoing or misconduct that leads to corrective action. It can pose risks to individual nurses and IPHCWs when they divulge malfeasance and/or unethical behavior by the organization for which they work, but there are ethical arguments that nurses owe it to their patients and even the health systems and hospitals for which they work to deter dangerous, unethical, and miscreant behavior by organizations and/or individual employees with whom they work (Wilmot, 2001). According to Ahern and McDonald (2002, p. 303), "Nursing codes of ethics bind nurses to the role of patient advocate and compel them to take action when the rights or safety of a patient are jeopardized."

## Conclusion

For professional nurses and IPHCWs, the three case studies provided contribute to an understanding of agenda setting and policy change by illuminating the importance of the Kingdon model, path dependency, focusing events, punctuated equilibrium, and policy entrepreneurship. Nurses and IPHCWs bring a unique and trusted perspective to policy deliberation and development because of their training, values, ethics, and experiences. Knowing how and when to push for proposals that would improve health systems, job satisfaction, and public health is important, because nurses and IPHCWs number in the millions. Nurses are essential in ensuring quality health care that is available and affordable, which is why the public trusts and respects nurses so highly. The potential for valuable and beneficial political influence is great. No elected official wants to be seen as opposed to or even unsupportive of nurses' interests. What is required is a basic understanding of what gets on policy agendas in health systems and legislative settings and how to get policymakers to pay attention to professional nurses and IPHCWs.

## Chapter Discussion Points

1. How can RNs, APRNs, and other interprofessional healthcare workers (IPHCWs) become better policy entrepreneurs?
2. What holds RNs, APRNs, and other IPHCWs back from influencing policymakers' agendas?
3. How can RNs, APRNs, and other IPHCWs become aware of factors in the problem stream to which Kingdon alluded?
4. Using the Kingdon model, diagram an example of policy streams that RNs, APRNs, and other IPHCWs could be advancing relative to their practice.
5. Describe how APRNs and other IPHCWs can become involved in the political stream. Commit to three actions that you will take in the upcoming month to demonstrate your increased involvement in the political stream.
6. Describe a recent or upcoming window of opportunity for RNs, APRNs, and other IPHCWs.
7. What issue or problem in your community would you want to spend time advocating for and why?
8. How could you use a model of innovation (e.g., CAPABLE) to develop a policy that would improve patient outcomes?
9. Identify two to three public policies where you live that impact the scope of practice of RNs, APRNs, and IPHCWs. List the steps necessary to improve these policies.
10. What other professional organization or interest group do you think APRNs and IPHCWs should align with strategically to advocate for policy change and why? Who would best complement nurses in an alliance?

## References

Ahern, K., & McDonald, S. (2002). The beliefs of nurses who were involved in a whistleblowing event. *Journal of Advanced Nursing, 38*(3), 303–309.

Aliberti, M. J. R., & Covinsky, K. E. (2019). Home modifications to reduce disability in older adults with functional disability. *JAMA Internal Medicine, 179*(2), 211–212.

American Association of Nurse Practitioners. (2019). Issues at a glance: Full practice authority. https://www.aanp.org/advocacy/advocacy-resource/policy-briefs/issues-full-practice-brief

Baumgartner, F. R. (2016). John Kingdon and the evolutionary approach to public policy and agenda setting. In N. Zahariadis (Ed.), *Handbook of public policy agenda setting* (pp. 53–66). Edward Elgar Publishing.

Baumgartner, F. R., & Jones, B. D. (1991). Agenda dynamics and policy subsystems. *Journal of Politics, 53*(4), 1044–1074.

Baumgartner, F. R., Jones, B. D., & Mortensen, P. B. (2018). Punctuated equilibrium theory: explaining stability and change in public policymaking. In C. M. Weible & P. A. Sabatier (Eds.), *Theories of the policy process* (4th ed., chapter 2). Taylor & Francis.

Beland, D., & Katapally, T. R. (2018). Shaping policy change in population health: Policy entrepreneurs, ideas, and institutions. *International Journal of Health Policy and Management, 7*(5), 369–373.

Birkland, T. A. (2016). *An introduction to the policy process: Theories concepts, and models of public policy making*. Routledge.

Brasil, F. P. (2017). Translating ideas into action. *Policy and Society, 36*(4), 504–522.

Brolan, C. E., & Hill, P. S. (2016). Universal health coverage's evolving location in the post-2015 development agenda. *Health Policy and Planning, 31*(4), 514–526.

Cammisa, A. M., & Manuel, P. C. (2013). *The path of American public policy*. Rowman & Littlefield.

Campos, P. A., & Reich, M. R. (2019). Political analysis for health policy implementation. *Health Systems & Reform*, 5(3), 224–235.

Cohen, M. D., March, J. G., & Olsen, J. P. (1972). A garbage can model of organizational choice. *Administrative Science Quarterly*, 17(1), 1–25.

Collins, S., & Hewer, I. (2014). The impact of the Bologna process on nursing higher education in Europe: A review. *International Journal of Nursing Studies*, 51(1), 150–156.

Dassah, E., Aldersey, H., McColl, M. A., & Davison, C. (2018). Factors affecting access to primary health care services for persons with disability in rural areas: A "best-fit" framework synthesis. *Global Health Research and Policy*, 3, Article number: 36.

Deleon, P., Schneider, A. L., & Ingram, H. (2007). Social construction and policy design. In P. A. Sabatier (Ed.), *Theories of the policy process* (Chapter 4). Taylor & Francis.

Fortinsky, R. H., & Robison, J. T. (2018). Targeting function at home in older adults: How to promote and disseminate promising models of care? *Journal of the American Geriatrics Society*, 66(3), 433–435.

Gawande, A. (2017, October 2). Is health care a human right? *The New Yorker*. https://www.newyorker.com/magazine/2017/10/02/is-health-care-a-right

Gregg, J., Miller, J., & Tennant, K. F. (2018). Nurse policy entrepreneurship in a rural community: A multiple streams framework approach. *OJIN: The Online Journal of Issues in Nursing*, 23(3).

Hacker, J. S. (2002). *The divided welfare state: The battle over public and private social benefits in the United States*. Cambridge University Press.

Hacker, J. S. (2010). The road to somewhere: Why health reform happened. *Perspectives on Politics*, 8(3), 861–876.

Hacker, J. S., & Pierson, P. (2018). The dog that almost barked: What the ACA repeal fight says about the resilience of the American welfare state. *Journal of Health Politics, Policy & Law*, 43(4), 551–577.

Hassmiller, S. B., & Kuehnert, P. (2020). Building a culture of health to attain the sustainable development goals. *Nursing Outlook*, 68(2), P129–P133.

Herweg, N., Hus, C., & Zohlnhofer, R. (2015). Straightening the three streams: Theorizing extensions of the multiple streams framework. *European Journal of Political Research*, 54(3), 435–449.

Jones, B. D. (2002). Bounded rationality and public policy: Herbert A. Simon and the decisional foundation of collective choice. *Policy Sciences*, 35(3), 269–284.

Kingdon, J. W. (1995). *Agendas, alternatives, and public policies*. New York, NY: Harper Collins College.

Kingdon, J. W. (2011). *Agendas, alternatives, and public policies* (2nd ed.). Pearson.

Leeuw, E., Clavier, C., & Breton, E. (2014). Health policy—why research and how: Health political science. *Health Policy Research and Systems*, 12, Article number: 55.

March, J. G., & Olsen, J. P. (2008). Elaborating the "new institutionalism." In S. A. Binder, R. A. W. Rhodes, & B. A. Rockman (Eds.), *The Oxford handbook of political institutions*. Oxford.

McIntyre, A., & Song, Z. (2019). The US Affordable Care Act: Reflections and directions at the close of a decade. *PLoS Medicine*, 16(2), e1002752.

Mettler, S., & Sorelle, M. (2018). Policy feedback theory. In M. Sorrelle & S. Mettler (Eds.), *Theories of the policy process* (4th ed., Chapter 3). Taylor & Francis.

Mintrom, M. (2019). So you want to be a policy entrepreneur? *Policy Design and Practice*, 2(4), 307–323.

Miyamoto, S., & Cook, E. (2019). The procurement of the UN Sustainable Development Goals and the American national policy agenda of nurses. *Nursing Outlook*, 67(6), P658–P663.

Monroy, V. (2020). Overwhelmed at the bedside. *American Journal of Nursing*, 120(5), 13.

National Council of State Boards of Nursing. (2019). *Number of active RN licenses by state*. https://www.ncsbn.org/Aggregate-RNActiveLicensesTable2019.pdf

NPR, Robert Wood Johnson Foundation, & Harvard T.H. Chan School of Public Health. (2016). *The workplace and health*. https://cdn1.sph.harvard.edu/wp-content/uploads/sites/21/2016/07/NPR-RWJF-Harvard-Workplace-and-Health-Poll-Report.pdf

Oberlander, J. (2010). Long time coming: Why health reform finally passed. *Health Affairs*, 29(6), 1112–1116.

Peterson, M. A. (2018). Reversing course on Obamacare: Why not another Medicare catastrophic? *Journal of Health Politics, Policy & Law*, 43(4), 605–650.

Peterson, M. A. (2020). The ACA a decade in: Resilience, impact, and vulnerabilities. *Journal of Health Politics, Policy & Law, 45*(4), 595–608.

Pierson, P. (2000). Increasing returns, path dependence, and the study of politics. *American Political Science Review, 94*(2), 251–267.

Rasheed, S., Ahtisham, Y., & Younas, A. (2020). Challenges, extent of involvement, and the impact of nurses' involvement in politics and policy making in last two decades: An integrative review. *Journal of Nursing Scholarship, 52*(4), online ahead of print.

Reinhart, R. J. (2020). *Nurses continue to rate highest in honesty, ethics.* Gallup Poll Social Series. https://news.gallup.com/poll/274673/nurses-continue-rate-highest-honesty-ethics.aspx

Rosenbaum, S. (2018). The (almost) great unraveling. *Journal of Health Politics, Policy & Law, 43*(4), 579–603.

Ruiz, S., Snyder, L. P., Rotondo, C., Cross-Barnet, C., Colligan, E. M., & Giuriceo, K. (2017). Innovative home visit models associated with reductions in costs, hospitalizations, and emergency department use. *Health Affairs, 36*(3), 425–432.

Sabatier, P. A. (1988). An advocacy coalition framework of policy change and the role of policy-oriented learning therein. *Policy Sciences, 21,* 121–168.

Salsberg, E., & Martiniano, R. (2018, May 9). Health care jobs projected to continue to grow far faster than jobs in the general economy. *Health Affairs Blog.* https://www.healthaffairs.org/do/10.1377/hblog20180502.984593/full/.

Scheufele, D. A., & Tewksbury, D. (2006). Framing, agenda setting, and priming: The evolution of three media effects models. *Journal of Communication, 57*(1), 9–20.

Schneider, A. L., & Ingram, H. M. (2005). *Deserving and entitled: Social constructions and public policy.* State University of New York Press.

Simon, H. A. (1995). Rationality in political behavior. *Political Psychology, 16*(1), 45–61.

Smith, S., Buchanan, H., & Cloutier, R. (2020). Virginia NP scope of practice: A legislative case study. *Nurse Practitioner, 45*(2), 33–37.

Sowers, K. W. (2016). Transformation of the American healthcare system: Implications for cancer care. *Seminars in Oncology Nursing, 32*(2), 79–86.

Spoelstra, S. L., Sikorskii, A., Gitlin, L. N., Schueller, M., Kline, M., & Szanton, S. L. (2019). Dissemination of the CAPABLE model of care in a Medicaid waiver program to improve physical function. *Journal of the American Geriatrics Society, 67*(2), 363–370.

Starr, P. (2013). *Remedy and reaction: The peculiar American struggle over health care reform.* Yale University Press.

Starr, P. (2017). *The social transformation of American medicine* (2nd ed.). Basic Books.

Szanton, S. (n.d.). *CAPABLE: Aging in place.* Johns Hopkins Solutions. https://www.johnshopkinssolutions.com/solution/capable/

Szanton, S. L., Leff, B., Wolff, J. L., Laken, R., & Gitlin, L. N. (2016). Home-based care program reduces disability and promotes aging in place. *Health Affairs, 35*(9), 1558–1563.

United States District Court for the Southern District of New York, NYSNA, Case No. 1:20-cv-03122-JMF. (2020). https://www.courthousenews.com/wp-content/uploads/2020/05/newyorknurses.pdf

Whitehead, D. (2003). The health-promoting nurse as a health policy career expert and entrepreneur. *Nurse Education Today, 23*(8), 585–592.

Wieble, C. M., & Sabatier, P. A. (2007). The advocacy coalition framework: Innovations and clarifications. In P. A. Sabatier (Ed.), *Theories of the policy process* (Chapter 7). Taylor & Francis.

Wilmot, S. (2001). Nurses and whistleblowing: the ethical issues. *Journal of Advanced Nursing, 32*(5), 1051–1057.

Wisconsin Supreme Court, Case No. 2020AP000765-OA. http://www.thewheelerreport.com/wheeler_docs/files/043020wscwpha.pdf

# Online Resources

The following websites are useful sources for keeping up with health policy news and developments.

**American Academy of Nursing, Policy & Advocacy News:** www.aannet.org/news/policy-news

**American Association of Colleges of Nursing, Federal Policy Agenda:** www.aacnnursing.org/Policy-Advocacy/About-Government-Affairs-and-Policy/Federal-Policy-Agenda

Centers for Disease Control and Prevention (CDC), Preventing Chronic Disease: www.cdc.gov/pcd/index.htm
Congress.gov, The Legislative Process, Calendars and Scheduling: www.congress.gov/legislative-process/calendars-and-scheduling
HealthAffairs blog: http://healthaffairs.org/blog/
Kaiser Health News: http://kaiserhealthnews.org
National Conference of State Legislators, State Legislative Calendar: www.ncsl.org/research/about-state-legislatures/2020-state-legislative-session-calendar.aspx
National League for Nursing: www.nln.org/advocacy-public-policy/legislative-issues
*New York Times*, Money & Policy: www.nytimes.com/pages/health/policy/index.html
*PBS NewsHour*, Health: www.pbs.org/newshour/health
Robert Wood Johnson Foundation, Health Policy in Brief: www.rwjf.org/en/topics/rwjf-topic-areas/health-policy.html
Science Daily, Health Policy News: www.sciencedaily.com/news/health_medicine/health_policy/
Vox, Health Care: www.vox.com/health-care
*Wall Street Journal*, Health: http://online.wsj.com/public/page/news-health-industry.html

# CHAPTER 4

# Policy Analysis and Design

AnnMarie L. Walton

## KEY TERMS

**117th Congress:** The current legislative branch of the U.S. federal government composed of the Senate and the House of Representatives. It convened on January 3, 2021, and will end on January 3, 2023. The next Congress (118th) will meet in Washington, D.C. from January 3, 2023, to January 3, 2025.

**Centers for Medicare and Medicaid Services (CMS):** An agency within the U.S. Department of Health and Human Services, and therefore part of the executive branch of government. Responsible for managing the Medicare and Medicaid social health insurance programs.

*Federal Register:* The daily journal of the U.S. government that is prepared and published by the Office of the Federal Register each federal workday.

**Health disparities:** Preventable differences in the burden of disease, injury, violence, or opportunities to achieve optimal health that are experienced by socially disadvantaged populations. They are by definition inequitable and are directly related to the historical and current unequal distribution of social, political, economic, and environmental resources (Centers for Disease Control and Prevention [CDC], 2018).

**Health services research:** A multidisciplinary scientific field that examines a multitude of factors, systems, and processes in the delivery of health care. Nursing scientists are active in this area of research, trying to provide a means to address health services problems.

**Legislative language:** The characteristics of legislative language are derived from its role in the institution of law. Scholars have called it a complex, intricate, and bizarre style of language. Words are uncommon, sentences are long and complex, repetition and the passive voice are used, and the words seem to lack humanity. Legislative language is difficult to decipher (Maley, 1987).

**Model legislation:** Legislation that is authored by various organizations to establish an example for the creation of laws regarding a specific policy issue. Sometimes the organizations are professional organizations seeking to advance policies to protect their members in numerous states, other times they may be special interest groups that want government to help them achieve a goal. Nurses and nursing professional organizations can also participate in the policy design process in this way.

**Policy tools:** Those methods chosen by policymakers to help solve a problem or social issue. These tools differ based on chosen conceptual frameworks of political science theorists.

**Quadruple aim:** Four-part goal of enhancing the patient experience, improving population health, reducing per capita costs, and improving the work life of healthcare providers.

**Structural racism:** A system in which public policies, institutional practices, cultural representations, and other norms work in various, often reinforcing ways to perpetuate racial group inequity. It identifies dimensions of history and culture that have allowed privileges associated with "whiteness" and disadvantages associated with "color" to endure and adapt over time (Lawrence et al., 2004).

**Title:** Term used in reference to a federal code that refers to a broad subject heading under which the law is classified (e.g., crimes and criminal procedures). When used in reference to an act, the term means a large portion or section of the act (e.g., Title IX, which relates to sex and education, but is actually a follow up to the much broader Civil Rights Act of 1964).

**Unfunded mandate:** A statute or regulation that requires a state, local government, organization, or individual to perform certain actions, with no money provided for fulfilling the requirements.

# Introduction

In today's world and political climate, it is imperative that healthcare providers, administrators, and educators be knowledgeable about and active in the policy process, particularly as it relates to their professional work. The purpose of this chapter is to examine public policy formulation processes and tools that governments use to solve large and complex societal problems. Referring to the policy process model, we will be discussing policy analysis and strategy and policy development (**Figure 4-1**).

The scope of the federal government's involvement in social issues in the United States expanded rapidly in the 20th and 21st centuries. The development of federally funded public programs such as Medicare and Medicaid in 1965 made a major impact on how health care is delivered by providers and accessed by the public. National costs for health care began rising immediately after the advent of Medicare and had swelled to $3.6 trillion, or $11,172 per person, by 2018, more than twice the rate of most other developed countries. By 2028, healthcare spending is expected to reach $6.2 trillion and account for nearly one-fifth of the Gross Domestic Product (California Health Care Foundation, 2020). Public policy related to financing health care not only must ensure access and quality, but also bend the cost curve downward.

The creation of Medicare and Medicaid was preceded by efforts in the early 20th century to provide a "safety net" for more Americans in terms of ability to afford health care. The concept of a national health insurance program for Social Security beneficiaries was first proposed by the Surgeon General in 1937 (Centers for Medicare and Medicaid Services [CMS], 2015). Ten years later, a federal agency was created to administer programs in health, education, and social insurance. In the 1950s and 1960s, a social awareness of the need for a true

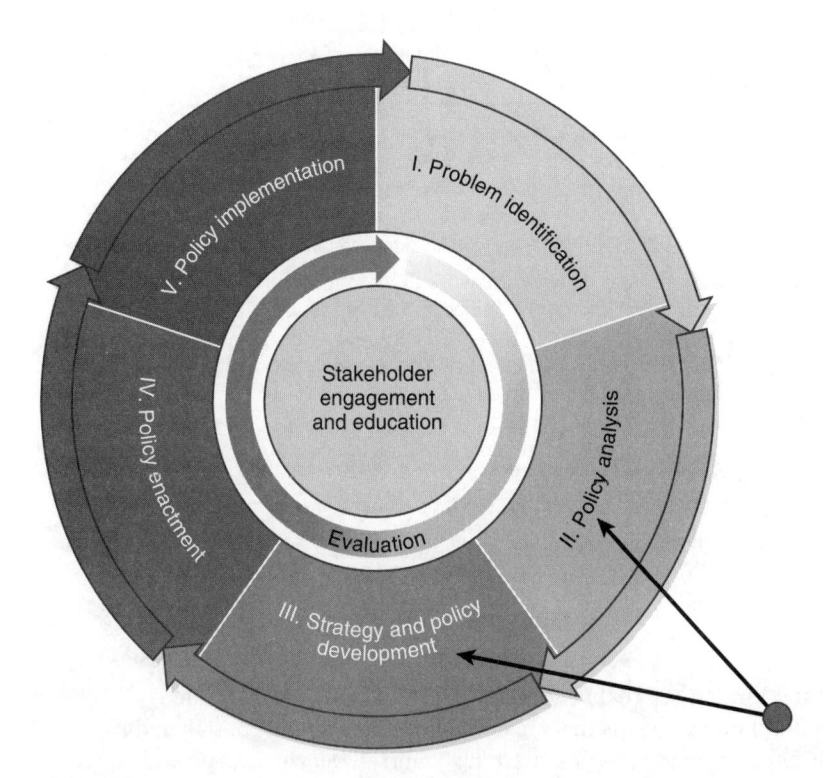

**Figure 4-1** Stages of the policy process: Policy analysis and design.

safety net emerged. By 1965, in response to this pressure, Congress had enacted legislation creating Medicare and Medicaid as Title XVIII and Title XIX of the Social Security Act, granting hospital insurance (Part A) and medical insurance (Part B) to nearly all Americans older than age 65. See the **Spotlight** box for an example of another legislative **title** important to nursing.

According to the **Centers for Medicare and Medicaid Services (CMS)**, in 1965 large numbers of the elderly were living in poverty and a majority had no health insurance. In addition to extending health insurance and coverage to this population group, the Medicare program helped to desegregate hospitals, which were financially motivated to integrate given the generous Medicare reimbursements offered in exchange for compliance with the Civil Rights Act of 1964. Facility costs in the form of building and renovating structures were high, and Medicare reimbursement could provide more than half of a hospital's income (Smith, 2005)—an attractive lure for hospitals.

All health insurers tend to follow and adopt whatever Medicare will reimburse, making the deliberations regarding this publicly funded program critical to the health insurance benefits available to the vast majority of all insured Americans. The passage of the Patient Protection and Affordable Care Act (ACA) in 2010 has also had a huge impact on health insurance. Since the passage of the ACA, it is estimated that 20 million people have become newly insured, and another 24 million have gained access to subsidized or free

> **Spotlight:** Title VIII of the Public Health Service Act
>
> "House Passes Nursing Workforce Reauthorization Act" was a recent headline on a nursing organization's website. Nursing leaders and educators advocate for inclusion of Title VIII funds in every congressional budget. The Title VIII referred to is contained within the Public Health Service Act. Title VIII funding extended until 2022 directs the Health Resources Services Administration to:
>
> - Reauthorize nursing workforce development programs that support the recruitment, retention, and advanced education of skilled nursing professionals.
> - Extend advanced education nursing grants to support clinical nurse specialists and clinical nurse leaders.
> - Define nurse-managed health clinics.
> - Add clinical nurse specialists to the National Advisory Council on Nurse Education and Practice.
> - Reauthorize loan repayments, scholarships, and grants for education.
>
> These types of programs are funded because nursing is considered as essential to the nation's health. Similar funding is appropriated to medical education under Title VII of the Public Health Service Act.

care through tax credits and Medicaid expansion. Health care is fraught with a multitude of factors that are difficult to identify and control, and the issue of healthcare reform has polarized the country. Policymakers on both sides of the political spectrum continue to call for reforms to the ACA, including repealing the ACA with no replacement, replacing the ACA with a single-payer system, and repairing the ACA with other measures that address coverage expansion (RAND, 2019).

Policies related to improving access to affordable, quality health care must address the following issues:

- How can health system performance be optimized to achieve the **quadruple aim**—enhancing the patient experience, improving population health, reducing costs, and improving the work life of healthcare providers?
- How can enough public funding be provided for basic and clinical research, provider education and professional development programs, and loan forgiveness for professionals who are practicing in underserved areas?
- How can the millions who remain uninsured be covered?

The United States has one of the most sophisticated healthcare systems in the world with respect to innovation, health information technology, and preparation of healthcare professionals. However, with regard to numerous health indices that evaluate the overall health of a country, the United States rates comparatively low. For example, the average life expectancy for females in the United States is 81 years, whereas in Japan, Canada, and the Netherlands—all of which are also developed countries—female life expectancy is 87.1, 84.7, and 83.2 years, respectively (World Health Organization [WHO], 2018). The United States also has high infant mortality compared to other industrialized countries, most likely due to high rates of birth defects, preterm birth, and maternal pregnancy complications (Centers for Disease Control and Prevention [CDC], 2019).

The U.S. healthcare system continues to evolve and will continue to benefit from improvements made to its performance, effectiveness, and efficiency by way of evidence-based policymaking. Efforts have been made by previous administrations to address the issues of access, cost, and quality—often referred to as the "three pillars" of healthcare policy—but past policy proposals have reflected the prevailing political philosophies and ideologies popular at the time. For example, government programs in the 1960s, under Democratic administrations, reflected an ideology wherein there was less concern with outcome-based planning and more concern with access. Two decades later, under a Republican administration, regulatory efforts attempted to reduce costs through outcome-based choices, individual responsibility for cost, and smaller expansion of healthcare coverage. Notably, in the last decade the work life of providers has been recognized as a pillar. Policy changes designed to influence one of the (now) four pillars—access to care, quality of care, cost of care, and the work life of providers—inevitably affect all four; that is, none of the pillars may be altered without consequences to the others.

One factor that inhibits the success of public policy is the inability to predict consumer behavior and participation in a given social program. Policies are usually designed to influence behavior and motivate individuals to do what they ordinarily might not do. Although many studies regarding the policy process have been conducted, few have examined the process of policy design specific to individual issues of health care.

The focus of most policy studies has been on the implementation of effective programs, and data have been gathered on statistical outcomes. A policy may be more successful if its design is incorporated into all phases of the policy process. For example, in the agenda-setting phase, the problem or social issue could be stated in such a way that it will capture the attention of lawmakers and framed so that government response will be feasible and adaptable. During the implementation phase, the policy's design provides guidance and an overall picture of the plan by specifying the intended outcomes. During the evaluation phase, the program objectives are clearly identified and measurable to ensure that the proposed change produces the desired outcome.

Public policy is, by its nature, complicated. Many social problems do not have simple solutions. If they did, more than likely the efforts to address those problems would take the form of a guideline, recommendation, or rule implemented by the private sector. Health care is perhaps the most convoluted of public issues because it is affected by a multitude of factors, such as state, federal, and international economies; social movements; education; resources; and religion. As a result, solutions that seek to provide accessible, affordable, and quality health care without leaving a large segment of the population uninsured, driving up the costs of health care, and sacrificing quality are often complicated, fragmented, and difficult to implement across various healthcare settings and populations. The nursing profession should engage in providing stories, interpreting data, and adding insight to help policymakers design the most effective policies to improve access and quality and reduce costs.

## The Policy Design Process

Policies reflect evidence-based data as well as public opinion. Thought leaders and policy makers comprise a collection of stakeholders whose task is to find solutions to problems that cannot be resolved by nongovernmental or philanthropic organizations. Policies that address social problems in the United States usually are formulated by a combination of legislators and aides, the executive branch, and special interest groups and advocates at both the federal and the state levels. Policies may subsequently be altered or struck down by the judicial branch (i.e., the courts). In a classic discussion about laws, regulations, and social programs, Theodore Lowi (1972) identified four types of policies—distributive, redistributive, regulatory, and constituent—to describe the complexity and richness of government efforts to influence citizen behavior and achieve policy purposes. Commonly used government techniques such as standards, direct expenditures or subsidies, sanctions or taxation, public corporations, contracts, grants, arbitration, moral suasion, education, licensing, and certification are all methods to achieve social goals. Other classic work by political scientists Doern and Wilson (1974) proposed that all policy tools or instruments could be arranged along a coercion continuum, and that policies would shift over time from less coercive to more coercive.

Professional experts such as registered nurses are often asked to serve as panel members or consultants or to serve on committees that provide input to policymakers. Individual nurse leaders also are increasingly playing leadership roles in critical policy arenas. For example, under the Obama administration, Marilyn Tavenner became the first nurse to lead the CMS, while Lieutenant General Patricia Horoho became the first nurse appointed as the Surgeon General for the U.S. Army.

State nurses' associations also have increasingly taken on a leadership role in advocating directly for change, leaving the sidelines of simply monitoring policy proposals under consideration. Nurses, and organizations representing nurses, advocate for policies that may be seen as self-serving and are frequently born from clinical practice experiences. Policies that include advanced practice registered nurses (APRNs) in reimbursement models, eliminate supervisory requirements, or eliminate barriers to full scope of practice fall into this category. Other policy examples at the state level include those that make it a felony to assault a healthcare worker and those that mandate the use of lift equipment. Very often, nursing professional organizations are able to share and borrow **model legislation** from other states that have made similar efforts.

Labor unions (collective bargaining units) representing registered nurses often advocate for policies at the state level that may improve working conditions for nurses, with staffing ratios being a perennial topic of debate. Even the existence of labor unions varies by state, and 24 states have enacted "right-to-work" laws that ensure that healthcare facilities cannot exclude workers who want to work there without being part of a union. The proliferation of participants in policy formation makes systematic program design that is focused on outcomes difficult to achieve. In her classic research, Safriet (2002) reported that most social issues are not brought to the attention of policymakers until there is a crisis with multiple causative factors. The decisions that relate to, or have an impact on, perceived social problems often are made hastily because of lack of information, constituency impatience, and lack of expertise.

Much policy that regulates nursing practice is determined at the state level, and the policy process conducted there is no less complicated than at the federal level. As of 2020, legislative efforts to support full-practice authority for APRNs in North Carolina had been underway for more than 5 years. In the 2016–2017 legislative session of the North Carolina General Assembly, legislation was introduced that would have made several changes to North Carolina's Nursing Practice Act, including eliminating barriers to the full scope of practice for APRNs in the state. Nursing advocates, including the North Carolina Nurses Association and the North Carolina Association of Nurse Anesthetists, played a significant role in designing the legislation to overhaul the existing law and expand the scope of practice of APRNs. In that session, advocates for change were bolstered by an economic analysis showing North Carolina could significantly reduce healthcare spending by removing physician supervision of APRNs in the state (Conover & Richards, 2015). Advocacy efforts in North Carolina continued and the legislative effort became known as the SAVE Act in the 2019–2020 legislative session (NC HB185, NC SB143). HB185 contains nine pages of dense **legislative language**, making it difficult to understand and digest, and covers definitions of APRNs, population focus areas, and fees (see **Figure 4-2**).

The prominence of nurses and nursing during the COVID-19 pandemic may well influence the aforementioned legislation. A pandemic, as a public health emergency, captures the attention of the public and of lawmakers. In fact, the National Academy of Medicine incorporated emerging evidence about the impacts of COVID-19 and nurses' roles in the crisis and delayed the periodic consensus study, *Future of Nursing 2020–2030*, which was originally to be released in December 2020, until May 2021. We can hold some hope that attention, evidence, and the consensus study might promote the status of APRNs in a number of states.

# Research Informing the Policy Process

**Health services research** is typically defined as a multidisciplinary scientific field that examines a multitude of factors, systems, and processes in the delivery of health care. More specifically, nursing health services research can inform policymakers of clinical practice areas that involve the direct patient care experience of the nursing community (Jones & Mark, 2005). In their assessment, Jones and Mark note that nursing health services research can lead to the development of knowledge that improves access, health, and patient safety, among other things. Over the long term, they argue, such research can improve nursing care and patient outcomes—two broad policy issues that benefit in some ways from state or federal regulation. The example of including Conover and Richards' work on cost in conversations about legislation related to scope of practice for APRNs is a good example of the application of research to the policy process.

117th CONGRESS
1st Session

H. R. 598

To amend titles XVIII and XIX of the Social Security Act to improve the quality of care in skilled nursing facilities under the Medicare program and nursing facilities under the Medicare program during the COVID-19 emergency period, and for other purposes.

---

IN THE HOUSE OF REPRESENTATIVES
January 28, 2021

Ms. Schakowsky (for herself and Mr. Takano) introduced the following bill; which was referred to the Committee on Ways and Means, and in addition to the Committee on Energy and Commerce, for a period to be subsequently determined by the Speaker, in each case for consideration of such provisions as fall within the jurisdiction of the committee concerned

---

**A BILL**

To amend titles XVIII and XIX of the Social Security Act to improve the quality of care in skilled nursing facilities under the Medicare program and nursing facilities under the Medicare program during the COVID-19 emergency period, and for other purposes.

*Be it enacted by the Senate and House of Representatives of the United States of America in Congress assembled,*

SECTION 1. Short title.

This Act may be cited as the "Quality Care for Nursing Home Residents and Workers During COVID-19 and Beyond Act".

TITLE I—Addressing COVID-19

SEC. 101. Improving quality of care in skilled nursing facilities and nursing facilities during COVID-19 emergency period.

(a) Medicare.—Section 1819 of the Social Security Act (42 U.S.C. 1395i-3) is amended by adding at the end the following new subsection:

"(k) Additional requirements during certain public health emergency.—

"(1) SKILLED NURSING FACILITIES.—

"(A) IN GENERAL.—During the portion of the emergency period defined in paragraph (1)(B) of section 1135(g) beginning on or after the date of the enactment of this subsection, a skilled nursing facility shall comply with the quality of care requirements described in subparagraph (B), the worker safety requirements described in subparagraph (C), and the transparency requirements described in subparagraph (D).

**Figure 4-2** Example of legislative language.

"(B) QUALITY OF CARE REQUIREMENTS.—The quality of care requirements described in this subparagraph are each of the following:

"(i) Employ, on a full-time basis, an onsite infection preventionist who—

"(I) has primary professional training in nursing, medical technology, microbiology, epidemiology, or other related field;

"(II) is qualified by education, training, experience or certification; and

"(III) has completed specialized training in infection prevention and control.

"(ii) In the case of a resident who elects to reside with a family member of such resident for any portion of the emergency period described in subparagraph (A), guarantee the right of such resident to resume residency in the facility at any time during the 180-day period immediately following the end of such emergency period.

"(iii) Notwithstanding subparagraphs (A) and (B) of subsection (c)(2), permit a resident to remain in the facility and not discharge or transfer the resident from the facility unless—

"(I) the State survey agency approves the discharge or transfer;

"(II) in the case of a transfer, the transfer is to a facility dedicated to the care of residents who have been diagnosed with COVID-19 if the resident has been diagnosed with COVID-19, or a facility dedicated to the care of residents who have not been diagnosed with COVID-19 if the resident has not been diagnosed with COVID-19;

"(III) before effecting the discharge or transfer, the facility records the reasons in the resident's clinical record;

"(IV) at least 72 hours in advance of the discharge or transfer, the facility provides a notice of the discharge or transfer to the resident (or legal representative of the resident, if applicable), including the reasons therefor and the items described in clause (iii) of subsection (c)(2)(B); and

"(V) the resident (or legal representative of the resident, if applicable) acknowledges receipt of the notice described in subclause (IV) and provides written consent to the discharge or transfer.

"(iv) Test (on a weekly basis) each resident for COVID-19, or, in the case that the facility does not have a sufficient number of testing kits for COVID-19, screen each resident for symptoms of COVID-19 and report (on a daily basis until the facility has a sufficient number of such testing

**Figure 4-2** Continued.

Health services researchers such as Donald Taylor, Linda Aiken, Peter Buerhaus, and Erin Fraher inform policy in myriad ways, ranging from identifying a problem, to weighing the risks and benefits of possible solutions, to providing estimates for how much a solution may cost government and society (Clancy et al., 2012). Such research often relies on large national data sets that offer insight into a particular problem. Clinical nurses are also key to the provision of that data. Take, for example, the Agency for Healthcare Research and

Quality (AHRQ), the federal agency responsible for producing evidence-based information to make health care safe, high quality, and accessible. The AHRQ is part of the Department of Health and Human Services (HHS), which is under the executive branch of the government and its directives. For most of us, those agencies and their functions seem far from our day-to-day work. However, AHRQ gives researchers and policymakers the most complete data on the cost and use of health care and health insurance coverage in the United States (AHRQ, 2020a). One of the sources the AHRQ uses is the Medical Expenditures Panel Survey (MEPS), which consists of large-scale surveys of families and individuals, their healthcare providers, and employers across the country. The AHRQ also gathers data to produce the National Healthcare Quality and Disparities Reports housed on the AHRQ website and retrievable at www.ahrq.gov/research/findings/nhqrdr/index.html (AHRQ, 2020b). These annual reports offer summarized data that can stimulate ideas for further study or research as well as cursory analyses to jump-start projects for the improvement of patient care. The reports provide reliable and updated data that can lead to meaningful policy changes in improving care, lowering costs, and reducing health disparities. Nurses are part of contributing to the data included, nurse scientists are part of analyzing these data to answer health services research–related questions, and then part of programs and policies created to improve health care. While these large federal data sets may seem far from our daily work, nurses contribute to and are impacted by these data and the policies data inform every day.

# Public Opinion Informing the Policy Process

Anne Schneider and Helen Ingram (1993) theorized in some of their earliest work that policymakers are more likely to craft and support public policy that benefits the "advantaged" and punishes the "deviants" to ensure their future electoral success. They posit that society can be divided into four groups; "the advantaged" (politically influential and of whom the public has a positive view—scientists, veterans, businesses, the elderly), "the dependent" (politically weak but viewed positively—children, mothers, the disabled), "the contenders" (politically strong but perceived negatively—the rich, big unions, minority interest groups), and "the deviants" (politically weak and of whom the public has a negative view—criminals, drug addicts, gangs). Therefore, it is not hard to see how policies further health disparities if the voices and work of the strong/positive construct group are those most often heard and attended to. We can think about policies that have been around for a long time, such as Social Security and Disability Insurance (SSDI), and how the population who benefits from that policy and who it serves has not changed much over time. We can compare that to Aid to Dependent Children (which began in 1935 to support young, white widows in wartime) and today is known as "social welfare" (or simply "Welfare"), predominantly serving minority single mothers, and the difference in social construction of that group as irresponsible or immoral.

Population-based approaches to health policy specifically examine the health outcomes of a group and the distribution of health outcomes within that group. In so doing, many of the social contributors to health arise, such as education, access to healthy food, economic opportunities, and structural racism, to name a few. In order to solve many of these problems that contribute to disparate health outcomes between groups, we must go beyond policies that fall in the health sector to those in the housing, education, parks, transportation, and criminal justice sectors among others. A "health-in-all-policies" approach, as proposed by the American Public Health Association, "is a collaborative approach to improving the health of all people by incorporating health considerations into decision-making across sectors and policy areas" (APHA, 2020). It ensures that policymakers are informed about and consider health, equity, and sustainability consequences of various policy options during the issue analysis and policy development process. This approach is a way to ensure that some of the tendency to further policies that support some groups over others are consciously reviewed. Nurses can advocate in this regard by making patients and their circumstances real and alive to policymakers. Sharing a real story about a patient who cannot afford needed medication due to its cost, coupled with caring for dependents, working one or more low-wage jobs, and not qualifying for Medicaid, helps policymakers acknowledge the myriad social contributors to health and may help to shift a policymaker's perspective from that patient as a deviant to at least a dependent or a contender in the model proposed by Schneider and Ingram.

# The Design Issue

Unclear mandates often result in a mismatch between legislative intent and bureaucratic behavior. For instance, Congress enacted the Emergency Medical Treatment and Labor Act (EMTALA) in 1986 as a part of the Consolidated Omnibus Budget Reconciliation Act (COBRA) to ensure access to emergency care for patients with unstable conditions. Although the legislation requires hospitals to provide specific emergency services to patients seeking treatment, regardless of their citizenship, legal status, or ability to pay, the federal government does not reimburse for the cost of that care. EMTALA was intended to eliminate the practice of hospitals refusing to accept or treat unstable patients without proof of insurance (also known as "dumping patients"); patients were sometimes sent over long distances to a public or county hospital. Despite the good intentions to ensure care for those in need, an **unfunded mandate** puts pressure on hospitals, which can face high costs when they are required to provide uncompensated care. An unintended consequence of EMTALA is the public's general belief that everyone in the United States can get all the care they need if they show up at an emergency department. However, this is not the case. The EMTALA policy design did not include specific content about reimbursement (**Figure 4-3**).

Policy design became a focus of research studies several decades ago. Linder and Peters (1987), whose work established a classic starting point for design research, reported that poor policy design is often the reason for policy failure.

## Chapter 4 Policy Analysis and Design

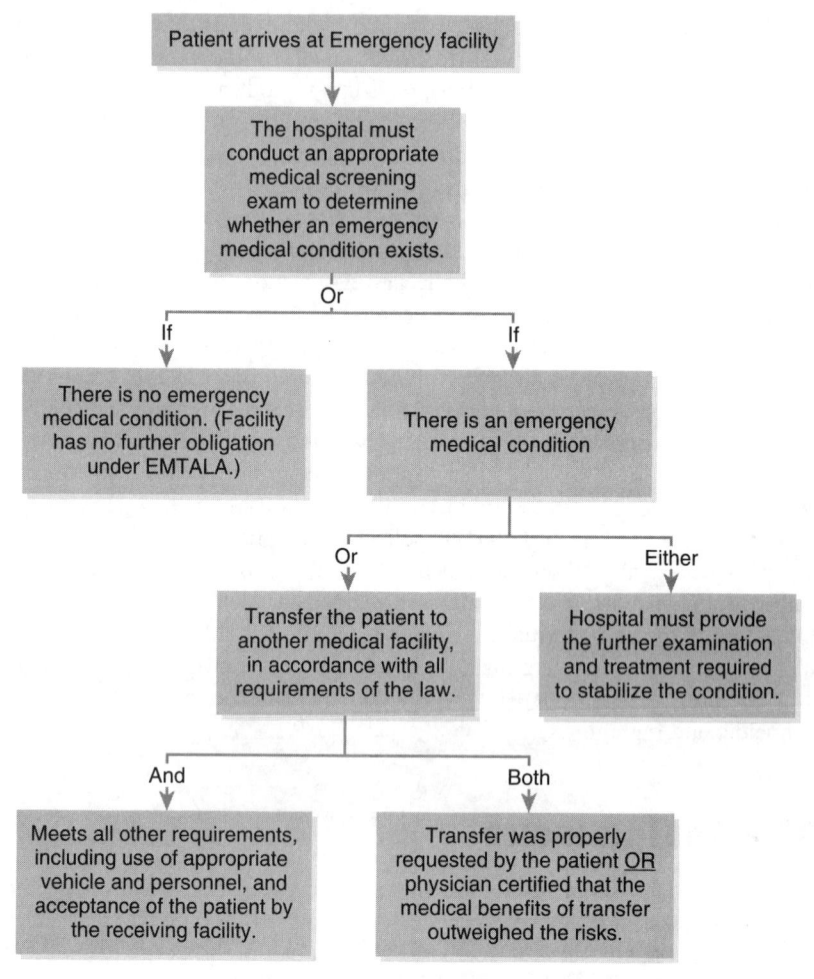

```
Patient arrives at Emergency facility
              ↓
The hospital must conduct an appropriate medical screening
exam to determine whether an emergency medical condition exists.
              Or
       If           If
       ↓            ↓
There is no      There is an emergency
emergency        medical condition
medical
condition.
(Facility has
no further
obligation under
EMTALA.)

From "There is an emergency medical condition":
              Or              Either
              ↓               ↓
Transfer the patient to     Hospital must provide
another medical facility,   the further examination
in accordance with all      and treatment required
requirements of the law.    to stabilize the condition.

           And                      Both
           ↓                         ↓
Meets all other requirements,   Transfer was properly
including use of appropriate    requested by the patient OR
vehicle and personnel, and      physician certified that the
acceptance of the patient by    medical benefits of transfer
the receiving facility.         outweighed the risks.
```

*Note: These requirements apply to all patients and to every hospital that has an emergency departmentand participates in the Medicare program.*

**Figure 4-3** The COBRA antidumping law (EMTALA).

These scholars noted that the best bureaucracies in the world may not be able to achieve desired goals if an excessively ambitious policy is used (i.e., the problem is too complex for a single policy or agency). Also, if there is a misunderstanding of the nature of the problem, inappropriate policies may be formulated. Linder and Peters proposed that implementation should be examined but only as one of the conditions that must be satisfied for successful policymaking. They maintained that by shifting the focus of study to policy design, more reliable and explicit answers can be found, leading to greater chances of policy success.

The design phase remains an integral part of the policy process. An understanding of the policy tools or instruments chosen for policy design and the underlying assumptions of policymakers during the design process are critical to an understanding of the overall policy process.

# Policy Instruments (Government Tools)

The study of the instruments or tools by which the government achieves desired policy goals has shed light on lawmakers' intentions during policymaking and has allowed researchers to infer the predictive capabilities of tools. Two scholars proposed a framework for studying policy based on policy tools. Schneider and Ingram (1990), in their classic work, offer a framework to analyze implicit or explicit behavioral theories found in laws, regulations, and programs. Their analysis uses government tools or instruments and underlying behavioral assumptions as variables that guide policy decisions and choices. Their contention is that target group compliance and utilization are important forms of political behavior that should be examined closely. When these tools are combined with process variables such as competition, partisanship, and public opinion, Schneider and Ingram argue, the tools approach moves policy beyond considering the standard analysis and improved frameworks. They note that policy tools are substitutable, and states often use a variety of tools to address a single problem.

To understand which tools are most efficient, emphasis should be placed on using them in conjunction with a particular policy design. According to Howlett, Mukherjee, and Rayner (2014), **policy tools**—that is, those methods chosen by policymakers to help solve a problem or social issue—are so critical in policy design that policy implementation cannot be achieved without them.

Howlett (2011) describes five broad categories of policy tools used by governments in designing policy: authority, incentive, capacity building, symbolic or hortatory, and learning. Professional nurses can use their knowledge of policy tools to make suggestions and recommendations to government leaders who are designing policies and programs.

## Authority Tools

Authority tools are used most frequently by governments to guide the behavior of agents and officials at lower levels. Authority tools are statements backed by the legitimate power of government that grant permission and prohibit or require action under designated circumstances. An example of an authority tool is a law, regulation, or mandate that requires vaccination for daycare and school entry.

## Incentive Tools

Incentive tools assume that individuals have access to the resources they desire most and will not be motivated positively to take action without encouragement or coercion. Having access to what is most desired leads to wanting to get the greatest value for each expenditure. Incentive tools rely on tangible payoffs (positive or negative) as motivating factors. Incentive policy tools manipulate tangible benefits, costs, and probabilities that policy designers assume are relevant to the situation. Incentives assume individuals have the "opportunity to make choices, recognize the opportunity, and have adequate information and decision-making skills to select from among alternatives that are in their best interests" (Schneider & Ingram, 1990, p. 516). An example of an incentive tool is payment or reimbursement for travel costs to eligible veterans seeking health care at Veterans Affairs medical centers. However, if transportation is a barrier to accessing primary care (in that transportation options do not exist, regardless of cost), the outcome from an attempt to use this particular incentive may fail.

## Capacity-Building Tools

Capacity-building tools provide information, training, education, and resources to enable individuals, groups, or agencies to make decisions or carry out activities. These tools assume that incentives are not an issue and that target populations will be motivated adequately. For capacity-building tools to work, populations must be aware of the risk factors inherent in the tools and the ways in which these tools can help. Capacity-building tools focus on education and technical support. For example, information may point out the dangers of drugs and addiction to the target population through brochures, email, online videos, or other presentations. The underlying assumption is that information regarding the importance of addiction prevention and cessation is considered valuable, and users will abstain from or stop using these substances to protect their health. Capacity-building tools also are used to encourage people to recognize the value of health care and to sign up for healthcare insurance.

## Symbolic or Hortatory Tools

Symbolic or hortatory tools assume that people are motivated from within and decide whether to take policy-related actions on the basis of their beliefs and values. An example of this type of tool is the use of lower-number legislative bills reserved by congressional leadership. Procedural rules in the U.S. House of Representatives allow certain bill numbers, such as House of Representatives (H.R.) 1, to be reserved and assigned to significant legislation. For example, Congress approved an H.R. 1, the Medicare Prescription Drug, Improvement, and Modernization Act of 2003, to create the Part D program under Medicare. Some of the lowest bill numbers are also reserved for use by leadership in the U.S. Senate (Congress.gov, n.d.). The way in which bill numbers are assigned indicates their legislative significance (often symbolic) and signals that certain policy changes are a high priority for the majority party.

Another hortatory tool is a federal request for proposals to research a particular topic of significant interest to the government. Universities capable of conducting such research will apply for available grant awards, both to undertake the research and to enjoy the benefits that accompany such funding. Implementation of policies is also more effective when the policy is consistent with the mission, values, and real-world experiences of those who must implement them. Consideration of beliefs and values of those who will ultimately be responsible for implementation is critical in the policy analysis and design phases.

Executive orders from the president might also be considered symbolic tools. They clearly express the values and desires of the president and his or her supporters, and they can have significant influence on the internal affairs of the government, for example, by specifically stating the degree to which legislation will be enforced. That said, they are subject to judicial review and can be overturned if they are deemed unconstitutional. They are not supported by Congress, they do not go through the federal budgeting and appropriations process, and they have expiration terms. Usually, a new president reviews all executive orders in his or her first weeks of office and can revoke, modify, or make exceptions to them. An executive order keeps priorities of the president in the awareness of policymakers longer and may lead to legislation down the road. A recent example of executive orders that have kept the attention of policymakers is the Deferred Action on Childhood Arrivals, or DACA, program. President Obama issued it as an executive order in 2012 after the Development, Relief and Education for Alien Minors (DREAM) Act did not pass in Congress several times. In 2017, President Trump wrote a new executive order to end the DACA program. Several lawsuits were filed over the termination of DACA. In 2020, two federal courts ruled against the Trump administration. For the last decade, these executive orders have helped keep immigration issues unique to children in the eye of policymakers. The number of executive orders made by each administration can also demonstrate how much difficulty the administration has had in getting policy passed. For example, the Reagan administration made 381 executive orders, the (G.W.) Bush administration made 291, the Obama administration made 276, the Clinton administration made 254, the Trump administration made 220, and the (G.H.W.) Bush administration only 166. To date, the Biden administration has made 32. Governors can also make executive orders at the state level, some of which are subject to legislative review. These are used at the state level usually during natural disasters, to create advisory committees, or to address management and administrative issues. Executive orders, along with presidential proclamations and other documents, are announced to the press and entered into the **Federal Register** (see www.federalregister.gov/presidential-documents).

## Learning Tools

These tools are used when the basis upon which target populations might be moved to take problem-solving action is unknown or uncertain. Policies that use learning tools often are open-ended in purpose and objectives and have broad goals. A needs assessment of the target population may be conducted by a task force, which provides knowledge and insight for policymakers. For example, if a community program addressing childhood obesity is proposed, a needs assessment must be conducted beforehand to determine which information is needed before a proposal is presented to the county council.

Policy tools are important resources for the professional nurse because experience using them can enlighten policymakers and persuade them to support or oppose a policy. Learning about the types of policy tools is similar to the education nurses provide to patients and families so that patients can make informed decisions. The education often includes the use of an enduring reference, such as a pamphlet, video, or website for future reference and consideration. Similarly, policy briefs, talking points, and fact sheets about specific health conditions often are given to policymakers to help them understand a health policy issue.

## Behavioral Dimensions

In addition to understanding the types and roles of tools in formulating policy, professional nurses must understand behavioral assumptions and the political context in which tools exist. The political climate in which social problems are addressed often prescribes the choice of tools to be implemented. Various tools are used when addressing social problems and result in differing outcomes when the tools are applied by different agencies, states, or countries. In the United States, for example, liberal policymakers are inclined to use capacity-building tools when developing policies for poor and minority groups, such as grants to communities for social programs, whereas conservative policymakers might use the same types of tools in developing policies applicable to businesses, such as strategic planning and business development activities.

### CASE STUDY 4-1: COVID-19, Disparities, and the CARES Act

In 2020, the United States began an era of managing the novel coronavirus (coronavirus disease 2019, or COVID-19) pandemic. As of February, 2021, it is estimated that there have been 27,993,504 cases of COVID-19 and 498,993 deaths in the United States (CDC, 2020a). The exact number of cases and deaths remains unknown and is challenged by the fact that some individuals have mild symptoms and do not seek medical care, as well as delays in reporting and testing, barriers to testing, and differences in how states report cases and/or deaths. Likewise, data on gender and race is challenging to collect. In the CDC data above, race/ethnicity is not specified in 53% of cases. All of this underscores the need for health services research and reliable data sources.

Mainstream media and academics are writing about the race-related **health disparities** in both COVID-19 cases and deaths. Some of the reasons noted for the disparities include that African Americans are more likely to live in more densely populated areas, are overrepresented in jails, are more likely to be employed in jobs where they cannot work from home or do not have paid sick leave, are more likely to have underlying health conditions, and are more likely to face racial bias that prevents them from getting proper treatment (CDC, 2020b). Advocates and academics alike are asking for more attention to be paid to these social contributors to health such as income, education, and **structural racism**. These persuasive writings by thought leaders and academics are a form of learning tool in the policymaking process.

Also at work in the policy design process in this case is public opinion. Consider the CARES Act (Coronavirus Aid, Relief, and Economic Security Act) that President Trump signed into law on March 27, 2020. Whose interests were addressed in the act and whose were not? As noted in this chapter, legislation often is dense and includes many details, and the CARES Act is 335 pages of legislative language. The act includes provisions for small businesses, retirees, credit protections, provisions for student loan relief, and tax provisions for individuals. It provides $2 trillion

Anthony Fauci, MD, director of the National Institute of Allergy and Infectious Diseases, answers questions about the government's response to the COVID-19 pandemic.
Courtesy of The White House.

in relief. Of that $2 trillion, the largest relief goes to individuals, followed by big corporations, small businesses, state and local governments, and then public health, education, and the safety net (Snell, 2020). Using the terminology coined by Schneider and Ingram, it is easy to see how the CARES Act supports the advantaged (small businesses, retirees) and to some extent the dependent (children), while not specifically addressing the needs of the contenders (minority groups dying at disproportionate rates from this disease), nor the deviants (incarcerated, homeless).

There are some authority tools at work in the COVID-19 pandemic, such as states closing public schools, libraries, and community centers. There are also hortatory tools that are in use in the CARES Act. The $100 billion given to hospitals to treat the disease and the $11 billion allocated for diagnostics, treatments, and vaccines demonstrates the prioritization of a focus on care and cure, a hortatory tool.

COVID-19 provides us with a contemporary example of a health crisis that clearly impacts and is impacted by nursing, uses a variety of the policymaking tools, and is influenced by public opinion on the issue. Looking at the CARES Act through the lens of policy design, it is possible to see how health disparities widen as a result of public opinion and how other policies that fall outside of those specifically related to health and health care can have a major impact on health outcomes.

# Conclusion

As a component of professional nursing, active participation in the policy process is essential in the formulation of policies designed to provide quality health care at sustainable costs to all individuals. To be effective in the process, RNs and APRNs must understand how the process works and at which points the greatest impact might be made. The design phase of the policy process is the point at which the original intent of a solution to a problem is understood and the appropriate tools are employed to achieve policy success. It is greatly impacted by public opinion on issues as well. Nurses, the most trusted profession, can do much to change public opinion on issues and influence policy.

## Chapter Discussion Points

1. Using the www.congress.gov website, identify a piece of proposed health policy legislation.
   a. Research the background for the problem or issue being addressed by the policy.
   b. Is there an evidence base to support the proposed policy?
   c. Based on your understanding of the behavioral assumptions underlying policymaking tools, predict the potential for success or failure of the policy. Identify policy variables that will affect its success or failure.
2. Using the www.congress.gov website, search the **117th Congress** to identify a policy (e.g., rule, regulation) that has been in use for several years yet has had little success. Identify the variables that may be inhibiting success and offer possible solutions.
3. How does the political climate affect the choice of policy tools and the behavioral assumptions made by policymakers?
4. Identify opportunities that are currently in place for RNs and APRNs to begin activity in policymaking.
5. Who is predominantly involved in designing health policy in the United States? Why do you think this is the case?

## References

Agency for Healthcare Research and Quality, U.S. Department of Health and Human Services. (2020a). *Agency for Healthcare Research and Quality: A Profile.* https://www.ahrq.gov/cpi/about/profile/index.html

Agency for Healthcare Research and Quality, U.S. Department of Health and Human Services. (2020b). *2018 National healthcare quality and disparities reports.* https://www.ahrq.gov/research/findings/nhqrdr/nhqdr18/index.html

American Public Health Association. (2020). *An introduction to health in all policies.* https://www.apha.org/-/media/files/pdf/factsheets/hiapguide_4pager_final.ashx?la=en&hash=A6776B82FCA90B3346A6B5851697ADEB2448D4E4

California Health Care Almanac. (2021). *2020 edition- Health care costs 101 US spending growth relatively steady in 2018.* https://www.chcf.org/publication/2020-edition-health-care-costs-101/

Centers for Disease Control and Prevention. (2018). *Health disparities.* https://www.cdc.gov/healthyyouth/disparities/index.htm

Centers for Disease Control and Prevention. (2019). *Infant mortality.* https://www.cdc.gov/reproductivehealth/maternalinfanthealth/infantmortality.htm

Centers for Disease Control and Prevention. (2020a). *Cases of coronavirus disease (COVID-19) in the U.S.* https://www.cdc.gov/coronavirus/2019-ncov/cases-updates/cases-in-us.html#1

Centers for Disease Control and Prevention. (CDC). (2020b). *COVID-19 in racial and ethnic minority groups.* https://www.cdc.gov/coronavirus/2019-ncov/need-extra-precautions/racial-ethnic-minorities.html

Centers for Medicare and Medicaid Services, U.S. Department of Health and Human Services. (2015, July). *Medicare and Medicaid milestones: 1937–2015*. https://www.cms.gov/About-CMS/Agency-Information/History/Downloads/Medicare-and-Medicaid-Milestones-1937-2015.pdf

Centers for Medicare and Medicaid Services, U.S. Department of Health and Human Services. (2019). *National health expenditures 2017 highlights*. https://www.cms.gov/files/document/highlights.pdf

Clancy, C., Glied, S., & Lurie, N. (2012). From research to health policy impact. *Health Services Research*, 47(1 Pt 2), 337–343.

Congress.gov. (2020). *Glossary*. Retrieved from https://www.congress.gov/help/legislative-glossary#r

Conover, C., & Richards, R. (2015). Economic benefits of less restrictive regulation of advanced practice registered nurses in North Carolina. *Nursing Outlook*, 63(5), 585–592.

Doern, G. B., & Wilson, V. S. (Eds.). (1974). *Issues in Canadian public policy*. Macmillan.

Howlett, M. (2011). *Designing public policies: Principles and instruments*. Routledge.

Howlett, M., Mukherjee, I., & Rayner, J. (2014). The elements of effective program design: A two-level analysis. *Politics and Governance*, 2(2), 1–12.

Jones, C. B., & Mark, B. A. (2005). The intersection of nursing and health services research: Overview of an agenda setting conference. *Nursing Outlook*, 53, 270–273.

Lawrence, K., Sutton, S., Kubisch, A., Susi, G., & Fulbright-Anderson, K. (2004). *Structural racism and community building*. The Aspen Institute. https://www.racialequitytools.org/resourcefiles/aspeninst3.pdf

Linder, S. H., & Peters, G. B. (1987). Design perspective on policy implementation: The fallacies of misplaced prescriptions. *Policy Studies Review*, 6(3), 459–475.

Lowi, T. J. (1972). Four systems of policy, politics, and choice. *Public Administration Review*, 11, 298–310.

Maley, Y. (1987). The language of legislation. *Language in Society*, 16(1), 25–48.

RAND Healthcare. (2019). *Healthcare reform*. https://www.rand.org/health-care/key-topics/health-policy/in-depth.html

Safriet, B. J. (2002). Closing the gap between can and may in health-care providers' scopes of practice: A primer for policymakers. *Yale Journal on Regulation*, 19, 301–334.

Schneider, A., & Ingram, H. (1990). Behavioral assumptions of policy tools. *Journal of Politics*, 52(2), 510–529.

Schneider, A., & Ingram, H. (1993). Social construction of target populations: Implications for politics and policy. *American Political Science Review*, 87(2), 334–347.

Schneider, A., & Ingram, H. (2005). *Public policy and the social construct of deservedness*. SUNY University Press.

Smith, D. B. (2005). The politics of racial disparities: Desegregating the hospitals in Jackson, Mississippi. *Milbank Quarterly*, 83(2), 247–269.

Snell, K. (2020). What's inside the Senate's $2 trillion coronavirus aid package. *NPR*. https://www.npr.org/2020/03/26/821457551/whats-inside-the-senate-s-2-trillion-coronavirus-aid-package

World Health Organization. (2018). *World health statistics 2018: Monitoring health for the SDGs*. https://apps.who.int/iris/bitstream/handle/10665/272596/9789241565585-eng.pdf?ua=1

# CHAPTER 5

# Policy Enactment: Legislation and Politics

**Amy L. Anderson**
With acknowledgment to the many contributions of Dr. Janice Lanier

## KEY TERMS

**527 organizations:** Organizations that are typically funded by big businesses, labor unions, and the super wealthy that use contributions to support issues and indirectly support candidates. They can accept unlimited contributions from anyone to influence elections and voting (Center for Responsive Politics, 2020e).

**Constituents:** Voters of a geographic region or community that are represented by an elected official and to whom the elected official is responsible.

**Interest groups:** Individuals, groups, or organizations with a common cause or issue that attempts to influence action on public policy. Also known as Special Interest Group or SIG.

*Frequently confused by students*

**Legislation:** A law enacted by a governing body or legislature. Legislation may be used to regulate, fund, grant, declare, or outlaw activities or programs. Legislators draft bills that must be voted on to enact legislation, that is, to create laws.

**Legislators:** Individuals elected by voters in a geographic region to represent the constituents at the state legislature or U.S. Congress. Legislators draft, debate, and vote on bills and resolutions.

**Legislature:** A group of individually elected representatives that are authorized by their constituency to draft, debate, and vote on legislation.

**Lobbyist:** An individual whose job is to influence legislators and decision-makers on public policy. They must be registered and follow a series of regulations to prevent misconduct.

**Political action committee (PAC):** A formal group or organization engaging with the political process to influence policymakers and to endorse candidates for political office. PACs pool member contributions to donate to campaigns, to push political initiatives, or to support legislation. A PAC usually represents a group of people with common interests and policy positions. PACs must register and follow strict state and federal laws.

**President pro tempore (U.S. Senate):** The majority party of the U.S. Senate elects a president each session. The president pro tempore fulfills duties as the lead officer of the Senate and is third in line of succession for the presidency.
**Speaker of the House (U.S. House of Representatives):** The majority party of the House of Representatives elects the speaker for each session. The speaker fulfills duties as the lead officer of the House of Representatives and is second in line of succession for the presidency after the vice president.
**Sponsor/cosponsor:** Each piece of legislation must be introduced, or sponsored, by an elected Member of Congress. If a bill has more than one sponsor, which is common, the sponsors are referred to as cosponsors. The sponsor and cosponsors work to get votes and move the bill through the legislative process.

# Introduction

Governments exist to govern, protect, and advance the interests of the people. The structure of a government determines the access points at which the public—including nurses—can participate to ensure informed decision making. All governments around the world are uniquely constructed. Because public policy and politics are intertwined, participating in policy work requires a strong understanding of the structure of government, the political process, and politics to advance sustainable legislation.

Although many nurses wish to avoid engaging in politics, legislative policies, regulations, administrative rules, and executive orders impact the lives and work of millions of registered nurses. Avoiding policy engagement subjects health professionals and their patients and families to legislative actions that can negatively affect the workplace and impede the care of everyday Americans.

Nurses at all levels of education should strive for engagement at every level of government to ensure that the voice of the profession is heard. What happens at the federal, state, and local levels impacts care delivery, patients and families, and work at the bedside. While each nursing voice and contribution is unique, together nurses can influence legislators to make positive change to the U.S. healthcare system.

For 18 years, the nursing profession has been ranked by the American people as the most trusted profession (Reinhart, 2020). People trust nurses and expect the profession to participate in policy work to advocate on their behalf for a better health system and improved health outcomes around the nation. Nurses are experts in care delivery and provide a unique and important perspective on the unintended consequences of legislation. By focusing on solving healthcare problems at the local, state, and federal levels, nurses can reduce the negative impact of poor legislation.

In this chapter, we will review the structures of our governments—federal, state, and local. The structural discussion will provide a strong reference point for students to discover the people/bureaucrats (those who are employed rather than elected to government positions) who control access to policymakers. After discussing the people who make our governments run, the chapter will focus on people, power, and the legislative process.

## Structure of Government: Federal, State, and Local

The U.S. Constitution created a federalist system, also known as federalism. The United States is a constitutional republic with democratically elected leaders and a separation of powers between the federal and state governments. Not a true democracy where election to office is by a simple majority vote, the Founders created an Electoral College for the election of the president. The framers created the Electoral College as a compromise between an election by popular vote and an election by a vote of Congress (National Archives, n.d.). The original format of the Electoral College was changed with the addition of the 12th Amendment to the Constitution, which provided separate and distinct Electoral College votes for president and vice president (National Constitution Center, n.d.). The U.S. Constitution allocates specific responsibilities to each branch of government (**Table 5-1**).

## The Executive Branch

The federal government is composed of three distinct branches with specific roles and responsibilities and a complex system of checks and balances (see **Figure 5-1**). The president holds the power in the executive branch, overseeing the armed forces as commander-in-chief and as head of state. The president also has the power to sign legislation into law, create executive orders, and veto bills from Congress (The White House, 2020a). The president works with the vice president, presidential cabinet, and agency executives to execute and enforce laws established by Congress. The executive branch (**Table 5-2**) oversees more than 4 million personnel working on the day-to-day administration of missions, programs, and responsibilities in the Executive Office of the President (headed by the president's Chief of Staff) cabinet departments, and executive agencies (The White House, 2020a). Members of the presidential cabinet are appointed by the president and confirmed by the Senate. Some other government agency positions require Senate confirmation, but not all are subject to this process.

Although the executive branch holds the responsibility for making federal appointments and ensuring the execution and enforcement of legislation, shared responsibility for federal agencies between the executive and legislative branches results in additional checks and balances for branches of government (The White House, 2020a). Note that although the bulk of federal agencies report to the executive branch, there is broad constitutional authority provided to Congress allowing for control through legislative powers. Congress may create agencies and define interactions with the executive branch informed by separation-of-powers principles (Congressional Research Services, 2018). Statutory authority informs and controls the federal agencies through structural design, limitations on agency appointments, protection from presidential removal of agency leadership (except for cause), defining jurisdiction, authority and regulation, procedural controls of decision making, and agency funding (Congressional Research Services, 2018). Although the executive branch can advise and discuss and debate positions and policies created within executive

**Table 5-1** The Three Branches of Federal Government

| | Executive | Legislative | Judicial |
|---|---|---|---|
| **Composition** | Office of the President and 15 executive departments (State, Treasury, Defense, Agriculture, Energy, Housing and Urban Development, Justice, Commerce, Education, Health and Human Services, Interior, Labor, Transportation, Veterans Affairs, and Department of Homeland Security) | Senate and House of Representatives known collectively as Congress with 535 elected Members | U.S. Supreme Court, federal district courts, and U.S. circuit courts of appeals |
| **Role in health policy** | Recommends legislation and promotes major policy initiatives. | Possesses the sole federal power to enact legislation and to tax citizens and allocate federal spending. | Judicial interpretations of the Constitution or various laws may have a policy effect. |
| | Implements laws and manages programs after they have been passed by Congress through regulation, oversight, and presidential funding priorities. | Originates and promotes major policy initiatives. | Resolves questions regarding agency regulations that may affect policy. |
| | Writes regulations that interpret statutes (laws). | Has the power to override a presidential veto. | |
| | Has the power to veto legislation passed by Congress. | | |
| **Restrictions to power** | Unable to enact a law without the approval of Congress (legislative branch). | U.S. Supreme Court may invalidate legislation as unconstitutional. | Unable to recommend or promote legislative initiatives. |

Produced with information gathered from The White House (2020a, b).

## 3 BRANCHES of U.S. GOVERNMENT

**Constitution** (provided a separation of powers)

**Legislative** (makes laws)
- Congress
- Senate
- House of Representatives

**Executive** (carries out laws)
- President
- Vice President
- Cabinet

**Judicial** (interprets laws)
- Supreme Court
- Other Federal Courts

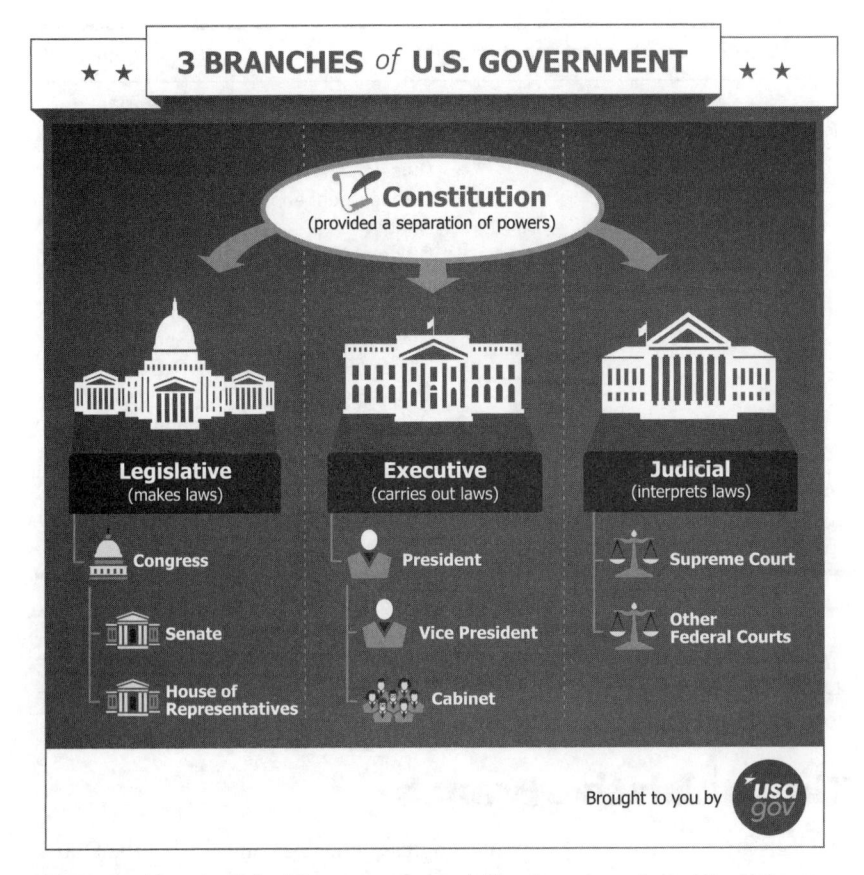

Brought to you by usa.gov

**Figure 5-1** How the United States is governed: The three branches of the U.S. government.

USA Government, Three Branches of the U.S. Government. https://www.usa.gov/branches-of-government.

**Table 5-2** Executive Branch Oversight

| President | Vice President | Executive Office of the President | Presidential Cabinet Members |
|---|---|---|---|
| ■ Vice president<br>■ Executive Office of the President<br>■ Presidential cabinet members<br>■ Heads of more than 50 executive agencies | ■ **President pro tempore (U.S. Senate)**<br>■ Prepared to assume role of president<br>■ Top adviser<br>■ Duties as assigned by the president | ■ White House Office<br>■ Office of the Vice President<br>■ Council of Economic Advisors<br>■ Council of Environment Quality<br>■ National Security Council<br>■ Office of Administration | ■ Department of Agriculture<br>■ Department of Commerce<br>■ Department of Defense<br>■ Department of Education<br>■ Department of Energy |

*(continues)*

**Table 5-2** Executive Branch Oversight                                         (continued)

| President | Vice President | Executive Office of the President | Presidential Cabinet Members |
|---|---|---|---|
|  |  | ■ Office of Management and Budget<br>■ Office of National Drug Control Policy<br>■ Office of Policy Development<br>■ Office of Science and Technology Policy<br>■ Office of the U.S. Trade Representative | ■ Department of Health and Human Services<br>■ Department of Homeland Security<br>■ Department of Housing and Urban Development |

Data from The White House. (2020, August 22). The White House- Executive Branch. whitehouse.gov: https://www.whitehouse.gov/about-the-white-house/the-executive-branch/

agencies, protections exist for agency employees and appointees through the statutory authority provided to Congress allowing for agencies to uphold positions without White House support.

# The Legislative Branch

The legislative branch is made up of Congress, which is composed of the House of Representatives and the Senate (**Table 5-3**). Congress has House Committees, Senate Committees, Joint Committees, and Commissions (**Table 5-4**). Some of the committees of specific interest to nurses and other healthcare professionals (where healthcare bills are introduced, reviewed, and moved forward) include the Senate Committee on Finance; the Senate Subcommittee on Health; the Senate Committee on Health, Education, Labor, & Pensions (HELP); the Senate Committee on Appropriations; the Senate Special Committee on Aging; the Senate Subcommittee on Labor, Health and Human Services, Education, and Related Agencies; the House Committee on Ways and Means; the House Subcommittee on Health; the House Committee on Appropriations; the House Subcommittee on Labor, Health and Human Services, Education, and Related Agencies; and the House Committee on the Budget (The White House, 2020b). Nurses can monitor these committees for significant federal legislation and work with professional organizations to influence policymakers on the issues.

# The Judicial Branch

The judicial branch of the federal government includes the Supreme Court; the Courts of Appeals; the District Courts; the Bankruptcy Courts; and Article I Courts, which include the U.S. Tax Court, the U.S. Court of Appeals for the

**Table 5-3** U.S. Congress: Senate and House of Representatives

| Senate | House of Representatives |
|---|---|
| Each state has two senators. 100 total Members. | There are 435 representatives (Number of representatives is based on state population as determined by the official U.S. Census conducted every 10 years). Redistricting or redrawing of district lines is subject to state law. |
| Senators serve 6-year terms. One-third are elected every 3 years. No term limits. | Representatives serve 2-year terms. Elected every 2 years. No term limits. |
| A president pro tempore is elected by the majority party each session. The vice president serves as the president of the senate. | **Speaker of the House** is elected every session from the majority party. |

Data from Congress. (2020, August 22). Committees of the U.S. Congress. Congress: https://www.congress.gov/committees

**Table 5-4** U.S. Congress Committees and Caucuses

| House | Senate |
|---|---|
| *Standing Committees* | |
| Agriculture | Agriculture, Nutrition, and Forestry |
| Appropriations | Appropriations |
| Armed Services | Armed Services |
| Budget | Banking, Housing, and Urban Affairs |
| Education and Labor | Budget |
| Energy and Commerce | Commerce, Science, and Transportation |
| Ethics | Energy and Natural Resources |
| Financial Services | Environment and Public Works |
| Foreign Affairs | Finance |
| Homeland Security | Foreign Relations |
| House Administration | Health, Education, Labor, and Pensions |
| Judiciary | Homeland Security and Governmental Affairs |

*(continues)*

**Table 5-4** U.S. Congress Committees and Caucuses  *(continued)*

| House | Senate |
|---|---|
| Natural Resources | Judiciary |
| Oversight and Reform | Rules and Administration |
| Rules | Small Business and Entrepreneurship |
| Science, Space, and Technology | Veterans' Affairs |
| Small Business | |
| Transportation and Infrastructure | |
| Veterans' Affairs | |
| Ways and Means | |
| **Special, Select, and Other Committees** | |
| House Permanent Select Committee on Intelligence | Aging (Special) |
| Select Committee on Climate Crisis | Caucus on International Narcotics Control |
| Select Committee on Modernization of Congress | Ethics (Select) |
| | Indian Affairs |
| | Intelligence (Select) |
| **Joint Committees** | |
| Joint Committee on Printing | |
| Joint Committee on Taxation | |
| Joint Committee on the Library | |
| Joint Economic Committee | |
| **Commissions** | |
| Commission on Security and Cooperation in Europe (U.S. Helsinki Commission) | Congressional Oversight Commission |
| Congressional-Executive Commission on China | |
| Tom Lantos Human Rights Commission | |

Data from Congress. (2020, August 22). Committees of the U.S. Congress. https://www.congress.gov/committees

Armed Forces, and the U.S. Court of Appeals for Veterans Claims (United States Courts, 2020). The federal judiciary resolves disputes about the U.S. Constitution and other federal laws as part of the system of checks and balances. Federal courts may review the constitutionality of legislation. The Supreme Court is the highest court in the United States as established by Article III of the U.S. Constitution. Below the Supreme Court are 94 district-level courts and 13 courts of appeal (United States Courts, 2020). The Supreme Court can choose whether to hear a case brought forward and has delivered decisions on numerous healthcare-related laws

## State and Local Governments

Other levels of government mirror the structure of the federal government with executive, legislative, and judicial branches. Although they are similar, each state has established individual state and local structures that may diverge from the federal government to some degree.

---

**Spotlight:** Historic Case Involves Unprecedented Legislative and Judicial Actions

In September 2004, 41-year-old Theresa (Terri) Mae Schiavo had been in a persistent vegetative state for 14 years after suffering cardiac arrest from a potassium imbalance. Her husband and legal guardian, Michael, had battled her parents, Bob and Mary Schindler, for 7 years over whether his wife should be allowed to die. Michael Schiavo, who had been wed to Terri for 18 years, said that his wife had previously told him that she would not want to be kept alive artificially. Physicians who testified on his behalf said she had no hope for recovery. She was fed through a tube but breathed on her own. However, the Schindlers maintained that their daughter could be helped with therapy.

Previous litigation and appeals included legislative and court actions in October 2003: Ms. Schiavo's feeding tube was removed, only to be reinserted 6 days later after the Florida **legislature**, in emergency session, passed a law that gave Governor Jeb Bush the power to intervene in the case. The governor ordered the feeding tube reinserted. The governor's office appealed to the Florida Supreme Court after a Pinellas County circuit court judge ruled in May that "Terri's Law" was unconstitutional, stating that the law violated the fundamental separation of powers between the executive and legislative branches and a violation of the right to privacy. Nineteen different Florida state court judges, at various times, considered the Schindlers' requests on appeal in six state appellate courts. Terri's Law was then struck down by the Florida Supreme Court.

Subsequently, U.S. District Court judge James Whittemore denied a temporary restraining order that would have forced the reinsertion of Schiavo's feeding tube. A three-judge panel of the 11th Circuit U.S. Court of Appeals upheld Whittemore's decision.

The case then moved to federal court in March 2005, following unprecedented action by Congress giving federal courts the authority to fully review her case. Following the Florida court's ruling, the U.S. Supreme Court rejected a petition forcing the reinsertion of Terri Schiavo's feeding tube. She died 13 days after the feeding tube was removed. Her illness and death were the focus of major medical, legal, theological, ethical, political, and social controversies.

Powers not held at the federal level are shared among state and local governments (The White House, 2020b). At the state or local level, the elected executive officials are a governor or mayor, whereas some areas of the country have municipalities, parishes, or county-elected officials (Porche, 2019). The legislative and judicial branches at the state level are like the federal system, with elected legislators meeting at the state capitols and an established judiciary with a state court system.

# The Legislative Process

## Legislation

Ideas for **legislation** come from many different places and people, such as a legislator's constituents, a special interest group, a lobbyist working for an organization, a story the legislator heard or a personal experience, or a concern for the future—all of these generate conversations that could result in a legislator introducing a bill. Nurses can be the impetus for a bill if they present an issue or idea to solve a problem to the legislator. Identifying problems that can be solved with existing resources or by fulfilling other obligations of the policymaker will help "sell" an idea increasing the chances of support.

Once an idea is identified, a bill is written by legislative counsel (see www.slc.senate.gov/Drafting/drafting.htm), the legislator or a group working with the legislator, and once complete, can be introduced to a chamber of Congress. Bills are required to have legislators sign on as a **sponsor/cosponsor**. Most states work in a similar way with a bicameral system of state government with two chambers, with the exception of Nebraska which has a unicameral system. Very few bills make it through all the stages of introduction, debate and review, amendment, and a vote by both chambers, resulting in few bills making their way to the president's or a governor's desk (United States Senate, 2020).

## Committees

The House and Senate leaders are voted into leadership positions by their colleagues. The majority party leadership selects committee chairs for the session while the minority party selects leaders called ranking members. These leadership positions are quite influential and prestigious. A committee chair (the chair is always a member of the political party with the majority of Members) has the authority to determine the focus and framework of the committee for the congressional session and determines which bills will be placed on the calendar for review and debate. A committee chair can determine the fate of a bill before it even gets to the committee and often receives significant contributions from special interest groups to support his or her reelection, allowing for more influence on committee direction. Reelection is always under consideration by lawmakers.

The committee will vote to accept or reject a bill after reviewing it. Committees can also make changes to the bill and language prior to sending the bill to the floor of the House or Senate. Members of Congress will then discuss and debate the bill. Changes and amendments can be proposed prior to placing the bill up for vote. If the bill is passed in the chamber, then it moves to the other chamber for consideration. If the bill is changed by the subsequent chamber, the bill will then have to go back through the process at the other chamber until both chambers agree on language and amendments of the bill. If a bill is changed by one chamber and not agreed upon by the other, then a conference committee made up of representatives from both chambers meets to reconcile the differences in the two versions of the bill. If reconciliation and agreement does not occur, a bill dies (USAGov, 2020).

If a bill passes in both the House and the Senate, it is sent to the chief executive who must sign a bill for it to become law. The chief executive—the president at the federal level and the governor at the state level—may veto any bill. If a bill is vetoed by the chief executive, the bill returns to the **legislature** for modification or a potential veto override. In the case of Congress, a veto override requires a two-thirds majority vote—referred to as a super majority—in both chambers for the bill to become a law (USAGov, 2020).

## Action on a Bill

The legislative process to make a bill a law must take place during the legislative cycle, which is 2 years (a biennium) at the federal level. It can take years to move a bill through the process, if a bill does not make it through during the biennium, the bill dies and it must be reintroduced in the next legislative cycle should the legislator wish to attempt to advance the bill again (**Figure 5-2**).

Although there are some subtle differences between the state and federal legislative process, the dynamics of politics can change the outcome of a bill or initiative whether at the state or federal level. If a bill is not placed on the calendar for introduction on the floor, the bill never sees the light of day. Politics plays a significant role in determining whether a bill will even be up for consideration. With much of the political process being done behind closed doors, relationships play a key role in advancing legislation.

> **Tracking a Bill**
>
> Go to https://Congress.gov.
>
> Select "Legislation" and search on a topic such as "health care."
>
> Example: H.R.4651 was the 4651st bill introduced in the 116th Congress.
>
> H.R.4651—116th Congress (2019-2020) American Healthcare Future Act of 2019. To amend the Internal Revenue Code with respect to Health Savings Accounts (HSA). Repeals requirement that individuals must be covered by a high deductible insurance plan, increases maximum contribution, allows those eligible for Medicare to have an HSA, allows HSAs to be used for health insurance purchase, provides cost-of-living adjustments, allows rollovers from Medicare Advantage Medical Savings Accounts, and allows HSAs to be used with direct primary care.
>
> Sponsor: Rep. Steve King (Introduced 10/11/2019)
>
> Status: Referred to the House Committee on Ways and Means on 10/11/2019

**Figure 5-2** How to find legislation.

## Funding Legislation: Winning a Seat at the Table

Winning an election at the local, state, or federal level can be very costly. Candidates must fundraise to run for office, and the price of an election can range from hundreds of thousands of dollars for a local or state position to millions for a congressional seat. In the 2018 elections, in Maryland's 6th District, now Representative David Trone (D) spent more than $18 million to win his seat, while the least expensive campaign was run by incumbent Jose Serrano (D), who won with a mere $240,000—a range of between $2.00 and $112.40 per vote (Berkowitz, 2019). Candidates cannot rely solely on individual campaign contributions by voters to meet the costs of running a campaign. Although some are wealthy enough to fund their own campaigns, like David Trone, most policymakers must rely on wealthy individuals or special interest groups and Political Action Committees (PAC) to contribute.

The amount of money flowing through the election system results in questions about whether a seat is won or bought. Is it the principles or positions that are winning, or just the individual with the most money to campaign? And after the election, what is the return on investment for those that funded a campaign? Contributions from different special interest groups and 527 organizations will continue to vary from election to election, and will likely be based on the candidates and the issues of the time, but billions of dollars are spent every year to influence through political contributions (Center for Responsive Politics, 2020b).

In 2010, the U.S. Supreme Court ruled on campaign finance law in *Citizens United v. Federal Election Commission*. This ruling struck down the law that prevented unions and corporations from using funds to directly influence elections through advocacy for or against candidates, stating that this was in essence a violation of free speech (National Constitution Center, 2019). This ruling allowed for unlimited spending by corporations or unions if the efforts were not coordinated with a political campaign. There has been support for disclosure of activity and sources of spending, and since the ruling the flow of money into campaigns has increased dramatically.

## Power: Who Has It? You Want It!

The system of government created by the Founders was intended to ensure direct influence on decision making by the people. However, because of the U.S. two-party system, politics has become an industry in which power is determined by selling a political brand with defined ideologies and value statements demonizing those who disagree (Gehl & Porter, 2020). Because of this duopoly, in order to advance legislation, common ground must be found to engage both parties in legislative action. In recent years, a clear majority in the legislature has resulted in partisan politics and difficulties passing and/or blocking legislation. According to Gehl and Porter (2020),

> The politics industry is driven by the same five forces that shape competition in any industry: the nature and intensity of rivalry, the power

Exercising Nursing Political Power

**Figure 5-3** Exercising nurse power.

of buyers, the power of suppliers, the threat of new entrants, and the pressure from substitutes that compete in new ways. The dynamic relationships among these forces determine the nature of industry competition, the value created by the industry, and who has the power to capture that value.

Parties are competing for constituents to win elections and the ability to pass or block bills—sometimes resulting in a win-lose proposition for the public interest (Gehl & Porter, 2020). The power to influence in this environment takes considerable effort and well-established relationships, as well as a deep understanding of the different perspectives of each party.

Many different powerful influences impact on decisions in the policy arena (**Figure 5-4**). Six types of power are typically used in leadership and politics: legitimate, expert, reward, informational, coercive, and referent. *Legitimate power* comes from a role or position. *Expert power* comes in the form of knowledge, experience on an issue, and expertise. *Reward power* is based on providing a type of incentive for compliance or agreement. *Informational power* is having information that someone else might not have that can create a bargaining situation or be provided as a favor. *Coercive power* results in the ability to apply pressure or punishment for not complying. *Referent power* is personality, persuasion, or inspiration that modifies behavior (Mind Tools, 2020).

Most policy in the U.S. government starts outside of formal legislative arenas and comes from events affecting Americans or from foreign influences

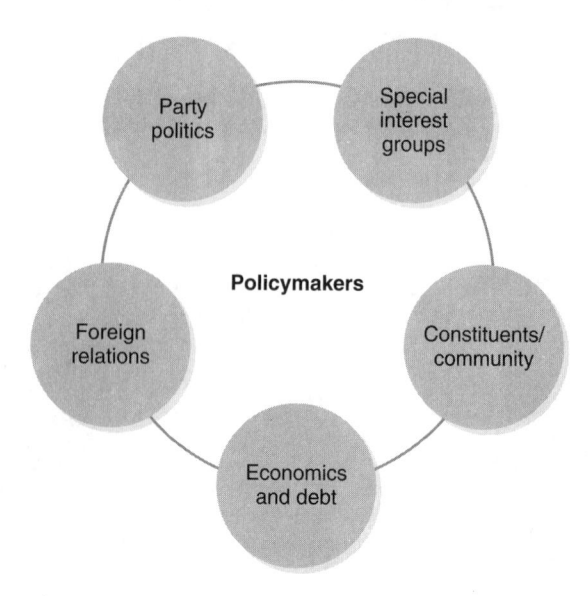

**Figure 5-4** Power influences.

wanting a piece of the pie (e.g., import/export taxes). Different types of power are used with legislators to gain action on issues. Power is essential to change. The nursing profession has the opportunity to work through different types of power to directly influence legislators and advance legislation.

## The People: Legislators

Although lawmakers, or **legislators**, play a significant role in the political process, other people in politics play an integral, influential, and sometimes underestimated role in getting legislation to a hearing or a vote. These other players are key to success on policy issues. Understanding the background, goals, and positions of the many different people that contribute to the final success of a bill is essential.

Researching and obtaining background information on each decision-maker is important to achieving policy influence or meeting a legislative goal. Technology allows for the identification of lawmakers at federal or state government websites using an address or ZIP code (Open States, 2020). Most government websites provide background information on the legislators and staff as well as photos and access to their voting records.

## The People: Legislative Staff

A federal legislator's staff typically includes a chief of staff, administrative assistants, legislative directors, a press secretary, legislative assistants (LAs), and committee staff (**Table 5-5**). Federal lawmakers maintain a staff in Washington, D.C., as well as a smaller staff in their local or district offices. State-level legislators may have only one staff member who is responsible for all office activities. Most staff are on-site at the legislative offices during all business days, unlike legislators who may travel home or be away during a recess. Although getting

**Table 5-5** Legislative Staff

| Staff Member | Role |
| --- | --- |
| Chief of staff | Senior staff person. Answers directly to the Member. |
| Administrative assistant | Oversight responsibilities for staff. |
| Legislative directors | Responsible for day-to-day legislative activities. |
| Press secretary | Responsible for press releases and public relations. |
| Legislative assistants/aides (LAs) | Responsible for specific legislative areas/issues (e.g., health, agriculture, Social Security). LAs have more than one area of responsibility. LAs provide staff assistance to the Member at committee hearings, write policy briefs, and prepare the Member's statements and witness questions. They may help draft bills by working in concert with the legislative council. |
| Committee staff | Support the work of Congressional committees. Separate staffs are allocated to the majority and minority parties, with a larger number serving the majority party. Their focus usually is narrower than the legislator's personal staff and they usually are older and more experienced. They plan the committee agenda, coordinate schedules, gather and analyze data, draft committee reports, etc. |

to know and communicating with legislators is vital, the importance of getting to know and engaging their staff should not be underestimated. A legislator's staff plays an important role in the political process and can be indispensable in advancing policy work.

A legislator's staff often provides detailed research and opinions on an issue to a legislator. It is not uncommon for a legislative aide to be responsible for a specific set of policy issues. In other words, they watch legislation, read bills, and advise the policymaker on different stakeholders' positions on an issue prior to a vote. With so many pieces of legislation to keep up with, legislators rely heavily on their staffs for key information and recommendations for voting positions. The legislative staff also controls who has direct access to the legislator with scheduling and can influence the priority given to issues and initiatives.

## The People: Constituents

It is not uncommon for **constituents**, including nurses, to be unaware of who their elected officials are and have had no interaction with the legislative staff advising the policymaker. Although most people know who the president is, Members of Congress who represent an area or region are not always as easily remembered by name. Some people will recognize their state or local leaders but not pay attention to who is representing them in Washington, D.C. This lack of knowledge often leads to issues being brought to the wrong level of government, impacting advocacy and poorly representing the profession.

For example, if a nurse is advocating for every school to employ a school nurse on-site, visiting a federal legislator would be ineffective because decisions regarding school legislation and regulations are made at the state and local levels. The congressional leader would not be able to move forward a change on this issue. The best policymakers to influence in this scenario are state or local lawmakers. To advance legislation, it is vital that the right issue is taken to the right person at the right level of government. Understanding the government's responsibilities at each level will help with taking the message to the right person.

Engaging constituents/voters to support an issue is an important way to gain momentum. Nursing groups have succeeded in advancing legislation by creating coalitions that include stakeholders from various perspectives and voting blocks. Finding individuals with common interest on an issue provides greater depth of insight and improves resources to influence lawmakers. It is not uncommon for bipartisan stakeholders to "reach across the aisle" (i.e., engage with the other party) to sign on to an important issue in order to expand their reach and influence on government officials to get a bill passed. Gale Adcock, FNP, a Member of the North Carolina House of Representatives (D–N.C. District 41), has a favorite saying, "I don't work across the aisle, I'm constantly *in* the aisle." She has represented her constituents in Wake County for three terms. By taking a bipartisan approach, coalitions working with lawmakers are showing the value of people over politics. This can result in increased support and an improved likelihood a bill may be passed.

## The People: Special Interest Groups

**Lobbyists** are often hired by special interest groups to influence the policymaking process. Professional lobbyists who are hired to work on an issue use the power of persuasion to move legislators to vote in a specific way. Because lawmakers themselves cannot be experts on all the issues and are often pressed for time before a vote, they may use lobbyists to gather information and knowledge about an issue.

Although anyone can lobby a legislator, professional lobbyists must be duly registered and adhere to rules and regulations regarding lobbying (National Council of State Legislatures, 2020). Nurses may not know all the lobbyists working on an issue, but as the complexity of a piece of legislation increases lobbyists become even more critical to passing the law. The greater the size and impact of the bill, the more input that is needed. Lawmakers will look to legislative staff and lobbyists to be informed prior to a vote.

Although some of the largest lobbying firms reportedly reside on K Street in Washington, D.C., influence may also come from individuals who have worked in government. It is not uncommon after leaving the public sector for government employees or officials to obtain jobs that have direct influence on government. Many of these individuals move in and out of the public and private sector. This is called the "revolving door in Washington." Lobbying firms recognizing the opportunity to gain influence by hiring a previous government official or staff member to represent and defend their interests, and government officials leaving the public sector enjoy the benefits of working for private firms (Center for Responsive Politics, 2020d).

Special **interest groups** (sometimes referred to as SIGs) are stakeholders attempting to gain influence on an issue. The Center for Responsive Politics provides an open source to review political contributions and lobbying investments by sectors, organizations, and some individuals. Financial influence can heavily impact policy decisions. Understanding the scale of the impact of special interest groups on health care requires a look at the financial spending of health professionals on lobbying (**Table 5-6**). Unfortunately, nurses have historically made a smaller financial investment in policymaking than other health professionals; reducing the overall influence of the profession at both the state and federal level (Center for Responsive Politics, 2020c).

Other special interest groups include the **political action committee (PAC)** and 527 organizations. PACs are formal action organizations that are often a separate entity from professional organizations that follow state and federal guidelines related to political activities. PACs and 527 organizations are specifically regulated to reduce corrupt practices. These organizations use contributions and resources to engage with, endorse, and support candidates for political office.

Advocacy groups tied to big business, labor, manufacturing, and the very wealthy are called **527 organizations**. These organizations are referred to by this name due to the governing section of the tax code that applies to these organizations. 527 groups have no limit to the amount they can raise, but they must be registered and disclose their contributions to the Internal Revenue Service (IRS; Center for Responsive Politics, 2020a). The funds are used for

**Table 5-6** Lobbying and Campaign Contributions by Health Professionals in 2019–2020

| Entity | Lobbying[a] | Campaign Contributions[b] |
|---|---|---|
| American Association of Nurse Anesthetists | $760,000 | $673,000 |
| American Association of Nurse Practitioners | $784,239 | $141,000 |
| American Nurses Association | $426,676 | $254,977 |
| American Medical Association | $20,910,000 | $615,299 |
| American Society of Anesthesiologists | $1,090,000 | $1,676,213 |

Data from Center for Responsive Politics. (2019). https://www.opensecrets.org/federal-lobbying/industries/summary?id=H01
[a]Total costs could include salaries, retainers, and expenses lobbyists incur as part of their jobs. They could also include developing materials to support an initiative, or studies/surveys commissioned to support or refute a position.
[b]Election cycle through August 2020 prior to 2020 election. Some contributions are categorized as individual.

political activities such as voter mobilization and ad campaigns but cannot be directly donated to political candidates (Center for Responsive Politics, 2020e).

Registered nurses constitute a special interest group: PACs and lobbyists work to move nursing's policy agenda forward. In 2021, three registered nurses served in the House of Representatives: Eddie Bernice Johnson (D-Texas District 30), Lauren Underwood (D-Illinois District 14), and Cori Bush (D-Missouri District 1). Congresswoman Johnson was the first nurse elected to Congress. All are trailblazers for the profession in politics (American Nurses Association, 2020b). At the time of publication, no registered nurses served in the Senate.

## Political Strategy

Understanding the process and structure of government is only part of the picture. Success in influencing health policy requires knowledge of the political environment, political players, and the political climate. Knowing when to strike, which stakeholders will have the most impact, who can and will work together, what the opposition's strengths and weaknesses are, and funding of efforts to get legislation passed are all part of political strategy. Although nurses should cultivate individual relationships with the legislators and government officials that represent them, the strategy of introducing and advancing a bill idea can sometimes be frustrating and not well received without greater support from the nursing community or a professional organization.

Participation in politics is complex and is often seen as requiring shrewdness. Political expediency will often result in compromises such as in bill language or amendments with unwanted changes that disappoint. Success at the policy table requires establishing a strategy and planned responses to stakeholders, unexpected changes in a bill, and the opposition's research and messaging. Investing in political planning requires both funding and time to become politically astute (**Figure 5-5**). Being politically astute involves having a set of skills, knowledge, and judgments about the interests, goals, and values of stakeholders. This astuteness brings self-awareness, self-control, and influence to policy work.

- Issues always have at least two sides, and maybe more, that are reasonable depending on one's point of view and experiences. You should be knowledgeable of all sides to an issue.
- Listen to what people are saying with an analytical ear. Critical thinking is not just for the clinical practice setting. Apply theories and concepts about policymaking to the issues being considered. Use therapeutic communication techniques.
- Utilize a variety of sources; do not just rely on those that are consistent with your own ideology. Most sources have a bias, so broaden your reading and listening to get a more complete perspective and perhaps a bit closer to the truth. Always consider the source of the information provided.
- Connect with others who are involved in the policymaking side of the profession. Share what you learn with colleagues. Become involved in local commissions, councils, and committees.

**Figure 5-5** Political astuteness.

Professional nursing organizations are usually represented by "government affairs" personnel and elected officers. Often, an organization will engage membership to reach out to legislators to establish relationships and research a legislator's position on healthcare issues. This engagement can be through committee work or policy sentinels. If nurses are interested in working to get legislation passed, a good place to start the work is through the American Nursing Association (ANA) and its affiliates or through a specialty nursing organization.

Although nurses can and should take an issue directly to a legislator in order to make change, nurses and nursing organizations must engage with experts in policy and politics to guide the entirety of the bill process. Members of the profession must be willing to invest in relationships with political advisers to improve the chance of a successful outcome. Consultants help with unified and directed messaging that is better received by specific legislators and aids in identifying strategic alliances with common interests to increase influence and expand the reach of the nursing organization. Outside perspectives and expertise may be necessary to maneuver the "game" of politics and advance a bill, but hiring consultants comes at a cost, requiring political contributions from nurses to their professional nursing organization's PACs or the organization working on the issue.

## Nurses Engaged in Legislative Policy Change

At the federal level, nursing organizations are working to make improvements through legislation on workforce, safety, staffing, gun violence, environmental health, and nursing education, among other issues (American Nurses Association, 2020a). Organizations such as the American Nurses Association, the American Organization of Nursing Leadership, the American Academy of Nursing, the National League for Nursing, the American Association of Colleges of Nursing, the American Association of Nurse Practitioners, and others, set federal policy priorities and engage with federal legislators to influence changes that affect nursing and patients and families. Nurses engage in legislative action on behalf of the Nursing Workforce Development programs of Title VIII of the Public Health Service Act and its amendments in the Nursing Reauthorization Act. Title VIII funding supports critical programs in nursing education as well as efforts to bolster the nursing workforce caring for rural and underserved populations. The 2019 version of the Nursing Reauthorization Act also defined nurse-managed clinics, included recognition of all four advanced practice registered nurse roles, and allowed clinical nurse leaders access to educational grants (American Organization of Nurse Leaders, 2020). Title VIII programs fall under the jurisdiction of the Health Resource Services Administration (HRSA), an agency of the U.S. Department of Health and Human Services (HRSA, 2018) (**Figure 5-6**).

At the state level, state nursing organizations and nurses work on issues such as regulatory requirements, workforce safety, staffing measures, scope of practice, workforce shortages, and the nursing education pipeline. Some issues are similar to what is being worked on at the federal level, but state

**Figure 5-6** Title VIII Nursing Workforce Development programs within HRSA's Division of Nursing and Public Health.

organizations target legislation that impacts nurses working in one state. Scope of practice is a state-level issue and is not in the purview of federal legislators. On March 11, 2021, legislators, outside organizations, and the North Carolina Nurses Association (NCNA) announced the introduction of the SAVE Act, a bill to grant full-practice authority for Advanced Practice Registered Nurses. When the 2020 session ended, the bill was effectively killed and was forced to be reintroduced in 2021. This bill is the centerpiece of NCNA's legislative agenda and has been one of NCNA's highest priorities for several years.

# Conclusion

Building relationships with legislators, legislative staff, policy experts, and key stakeholders is paramount to success in the political arena. While quid pro quo exists in the halls of Congress and at the state houses, the advancement of a policy agenda requires playing the political game and fully participating by bringing policy solutions and support to policymakers. Nurses who wish to enter the policy arena should be fully prepared and educated on the issues, bring facts and data to support their positions, and provide impactful stories on how the problem affects the public.

Changes that improve the lives of patients, families, and the nursing community may take time and an incremental approach to succeed. Often nurses get discouraged that their solution cannot be accomplished in a single legislative session. Policy change is a long game full of moves and countermoves to gain ground. Compromise is not loss—it is a necessary tool to move a policy agenda forward based on the political will and climate. Every battle won—no matter how small—will typically provide an advantage in the next session. Remaining committed to the long-term goal and being open to the many steps it may take to arrive requires resiliency. Policy work is not for the easily discouraged.

Nurses are needed to provide perspective and context on health policy and healthcare legislation. The profession should support nurses who participate in health policy and politics through academic scholarship, leadership plans, and promotion. By encouraging and positioning nurses at the table across all levels of government, the profession can change the dynamics and instigate a sea change toward a better system for all (Anderson et al., 2020).

Finding common ground and looking for measures that will appeal to both sides of the aisle will result in greater success. The profession needs nurses from the entirety of the political spectrum voicing ideas to move forward substantive change. The nursing community should recognize the unique and significant contributions of all nurses engaging in policy and politics and commit to increased awareness, recognition, and investment in policy initiatives to advance important legislative changes. Nurses must think politically, use strategy to develop a plan, and play the political game to be effective. After all, what happens in Congress, the state houses, and at the city council impacts the delivery of patient care—whether nurses engage or not.

## CASE STUDY 5-1: Workplace Safety

Many hospitals and clinics in the state have been eager to avoid reporting assaults on healthcare workers in their facilities due to concerns with bad publicity. Professional organizations representing nurses have convened a committee to discuss possible solutions, but no action has been taken at the state level, and no legislators have been willing to sponsor a bill.

Although nurses in the state are considered to be part of a protected class, like teachers and police officers, the offense is considered a misdemeanor, not a felony. The nursing organizations would like to see a bill that requires any attack on a nurse or healthcare worker to be considered a felony.

A recent case of violence against a nurse in the emergency room that was picked up by the media has prompted a legislator to contact local nurses to discuss the prevalence of the issue in health care. The legislator is facing a tough reelection campaign and wishes to make this issue a part of her reelection campaign. The professional organizations have met with this legislator in the past, and she has not always been supportive of the nursing community or healthcare legislation. The legislator has also asked for political campaign contributions from the state nursing organization's PAC, but no money has been contributed to this legislator in the past and it is possible the legislator will lose the race.

### Case Study Discussion Questions

1. As a member of the government affairs committee and regional representative for your state nursing organization, you have been asked to visit with the legislator about the issue. What are some questions that you will prepare to ask at the visit?

2. After the first meeting, the legislator has asked for nurses to develop a position and talking points related to this issue to present to a possible cosponsor. What are some key points that need to be made on this issue?
3. The legislator asks for a political contribution from the nursing organization. The government affairs committee is considering this request. What concerns might the committee have? How could the decision impact the possible legislation?
4. If the legislator is reelected, what is the process to get the bill advanced?

## Chapter Discussion Points

1. Compare and contrast the federal government and the state system in which you reside. Consider how your state differs from other states. Think about the checks and balances of the three branches of the federal government and how they work together to govern and maintain laws.
2. Identify a healthcare or nursing issue of interest and determine who the stakeholders are. Think about the many industries an issue might impact, and include a variety of individuals and organizations.
3. Identify a healthcare bill using the www.congress.gov website. Track the progress of the bill and the next steps to getting the bill passed.
4. Analyze the role of nurses in policy and politics. Discuss how nurses can be more involved in health policy and politics.
5. Watch the movie, *And the Band Played On* (1993), about the onset of the HIV/AIDS crisis. Knowing that the Centers for Disease Control and Prevention (CDC) is an agency within the executive branch, discuss the politics involved in notifications and public health warnings, protecting the nation's blood supply, and engaging in global politics. The movie is available on YouTube.

## References

American Nurses Association. (2020a). *Get involved*. https://www.nursingworld.org/practice-policy/advocacy/federal/

American Nurses Association. (2020b). *Nurses serving in Congress*. https://www.nursingworld.org/practice-policy/advocacy/federal/nurses-serving-in-congress/

American Organization of Nurse Leaders. (2020). *Title VIII Reauthorization*. https://www.aonl.org/advocacy/key-issues/title-viii-reauthorization

Anderson, A. L., Waddell, A., Brennan, P., Burnett, C., Anderson, C., & Short, N. (2020). Advancing health policy education in nursing: American Association of Colleges of Nursing Faculty Policy Think Tank. *Journal of Professional Nursing, 36*(5), 100–105.

Berkowitz, B. A. (2019, November 15). How to run for Congress. *The Washington Post*. https://www.washingtonpost.com/politics/2019/11/15/how-run-congress/?arc404=true

Center for Responsive Politics. (2020a). *527 basics*. https://www.opensecrets.org/527s/basics.php

Center for Responsive Politics. (2020b). *Influence and lobbying*. https://www.opensecrets.org/influence/

Center for Responsive Politics. (2020c). *Nurses: Top contributors to federal candidates, parties, and outside groups*. http://www.opensecrets.org/industries/contrib.php?ind=H1710

Center for Responsive Politics. (2020d). *Top industries*. http://www.opensecrets.org/revolving/top.php?display=I

Center for Responsive Politics. (2020e). *Top organization contributions to 527 committees, 2018 election cycle.* https://www.opensecrets.org/527s/527contribs.php
Congress.gov. (2020a). *Committees of the U.S. Congress.* https://www.congress.gov/committees
Congress.gov. (2020b). *S.1399—Title VIII Nursing Workforce Reauthorization Act of 2019.* https://www.congress.gov/bill/116th-congress/senate-bill/1399/actions
Congressional Research Services. (2018). *Congress's authority to influence and control executive branch agencies.* Author.
Florida Senate. (2020). *CS/CS/HB 607: Direct Care Workers.* https://www.flsenate.gov/Session/Bill/2020/607
Gehl, K. M., & Porter, M. E. (2020, July–August). Fixing U.S. politics. *Harvard Business Review.* https://hbr.org/2020/07/fixing-u-s-politics
Russell, S. (2018). HRSA and the Title VIII Nursing Workforce Programs. *Health Resources and Services Administration.* https://www.hrsa.gov/sites/default/files/hrsa/advisory-committees/nursing/meetings/2018/Title-VIII-nursing-workforce-programs-final-2018.pdf
Mind Tools. (2020). *French and Raven's Five Forms of Power.* https://www.mindtools.com/pages/article/newLDR_56.htm
National Archives. (n.d.). *Electoral College.* https://www.archives.gov/electoral-college/about
National Constitution Center. (n.d.). *12th Amendment election of president and vice president.* Interactive Constitution. https://constitutioncenter.org/interactive-constitution/amendment/amendment-xii
National Constitution Center. (2019, September 6). *Citizens United v. Federal Election Commission.* https://constitutioncenter.org/interactive-constitution/educational-video/citizens-united-v-federal-election-commission
National Council of State Legislatures. (2020, August 8). *Lobbyist registration requirements.* https://www.ncsl.org/research/ethics/50-state-chart-lobbyist-registration-requirements.aspx
Open States. (2020). *Find my legislator.* https://openstates.org/find_your_legislator/
Porche, D. J. (2019). Executive offices: State and local governmental level. In D. J. Porche (Ed.), *Health policy application for nurses and other health professionals* (pp. 49–66). Jones & Bartlett Learning.
Reinhart, R. J. (2020, January 6). Nurses continue to rate highest in honesty, ethics. Gallup. https://news.gallup.com/poll/274673/nurses-continue-rate-highest-honesty-ethics.aspx
The White House. (2020, August 22a). *The White House- Executive Branch.* https://www.whitehouse.gov/about-the-white-house/our-government/
The White House (2020, August 22b). *The White House- Legislative Branch.* https://www.whitehouse.gov/about-the-white-house/our-government/the-legislative-branch/
Thomas, K. (2020, March 24). *Florida nurse practitioners gain full practice authority.* Daily Nurse: The Pulse of Nursing. https://dailynurse.com/florida-grants-advanced-nps-full-practice-authority/
United States Courts. (2020, August 23). *Court role and structure.* https://www.uscourts.gov/about-federal-courts/court-role-and-structure#:~:text=The%20federal%20judiciary%20operates%20separately,them%20as%20the%20Constitution%20requires.&text=The%20judicial%20branch%20decides%20the,other%20disputes%20about%20federal%20l
United States Senate. (2020, August 20). *Responsibilities of the Legislative Drafter.* https://www.slc.senate.gov/Drafting/drafting.htm
United States Senate. (2020, August 20). US Senate. https://www.senate.gov/reference/glossary_term/caucus.htm

## Online Resources

**American Association of Critical-Care Nurses, Policy & Advocacy:** www.aacn.org/policy-and-advocacy
**American Nurses Association, Advocacy:** www.nursingworld.org/practice-policy/advocacy/
**American Association of Nurse Anesthetists, Advocacy and Policy:** www.aana.com/advocacy
**American Association of Nurse Practitioners, AANP Advocacy:** www.aanp.org/advocacy
**American Organization for Nursing Leadership, AONL Advocacy Center:** www.aonl.org/aonl-advocacy
**Campaign for Action:** https://campaignforaction.org
**Center for Responsive Politics, OpenSecrets.org:** www.opensecrets.org

Congress.gov: www.congress.gov

National Council for State Boards of Nursing, Policy and Government: www.ncsbn.org/policy-and-government.htm

National League for Nursing: www.nln.org/advocacy-public-policy/government-affairs-action-center

Open States, Find Your Legislators: https://openstates.org/find_your_legislator/

Supreme Court of the United States: www.supremecourt.gov

The White House: https://www.whitehouse.gov

# CHAPTER 6

# Policy Implementation: Avoiding Policy Failure

Leslie Sharpe

## KEY TERMS

**Bottom-up:** A framework that views policy implementation at the level of the implementers and the actual implementation process.
**Deflection of goals:** A type of maneuver used in policy implementation that creates changes in the original goals.
**Dissipation of energies:** Actions used by implementation players that can impede, delay, and/or cause the collapse of a program.
**Diversion of resources:** A type of maneuver used in policy implementation to win favor related to budget decisions.
**Implementation:** The time period following the decision to adopt a new policy or guideline until the users have fully and consistently adopted the policy into practice.
**Implementation climate:** The shared perception by organizational members that the innovation to be implemented is an organizational priority.
**Implementation effectiveness:** The regularity and consistency with which the targeted organizational members use the innovation or policy.
**Implementation science:** The study of implementation of healthcare policies and evidence-based guidelines from research into practice.
**Innovation–values fit:** The perception that the innovation or policy is consistent with the mission and values of the organization.
**Policy failure:** Failure to achieve the intended (or essential) goals of the policy or legislation.
**Policy implementation research:** Research that studies the implementation of laws, rules, and regulations.
**Top-down:** A framework that views policy implementation as an administrative process with the focus on the goals and direction of policy.

# Introduction

Healthcare policy implementation is complex, requiring coordination by multiple organizations and stakeholders to achieve benefits. Often, complex innovative policies are adopted with great anticipation and fanfare only to fail during implementation. Enactment of a policy or legislation does not guarantee that it will be a success. Governments often create policies that rely on implementation by arm's-length organizations and require practice changes on the part of different segments of the healthcare system without understanding the differences in, and complexities of, these agencies. Examples of recently implemented health policies include opioid legislation, Medicaid expansion in most states, coronavirus aid and relief (CARES Act), relaxed telehealth rules, loan repayment programs for health professional education, safeguards for first responders, and major building projects within the Veterans Administration (for a full list of public laws passed during a particular congressional session refer to www.congress.gov/public-laws/). Essential components that are useful in implementing health policy include innovation, a technical (how-to) package, communication, partnerships, management, and political commitment.

Why is understanding the process of policy implementation important for nurses? Nurses make up the largest segment of health professionals in the United States—3.6 million strong (American Nurses Association [ANA], 2017). Burke (2016) reflects that "through policy work, nurses can and should influence practice standards and processes to assure quality of care. Nurses who influence health policy help shape the care that will be provided today and tomorrow." However, Cramer (2002) noted that nurses are disproportionately underrepresented in actively shaping health policy. In a study on nursing and the media, Woodhull (1997) analyzed 20,000 articles (2,600 health articles) published in 16 U.S. newspapers, magazines, and health trade publications in September 1997. Less than 1% of the articles in major magazines referenced a nurse; nurses were referenced in less than 4% of the 2,101 newspaper health articles from 7 newspapers across the United States. Nursing leaders have called for journalists to develop more effective communication channels for nurses and those they both serve. Unfortunately, not much has changed since 1997: Diana Mason and colleagues (2018a) reported in the Woodhull Study Revisited that even after 20 years, nurses are rarely quoted in healthcare articles (2% of quotes) and that nurses are totally invisible as sources in articles about healthcare policy. They assert that "nurses may be shirking their social responsibility to advocate for the health of people if they are not proactive in accessing and responding to journalists" (Mason et al., 2018b). As policy implementers, patient advocates, and healthcare consumers, nurses are overwhelmingly qualified to sit at the table as experts in health policy planning and implementation. It's high time we find the courage to lead and "unleash the power of nursing" (McLemore, 2020).

It is difficult to discuss policy implementation in isolation, because the success of implementation relies heavily on the design/planning process as well as on feedback from stakeholders and the evaluation process. Without adequate foresight and planning to address potential barriers, implementation can fail miserably. The evaluation framework developed by the Centers for Disease Control and Prevention (CDC, n.d.) recommends that the implementation evaluation questions be considered as early as the planning stage. For example, are the steps of the implementation process clearly outlined? Are the necessary resources available for policy implementation? Formulating these questions at the beginning will facilitate a smooth planning and implementation process to enhance the likelihood of success.

The focus of this chapter is on policy implementation (**Figure 6-1**). Policy implementation occurs when an individual, group, community, or government operationalizes a policy to protect and promote the health of individuals and the community. Often, health policy is implemented as a social program or as a series of programmatic activities. The policymaking process is cyclical, dynamic, imperfect, and often complex. The relative success or failure of a policy or program depends heavily on what happens during the implementation process—that is, how the organization carries out the instructions indicated in the policy/program. Howlett (2019) defines **implementation** as "the effort, knowledge and resources devoted to translating policy decisions into action" (p. 407). But how is a policy implemented once it has gone through the

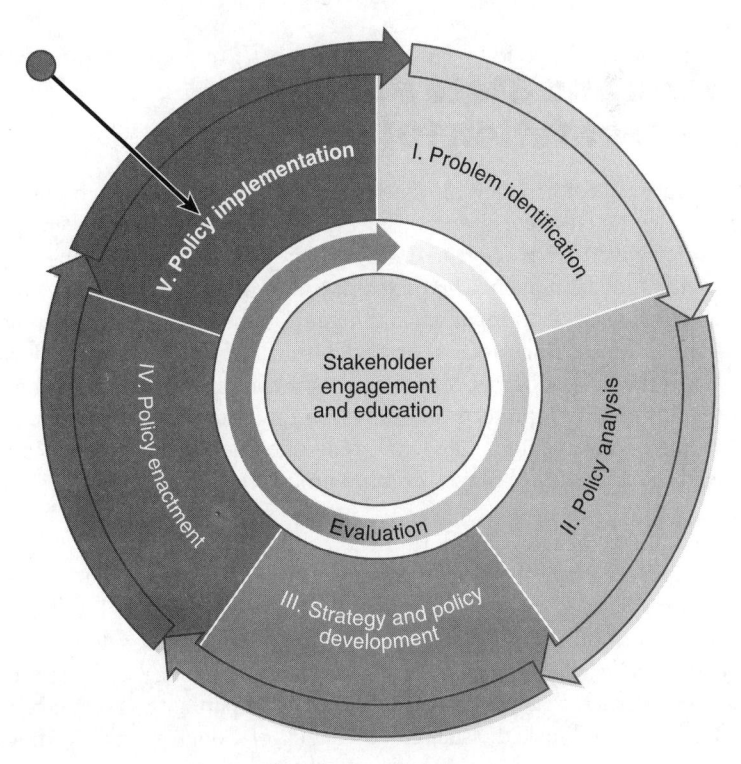

**Figure 6-1** The policy process: Policy implementation.

previous stages of the policy process? Specific steps in policy implementation include educating those affected by the new policy, changing current systems to adapt to the new policy, and monitoring for compliance with the policy (CDC, 2019).

Policies come in many forms: some are statutory, resulting from legislative enactment or permanent rule; others are nonstatutory in origin, such as procedural manuals and institutional guidelines. Health policies reflect the mix of public health needs and desires of special interest groups and often impact the choice of who will receive health care and how, when, and where the that care will be delivered. Implementation is about determining who participates (including both actors and organizations); why and how they participate (including procedures and techniques that reflect command, control, and incentives); and with what effect, meaning the extent to which the policy or programmatic goals have been supported. The observed output and the measurable change(s) constitute the outcome of policy implementation. The implementation of health-related laws, as well as rules and regulations, can change the physical environment in which people live and work, impact behavior, affect human biology, and influence the availability and accessibility of health services (Longest, 2010). The majority of the top 10 public health achievements in the 20th century were policy driven; examples include vaccinations, tobacco use reduction, improved workplace safety, and improved motor vehicle safety (Klausner, 2017; Nilsen et al., 2013).

## Federal and State Policy Implementation 101

Formulation of health policy on the federal and state levels can originate in either the legislative (senate or house) or executive (president or governor) branches of government (Gostin, 1995). Policy can be further refined or altered by the judicial branch. The preferences and influence of interest groups, political bargaining, and individual and organizational biases play a significant role in the policymaking process, especially during implementation. Ideology often poses the biggest barrier to unbiased formulation and implementation of health policy that truly protects and promotes the health of populations. Some policies, once implemented, may have unintended negative consequences and may need the advocacy of nurses or other groups to step in and campaign for change.

Much of U.S. health policy formulation and implementation is initiated in the U.S. Congress. Like the executive branch, Congress has access to extensive information gathering capabilities from objective resources to analyze scientific data in the creation of sound policy. However, politics often gets in the way of science. The legislature may be dominated by one political party and ideological beliefs, such that policymaking may lack impartiality: implementation of policies may be blocked, "starved" by a lack of Congressional funding, or repealed. Disparate ideals in Congress can also pose major obstacles in passing and implementing policy, such as the failure to reach a timely agreement to replace an expired relief bill providing unemployment benefits during the COVID-19 pandemic (Horsley, 2020).

In unprecedented times, such as a natural disaster, the federal government and states have the option to activate emergency powers to protect the health and safety of citizens (Haffajee & Mello, 2020). An example is the state of emergency declarations by states, localities, and the federal government that enabled drastic measures of closing schools and businesses, mandating masks, and implementing physical distancing measures to help control the spread of the novel coronavirus. The president also has the option of invoking the Defense Production Act (DPA) to direct private companies to prioritize government contracts to allow more rapid production of critical medical equipment and supplies and to purchase and rapidly distribute testing supplies to respond to a national emergency, such as the pandemic (Tucker, 2020). However, this is an option, not a requirement, and the DPA was not exercised until well into the COVID-19 pandemic. A lack of action at the federal level of government generally signals to states to act on their own. For example, early during the COVID-19 pandemic, states procured their own medical supplies and often competed with each other (or the federal government) for limited supplies (Haffajee & Mello, 2020; Richardson, 2020; U.S. Department of Health and Human Services [HHS], 2020).

In terms of health policy on the federal level, note that not all health programs are assigned to the U.S. Department of Health and Human Services (HHS) for implementation. Six major government healthcare programs provide services to over 40% of Americans: Medicare, Medicaid, the Children's Health Insurance Program (CHIP), TRICARE, the Veterans Health Administration (VHA), and the Indian Health Service (IHS; Rosso, 2020). Congress can order pilot programs, demonstrations, or full implementation of policy by any of these six programs. For example, the decision may be made to assign implementation of a program to the Department of Defense (DOD) or the Department of Veterans Affairs (VA). If implementation is successful with this population, the hope is that the broader health community will be more willing to adopt these programs. Examples of program implementation that relate to health but are carried out by other agencies include TRICARE, which is administered by the Defense Health Agency (TRICARE, 2018), and the Supplemental Nutrition Assistance Program (SNAP, formerly known as the food stamp program), which is administered by the U.S. Department of Agriculture. These decisions regarding implementation of policy may be very political in nature, but they are often quite strategic when positioning programs for success.

At times, federal policy implementation may not always translate well on the state level. It may also struggle when the urgency of the situation necessitates more immediate action rather than waiting for agreement from all parties on the federal level. Beneficial strategies that may enhance the likelihood of successful implementation include state innovation waivers, allowing states to act as "laboratories of democracy."

State innovation waivers are a creative strategy to assist with implementation of federal policy on the state level when states encounter challenges in implementation of a federal program. Section 1332 of the Patient Protection and

Affordable Care Act (ACA) created state innovation waivers to give states flexibility in achieving the core features of ACA healthcare reform and coverage but giving them the option of modifying how they provided that coverage (Dean & Sung, 2019). Alaska, for example, utilized a state innovation waiver by collaborating with the Centers for Medicare and Medicaid Services (CMS) to develop a program to help apportion the costs of high-cost enrollees and lower premiums.

*An appendix to this chapter provides an overview of how the ACA has been implemented in the decade since it became law. The ACA has become the very fabric of the U.S. healthcare system. Repeal at this time would cause upheaval and chaos. Take a look at the 10 titles of the ACA and determine what you think should be done to strengthen our healthcare system.*

States are often referred to as the laboratories of democracy—where policies can be implemented on a pilot scale before being rolled out to the entire country (Salam, 2013). Blakeman (2020) argues that "our states—because of their diversity—are the best place for novel solutions to complex problems." Although many argue that federal action is warranted in response to the pandemic, Blakeman (2020) responds that states and local governments are best positioned to respond to the needs of their constituents:

> A state that finds a better way of doing something for their own population can be a model for dealing with similar challenges by other states. Dividing and conquering can be a smart strategy. It is better to have 50 states working separately and together at a time of crisis than sitting back waiting for "one size fits all" solutions dictated from a federal government that surely is not tailored to the individuality of the states that comprise the Union.

The final branch of government that affects the implementation of health policy is the judicial branch. The court system is often called on to intervene when a policy may intrude on basic human rights or when the programs or policies are not implemented according to the original intent. Challengers to implementation may have to turn to the judiciary for resolution of their protests. Although many may perceive the court system as being impartial, it is important to remember that judges in the higher courts are appointed by political figures, have no accountability to the public, hold long-term appointments, have minimal experience in scientific thinking, and rarely have any expertise in health issues. Despite these concerns, the judiciary has contributed to health policy in the areas of reproductive rights, the right to die, and mental health. **Figure 6-2** is a cartoon criticizing the 2019 Supreme Court decision that partisan redistricting is a political question, not reviewable by federal courts, and that those courts cannot judge if extreme gerrymandering violates the Constitution.

## Conceptual Framework

Helfrich and colleagues (2007) adapted Klein and Sorra's (1996) framework for innovating implementation from the manufacturing setting to the healthcare

*Conceptual Framework* **127**

**Figure 6-2** Decision by the Supreme Court of the U.S. affects policy implementation.
Reproduced from Steve Sack, *The Minneapolis Star-Tribune*, MN.

setting (see **Figure 6-3**). They found that several factors are essential to ensure effective implementation, including clear communication of the rationale and priority for the innovation. Factors that enhance communication include learning about the guideline/policy through group interactions, positive staff attitudes/beliefs, the presence of champions, support from leadership at all levels of the organization, and interprofessional teamwork and collaboration (Ploeg et al., 2007). The **implementation climate**—that is, the perception of the targeted users that the new policy is beneficial, supported, and expected—is a critical factor in determining the effectiveness of the implementation (Klein & Sorra, 1996). Helfrich and colleagues expanded Klein and Sorra's framework by exploring the **innovation–values fit**, that is, the perception that the innovation or policy is consistent with the mission and values of the organization, and the use of champions and their impact on implementation climate. They found that the implementation climate was enhanced if the innovations–values fit was strong and champions were used to promote the innovation. According to their research, a stronger implementation climate is more likely to contribute to higher **implementation effectiveness**. Additionally, making changes incrementally rather than as radical change facilitates implementation as well (Ploeg et al., 2007).

Successful implementation depends heavily on the manipulation of many variables. These variables include private agencies and groups that are often contractors for carrying out policies; the target groups themselves; public attitudes; resources; the commitment and leadership of officials; and the socioeconomic, cultural, and political conditions in the environment in

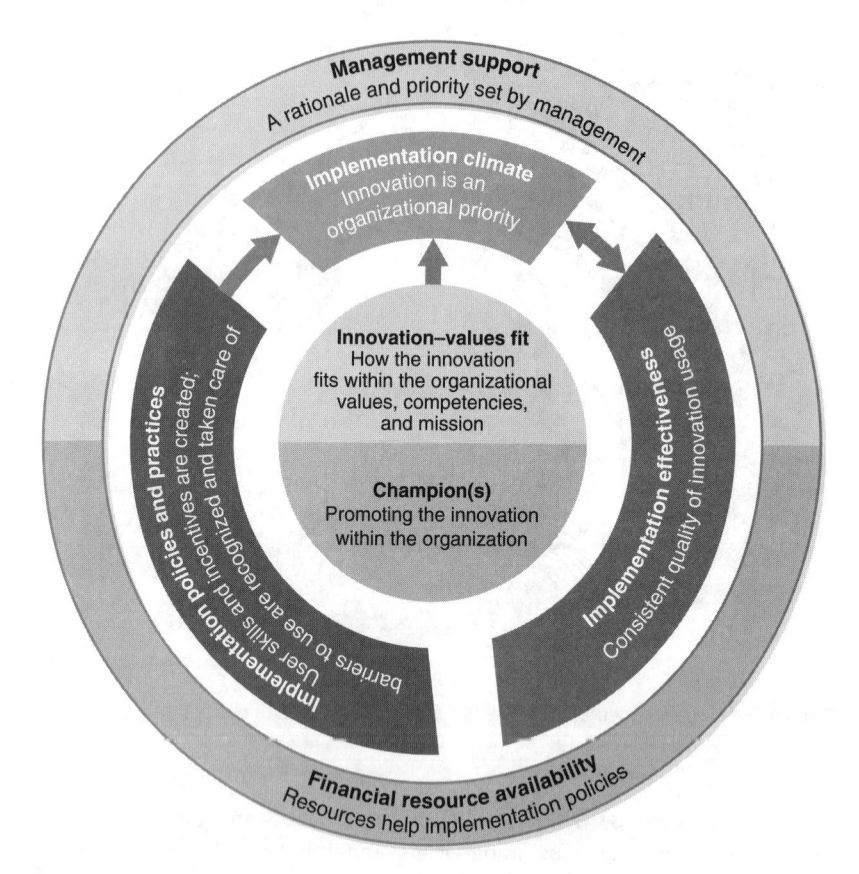

**Figure 6-3** Conceptual framework of complex innovation implementation.

Data from Helfrich, C. D., Weiner, B. J., McKinney, M. M., & Minasian, L. (2007). Determinants of implementation effectiveness: adapting a framework for complex.

Inner circle labels:
- **Management support** — A rationale and priority set by management
- **Implementation climate** — Innovation is an organizational priority
- **Innovation–values fit** — How the innovation fits within the organizational values, competencies, and mission
- **Champion(s)** — Promoting the innovation within the organization
- **Implementation effectiveness** — Consistent quality of innovation usage
- **Financial resource availability** — Resources help implementation policies
- **Implementation policies and practices** — User skills and incentives are created; barriers to use are recognized and taken care of

which the policies are supposed to operate (Palumbo et al., 1990). The presumption that regulations and policies are enacted according to their original intent turns out to be fallacious in many cases. Those who implement policy are rarely involved in in the planning phase, potentially hindering successful implementation (Mwisongo et al., 2016). The conscious or unconscious refusal to follow the policy directives can result in noncompliance or failure, making the actual implementation process far from what the policymakers originally envisioned.

The majority of problems that interfere with policy implementation are "people problems," referring to those individuals who interact with the recipients of the policy or program. Personal attitudes and perceptions come into play during policy implementation. Implementers must practice coping strategies such as negotiation and may find themselves in unforeseen circumstances or confronted with rules that are often vague but with which they are compelled to comply. Implementers see themselves as required to interpret the policy involved in a creative but justifiable way. Sometimes they may be working with scarce resources. When faced with these kinds of pressures, implementers may decide to alter the policy/procedure based on their perception of shortcomings in the policy. These perceptions of policy shortcomings may reflect the implementers' desire to enhance their professionalism, strengthen leadership, and perhaps restructure the organization (Hill & Hupe, 2002). In essence, public employees or frontline workers, often referred to as "street-level bureaucrats," function as policy decision-makers because they wield considerable discretion in the day-to-day implementation of public programs or policies as they interact with the recipients of those policies (Tummers & Bekkers, 2014).

Bardach (1977), in his classic study of implementation, describes political factors and maneuvers that can impede implementation of policies and result in poor performance, escalating costs, and delays. Types of maneuvers that may derail policy implementation include diversion of resources, deflection of goals, and dissipation of energies.

**Diversion of resources** manifests itself in several ways. Organizations and individuals who receive government money tend to provide less in the way of exchange for services for that money. Playing the budget game is another diversion. Persons responsible for the budget do what they can to win favor in the eyes of those who have power over their funding. Incentives shaped for implementers by those who control their budgets influence what the implementers do with respect to executing policy mandates.

During the implementation phase, goals often undergo some change resulting in the second type of maneuver—**deflection of goals**. The change in the goals can be the result of multiple factors: (1) a perception that the original goals were too ambiguous or too specific; (2) goals that were based on a weak consensus; (3) goals that were not thought out sufficiently; (4) the organization realizes the program will impose a heavy workload; (5) the program causes controversy; or (6) the required tasks are too difficult for the workers to perform. An agency may try to shift implementation of certain unattractive elements to different agencies. If no one wants the responsibility of taking charge of those elements, consumers get the runaround and each agency involved can claim it is not their problem (Bardach, 1977).

The third maneuver—**dissipation of energies**—wastes a great deal of the implementers' time. Dissipation of energy occurs when implementers avoid responsibility, defend themselves against others, and set themselves up for advantageous situations. Some may use their power to slow or stall the progress of the program until their own terms are met. This action can lead to delay, withdrawal of financial and political support, or total collapse of a program.

To enhance successful implementation, allocation of adequate financial resources to support the new innovation or policy is essential (Helfrich, 2007). For policy implementation in communities, financial support from professional associations and partnerships across agencies and sectors is important. Additionally, implementing agencies must have the authority, personnel, information and expertise, and technology to implement the policy effectively (Longest, 2010). Some states have formed implementation support centers to assist with the challenges associated with the effective delivery of governmental programs and to reduce barriers to implementation (Pew Charitable Trusts, 2017). These centers assist agencies tasked with implementation of programs with staff training, technical assistance, and the creation of tools and processes to assist with implementation oversight. If those working at the front lines "ultimately translate policy intentions into practice, influencing the lived experience of patients and citizens" (Gilson, 2016, p. 188), then we must consider that adopting a participatory approach to policymaking and implementation by including implementers in the planning process may improve the implementation process (Mwisongo et al., 2016).

So, what is considered **policy failure**? Success or failure often depends on which benchmarks are used. McConnell (2015) argues that "failure is rarely all or nothing" and proposes the following definition for policy failure: "A policy fails, even if it is successful in some minimal respects, if it does not *fundamentally achieve the goals that proponents set out to achieve* [emphasis added], and opposition is great and/or support is virtually non-existent" (p. 230). When a policy implementation is examined, one question that begs discussion is the notion of what is considered acceptable compliance with the policy. Is 100% compliance realistic? For example, is a vaccine policy successful if 75% of children are vaccinated while 25% of children have proper paperwork documenting religious, medical, or conscientious objection to vaccines? If that is not considered successful, which measures need to be taken to get closer to an acceptable compliance rate? Who determines what is acceptable (and based on which data)? Does the policy need to be reexamined? How often should a policy be reexamined? Is this a policy, person, or systems problem? Do the measures of success need to be reconsidered or redefined?

Policy failure has often been viewed from the opposing perspectives of "top down" or "bottom up" (Nilsen et al., 2013). In the **top-down** approach, failure is viewed as an administrative or policymaker issue, such as insufficient funding appropriated, poor planning, or flawed policy. The **bottom-up** perspective lays more of the blame with those who implement the policy. When contemplating the success or failure of policy implementation, McConnell (2015) suggests that failure be evaluated on a continuum of tolerable failure to complete failure by exploring the following questions:

- Did the policy, as implemented, meet the original objectives?
- Was it implemented as intended?
- Did it benefit the intended target group?
- Did it provide benefits that outweigh the costs?
- Did it satisfy criteria that are highly valued in that policy sector?
- Did it meet legal, moral, or ethical standards?
- Did it garner support from key stakeholders in that sector?
- Did it improve on the previous state of affairs?
- Did it improve by comparison to a similar jurisdiction?

# Policy Implementation Research Versus Implementation Science

Helfrich and colleagues' (2007) conceptual framework illustrates the determinants of complex innovation implementation in large organizations; however, this framework can also be useful when evaluating unsuccessful policy implementation to determine whether the failure is due to poor implementation or flaws in the innovation or policy (refer to Figure 6-2). The body of evidence from implementation research in health care is growing, including research about factors influencing nursing's implementation of evidence into practice. It is important when discussing policy implementation and policy failure to distinguish between policy that comes in the form of laws, rules, and regulations ("Big P" policies) versus healthcare policies and guidelines used in research and clinical practice ("small p" policies) (Nilsen et al., 2013). Understanding the difference between *implementation science* and *policy implementation research* will be helpful when considering strategies to avoid implementation failure.

**Implementation science** plays a crucial role in reducing "the gap between what has been shown in research to be effective and what is actually practiced in healthcare" (Nilsen et al., 2013, p. 1). Implementation science is often used to test effectiveness of strategies to achieve change in clinical practice—its origins can be traced to evidence-based medicine and practice. The Patient-Centered Outcomes Research Institute (PCORI) and the Center for Medicare and Medicaid Innovation (the Innovation Center) rely heavily on implementation science to achieve common goals of improving health care and outcomes for patients and communities (CMS.gov, n.d.; PCORI, 2020). Those who carry through evidence-to-practice are generally individual healthcare practitioners, and the intended targets of implementation science are the patients, organizations, or institutions for the intended intervention or guideline. Implementation science tends to have a limited scope and time frame for implementation (Nilsen et al., 2013).

Whereas implementation science can be applied to improve the execution of evidence-based research to practice, **policy implementation research** is more applicable to Big P policy implementation. Policy implementation research emerged out of a need to investigate why Big P policy often evolves, changes, or unfolds as fundamentally changed from the original intent of policymakers or thought leaders (Nilsen et al., 2013). Researchers are unable to control or manipulate variables when looking at Policy implementation studies. Whereas the object in implementation science is to improve a specific clinical practice (such as handwashing or the use of narrow-spectrum antibiotics for common infections in children), in Policy implementation research, the object is legislation, rules, or regulation. Policy implementation can be quite complex and rarely follows a linear process. The implementers in this setting are much more ambiguous, and may include "complex networks of individuals, organizations, and interorganizational relations" (Nilsen et al., 2013, p. 6). The targets in this area of research may be clients, recipients, community citizens, or organizations. Although Policy implementation research may be easily defined and concrete (e.g., seat belt laws), it can also be much broader and more nebulous, with a time frame for implementation spanning years.

Policy implementation is a complex process and one in which it is almost impossible to separate policies from politics. Many political barriers could potentially impede successful implementation. It is easy to understand why the U.S. public feels frustrated with government; this frustration reflects the perceived failure of government to turn promises into performance. Looking back at the list of key elements for successful implementation, think about what happens when legislation and policy, enacted in haste to respond to an emergency, leaves out an important target group. When Congress approved the emergency supplemental funding bill that allowed the expansion of telehealth services, it left out Federally Qualified Health Centers (FQHCs) and rural health clinics (RHCs) that serve underserved areas (Caravan Health, 2020). With this unintentional omission, providers would be inhibited from serving vulnerable populations in rural areas via telehealth. Because of vocal advocacy from providers and other supporters of FQHCs and RHCs, this oversight was corrected in the Coronavirus Aid, Relief, and Economic Security (CARES) Act of 2020.

## Power: What Is Needed to Get Policy Implemented?

Nurses, who think in terms of evidence and scientific facts, are often surprised that facts do not always win the day when it comes to policy and politics. Power and politics may seem like dirty words to many nurses: something to be avoided rather than studied and utilized. Power is one of the most important but least clear concepts in political science. Organizations operate by distributing authority and setting a stage for the exercise of power. It is no wonder that individuals who are highly motivated to secure and use power find a familiar and hospitable environment in politics and policymaking. A political pyramid exists when people compete for power in an environment of scarcity. In other words, people cannot get the power they want just by asking. Instead, they have to enter into the decisions on how to distribute authority in a particular formal organization structure. Scarcity of power arises under two sets of conditions: (1) where individuals gain power at someone else's expense, and (2) where there is a comparative gain resulting in a relative shift in the distribution of power. The fact that organizations are pyramids produces a scarcity of positions the higher one moves in the hierarchy. A factor that heightens the competition for power that is characteristic of all political structures is the incessant need to use whatever power one possesses. The most visible forms of power are measurable, but the most worrying and least visible often are not.

In public policy, the question of power arises when we ask: who are the policymakers? Who is responsible for policy change? Who is thought to be in charge, and who is actually in charge? We may also use discussions of power to explain why policies change or remain stable (Cairney, 2020).

Mwisongo and colleagues (2016) used Arts and Tatenove's (2004) conceptual framework on dimensions of power to describe how power influences policymaking. The authors maintain that power is central to policymaking and cannot be discounted. The concept of power encompasses a vast range of behaviors, including the ability to get what you want despite the resistance of others, the possession of authority based on consent, and the inability to exercise autonomy when subject to "structural" power.

The authors discuss three types of power: relational, dispositional, and structural. *Relational power* involves the interactions that exist between stakeholders and resources to achieve outcomes. *Dispositional power* refers to the person's hierarchical position in an organization that gives them legitimacy and authority in sharing knowledge and information as well as in allocating resources. *Structural power* involves relations in which one more powerful actor constitutes the identity, preferences, and capabilities of the other actor. Assessing structural power in conjunction with its counterpart, instrumental power, can provide strong leverage for explaining variation in health policy outcomes that affect health care. *Structural power* organizes and orchestrates the systemic interactions within and among groups, directing economic and political forces and ideological forces that shape public ideas, values, and beliefs. As nurses, we need to understand and recognize our power to claim our role in policymaking.

**Case Study 6-1** illustrates how citizens negatively affected by a policy can provide feedback and advocate for change through political activism. As you read the case, think about what type of power the senior citizens had and what structural power worked for (and against) their cause.

## CASE STUDY 6-1: When Policy Implementation Is Rejected by Citizens: Reinstatement of the Medical Expenses Deduction on North Carolina State Income Taxes

In 2013, the North Carolina General Assembly overhauled the state's tax code, which had been in effect since the 1930s. The proposed plan eliminated several deductions from individuals' state income taxes. The initial proposal eliminated deductions for mortgage and property taxes, contributions to nonprofit organizations, medical expenses, long-term care insurance, government and private retirement income, and contributions to the NC 529 college savings plans. In an effort to offset the elimination of these deductions, the proposal increased the standard deduction for single people from $3,000 to $7,500 and for married couples filing jointly from $6,000 to $15,000. Lobbyists for realtors and nonprofit organizations were successful in persuading the legislature to keep their deductions, although mortgage and property tax deductions were limited to $20,000. Senior citizens did not have anyone lobbying on their behalf, and most of the eliminated deductions affected them.

The N.C. General Assembly's fiscal research staff forecasted that taxpayers across all categories would see some slight reduction in their tax burden. However, they also acknowledged that those 65 and older might pay more because several of the categories affected them. In contrast, the N.C. Budget and Tax Center said those taxpayers making less than $84,000 would end up paying more in taxes. The majority of citizens 65 and older are in that category.

The legislation took effect in 2014. It turned out that almost all senior citizens suffered sticker shock when they filed their 2014 state income taxes. On average, their income tax increased by $1,800. That summer, the North Carolina Continuing Care Residents Association (NorCCRA) created a legislative committee and organized a letter-writing campaign to members of the House Appropriations Committee. Because nothing could happen in the 2014 short legislative session to remedy the perceived problems, the campaign was essentially an educational piece letting legislators know that residents would be back in the 2015 session seeking to reinstate the medical expenses deduction.

Sindy Barker, chair of the newly formed statewide Legislative Committee, had retired in 2006 after spending 19 years lobbying the N.C. General Assembly on behalf of the North Carolina Nurses Association. Her knowledge of how to successfully lobby for nursing issues enabled the NorCCRA Legislative Committee to develop a systematic plan for approaching members of the 2015 General Assembly.

Questions were raised as to whether an organization that had never lobbied before could pull together a successful lobbying effort, especially when there did not appear to be much support for its issue among members of the General Assembly. In fact, when HB46, Senior Tax Deduction for Medical Expenses, was introduced, the Fiscal Research Division said the state would lose $37.9 million in revenues from this deduction in 2015 alone. That forecast escalated to $44.1 million by fiscal year 2019–2020. Moreover, this loss to state revenues assumed that the deduction was reinstated only for citizens age 65 and older.

Members of the General Assembly did understand that a high percentage of senior citizens vote, and that retired individuals also have more time to make contact with their legislators. Over the course of several months, the 20,000 residents living in continuing care retirement communities (CCRCs) in North Carolina were asked to write 650 individual letters or emails to the following legislators:

- The 15 members of the House Committee on Aging, explaining the bill and then thanking them for a favorable report
- The 74 members of the Republican Caucus
- The 42 members of the House Committee on Finance
- The 81 members of the House Appropriations Committee
- All 120 Members of the House, thanking them for including the medical expense deduction in the budget
- The 50 Members of the Senate, asking them to include the medical expense deduction in their version of the budget
- The 83 members of the Budget Conference Committee, asking them to support the House version of the deduction with no cap
- The 170 members of the General Assembly, thanking them for reinstating the medical deduction in the final budget

One CCRC held a letter-writing party and sent 1,761 letters in one day. Several simply put out petitions for their residents to sign and then forwarded those letters to the appropriate legislators. The typical petition contained upward of 150 signatures. Members of the General Assembly soon realized this was an issue dear to the heart of many of their regular voters.

Ms. Barker, the Legislative Committee chair, brought her husband in a wheelchair to the General Assembly when she appeared before committees, and he became the face of what "high medical expenses" look like. The issue made the front page of several major state newspapers and was featured in online stories and local newscasts.

By the end of March 2015, NorCCRA had been joined in its campaign by AARP, N.C. Retired Government Employees, and organizations that represent children and adults with chronic diseases and disabilities. This coalition meant more letters, emails, and phone calls to legislators. In one week in April, they achieved more than 7,000 contacts, or approximately 40 contacts per legislator.

When the reinstatement of the medical expenses deduction was included in the House budget toward the end of May, the policy advocates were halfway home. It was not a very smooth ride, but by the middle of September the medical expenses deduction was reinstated in the final budget passed by the General Assembly.

The reinstatement of medical expenses deduction took effect for 2015 taxes, so 2014 was the only year with the higher increase. NorCCRA conducted another survey in 2016 following income tax filing in the spring. The senior citizens' average tax bill was $1,400 less than it had been in the previous year. The other deductions that were eliminated in 2013 remain in place, but the one that clearly had the biggest impact was the medical expenses deduction. Members of the General Assembly again received thank-you letters from NorCCRA, letting them know what a difference their legislation had made.

**Case Study Discussion Questions**

1. How can legislation with such negative consequences for a large group of citizens be prevented or stopped?
2. Using what you have learned about the policy process model so far, where do you think the N.C. General Assembly "went wrong" with the policy aimed at gaining more revenue from taxpayers?
3. Once the original policy to eliminate specific tax deductions was passed by the legislature, which steps in the implementation process might have prevented the backlash by citizens?
4. Why might forecasts regarding the impact of a policy be incorrect and lead to unintended consequences?
5. Were the consequences of the original legislation intended or unintended? Why or why not?

# Involving Nurses in Implementation

Despite the United Nations declaration of 2020 as "The Year of the Nurse and Midwife," and even in the midst of a global pandemic where the leadership of nurses "has been hugely consequential," nurses are unlikely to be consulted or mentioned in articles about policy-related health issues (Mason, 2020) and continue to have disproportionately low representation in leadership positions (boards of directors and trustees) of healthcare organizations (Benson & Hasmiller, 2016). Dr. Diana Mason asserts that nurses "have the expertise to know what matters for the health of patients, families, and communities and we want to be able to share it, be heard, and lead the changes that are needed in health care" (Mason, 2020).

# Conclusion

Policy implementation is the stage of the policy process immediately after passage of the law. The series of decisions and actions that occur during implementation will impact the extent to which the program goals are supported and the measurable change that occurs. In this stage, the content of the policy, and its impact on those affected, may be modified substantially or even negated. In analyzing this stage in the policymaking process, one needs to examine how, when, and where particular policies have been implemented.

Problems with policy implementation are widespread. During the implementation process, the political forces of individuals, groups, organizations, and sometimes governmental bodies are at work. These various forces may be trying to change the policy to meet their own needs and control a part of the implementation process. When the implementers are not working in concert to meet the intended legislative goals, the recipients lose. Remember, the entire nursing community and other health professionals can affect implementation in both positive and negative ways. As America's largest group of health professionals, you and your colleagues will find the confidence and courage to amplify nursing's voice, claim your role, and understand your power in shaping policy.

## Chapter Discussion Points

1. Find an example of recent legislation that affects your patients or your profession or select a recent law that you are interested in. Who were the champions for this legislation? What qualifies them to be champions? What qualities do they possess?
2. For the piece of legislation you selected, what steps were taken to improve the potential for successful implementation? What strategies would have improved the success of implementation?
3. For the piece of legislation you selected, what were the benchmarks for measuring the success of the implementation of the new policy or innovation? How would you rate the success or failure of the policy?

# Chapter Appendix

## Titles of the Patient Protection and Affordable Care Act

| Title | Directive | Implemented |
|---|---|---|
| Title I. Quality, Affordable Health Care for All Americans | Mandates shared responsibility. Asks all Americans to take responsibility for improving America's health care. In order to lower costs for all Americans and extend coverage to people with preexisting conditions, all Americans who can afford to purchase insurance will be asked to.<br><br>■ Required uninsured Americans to buy insurance or pay a tax.<br>■ Eliminates lifetime and unreasonable annual limits on benefits. In the past, more than 60% of bankruptcies were medical related, and three-quarters of those bankruptcies involved people with health insurance who had reached their coverage limits.<br>■ Ensures coverage of essential health services:<br>  • Ambulatory care services<br>  • Emergency services<br>  • Hospitalization<br>  • Maternity and newborn care<br>  • Mental health services and addiction treatment<br>  • Prescription drugs<br>  • Rehabilitation services and devices<br>  • Laboratory services<br>  • Preventive services, wellness services, and chronic disease treatment<br>  • Pediatric services<br>■ Requires insurance companies to safeguard benefits.<br>  • Parents can add children up to age 26 to their plans.<br>  • An insurer cannot drop a person's coverage if they get sick. The insurer cannot put a ceiling on lifetime coverage.<br>  • The insurer cannot deny coverage to those with preexisting conditions.<br>  • The insurer must cover wellness and pregnancy exams.<br>  • Insurance companies must spend at least 80% of premiums on medical services or rebate the rest back to policyholders. | ■ Federal government and some states established health insurance exchanges to allow consumers to compare health plans.<br>■ Congress repealed the tax penalty in 2019. |

| | | |
|---|---|---|
| Title II. The Role of Public Programs | Extends Medicaid, preserves CHIP, and simplifies enrollment for individuals and families.<br>■ Extended Medicaid coverage to anyone whose income is below 138% of the federal poverty level. It also allowed states to cover low-income adults without children. The federal government would pay 100% of the increased cost of Medicaid for the states until 2017. After that, the federal government reduced assistance and states that expanded Medicaid received more assistance than states that did not. | ■ In 2012, the U.S. Supreme Court ruled that states could not be forced to expand Medicaid. By 2020, 34 states had expanded Medicaid or received waivers from CMS to pilot other ways to increase access to Medicaid.<br>■ The uninsured rate among U.S. adults 18 years of age and older dipped to 8.5% by 2018. All states and the District of Columbia had a lower uninsured rate in 2019 than in 2010.<br>■ Hospitals incurred less uncompensated care costs and earned more Medicaid reimbursement for patients who would have otherwise been unable to pay for care. |
| Title III. Improving the Quality and Efficiency of Healthcare | Preserves, protects, and reforms Medicare.<br>■ Transforms healthcare delivery system.<br>■ Encourages the development of new patient care models. | ■ Hospital value-based purchasing started in 2013. A percentage of a hospital's payments are tied to the hospital's performance on quality measures related to common and high-cost conditions.<br>■ Established quality data reporting requirements for Medicare for physicians, hospitals, and rehab programs.<br>■ CMS Innovations Center established.<br>■ Shared savings programs (ACOs) established. |

*(continues)*

| Title | Directive | Implemented |
|---|---|---|
| | ■ Closes the doughnut hole for Medicare Part D. | ■ Hospital readmissions reductions program established.<br>■ Community-based transition programs established.<br>■ In 2011, Medicare beneficiaries got a 50% discount on brand-name prescription drugs during the coverage gap. In 2020, the discount is 75%. |
| Title IV. Preventing Chronic Disease and Promotion of Health | Promotes prevention, wellness, and the public health and provides an unprecedented funding commitment to these areas.<br>■ Uses national prevention and health promotion strategies to work to improve the health of Americans and reduce preventable illness and disability to keep Americans healthy and keep healthcare costs down.<br>■ Established the National Prevention, Health Promotion, and Public Health Council.<br>■ Increases access to preventive health services.<br>■ Supports programs for creating healthier communities. | ■ The Surgeon General heads the council, which is composed of the heads of 12 federal agencies plus any others deemed appropriate by the Surgeon General.<br>■ Provides funding for school-based health centers.<br>■ Supports oral healthcare prevention activities.<br>■ Medicare Annual Wellness visits.<br>■ Covers comprehensive tobacco-cessation services for pregnant women on Medicaid.<br>■ Authorizes states to purchase adult vaccines under CDC contracts. |

| | | |
|---|---|---|
| | | ■ Mandates nutrition labeling of standard menu items at chain restaurants.<br>■ Requires employers to provide time for breastfeeding mothers to express milk |
| Title V. Healthcare Workforce | Supports and expands the healthcare workforce.<br>■ Increases the supply of the healthcare workers, including primary care physicians, nurse practitioners, nurses, physician assistants, mental health providers, and dentists.<br>■ Enhances healthcare workforce education and training<br>■ Improves access to healthcare services.<br>■ Provides for healthcare workforce assessment. | ■ Federally supported student loan funds.<br>■ Nursing student loan program.<br>■ Loan repayment programs for providers working in underserved areas.<br>■ Support for nurse-managed health centers.<br>■ Funds training in several areas, including geriatric medicine, mental health, cultural competency, and dentistry.<br>■ Provides for nurse education, practice, and retention grants.<br>■ Nurse faculty loan program.<br>■ Helps fund and expand community health centers (safety net providers).<br>■ Mandates the collection of comprehensive workforce data in order for the healthcare workforce to meet the healthcare needs of individuals, including research on the supply, demand, distribution, diversity, and skills needs of the healthcare workforce. |

*(continues)*

| Title | Directive | Implemented |
|---|---|---|
| Title VI. Transparency and Program Integrity | Helps patients take more control of their healthcare decisions with informed decision making.<br><br>Physicians:<br>- Requires physicians to report any financial interest they have with imaging companies, etc., and to provide a list of alternative service providers to patients.<br>- Requires medical device makers, drug companies, etc. to reveal financial arrangements they have with physicians.<br><br>Nursing homes:<br>- Greater transparency in nursing homes by placing regulations and incentive programs to help improve quality control. Requires nursing facilities to implement compliance and ethics program for employees.<br><br>Provides physicians and other healthcare providers access to cutting-edge medical research to enhance informed decision making.<br><br>Includes Medicare, Medicaid, and CHIP program-integrity provisions.<br><br>Reins in waste, fraud, and abuse by imposing disclosure requirements to identify high-risk providers who have defrauded the American taxpayer. | - Enterprises that manage the prescription drug portion of Medicare or the state exchanges (such as pharmacy benefit managers) must report any financial concessions they receive from pharmaceutical companies.<br>- Provides for training and requires background checks for nursing home staff to reduce elder abuse.<br>- Established the Patient-Centered Outcome Research Institute (PCORI)<br>- Established procedures for screening providers and suppliers participating in Medicare, Medicaid, and CHIP, minimally including licensure checks.<br>- National provider identifier numbers required for all providers on enrollment applications for Medicare, Medicaid, CHIP.<br>- Requires face-to-face encounters with patients in order to certify home health services or durable medical equipment.<br>- Mandates timely submission of Medicare claims (<12 months). |

| | | |
|---|---|---|
| Title VII. Improving Access to Innovative Medical Therapies | Promotes innovation and saves consumers money. Ends anticompetitive behavior by drug companies that keeps effective and affordable generic drugs off the market.<br>■ Extends drug discounts to hospitals and communities that serve low-income patients.<br>■ Creates a pathway for the creation of generic versions of biological drugs so that doctors and patients have access to effective and lower-cost alternatives.<br>■ Requires competitive pricing for vaccines and hormone therapies. | ■ Provides critical-access hospitals, children's hospitals, stand-alone cancer hospitals, sole community hospitals, and rural referral centers 340B discounts. |
| Title VIII. Community Living Assistance Services and Supports Act | This title was intended to provide Americans with a new option to finance long-term services and care in the event of a disability.<br>■ Americans with disabilities were to receive a $50 daily payment to put toward assisted living. They were to pay premiums for 5 years and work for 3 of those years. | The title entered into force on January 1, 2011, but by October 1 it was determined to be unworkable. It could not compete with private-sector plans that offered better benefits. The title was repealed January 1, 2013. |
| Title IX. Revenue Provisions | Improved enforcement and closed loopholes in the tax code.<br>■ Reformed the excise tax on insurance companies.<br>■ Inclusion of cost of employer-sponsored health coverage on W-2.<br>■ Increased taxes on health savings account (HSA) distributions *not* being used for medical expenses.<br>■ Limited flexible spending account (FSA) contributions to $2,500 per year. | ■ Levied an excise tax of 40% on insurance companies selling plans with annual premiums above $8,500 for single coverage and $23,000 for family coverage. |
| Title X. Reauthorization of the Indian Health Care Improvement Act | Permanently reauthorized the Indian Health Care Improvement Act so it would no longer be at risk for losing funding and would allow the Indian Health Service to modernize services, including mobile health care, mental health counseling, and long-term in home or community care, and hospice services. | |

*Sources:* Native Voices. (2010). *2010: Indian Health Care Improvement Act permanently renewed.* https://www.nlm.nih.gov/nativevoices/timeline/599.html; ObamaCareFacts.com. (2015). *Summary of provisions in the Patient Protection and Affordable Care Act.* https://obamacarefacts.com/summary-of-provisions-patient-protection-and-affordable-care-act/; ObamaCareFacts.com. (2020). *Affordable Care Act summary.* https://obamacarefacts.com/affordablecareact-summary/

# References

American Nurses Association. (2017). *Advocacy: Becoming more effective*. http://www.nursingworld.org/MainMenuCategories/Policy-Advocacy/AdvocacyResources Tools

Arts, B., & Van Tatenhove, J. (2004). Policy and power: A conceptual framework between the 'old' and 'new' policy idioms. *Policy Sciences, 37*(3–4), 339–356. https://doi.org/10.1007/s11077-005-0156-9

Bardach, E. (1977). *The implementation game: What happens after a bill becomes a law.* MIT Press.

Benson, L., & Hassmiller, S. (2016, October). *Improve the patient experience—Ask a nurse to join the board.* https://www.nursesonboardscoalition.org/resources/for-organizations/

Blakeman, B. (2020, May 7). States are the laboratories of democracy. *The Hill.* https://thehill.com/opinion/judiciary/496524-states-are-the-laboratories-of-democracy

Burke, S. (2016). *Influence through policy: Nurses have a unique role.* https://nursingcentered.sigmanursing.org/commentary/more-commentary/Vol42_2_nurses-have-a-unique-role

Cairney, P. (2020). *Understanding public policy: Theories and issues* (2nd ed.). Red Globe Press.

Caravan Health. (2020, March 23). *Rural providers left out of new telehealth expansion—Caravan Health calls on Congress to fix ASAP.* https://caravanhealth.com/thought-leadership/articles/rural-providers-left-out-of-new-telehealth-expansion/

Centers for Disease Control and Prevention. (n.d.). *Step by step: Evaluating violence and injury prevention policies: Brief 4: Evaluating policy implementation.* https://www.cdc.gov/injury/pdfs/policy/Brief%204-a.pdf

Centers for Disease Control and Prevention. (2019). *What is policy implementation?* https://www.cdc.gov/policy/polaris/policyprocess/policy_implementation.html

Centers for Medicare & Medicaid Services. (n.d.). *The Centers for Medicare & Medicaid Innovation (the Innovation Center).* https://innovation.cms.gov/

Cramer, M. (2002). Factors influencing organized political participation in nursing. *Policy, Politics, & Nursing Practice, 3*(2), 97–107.

Dean, O., & Sung, J. (2019, September). *Health insurance state innovation waivers and older adults: A guide for states.* AARP Public Policy Institute. https://www.aarp.org/content/dam/aarp/ppi/2019/09/health-insurance-state-innovation-waivers-and-older-adults-state-guide.doi.10.26419-2Fppi.00081.003.pdf

Gilson, L. (2016). Everyday politics and the leadership of health policy implementation. *Health Systems & Reform, 2*(3), 187–193. https://doi.org/10.1080/23288604.2016.1217367

Gostin, L. (1995). The formulation of health policy by the three branches of government. In R. E. Bulger, E. M. Bobby, & H. V. Fineberg (Eds.), *Society's choices: Social and ethical decision making in biomedicine* (pp. 335–357). National Academies Press.

Haffajee, R. L., & Mello, M. M. (2020). Thinking globally, acting locally—the U.S. response to COVID-19. *The New England Journal of Medicine, 382,* e75. https://doi.org/10.1056/NEJMp2006740

Helfrich, C. D., Weiner, B. J., McKinney, M. M., & Minasian, L. (2007). Determinants of implementation effectiveness: Adapting a framework for complex innovations. *Medical Care Research and Review, 64*(3), 279–303.

Hill, M. J., & Hupe, P. L. (2002). *Implementing public policy: Governance in theory and in practice.* SAGE.

Horsley, S. (2020, August 7). *Congress fails to reach agreement on new COVID-19 relief bill.* NPR. https://www.npr.org/2020/08/07/900076328/congress-fails-to-reach-agreement-on-new-covid-19-relief-bill

Howlett, M. (2019). Moving policy implementation theory forward: A multiple streams/critical juncture approach. *Public Policy and Administration, 34*(4), 405–430. https://doi.org/10.1177/0952076718775791

Klausner, A. (2017). *CDC: The top 10 public health achievements in the 20th century.* https://www.berkeleywellness.com/healthy-community/health-care-policy/article/cdcs-top-10-public-health-achievements-20th-century

Klein, K., & Sorra, J. (1996). The challenge of innovation implementation. *Academy of Management Review, 21*(4), 1055–1080.

Longest, B. (2010). *Health policy making in the United States* (5th ed.). Health Administration Press.

Mason, D. J. (2020, June 26). Nurses lack representation in media: Recognize them for the leaders that they are. *USA Today*. https://www.usatoday.com/story/opinion/2020/06/26/nurses-leaders-medicine-but-overshadowed-media-column/3223242001/

Mason, D. J., Glickstein, B., Nixon, L., Westphaln, K., Han, S., & Acquaviva, K. (2018a). The Woodhull Study Revisited: Nurses' representation in health news media 20 years later. *Journal of Nursing Scholarship*, 50(6), 695–704. https://doi.org/10.1111/jnu.12429

Mason, D. J., Glickstein, B., Nixon, L., Westphaln, K., Han, S., & Acquaviva, K. (2018b). *Research brief: The Woodhull Study Revisited: Nurses' representation in health news media*. Center for Health Policy & Media Engagement, The George Washington University. https://nursing.gwu.edu/sites/g/files/zaxdzs1226/f/downloads/Woodhull_Study_Revisited_Research_Brief.pdf

McConnell, A. (2015). What is policy failure? A primer to help navigate the maze. *Public Policy and Administration*, 30(3–4), 221–242. https://doi.org/10.1177/0952076714565416

McLemore, M. (Guest), & Tayyeb, A. (Executive Producer). (2020, June 30). Dr. Monica McLemore [Season 1, Episode 10]. In *RN-Mentor Podcast*. https://www.alirtayyeb.com/rnmentor-podcast/dr-monica-mclemore-phd-mph-rn-faan

Mwisongo, A., Nabyonga-Orem, J., Yao, T., & Dovlo, D. (2016). The role of power in health policy dialogues: Lessons from African countries. *BMC Health Services Research*, 16(Suppl. 4), 213. https://doi.org/10.1186/s12913-016-1456-9

Native Voices. (2010). *2010: Indian Health Care Improvement Act permanently renewed*. https://www.nlm.nih.gov/nativevoices/timeline/599.html

Nilsen, P., Ståhl, C., Roback, K., & Cairney, P. (2013). Never the twain shall meet?—A comparison of implementation science and policy implementation research. *Implementation Science*, 8(63). https://doi.org/10.1186/1748-5908-8-63

ObamaCareFacts.com. (2015). *Summary of provisions in the Patient Protection and Affordable Care Act*. https://obamacarefacts.com/summary-of-provisions-patient-protection-and-affordable-care-act/

ObamaCareFacts.com. (2020). *AffordableCareActsummary*. https://obamacarefacts.com/affordablecareact-summary/

Palumbo, D. J., Calista, D. J., & Policy Studies Organization. (1990). *Implementation and the policy process: Opening up the black box*. Greenwood Press.

Patient-Centered Outcomes Research Institute. (2020). *Our vision and mission*. https://www.pcori.org/about-us/our-vision-mission

Pew Charitable Trusts. (2017). *4 ways implementation support centers assist in the delivery of evidence-based programs*. https://www.pewtrusts.org/en/research-and-analysis/fact-sheets/2017/07/4-ways-implementation-support-centers-assist-in-the-delivery-of-evidence-based-programs

Ploeg, J., Davies, B., Edwards, N., Gifford, W., & Miller, P. E. (2007). Factors influencing best-practice guideline implementation: Lessons learned from administrators, nursing staff, and project leaders. *Worldviews on Evidence-Based Nursing*, 4(4), 210–219.

Richardson, H. C. (2020, August 29). *Letters from an American*. https://heathercoxrichardson.substack.com/

Rosso, R. (2020). *U.S. health care coverage and spending, IF10830, April 14, 2020*. Congressional Research Service. https://fas.org/sgp/crs/misc/IF10830

Salam, R. (2013, March 17). 'Laboratories of Democracy' and What Works Where. *National Review*. https://www.nationalreview.com/the-agenda/laboratories-democracy-and-what-works-where-reihan-salam/

TRICARE. (2018). *About TRICARE*. https://www.tricare.mil/About#:~:text=TRICARE%20is%20managed%20by%20the,of%20Defense%20(Health%20Affairs)

Tucker, E. (2020, March 19). What exactly is the Defense Production Act? *Military Times*. https://www.militarytimes.com/news/your-military/2020/03/19/what-exactly-is-the-defense-production-act/

Tummers, L., & Bekkers, V. (2014). Policy implementation, street level bureaucracy, and the importance of discretion. *Public Management Review*, 16(4), 527–547.

U.S. Department of Health & Human Services. (2020, August 20). *Trump administration Uses Defense Production Act to aid our most vulnerable.* https://www.hhs.gov/about/news/2020/08/20/trump-administration-uses-defense-production-act-to-aid-our-most-vulnerable.html

Woodhull, N. (1997). The Woodhull Study on nursing and the media: Health care's invisible partner. *Sigma Theta Tau International.* https://sigma.nursingrepository.org/bitstream/handle/10755/624124/WoodhullReport1997.pdf?sequence=1

# CHAPTER 7

# Government Response: Regulation

Julia L. George and Catherine Moore

## KEY TERMS

**Administrative procedures act (APA):** A state or federal law that establishes rule-making procedures for its respective agencies.

**APRN Compact:** Adopted August 12, 2020, by the National Council of State Boards of Nursing. An agreement that allows an advanced practice registered nurse (APRN) to hold one multistate license with a privilege to practice in other compact states. It will be implemented when seven states have enacted the legislation.

**Board of Nursing (BON):** An executive branch state government administrative agency charged with the power and duty to enforce laws and regulations governing the practice of nursing in the interest of public protection.

**Certification:** A form of voluntary credentialing that denotes validation of competency in a specialty area, with permission to use a title.

**Licensure:** A form of credentialing whereby permission is granted by a legal authority to perform an act that would, without such permission, be illegal, a trespass, a tort, or otherwise not allowable.

**Multistate regulation:** A provision that allows a professional to practice in more than one state based on a single license.

**National Council of State Boards of Nursing (NCSBN):** A nonprofit, nongovernmental organization that provides a means by which state boards of nursing may discuss and act on matters of common interest, including development of licensing examinations.

**Nursing Regulatory Bodies (NRBs):** Jurisdictional governmental agencies in the 50 states, the District of Columbia, and four United States territories that are responsible for the regulation of nursing practice. Nursing Regulatory Bodies outline standards for safe nursing care and issue licenses to practice nursing (National Council of State Boards of Nursing, 2020a). A state Board of Nursing is an example of an NRB.

**PICOT:** An acronym that serves as a format or template to identify elements of or to ask a health policy question. It stands for *population, intervention, comparison, outcomes*, and *time*.

**Public rule hearings:** Meetings held by state or federal administrative agencies for the purpose of receiving testimony from witnesses who support or oppose regulations or to receive expert testimony.
**Practice act:** A law that regulates and defines legal responsibilities of the nurse and scope of practice. It is intended to protect the public from harm as a result of unsafe or unqualified nurses.
**Recognition:** A form of credentialing that denotes a government authority has ratified or confirmed an individual's credentials.
**Registration:** A form of credentialing that denotes enrolling or recording the name of a qualified individual on an official agency or government roster.
**Regulations (rules):** Orders or directives that provide details or procedures to operationalize a federal or state law (statute). A law directs an agency or government to develop and implement regulations/rules to achieve the purpose(s) of that law. Rules have the force and effect of law.
**Statutory authority:** The law or laws passed by Congress or a state legislature that specify the powers, duties, and functions that may be exercised by an agency (Stiff, 2020).

# Introduction

Regulation of the United States (U.S.) healthcare delivery system and of healthcare providers exists to protect the interests of public safety, but regulatory structures are extraordinarily complex. The vastness of the industry, the manner of healthcare financing, and the proliferation of laws and regulations that govern practice and reimbursement contribute to that complexity. This chapter focuses on major concepts associated with the regulation of healthcare professionals. Understanding licensure and credentialing processes and their impact on nursing is essential. Understanding how regulations affect the healthcare system and individual providers empowers nurses and other providers to advocate on behalf of consumers and the profession.

All healthcare professionals are licensed by state government agencies. Practice-specific boards or commissions (e.g., the North Carolina Board of Nursing) or multiprofessional boards (e.g., Michigan's Department of Licensing and Regulatory Affairs) are executive branch regulatory agencies that govern each profession with the goal of protecting the public. State practice–specific board processes are similar from state to state but vary to some extent because their laws are determined by individual state legislatures and their regulations are determined by the specific agency. **Nursing Regulatory Bodies (NRBs)** are jurisdictional governmental agencies in the 50 states, the District of Columbia, and four U.S. territories that are responsible for the regulation of nursing practice (National Council of State Boards of Nursing, 2020a). A state **Board of Nursing (BON)** is an example of an NRB.

# Health Professions Regulation and Licensing

## Definitions and Purpose of Regulation

Regulation is defined as "an act or process of control over something by rule or restriction" (Garner, 2014, p. 1475). Health professions regulation is needed as a mechanism to protect the interests of public safety. Because of the extraordinary diversity and variability in health professions education programs, licensure and other forms of credentialing vary as well. Laypeople cannot judge the competency of a health professional, nor determine whether that professional's practice meets acceptable and prevailing standards. For these reasons, as well as because of the potential risk for harm and of the intimate nature of nursing and health care, states protect the public by establishing laws to regulate the profession (Russell, 2012). Health professions regulation exists to safeguard the public by gatekeeping entry into the health professions and providing for ongoing maintenance of acceptable standards of practice for those professions. A **practice act**, and the rules written (legal-speak for this type of writing is *promulgated*) from the practice act, constitute government regulatory oversight of professions.

Practice acts vary by state, but most include the same basic elements (Russell, 2012):

- Creation of an agency/board that serves as the decision-making body
- Definitions, standards, and scopes of practice
- Scope of the board's power and authority and its composition
- Standards for educational programs
- Types of titles, licensure, and certification
- Title protection
- Licensure requirements
- Grounds for disciplinary action, including due process (remedies) for the licensee charged with violation of the practice act or regulations

Requirements for mandatory continuing education and/or competency requirements for licensure and relicensure are also found in practice acts.

An NRB's rule-making authority is specified in the practice act as one of its "powers and duties." The rule-making authority generally includes categories such as initial licensing requirements, standards of practice, delegation standards, requirements for prelicensure registered nurse (RN) and licensed practical nurse/licensed vocational nurse (LPN/LVN) educational programs, advanced practice registered nurse (APRN) standards and requirements for practice and prescribing, disciplinary procedures, and standards for continuing education or competence.

Not all state NRBs are granted **statutory authority** to express formal opinions; some must rely on the specific language in the practice act and regulations, the official opinions of an attorney general's office, or court decisions. It cannot be presumed that silence of the law on an issue implies legislative intent for the NRB to write a rule. When there is no prior statutory authority to address an issue, the

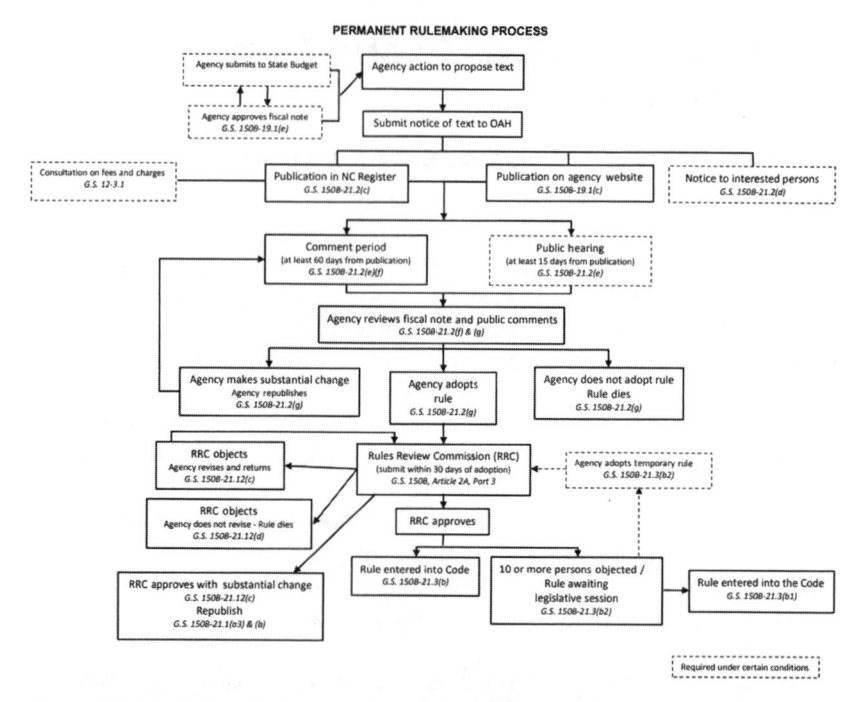

**Figure 7-1** North Carolina's permanent rule-making process.

Information for Rule-making Coordinators, Permanent Rule-making Process, North Carolina Office of Administrative Hearings, 2016

legislative process must be initiated to allow the agency authority to promulgate new, specific regulations. **Figure 7-1** outlines one state's permanent rule-making process. This is the process for agencies to follow when they have been given authority through the legislative process to promulgate new regulations.

## Methods of Professional Credentialing

Various methods are used to credential health professionals. The method accepted in a particular state is determined by the state government and is based on at least two variables: (1) the potential for public harm if safe and acceptable standards of practice are not met and (2) the profession's degree of autonomy and accountability for decision making. Historically, government agencies have been encouraged to select the least restrictive form of regulation to achieve public protection (Pew Health Professions Commission, 1994).

Today, four methods are used in the United States for credentialing and regulation of individual providers. These are described next, beginning with the most restrictive method and progressing to the least restrictive method.

### *Licensure*

A license is "a privilege granted by a state ... the recipient of the privilege then being authorized to do some act ... that would otherwise be impermissible" (Garner, 2014, p. 1059). **Licensure** is the most restrictive method of credentialing.

Anyone who practices within the defined scope must obtain the legal authority to do so from the appropriate administrative state agency. Licensure serves as a barrier to those who are unqualified to perform within a specific scope of practice. Licensure also protects the monetary interests of those who are licensed to perform certain acts by limiting economic competition with unlicensed individuals.

Licensure implies competency assessment at the point of entry into the profession. Applicants for licensure must pass an initial licensing examination, and then comply with continuing education requirements or undergo competency reassessment by the regulatory body that provides oversight for that profession. Because competency is unique to the individual professional and specialty, it is difficult to measure; most licensing agencies require mandatory continuing education in lieu of continued competency assessment for license renewal. Licensure offers the public the greatest level of protection by restricting use of a specific title and a scope of practice to professionals who meet these rigorous criteria and hold a current valid license. Unlicensed persons cannot identify themselves by the title identified in law (e.g., medical assistants cannot hold themselves out as nurses), and they cannot lawfully perform any portion of the scope of practice, unless their own practice act allows them to provide such services because of overlap.

Licensees are held accountable to practice according to provisions in law and rule, and to adhere to legal, ethical, and professional standards. A licensee holds greater public responsibility than an unlicensed citizen. Therefore, disciplinary action may be taken against licensees who have violated a law or rule. Notably, a revocable license means that that the legal authority (e.g., a BON) may divest the licensee of the license if it is deemed that the license holder has violated a law or regulation and that it is in the best interest of the public. Health professions are largely regulated by licensure because of the high risk of potential for harm to the public if unqualified or unsafe practitioners are permitted to practice.

## *Registration*

**Registration** is the "act of recording or enrolling" (Garner, 2014, p. 1474). Registration provides for a review of credentials to determine compliance with criteria for entry into a profession and permits the individual to use the title "registered." Registration provides title protection but does not preclude individuals who are not registered from practicing within the scope of practice, so long as they do not use the title "registered" or misrepresent their status.

Registration does not necessarily imply that prior competency assessment has been conducted. Some state laws may have provisions for removing incompetent or unethical providers from the registry or for "marking" the registry when a complaint is lodged against a provider. However, removing the person from the registry does not assure public protection, because the individual may practice without use of the title. An exemplar is the states' Nurse Aide Registry, which tracks individuals who have met criteria to be certified for employment in long-term care settings; this registry was required by the federal Omnibus Budget Reconciliation Act of 1987.

## Certification

A certificate is "an official document stating that a specified standard has been satisfied" (Garner, 2014, p. 275). In nursing, **certification** usually refers to the voluntary process requiring completion of a specialty-focused education program, competency assessment, and practice hours. This type of certification in nursing, granted by proprietary professional nursing organizations, attests that the individual has achieved a level of competence in nursing practice beyond entry-level licensure.

Certification awarded by proprietary organizations does not have the force and effect of law. However, the term *certification* may also be used by state government agencies as a regulated credential; states may offer a *certificate of authority* or an otherwise-titled certificate to practice within a prescribed scope of practice. In this case, certification is required by law for practice in the specific role. For example, an APRN may need to hold a certificate as a nurse practitioner (NP) from a proprietary organization to qualify for a certificate of authority from a state NRB to practice as an NP in that state. Most states have enacted regulations requiring nationally recognized specialty nursing certification for an APRN to be eligible to practice in the advanced role. Astute consumers may ask whether a provider is certified as a means of assessing competency to practice. Employers also use certification as a means of determining eligibility for certain positions or as a requirement for internal promotion.

Professional standards of practice and codes of ethics exemplify professional self-regulation. National professional organizations set standards for specialty practice. By means of the certification process, these organizations determine who may use the specialty titles within their purview. Documentation of continuing education and practice competency or reexamination is usually required for periodic recertification. Standards are periodically reviewed and revised by committees of the membership to ensure that they reflect current practice. Certification requirements may act as a barrier to entry into a profession. Proprietary organizations profit from certification processes. Policymakers sometimes hesitate when analyzing workforce shortages for professions in which there may be voluntary "certification-creep"; that is, the tendency to require more and more proofs of competency, credentials, or continuing education.

## Recognition

**Recognition** is "confirmation that an act done by another person was authorized ... the formal admission that a person, entity, or thing has a particular status" (Garner, 2014, p. 1463). Official recognition is used by several NRBs as a method of regulating APRNs and implies that the board has validated and accepted the APRN's credentials for the specialty area of practice. Criteria for recognition are defined in the practice act and may include requirements for certification.

# History of Health Professions Regulation

Physicians were the first healthcare professionals to gain legislative recognition for their practice. Most states had physician licensing laws in place by the early 1900s. Nursing soon followed suit. The earliest nursing regulation was enacted in Cape Town, South Africa, in 1891, followed by New Zealand in 1901. The first nursing regulation in the United States occurred in 1903, with North Carolina, New Jersey, New York, and Virginia enacting laws (Dorsey & Schowalter, 2008; Pollitt, 2014; Russell, 2017). By the 1930s, state licensing for nurses had been enacted in 40 states (Hartigan, 2011). Physician scopes of practice are broad; they are unlimited in many states. Historically, this has been problematic for nursing and other nonphysician healthcare providers seeking to define their unique scope, particularly in areas that may overlap with physicians' services. That history of nursing regulation has been characterized by efforts to accommodate this medical preemption (Safriet, 1992).

Early nursing regulation was permissive (voluntary). Systems were developed that allowed nurses to register with a governing board—hence the title "registered nurse." In some states, nurses were registered by the medical board before separate boards of nursing were established. Registration is a minimally restrictive form of state regulation and does not usually require entrance qualification (e.g., examination). Between the 1930s and 1950s, states enacted mandatory licensure laws—Nursing Practice Acts (NPAs)—requiring practicing nurses to obtain licensure with the state NRB.

## *Professional Self-Regulation*

Self-regulation occurs within a profession when its members establish standards, values, ethical frameworks, and safe practice guidelines exceeding the minimum standards defined by law. This voluntary process plays a significant role in the regulation of the profession, equal to legal regulation in many ways. By the 1940s, the need for a standardized licensure exam had become apparent. In 1944, the State Board Test Pool Examination was established by the National League for Nursing (NLN). The State Board Test Pool Examination ensured standardization and relieved state NRBs of the burdens associated with each NRB writing and grading the examination. Over the years, questions about the potential for conflict of interest were raised. Although individual NRBs set their own passing standards, authority for the creation and control of the examination had been absorbed by a professional association (the NLN). This relationship set up conflicts between governmental regulation and professional self-regulation, which should be separate and independent. Concurrently, NRB leaders created a forum in which they could meet and discuss matters of common interest, although that forum was structured as a council of the American Nurses Association. This created additional conflict between NRBs' prescribed governmental duty to establish licensure standards and professional associations' rights and responsibilities to remain independent of governmental influence.

## *National Council of State Boards of Nursing*

To address these issues, in 1978, the **National Council of State Boards of Nursing (NCSBN)** formed with the assistance of a Kellogg Foundation grant. The NCSBN is an autonomous nonprofit organization that represents the states' interests rather than those of professional nursing organizations (Hartigan, 2011). Members of the organization include the NRBs in the 50 states, the

District of Columbia, and four U.S. territories. The purpose of the NCSBN was described as lessening the burdens of government by providing an organization through which NRBs act on matters of common interest and concern affecting the public health, safety, and welfare, including the development of nursing licensing examinations (Dorsey & Showalter, 2008). Through the years, the NCSBN has grown into an international nursing organization with a vision to advance regulatory excellence worldwide. In addition to test development, the NCSBN developed a database to provide access to licensure and disciplinary information. The organization also developed continuing education resources and practice guidelines. Research has become an integral part of the work of NCSBN, and a worldwide regulatory atlas has also been introduced (National Council of State Boards of Nursing [NCSBN], 2020e).

### National Council Licensure Exam (NCLEX)

The State Board Test Pool Examination was the national licensing examination when the NCSBN was organized in 1978. The NCSBN assumed ownership of the national licensing examinations in 1978. By 1982, the NCSBN changed the test name to the National Council Licensure Exam (NCLEX). The NCSBN established an Examination Committee to address security concerns of the exam, to evaluate test validity and reliability, and to develop a test plan. By 1991, the NCSBN Delegate Assembly, composed of representatives from NCSBN membership organizations, voted to move from a paper-and-pencil examination to computerized adaptive testing (CAT). By 1994, nursing became the first healthcare profession in the United States to move the licensing examination to CAT (Dorsey & Schowalter, 2008). The NCLEX has continued to be administered through CAT. The NCSBN is developing a "New Generation NCLEX," which will be introduced in 2023 at the earliest. The 2013–2014 Strategic Practice Analysis highlighted the increasingly complex decisions a newly licensed nurse must make. Testing research by the NCSBN has shown that clinical judgment and decision making in practice can be reliably assessed. As a result, the New Generation NCLEX will ask better questions to help nurses think critically when providing care and make the right decisions (NCSBN, 2020f).

## Regulation Versus Legislation

The legislative and regulatory processes operate in parallel. Both are public processes and equally powerful; however, the processes differ in important ways. Legislation is shaped by elected lawmakers—for example, state legislators or Members of the U.S. Congress. Laws are written in general terms to ensure applicability over time and to establish public policy. Regulations emerge from the law's rule-making authority and shape the details of implementation.

The legislative process is the first step in this two-layer process. Lawmakers introduce bills and shepherd them through the complex legislative process. The process begins when one or more legislators from the same chamber sponsor introduction of a bill during a legislative or congressional session. Bills may address issues of interest to the sponsoring legislator or of concern to the sponsor's constituents. Bills can be amended, substituted, or "die" at any number of points during the session. Checks and balances are built into the process: bills must be scrutinized by both houses and successfully navigate through committees during which testimony is heard. If they are passed by both houses and signed by the president or governor, they are enacted ("enrolled") and become law. Bills must pass during the session in which they are introduced; otherwise, they "die," with the docket for that congressional session or state general assembly being cleared, and the bill must be reintroduced in a subsequent session. The terms *legislation, act, law,* and *statute* are synonyms. *Legislation* also refers to both a bill-in-progress and a law that has been enacted. When referring to laws regulating professions, the term *practice act* is used.

Once signed into law, statute implementation is generally the responsibility of an administrative agency. Administrative agencies execute their responsibilities by enforcing both law and regulations. **Regulations (rules)** enable reasonable implementation of the law. Note that the terms *regulation* and *rule* are also used interchangeably. Whereas a law is written in broad language, regulations are detailed and specify how the law will be put into practice. An administrative agency's authority to write and implement regulations is established in the laws that create the agency. For example, nursing practice acts generally require the NRB to write rules with criteria that applicants must meet to be eligible to sit for licensure examinations and for issuing licenses. Rules amplifying that provision of law outline specific eligibility criteria and application procedures, designate approved examinations (e.g., NCLEX for RNs and LPNs or national certification examinations for APRNs), and include renewal procedures and fees.

The regulatory and legislative processes differ in other ways. Rulemaking is not dependent on legislative session schedules; rules may be written (or rewritten) at any time by an administrative agency. In addition, regulations adhere to **administrative procedures act (APA)** requirements; some states require evaluation and revision of regulations on a predictable schedule to ensure that regulations reflect the current environment.

Like lawmaking, regulation promulgation is a public process and is described in greater detail later in this chapter. The rule-making process, like lawmaking, also includes structures to ensure checks and balances. For example, a nonbiased government body, such as North Carolina's Rules Review Commission, may be charged with oversight; it reviews all administrative regulations to ensure that (1) the filing administrative agency does not exceed its statutory authority, and (2) proposed regulations do not encroach on other laws or regulations.

If an administrative agency finds its regulations are inadequate to serve the needs of the public, and if the law does not support the additional rule-making authority it needs, it may seek statutory modification to add a section in the law that allows additional rule-making authority. To do so requires the agency to seek law change through the full legislative process. For nursing, this may include what is known as opening the NPA. Both laws and regulations have the same legal force and effect. Therefore, even though regulations are written by a government agency rather than a legislative body, regulations carry great weight because their origin stems from the law that provided the agency with its rule-making authority. From here forward, the term *law* will be used instead of *legislation*, but *regulation* and *rule* will be used interchangeably. There are uses for which the term *rule* is preferable (e.g., *rule-making authority*).

## Strengths and Weaknesses of the Regulatory Process

The regulatory process is somewhat more well-ordered than the legislative process in that it is directed by state or federal administrative procedures acts. These procedures guarantee opportunities for comment and public input. The regulatory process also includes built-in delays and time constraints that slow the process of developing and implementing regulations.

However, administrative agencies are able to exert a great deal of control over the rule-drafting process. Agency staff have an interest in ensuring that the final regulation has sufficient detail so that it can be reasonably enforced. It is possible that agency staff, although skilled regulators, may not be knowledgeable about a regulation's impact from the practitioners' point of view. If the agency did not invite stakeholders to assist with the original drafting of the regulation, then public input during the comment period is especially important.

---

**Spotlight:** Nurse Legislator Champions Legislation to Update North Carolina's Nursing Practice Act

State Representative Donna McDowell White, RN, is known in North Carolina as a strong advocate for the health and safety of the public. Her background as a public health nurse is reflected in her work on issues concerning the welfare of North Carolina's youngest citizens to its oldest. Representative White is currently serving as the only legislator on the North Carolina governor's Task Force on Safer Schools; she also serves on the Johnston County Opioid Task Force. She is also a founding member of the Johnston Network on Aging. Her work history with North Carolina's elderly population includes the establishment of practice standards for geriatric case management; she is also known for developing the Victims Assistance Program, which is now used statewide to assist elder victims of telemarketing fraud and scams.

In 2019, Representative White championed legislation to protect the safety of the public and to enhance the operational efficiency of the North Carolina Board of Nursing (NCBON). As of 2019, the North Carolina NPA had not been updated for several years. Due to the leadership and determination of Representative White, the revised regulations in the North Carolina NPA included provisions which modernized outdated (pre-HIPAA) language within the NPA, clarified the subpoena power and disciplinary authority of the NCBON, and specified confidentiality protections for materials gathered by the NCBON. An additional provision of this legislation was the inclusion of a section that granted the NCBON authority to create waivers to allow emergency health services to the public during a declared state of emergency. This provision was key in providing the NCBON with the authority to efficiently implement waivers to address the nursing workforce needs during North Carolina's response to the COVID-19 pandemic.

In addition to enforcement, administrative agencies may have legislative authority to interpret regulations. Sometimes regulations may be misinterpreted by agency staff or board members, resulting in the imposition of a new meaning that is not aligned with the original intent of the regulation. These interpretations may be published as opinions, interpretive statements, and/or declaratory rulings of the board. Opinions of the attorney general or a court of law may also misinterpret the original legislative intent, but the judicial branch of government is more likely to apply sound legal standards to its fact-finding and conclusions of law. Regardless, official opinions carry the force and effect of law even if they are not promulgated as regulations.

## The State Regulatory Process

The 10th Amendment of the U.S. Constitution specifies that all powers not specifically vested in the federal government are reserved for the states. One of these powers is the duty to protect its citizens (police powers). This power is translated in the form of states' authority and interest in regulating the professions to protect the health, safety, and welfare of their citizens. Administrative agencies are given referent power, through their legislatively enacted practice acts, to promulgate (write) regulations and enforce both the laws and the regulations for which they are responsible. These administrative agencies have been called the "fourth branch" of government because of their significant power to execute and enforce the law.

## Nursing Regulatory Bodies

Nurse practice acts vary by state, but all NPAs include the major provisions discussed earlier in this chapter. Provisions included in NPAs focus on a central mission—protection of the public safety. There are 58 NRBs in the United States, including those in the 50 states, the District of Columbia, and the U.S. territories; each of these is known as a *jurisdiction*. Each NRB is a member of the NCSBN. Some states have separate boards for licensing RNs and LPNs/LVNs. Several states regulate RNs and/or LPNs/LVNs through multiprofessional boards that have jurisdiction over a variety of licensed professionals, such as physicians, nurses, and dentists. As members of the NCSBN, NRBs represent the interest of public safety by providing oversight of the construction and administration of the NCLEX.

## Composition of Nursing Regulatory Bodies

Nursing regulatory bodies are generally composed of licensed nurses and consumer members. In most states, the governor appoints members. An exception is North Carolina, where the majority of board members are elected by nurses licensed to practice in the state; the governor, speaker of the house, and president pro tempore of the North Carolina senate each appoint one of the three public members to the NRB (North Carolina Nursing Practice Act, 1981/2019; Russell, 2017). Some NPAs designate specific board member representation—for example, from advanced practice nursing or nursing education, and in the case of joint boards, representation from LPNs/LVNs in addition to RNs/APRNs. In other states, criteria for appointment comprise only licensure and state residency.

## Serving on Boards and Commissions

One way to actively participate in the regulatory process is to seek appointment to the state BON or to other health-related boards or commissions. Appointments to boards and commissions should be sought strategically. It is important to select an agency with a mission and purpose consistent with your own interests and expertise. Because most board appointments are gubernatorial or political appointments, it is important to obtain endorsements from legislators, influential community leaders, and professional associations. Individuals seeking appointment are more likely to acquire endorsements if they have an established history of service to the professional community (see **Spotlight**).

## Board Meetings

Most state administrative procedures acts require boards to post public notice of meetings and make agendas available, usually 30 days prior to the meeting. State government agencies must comply with open meeting ("sunshine") laws, which permit the public to observe and/or participate in board meetings. Board meetings may vary in their degree of formality. Public participation is usually permitted, but open dialogue between board members and the public is generally limited. Opportunities to address the board may be scheduled on the meeting agenda (e.g., during an "open forum" time) and may require advance notification of the individual's name, topic, and the organization represented (if applicable). Boards may go into closed executive session for reasons specified in the state's APA (e.g., to obtain legal advice, conduct contract negotiations, and discuss disciplinary or personnel matters). Boards must comply with APA regulations regarding subject matter that may be discussed in an executive session and report out of executive session when the public session resumes.

---

**Spotlight:** Nurses on Boards Coalition Success

The Nurses on Boards Coalition (NoBC) represents national nursing and other organizations working to build healthier communities in America by increasing nurses' presence on corporate, health-related, and other boards, panels, and commissions. The coalition's original goal was to help ensure that nurses filled at least 10,000 board seats by 2020, as well as raise awareness that all boards would benefit from the unique perspective of nurses to achieve the goals of improved health and efficient and effective healthcare systems at the local, state, and national levels.

The Nurses on Boards Coalition first convened in 2014 in response to the landmark 2010 Institute of Medicine report, *The Future of Nursing: Leading Change, Advancing Health*, which recommended increasing the number of nurse leaders in pivotal decision-making roles on boards and commissions that work to improve the health of everyone in America. The Campaign for Action, an initiative of the AARP Foundation, the AARP, and the Robert Wood Johnson Foundation initially brought the groups together as part of their collaborative effort to implement the recommendations of the IOM report through the *Future of Nursing: Campaign for Action*.

By January 20, 2020, 10,023 RNs/APRNs had been newly placed on boards (does not include board and governance roles where nurses already have a significant presence within the nursing profession). Over 20,000 RNs/APRNs are registered with the NoBC. You can register your interest in serving too. Registration does not mean that you are automatically matched to a Board; it means that you receive timely updates about available Board positions to which you may choose to apply.

Board meeting participants include board members (appointed or elected), board staff (employees of the board), and legal counsel for the board. Legal counsel advises the board on matters of law and jurisdiction. Some boards may have "staff" counsel, but many state boards receive advice only from an assigned representative of the state attorney general's office, known as an assistant attorney general. All voting is a matter of public record, and board action occurs only in open public session. When board members vote, they must consider implications for the public welfare and safety, the legal defensibility of the outcome of the vote, and potential statewide impact of the decision. The board must act only within its legal jurisdiction.

Boards may publish action summaries of board meetings in their newsletters, in addition to articles written by board members and staff that explain law and rule. Newsletters typically include disciplinary actions taken against licensees during board meetings. The nature of the offense is included in some states' newsletters. Some states mail newsletters to licensees, but many BONs now make newsletters available only electronically.

## Monitoring the Competency of Nurses: Discipline and Mandatory Reporting

Licensed nurses are accountable for knowing the laws and regulations governing nursing in the state of licensure and for adhering to legal, ethical, and professional standards of care. Some state regulations include standards of practice; other states may refer to professional or ethical standards established by professional associations. Employing agencies also define standards of practice through policies and procedures, although these are separate from, in addition to, and superseded by the state's NPA and regulations.

Most NPAs include provisions for mandatory reporting that require employers to report violations of the NPA or regulations to the NRB. Licensed nurses also have a moral and ethical duty to report unsafe and incompetent practice to the NRB. In addition, the public may file complaints of licensees with NRBs. The NPA provides the NRB with authority to investigate complaints against licensees and potentially take action on the license, including the license or certificate to practice as an APRN. State administrative procedures acts ensure that the licensees subject to disciplinary action are provided due process. When a nurse is found, through the administrative processes, to have violated provisions of the NPA or regulations, the NRB can take action on the license; these actions may include a reprimand, fine, suspension, suspension of license with stay (i.e., probation), permanent revocation of license, or any other action permitted by the NPA.

A nurse who holds a multistate license (i.e., a license that permits a nurse to practice in more than one state in accordance with a multistate compact agreement) is held accountable for knowing and abiding by the laws and regulations of the state of original licensure as well as the compact state in which the nurse practices. Multistate regulation is discussed in more detail later in this chapter. Nurses with multistate licenses should be aware that ignorance of the law in any state of licensure and/or practice does not excuse misconduct.

## Changing the Rules
### Revising or Instituting New State Regulations

State agencies exercise their authority and duty to promulgate regulations amplifying their laws by following the state's APA. The APA of each state specifies the rule-making process. Rule-making processes differ from state to state. For example, some states designate government commissions or committees as the authorities for review and approval of regulations, whereas other states submit regulations to the general assembly or to committees of the legislature. Nevertheless, all state rule-making processes share the following common elements:

- Public notice that a new regulation or modification of an existing regulation has been proposed
- Opportunity to submit written comment or testimony
- Opportunity to present oral testimony at a rules hearing
- Agency filing of the rule in final form
- Publication of the final regulation in a state register or bulletin

Public comment may be very influential in determining the final outcome. The administrative agency drafting the regulation has discretion in determining which amendments are made and may make amendments based on public input prior to final filing. The time frame for implementation of new or revised regulations varies according to the state's APA. Generally, effective dates are within 30 to 90 days of publication of the final regulation. In some states, the agency is required to prepare a fiscal impact statement, providing an estimate of the costs that will be incurred as a result of the rule, both to the agency and to the public.

### Board Rule-Making Processes

Nursing regulatory bodies make regulatory decisions using methods similar to those used by other public officials in executive branch agencies. When drafting new rules or revising existing rules, NRBs examine matters of public safety and issues administering existing regulations, invite comment from stakeholders (in particular, nursing organization representatives), and may seek counsel from NRB advisory committees or task forces. Leveraging participation opportunities early in the rule-drafting process is important, in addition to providing testimony during formal hearings. It is also imperative to appreciate that the process becomes complex when it is confounded by the perspectives, values, and ethics of a variety of stakeholders. Because rule making involves dealing with both political complexities and content issues, NRBs may use policy design or process models to facilitate decision making. Using a process model that is both familiar in nursing and adaptable to the health policy arena—for example, evidence-based practice (EBP)—can facilitate an NRB's rule making because it provides an organized framework for problem solving.

The South Dakota BON successfully used an evidence-informed health policy (EIHP) model to analyze its policy for allowing registered nurses to delegate diabetes care for schoolchildren to trained unlicensed personnel. Evaluation of the policy is an example of how to use such a model to promote evidence-based nursing regulation (Damgaard & Young, 2017). The EIHP model is adapted from Melnyk and Fineout-Overholt's (2015) EBP model, and is a paradigm and problem-solving approach to health policy decision making. Like EBP, EIHP combines the use of evidence with issue expertise and stakeholder values and ethics to inform and leverage policy discussion and negotiation. The hoped-for outcome is the best possible health policy agenda and improvements (Loversidge, 2016b). Using the term *informed* rather than *based* shifts the focus of evidence to its realistic uses in policy arenas, which include informing and influencing stakeholders, as well as mediating dialogue; it also acknowledges the complexity of multiple factors, relationships, and rapidly shifting priorities inherent in the political process (Loversidge, 2016a).

Because EIHP is a full-cycle process model, it can facilitate decision making throughout the phases of regulation promulgation, rollout, implementation, and evaluation. The model includes three components and seven steps, summarized in **Table 7-1**. In particular, it makes use of the **PICOT** mnemonic in addressing the question of interest. As used in health policy, the "P" part of the question, the *population of interest*—generally focuses on the consumer. The "I" (*intervention*) refers to the policy change. The "C" is the *comparison*—the current policy or lack thereof. The "O" component describes the anticipated *outcome* after policy implementation (Loversidge, 2016b). The "T" is the *time* needed to implement the policy.

## Providing Public Comment

Regulatory agencies provide a small window of opportunity for public comment. Most comment periods last 30 days from the date of publication of the proposed regulation. However, longer comment periods are sometimes permitted if the agency anticipates the issue will draw strong public interest or involves controversy. **Public rule hearings** are held by the agency proposing the regulation. Public agencies must comply with APA regulations regarding

**Table 7-1** Loversidge's Evidence-Informed Health Policy Model

| Components of the EIHP | Steps of the EIHP |
|---|---|
| ▪ *External evidence*: Includes best research evidence, evidence-informed relevant theories, and best evidence from opinion leaders, expert panels, and other relevant sources.<br>▪ *Issue expertise*: Includes data from sources such as professional and healthcare associations/organizations and government agencies; also includes professions' understanding/experience with the issue; may include other data resources.<br>▪ *Stakeholder values and ethics*: Considers the values and ethics of healthcare providers, policy shapers, healthcare consumers, and others. | ▪ *Step 0*: Cultivate a spirit of inquiry in the policy culture or environment.<br>▪ *Step 1*: Identify the policy problem; ask a policy question in the form of a PICOT question.<br>▪ *Step 2*: Search for/collect relevant/best evidence.<br>▪ *Step 3*: Perform a critical appraisal of the evidence.<br>▪ *Step 4*: Integrate best evidence with issue expertise and stakeholder values and ethics; the result will be the desired health policy decision/change.<br>▪ *Step 5*: Contribute to the health policy development/implementation process.<br>▪ *Step 6*: Frame the policy change for dissemination.<br>▪ *Step 7*: Evaluate the effectiveness of the policy change and disseminate the findings. |

Data from Loversidge, J. M. (2016a). An evidence-informed health policy model: Adapting evidence-based practice for nursing education and regulation. *Journal of Nursing Regulation, 7*(2), 27–33.

public hearings. Federal agencies are generally required to hold a hearing when a numeric threshold is reached (i.e., a certain number of individuals or agency/organization representatives officially request to offer testimony to the agency about an issue). Written comments received by the agency are made a part of the permanent record and by law must be considered by the agency's board or commission members prior to publication of the final regulation. A final regulation can be challenged in the courts if the judge determines the agency did not comply with the APA or ignored public comments.

## Locating Information

Each state government periodically publishes a document containing notices, proposed regulations, final regulations, and emergency regulations. The publication cycle for this document—usually called the State Register or State Bulletin—can be obtained by accessing the state legislative printing office/website or the state legislative information system office/website. Federal regulatory information is available online: The National Archives manages the Code of Federal Regulations (CFR) website, and the U.S. Government Publishing Office oversees the eCFR website.

Because state and federal agencies promulgate numerous regulations, it is in one's best interest to belong to at least one national professional organization, most of which employ professional lobbyists who track legislation, monitor agencies' rule making, and report to their membership. Some state organizations employ such lobbyists; many others do not have the financial resources to do so. Specialty organizations' newsletters and journals and legislative subscription and monitoring services and bulletins can be relied upon to summarize proposed regulation content and track status progress.

## Emergency Regulations

Provisions for promulgating emergency regulations are defined at both the state and federal levels. Emergency regulations are enacted when an agency determines that the public welfare is in jeopardy and the regulation will serve as an immediately enforceable remedy. Emergency regulations usually take effect upon their date of publication, are generally temporary, and are effective for a limited time period (usually 90 days), with an option to renew them. Emergency regulations must be followed with permanent regulations that are promulgated in accordance with the usual APA requirements.

## Monitoring State Regulations

Administrative agencies promulgate hundreds of regulations each year. In this rapidly changing healthcare environment, conflicts related to definitions and scopes of practice, right to reimbursement, and requirements for supervision and collaboration may occur. Regulations that affect nursing practice may be implemented by a variety of agencies. Knowing which agencies regulate health care, healthcare delivery systems, and professional practice, and monitoring legislation and regulations proposed by those agencies, is important for safeguarding practice. Chief among the agencies that should be tracked are the health professions licensing boards, state agencies that govern licensing and certification of healthcare facilities, agencies that administer public health services (e.g., public health, mental health, and alcohol and drug agencies), and agencies that govern federal/state contribution program reimbursement (e.g., Medicare and Medicaid).

APRNs should be aware of regulations that mandate benefits or reimbursement policies and lobby for their inclusion as potential recipients of these benefits or funds. Several states have instituted open-panel legislation, known as "any willing provider" and "freedom of choice" laws. These bills mandate that any provider who is authorized to provide the services covered in an insurance plan must be recognized and reimbursed by the plan. Conversely, insurance companies and business lobbyists oppose this type of legislation. As managed care contracts are negotiated, APRNs must ensure that their services are given fair and equitable consideration. Other important areas for nurses include workers' compensation participation and liability insurance laws.

In summary, agencies that may potentially promulgate regulations that could have implications for APRN and RN practice or reimbursement should be monitored. **Table 7-2** provides some key questions to consider when analyzing

**Chapter 7** Government Response: Regulation

**Table 7-2** Analyzing Regulations

| Inquiry | Example Analysis |
|---|---|
| 1. Which government agency wrote the regulation? | The NC Board of Nursing created the rule. |
| 2. What is the source of the agency's authority (the law that provides the agency's rule-making authority)? | NC § 90-171.23. Duties, powers, and meetings. (b)(3) states the following: Adopt, amend or repeal rules and regulations as may be necessary to carry out the provisions of this Article. |
| 3. What is the intent or rationale of the regulation, and is it clearly stated? | The regulation was written as part of the response to the declared COVID-19 State of Emergency and at the request of the Secretary of the Department of Health and Human Resources. Furthermore, a joint statement on ordering, prescribing, or dispensing COVID-19 medications was released by the American Medical Association, the American Pharmacists Association, and the American Society of Health-System Pharmacists prior to the date that the regulation was written: www.ama-assn.org/delivering-care/public-health/joint-statement-ordering-prescribing-or-dispensing-covid-19<br>Section (d) of the rule clearly states "a nurse practitioner shall not prescribe a Restricted Drug for the prevention of, or in anticipation of, the contraction of COVID-19 by someone who has not yet been diagnosed." |
| 4. How does the regulation affect the practice of nursing? Does it constrain or limit practice? | The regulation constrains practice—provides guidelines for the prescribing of certain "restricted drugs," which should be "consistent with the evidence" of their use. |
| 5. Is the language in the regulation clear or ambiguous? Can the regulation be interpreted in different ways? | The language in the regulation is clear. |
| 6. Are there definitions within the legislation to clarify terms? | Definitions are provided specifying the actual "restricted drugs" referenced within the rule. |
| 7. Are any important points (especially for RNs and APRNs) omitted? | No. |
| 8. Is there sufficient lead time to comply with the regulation? | The rule was adopted as an Emergency Rule, effective April 21, 2020, and as a Temporary Rule on June 26, 2020. |
| 9. What is the fiscal impact (direct and indirect costs) of the regulation? | Although the fiscal impact of the regulation is unclear, the rule is part of an effort to assist with proper stewardship of healthcare resources during the State of Emergency. Adherence to the rule will prevent supply disruptions of the medications specified, especially to patients who use the medications for documented chronic conditions. |

a regulation for its impact on nursing practice. An example analysis is provided within the table using a regulation that was created during the COVID-19 pandemic (COVID-19 Drug Preservation Rule, 2020).

## The Federal Regulatory Process

The federal government has become a central factor in health professions regulation. A number of forces have influenced this trend; however, the advent of the Medicare and Medicaid programs was especially significant. Federal initiatives that have grown from these programs include cost containment (prospective payment program), consumer protection (combating fraud and abuse program) (Jost, 1997; Roberts & Clyde, 1993), and the initiatives and programs included in the Patient Protection and Affordable Care Act of 2010 (ACA), along with the Health Care and Education Reconciliation Act of 2010 (U.S. Department of Health and Human Services [DHHS], n.d.).

In July 2001, the Centers for Medicare and Medicaid Services (CMS) replaced the former Health Care Financing Administration (HCFA). As a result of its reformulation, this agency now provides increased emphasis on responsiveness to beneficiaries, providers, and quality improvement. In 2003, President George W. Bush signed the Medicare Prescription Drug, Improvement, and Modernization Act (MMA) into law. The act created a prescription drug benefit for Medicare beneficiaries (Medicare Part D) and established the Medicare Advantage program (Medicare Part C) (O'Sullivan et al., 2004), effectively providing seniors with prescription drug benefits and more choice in accessing health care beginning in 2006.

As Medicare has evolved, the practice of APRNs has likewise been influenced by changes in Medicare reimbursement policy. In 1998, when Medicare reimbursement reform was enacted, APRNs won the right to be directly reimbursed for provision of Medicare Part B services that, until that time, had been provided only by physicians. In addition, the reform lifted the geographic location restrictions that had limited patient access to APRNs. More recent revisions to the required qualifications, coverage criteria, billing, and payment for Medicare services provided by APRNs are specific, depending on whether the APRN is a certified registered nurse anesthetist, nurse practitioner, certified nurse midwife, or clinical nurse specialist. Reimbursement for APRNs has generally improved; for example, NP services are now paid at 80% of the lesser of the actual charge or 85% of the fee schedule amount that a physician is paid (U.S. DHHS, CMS, 2016). However, APRNs continue to lobby for reimbursement at 100% of the amount paid to physicians.

The Veterans Health Administration, the Indian Health Service, and the uniformed armed services are also regulated by the federal government. Large numbers of health professionals, many of whom are nurses/APRNs, are employed by these federal agencies and departments. Federally employed health professionals must be licensed in at least one state/jurisdiction. These individuals are subject to the laws of the state in which they are licensed and the policies established by the federal system in which they are employed. However, the state of licensure need not correspond with the state in which the federal facility or department resides, because practice that occurs on federal property is not subject to state oversight. This status reflects the Supremacy Clause of the U.S. Constitution, Article VI, Paragraph 2, which established that federal laws generally take precedence over state laws (Legal Information Institute, n.d.). State laws in conflict with federal laws cannot be enforced.

The Commerce Clause of the U.S. Constitution limits the ability of states to erect barriers to interstate trade. Courts have determined that the provision of health care constitutes interstate trade under antitrust laws, which, in turn, sets the stage for the federal government to preempt state licensing laws regarding the practice of professions across state boundaries if future circumstances make this a desirable outcome for the nation. The impact of technology on the delivery of health care—for example, telehealth—allows providers to care for patients in remote environments and across the geopolitical boundaries defined by traditional state-by-state licensure. This raises the question as to whether the federal government would have an interest in interceding in the standardization of state licensing requirements to facilitate interstate commerce. If this occurred, the federal government would be in the position of usurping what is presently the state's authority.

Licensing boards have an interest in avoiding federal intervention and are beginning to identify ways to facilitate the practice of telehealth while simultaneously preserving the power and right of the state to protect its citizens by regulating health professions at the state level. One approach to nursing regulation that addresses this conundrum is multistate regulation, which is discussed later in this chapter.

## Federal Rule Making

The federal regulatory process is established by the federal Administrative Procedures Act. In this process, a Notice of Proposed Rulemaking (NPRM) is published in the *Federal Register*, the daily (during business days) journal of the U.S. government containing new executive orders, presidential proclamations, rules and regulations, proposed rules, notices, and meetings affected by the Sunshine Act. The NPRM includes information about the substance of intended regulations and information about public participation in the regulatory process, including procedures for attending meetings or hearings and for providing comment. Federal regulatory information is available online via the Code of Federal Regulations website (**Figure 7-2**).

An agency writing proposed rules is mandated to consider all public comments; the amendments to draft regulations may be made based on public input if warranted. The *Federal Register* provides agency contact information on its website, making it feasible for the public to provide comment on proposed regulations. Only written comments are included in the public record, although agencies may permit oral comments if time is short. Instructions for submitting electronic comments or written submissions by mail, hand delivery, or courier are generally included the filing agency's *Federal Register* webpage. Comments received after the comment period posted in the *Federal Register* is closed can be legitimately disregarded by the agency. The agency publishes final regulations

**Figure 7-2** The *Federal Register* website.
*Federal Register.* Retrieved from https://www.federalregister.gov/

in the rules and regulations section of the *Federal Register*. Rules become effective 30 days after they are filed in final form by the agency and published in the *Federal Register* (**Figure 7-3**).

# Regulation in a Transforming Healthcare Delivery System

## History

Following a 1995 Pew Task Force report on healthcare workforce regulation reforms, the Institute of Medicine (IOM), now known as the National Academy of Medicine, issued a number of reports related to safety in healthcare systems, known as the Quality Chasm Series. Several of these reports made recommendations with regard to regulation. For example, in its first report, *To Err Is Human*, the IOM called for licensing and certification bodies to pay greater attention to safety-related performance standards and expectations for health professionals (Kohn et al., 2000).

A consensus report entitled *The Future of Nursing: Leading Change, Advancing Health* was jointly issued by the Robert Wood Johnson Foundation and the IOM in October 2010. This landmark report focused singularly on nursing and provided four key messages to guide changes and remove barriers that prevent nurses from being able to function effectively in a rapidly evolving healthcare system:

- Nurses should be enabled to practice to the full extent of their education and training.
- Nurses should be able to access higher levels of education and training in an improved education system that allows for academic progression.
- Nurses should be full partners in the interprofessional redesign of the U.S. healthcare system.
- Effective workforce planning and policymaking need better data collection and information infrastructures.

**168** **Chapter 7** Government Response: Regulation

**Figure 7-3** The federal rule-making process.

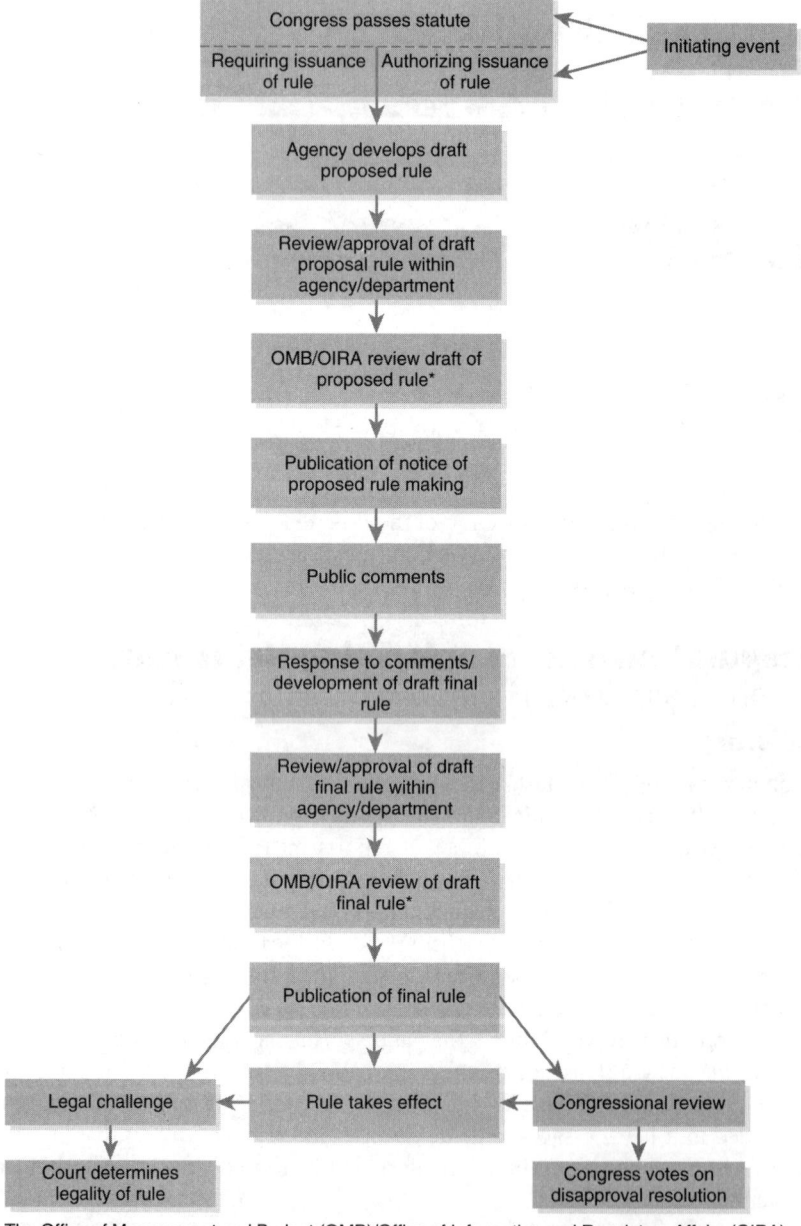

* The Office of Management and Budget (OMB)/Office of Information and Regulatory Affairs (OIRA) reviews only significant rules and does not review any rules submitted by independent regulatory agencies.

Carey, M. P. (2013). The federal rulemaking process: An overview. Congressional Research Service, the Library of Congress.

Eight recommendations for fundamental change are found in the report, along with related recommended actions for Congress, state legislatures, the CMS, the Office of Personnel Management, the Federal Trade

Commission (FTC), and the Antitrust Division of the Department of Justice. The recommendation most relevant to regulation is the first: to remove scope-of-practice barriers. Another recommendation with implications for regulation is the call to prepare and enable nurses to lead change to advance health; that is, the voice of nurses should be among those considered in health policy decision making, and nurses should actively serve on advisory committees, commissions, and boards where policy decisions are made to advance health systems to improve patient care (IOM, 2010). Finally, the suggestion to build an infrastructure for the collection and analysis of interprofessional healthcare workforce data has implications for regulation (IOM, 2010). Regulatory boards often survey their licensees as a part of renewal, providing excellent sources of workforce data. Progress toward accomplishment of the *Future of Nursing* report recommendations has been made. Information on *Future of Nursing* initiatives is available through the Future of Nursing: Campaign for Action website (https://campaignforaction.org). Additionally, Dr. Sue Hassmiller and the National Academy of Medicine will release a report card on the success or failure of these initiatives in 2021 titled *Future of Nursing Report Card: Progress After 10 Years*.

Another area ripe for regulatory reform relates to structures that encourage interprofessional collaboration. The Josiah Macy Jr. Foundation, an organization dedicated to improving the health of the public through the advancement of health professions education, has been instrumental in providing direction for regulatory reform. In 2013, the foundation held a consensus conference with health professions education leaders to discuss a vision for a joint future of healthcare practice and education. Recommendations for action in five areas were made; one of these was to "revise professional regulatory standards and practices to permit and promote innovation in interprofessional education and collaborative practice" (Josiah Macy Jr. Foundation, 2013, p. 2). The foundation's current 10-year plan includes three main objectives: promoting equity, increasing collaboration, and navigating ethical dilemmas. Work related to these objectives reflects the organization's belief that "applying the latest knowledge, clinical learning environments can improve outcomes for patients, health care professionals, and communities they serve" (Josiah Macy Jr. Foundation, n.d.). Additional information on the current strategic plan of the organization may be found at https://macyfoundation.org/about/our-strategic-plan.

These reports and recommendations provide a substantive body of evidence that can be leveraged for health professions regulatory reform, thereby ensuring that these professions can meet the needs of healthcare consumers. Nurses have a window of opportunity to act on these recommendations, but they must be open to the notion that collaboration with other health professions is essential if new regulatory models are to emerge. Regulation determines who has access to the patient, who serves as gatekeeper in a managed care environment, who is reimbursed, and who has autonomy to practice. Nurses must be visible participants in the political processes that determine the scope of their practice and which impact consumer choice and safety.

## Regulatory Reform: Exemplar Issues
### NC Dental Exemplar

In the United States, licensing boards are often dominated by individuals who are active in the profession that the licensing board is charged with regulating (Federal Trade Commission [FTC], 2015). Regulation of professional services through licensure and defined scopes of practice is a practice, in the name of public protection, that states have engaged in within the capacity of state sovereignty. Such regulatory practices control who can provide services and restrict competition of the regulated professions (Abram, 2015). According to the state action doctrine (*Parker v. Brown*, 1943), states are immune from federal antitrust prosecution when they regulate industries and professions under laws that provide regulatory authority to restrict competition.

The 2015 U.S. Supreme Court decision in *North Carolina State Board of Dental Examiners v. Federal Trade Commission* created uncertainties related to the ability of regulatory agencies to cite state action doctrine. An antitrust complaint filed by the FTC argued that the North Carolina Board of Dental Examiners (NCBDE) had violated the FTC Act for excluding nondentists from the teeth-whitening services market (Abram, 2015; Livanos, 2016). Ultimately, the U.S. Supreme Court ruled in favor of the FTC. The final ruling noted that because a controlling number of the NCBDE members are active market participants in the occupation regulated by the NCBDE, state-action antitrust immunity can only be cited if the board is subject to active supervision by the state.

### Scope-of-Practice Exemplar

The *Future of Nursing* progress report (IOM, 2016) noted that only minimal change in expansion of nurses' scopes of practice had been accomplished since the original report in 2010. APRNs continue to struggle with these issues, although progress has been made in some states as well as at the federal level. A 2014 report from the FTC provided an analysis of the consequences of continuing to impose restrictions on APRNs' scopes of practice. The report noted associations between mandatory physician supervision/collaborative practice agreement regulations and restriction of independent APRN practice. The FTC (2014) projected that these environmental factors would likely lead to decreased access to healthcare services, higher costs, and reduced quality of care, leading to minimization of nursing's ability to innovate in the delivery of health care.

The Department of Veterans Affairs (VA) finalized a regulation in 2016 that allowed for the full scope of practice for APRNs with the exception of certified registered nurse anesthetists (CRNAs) (Dickson, 2016). On April 21, 2020, the Veterans Health Administration issued a directive that included guidance to encourage VA medical facilities to allow healthcare professionals within their facilities to practice within the full scope of their license, registration, or certification, with the goal of increasing access to health care for VA beneficiaries (Veterans Health Administration, 2020). Additionally, the Office of the Under Secretary for Health sent a memorandum to leaders within the VA, including comments to strongly encourage VA medical facilities to use the authority granted within the directive to amend medical facility bylaws to allow CRNAs to have full practice authority to the extent that is within the full scope of their license (if their state license permits independent practice) (Stone, 2020). This guidance was applicable to 18 states that had permanently granted full practice authority and 9 states that granted temporary full practice authority during the COVID-19 pandemic (listed in the VA guidance as of April 21, 2020) (Panangala & Sussman, 2020; Veterans Health Administration, 2020). The VA noted that the full practice authority will remain during the duration of the public health emergency caused by the pandemic. However, Panangala and Sussman (2020) noted that it was expected that the VA medical facilities would revert back to standard bylaws at the end of the public health emergency.

## Interstate Mobility and Multistate Regulation Exemplar

The Nurse Licensure Compact (NLC) model, adopted by the NCSBN, is a mutual recognition model of **multistate regulation** and licensure for RNs and LPNs. States adopting the model voluntarily enter into an interstate compact, which is a legal agreement between states to recognize the license of another state and allow for practice between states. This allows nurses to possess a "home state" license and practice in a remote state without obtaining or paying for an additional license. The original NLC was first implemented in 2000. When momentum slowed, NCSBN revised the NLC language and included Uniform License Requirements and other improvements. As a result of that change, there are currently 34 states in the NLC, with additional states joining each year (NCSBN, 2020g).

In May 2015, NCSBN approved the **APRN Compact**, which would allow APRNs to hold one multistate license and extend privileges to practice in other APRN Compact states (NCSBN, 2017). To participate in this system, state NPAs would need to be revised to include the Uniform APRN Requirements. Currently, only three states (North Dakota, Idaho, and Wyoming) have legislated the APRN Compact. The original APRN Compact required a minimum of 10 states in order to implement. After the three initial states, APRN Compact legislation ground to a halt. Unfortunately, over recent years states that have been successful with passing legislation for full practice authority have done so with an agreement for a transition to practice. Those states were then ineligible for the APRN Compact, as it required full practice authority upon licensure. As a result, there has been no further success in passing an APRN Compact. The NCSBN convened a task force to revise the APRN Compact language, allowing for 2,080 hours of experience (no supervision required) in order to qualify for a multistate license. This compact language also reduced the number of states needed for implementation from 10 to 7. The revised APRN Compact was approved at the 2020 NCSBN Delegate Assembly (NCSBN, 2020d).

## COVID-19 Pandemic Exemplar

The first case of COVID-19 was reported in China on December 31, 2019 (World Health Organization [WHO], 2020). The United States had its first laboratory-confirmed COVID-19 case on January 20, 2020, which was then reported to the Centers for Disease Control and Prevention (CDC) on January 22, 2020 (Stokes et al., 2020). Health and Human Services Secretary Alex Azar called on states to reduce regulatory barriers that inhibit access to care during the response to COVID-19 (Azar, 2020). States had a variety of responses to this request, both temporary and permanent. Governors, state legislatures, regulatory boards, etc. each acted within their capacities to address needs for access to care. Temporary or permanent lifting of restrictions to scope of practice, practice across state lines, and the use of telehealth are a few of the actions taken by states in response to the pandemic (NCSBN, 2020b, 2020c). The increased adoption of telehealth is one of the response strategies that may have lasting long-term implications for the U.S. healthcare system (CDC, 2020; Perez, 2020).

### Electronic Access to Healthcare Services Exemplar

The impact of technology on the delivery of health care, including telehealth, was mentioned earlier in this chapter in the context of questions about whether the federal government has an interest in interceding in the standardization of state licensing requirements to facilitate interstate commerce. Such action would preempt the states' authority to license health professionals. However, the states maintain their right to protect their citizens. Today, nurses who live in one multistate-regulation state and practice telehealth in another multistate-regulation state have the benefit of multistate regulation (but must affirm licensure in the second state). Where no multistate compact exists between states, however, the nurse must generally seek licensure in the state in which the patient resides.

During the COVID-19 pandemic, two pieces of legislation were passed to promote the use of telehealth by providing funding and waivers to allow the use of telehealth as part of the COVID-19 response: the Coronavirus Preparedness and Response Supplemental Appropriations Act (H.R.6074) and the Coronavirus Aid, Relief, and Economic Security (CARES) Act (H.R.748) (Perez, 2020). These policy changes, in addition to changes implemented at the state level regarding telehealth, have reduced barriers to telehealth access and may have long-term implications to the way telehealth is used in the delivery of acute, chronic, primary, and specialty care (CDC, 2020; NCSBN, 2020b, 2020c).

## Conclusion

The capacity to adapt is crucial in an era of rapid change. Today's politically astute nurses have many opportunities to influence state and federal health policies and regulations to allow the public greater access to affordable, quality health care. Familiarity with the regulatory process will give registered nurses and APRNs the tools needed to navigate this dynamic environment with confidence. Knowing how to monitor the status of critical issues involving scopes of practice, licensure, and reimbursement will allow RNs and APRNs to influence the outcomes of debates on those issues. Participation in professional nursing organizations provides the foundation for strong coalition building and a power base from which to effect change in the political and regulatory arenas. Participation also gives members ready access to a network of colleagues, legislative affairs information, and professional and educational opportunities. Although supporting the profession through participation is central, it is equally important to remember that each professional nurse has the ability to make a difference.

## Chapter Discussion Points

1. Compare and contrast the legislative and regulatory processes.
2. Discuss multistate practice via interstate compacts, including positions of support and opposition to interstate compacts.
3. Contrast the BON and the national or state nurses' association vis-à-vis mission, membership, authority, functions, and source of funding.
4. The NCSBN continues to track APRN Consensus Model* implementation status across the United States. Evaluate the status of your state with regard to implementation of the recommend provisions within the APRN Consensus Model. The following is a useful resource to assist with your evaluation: National Council of State Boards of Nursing, *APRN Implementation Status*, www.ncsbn.org/5397.htm.

## CASE STUDY 7-1: Practice Waivers During Emergency

The COVID-19 pandemic required a coordinated response to facilitate the abilities of states to address healthcare workforce needs and promote access to care during the crisis. One role of NRBs within this context was the creation of regulatory waivers in response to the lack of available testing sites for nurse licensure exams and APRN certification exams. A state must grant an NRB the authority to create waivers in order for the NRB to pursue such action. Authority may be granted through statute or via an executive order issued by the governor of a state. One state recently enacted legislation that included provisions granting the NRB authority to waive requirements in the NPA to allow emergency health services to the public if a state of emergency is declared. Pursuant to the authority granted to the NRB under the new law, the NRB created such waivers for LPNs, RNs, certified registered nurse anesthetists, and clinical nurse specialists. Certified nurse practitioners (CNPs) are jointly regulated by the NRB and medical board (MB) in the state. The MB has similar emergency

---

* Although the APRN Consensus Model was developed in 2008, many states have not yet fully implemented the provisions within the model. Additionally, the NCSBN made revisions in 2020 with regard to the model language for APRN Compact legislation in hopes that this will assist with states adopting the APRN compact (and APRN Consensus Model).

provisions in statute which allow for the creation of waivers; the NRB and MB worked collaboratively to create the waivers for CNPs during the pandemic.

Certified nurse midwives (CNMs) are regulated by a separate regulatory board in the state, the statutory provisions for the CNM regulatory board do not include the authority to create waivers.

### Case Study Discussion Questions
1. Discuss other potential remedies that are available to the CNM regulatory board to pursue the ability to temporarily waive CNM regulations during the declared state of emergency.
2. Discuss the supporting evidence that the CNM regulatory board should include in prepared comments for a public hearing to pursue the statutory authority to grant emergency waivers.
3. The BON and MB worked collaboratively to create the CNP waivers. Discuss the potential implications of the requirement for joint regulatory authority in this situation.

# References

Abram, T. G. (2015). *North Carolina Board of Dental Examiners v. Federal Trade Commission*: State boards of nursing face increased exposure to antitrust claims. *Journal of Nursing Regulation*, 6(2), 25–27. https://doi.org/10.1016/S2155-8256(15)30383-5

Azar, A. (2020, March 24). *HHS secretary letter to states licensing waivers*. https://www.ncsbn.org/HHS_Secretary_Letter_to_States_Licensing_Waivers.pdf

Carey, M. P. (2013). *The federal rulemaking process: An overview*. Congressional Research Service Report RL32240. http://www.fas.org/sgp/crs/misc/RL32240.pdf

Centers for Medicare and Medicaid Services (CMS). (2014). *History*. Retrieved from https://www.cms.gov/About-CMS/Agency-information/History/

Centers for Disease Control and Prevention. (2020). *Using telehealth to expand access to essential health services during the COVID-19 pandemic*. https://www.cdc.gov/coronavirus/2019-ncov/hcp/telehealth.html

*COVID-19 Drug Preservation Rule*, 21 NCAC 36.0817. (2020). http://reports.oah.state.nc.us/ncac/title%2021%20-%20occupational%20licensing%20boards%20and%20commissions/chapter%2036%20-%20nursing/21%20ncac%2036%2020.0817.pdf

Damgaard, G., & Young, L. (2017). Application of an evidence-informed health policy model for the decision to delegate insulin administration. *Journal of Nursing Regulation*, 7(4), 33–33. https://doi.org/10.1016/S2155-8256(17)30019-4

Dickson, V. (2016, December 13). VA finalizes rule that extends scope of nurse practice. *Modern Healthcare*. https://www.modernhealthcare.com/article/20161213/NEWS/161219974/va-finalizes-rule-that-expands-scope-of-nurse-practice

Dorsey, C. F., & Schowalter, J. M. (2008). *The first 25 years: 1978–2003*. National Council of State Boards of Nursing. https://www.ncsbn.org/25Years_13.pdf

Federal Trade Commission. (2014). *Policy perspectives: Competition and the regulation of advanced practice nurses*. https://www.ftc.gov/system/files/documents/reports/policy-perspectives-competition-regulation-advanced-practice-nurses/140307aprnpolicypaper.pdf

Federal Trade Commission. (2015). *FTC staff guidance on active supervision of state regulatory boards controlled by marked participants*. https://www.ftc.gov/system/files/attachments/competition-policy-guidance/active_supervision_of_state_boards.pdf

Garner, B. A. (2014). *Black's law dictionary* (10th ed.). Thomas Reuters.

Hartigan, C. (2011). APRN regulation: The licensure–certification interface. *AACN Advanced Critical Care*, 22(1), 50–65.

Institute of Medicine. (2010). *The future of nursing: Leading change, advancing health*. National Academies Press.

Institute of Medicine. (2016). *Assessing progress on the Institute of Medicine report: The Future of Nursing.* National Academies Press.
Josiah Macy Jr. Foundation. (n.d.). *Knowing better, doing better.* https://macyfoundation.org/about/our-strategic-plan
Josiah Macy Jr. Foundation. (2013). *Conference summary: Transforming patient care: Aligning interprofessional education with clinical practice redesign.* https://macyfoundation.org/publications/aligning-interprofessional-education
Jost, T. S. (1997). *Regulation of the health professions.* Health Administration Press.
Kohn, L. T., Corrigan, J. M., & Donaldson, M. S. (Eds.). (2000). *To err is human: Building a safer health care system.* National Academies Press.
Legal Information Institute. (n.d.). *Supremacy Clause.* https://www.law.cornell.edu/wex/supremacy_clause#:~:text=Article%20VI%2C%20Paragraph%202%20of,laws%2C%20and%20even%20state%20constitutions
Livanos, N. (2016). State board shake-up: Legislative action in the wake of North Carolina Board of Dental Examiners v. Federal Trade Commission. *Journal of Nursing Regulation, 7*(1), 59–62. https://doi.org/10.1016/S21558256(16)31043-2
Loversidge, J. M. (2016a). A call for extending the utility of evidence-based practice: Adapting EBP for health policy impact. *Worldviews on Evidence-Based Nursing, 3*(6), 399–401. https://doi.org/10.1111/wvn.12183
Loversidge, J. M. (2016b). An evidence-informed health policy model: Adapting evidence-based practice for nursing education and regulation. *Journal of Nursing Regulation, 7*(2), 27–33. https://doi.org/10.1016/S2155-8256(16)31075-4
Melnyk, B. M., & Fineout-Overholt, E. (2015). *Evidence-based practice in nursing and healthcare: A guide to best practice* (3rd ed.). Lippincott Williams & Wilkins.
National Council of State Boards of Nursing. (2017). *APRN compact.* https://www.ncsbn.org/aprn-compact.htm
National Council of State Boards of Nursing. (2020a). *About U.S. nursing regulatory bodies.* https://www.ncsbn.org/about-nursing-regulatory-bodies.htm#:~:text=Nursing%20Regulatory%20Bodies%20(NRBs)%20are,the%20regulation%20of%20nursing%20practice.&text=NRBs%20achieve%20this%20mission%20by,issuing%20licenses%20to%20practice%20nursing
National Council of State Boards of Nursing. (2020b). *State response to COVID-19.* https://www.ncsbn.org/State_COVID-19_Response.pdf
National Council of State Boards of Nursing. (2020c). *State response to COVID-19 (APRNs).* https://www.ncsbn.org/APRNState_COVID-19_Response_6_26.pdf
National Council of State Boards of Nursing. (2020d). *NCSBN considers pertinent association business with its members at its 2020 annual meeting.* https://www.ncsbn.org/14928.htm
National Council of State Boards of Nursing. (2020e). *NCSBN's global regulatory atlas.* https://www.regulatoryatlas.com/
National Council of State Boards of Nursing. (2020f). *Next generation NCLEX project.* https://www.ncsbn.org/next-generation-nclex.htm
National Council of State Boards of Nursing. (2020g). *Nurse licensure compact.* https://www.ncsbn.org/nurse-licensure-compact.htm
*North Carolina Board of Dental Examiners v. Federal Trade Commission*, 574 U.S.__(2015). https://www.supremecourt.gov/opinions/14pdf/13-534_19m2.pdf
North Carolina Board of Nursing. (2020). *Homepage.* https://www.ncbon.com//
North Carolina Nurses Association. (2020). *About NCNA.* https://ncnurses.org/about-ncna/about-/ncna/
North Carolina Nursing Practice Act, NC Stat § 90-171.19 – 90-171.49 (1981 & rev. 2019). https://ncleg.gov/EnactedLegislation/Statutes/PDF/BySection/Chapter_90/GS_90-171.21.pdf
North Carolina Office of Administrative Hearings. (2016). *Permanent rulemaking process.* https://files.nc.gov/ncoah/documents/Rules/Rules---Rulemaking-Chart---Permanent-Rule.pdf
O'Sullivan, J., Chaikind, H., Tilson, S., Boulanger, J., & Morgan, P. (2004). *Overview of the Medicare Prescription Drug, Improvement and Modernization Act of 2003.* Congressional Research Service. Order Code RL31966. Washington, DC: Library of Congress.
Panangala, S. V., & Sussman, J. S. (2020). *Full practice authority for VA registered nurse anesthetists (CRNAs) during the COVID-19 pandemic.* Congressional Research Service Report No. IN 11408. https://crsreports.congress.gov/product/pdf/IN/IN11408

Parker v. Brown. 317 U.S. 341. (1943). https://supreme.justia.com/cases/federal/us/317/341//
Perez, K. (2020). *Six major long-term implications for the nation's healthcare system post-COVID-19.* Healthcare Financial Management Association. https://www.hfma.org/topics/financial-sustainability/article/6-major-long-term-implications-for-the-nation-s-healthcare-syste.html
Pew Health Professions Commission. (1994). *State strategies for health care workforce reform.* UCSF Center for Health Professions.
Pollitt, P. (2014). *The history of professional nursing in North Carolina 1902–2002.* Carolina Academic Press.
Roberts, M. J., & Clyde, A. T. (1993). *Your money or your life: The health care crisis explained.* Doubleday.
Russell, K. A. (2012). Nurse practice acts guide and govern nursing practice. *Journal of Nursing Regulation, 3*(3), 36–42. https://doi.org/10.1016/S2155-8256(15)30197-6
Russell, K. A. (2017). Nurse practice acts guide and govern: Update 2017. *Journal of Nursing Regulation, 8*(3), 17–25. https://doi.org/10.1016/S2155-8256(17)30156-4
Safriet, B. K. J. (1992). Health care dollars and regulatory sense: The role of advanced practice nursing. *Yale Journal of Regulation, 9*(2), 419–488. https://digitalcommons.law.yale.edu/yjreg/vol9/iss2/5
Stiff, S. M. (2020). *Congress's power over appropriations: Constitutional and statutory provisions.* Congressional Research Service Report No. R46417.
Stokes, E. K., Zambrano, L. D., Anderson, K. N., Marter, E. P., Raz, K. M., Felix, S. E. B., Tie, Y., & Fullerton, K. E. (2020). Coronavirus disease 2019 case surveillance—United States, January 22–May 30, 2020. *Morbidity and Mortality Weekly Report, 69*(24), 759–765. http://dx.doi.org/10.15585/mmwr.mm6924e2
Stone, R. A. (2020). *Memorandum: CRNA practice during the COVID-19 national emergency.* https://www.aana.com/docs/default-source/fga-aana-com-web-documents-(all)/fpa-eic-memo-april-21-2020d211058aa3a54e9d9886951118017934.pdf?sfvrsn=fb4759a6_0
U.S. Department of Health and Human Services (DHHS). (n.d.). *Read the Affordable Care Act.* https://www.healthcare.gov/where-can-i-read-the-affordable-care-act/
U.S. Department of Health and Human Services (DHHS), Centers for Medicare and Medicaid Services (CMS). (2016, October). *Advanced practice nurses, anesthesiologist assistants, and physician assistants. Medical Learning Network.* ICN901623. https://www.cms.gov/Outreach-and-Education/Medicare-Learning-Network-MLN/MLNProducts/Downloads/Medicare-Information-for-APRNs-AAs-PAs-Booklet-ICN-901623.pdf
Veterans Health Administration. (2020). *Directive No. 1899(2).* https://www.va.gov/vhapublications/publications.cfm?pub=1
World Health Organization. (2020). *WHO timeline—COVID-19.* https://www.who.int/news-room/detail/27-04-2020-who-timeline---covid-19

# Online Resources

National Council of State Boards of Nursing (NCSBN)

- **About U.S. Nursing Regulatory Bodies**: www.ncsbn.org/about-nursing-regulatory-bodies.htm
- **APRN Consensus Implementation Status**: www.ncsbn.org/5397.htm
- **Emergency Response by States and Nurses**: www.ncsbn.org/14508.htm#14523
- **Global Regulatory Atlas**: www.regulatoryatlas.com/
- **Model Acts**: www.ncsbn.org/model-acts.htm
- **Occupational Licensing Reform**: www.ncsbn.org/occupational-licensing-reform.htm
- **University of Minnesota Law School, Federal Administrative Law Research Guide**: https://libguides.law.umn.edu/c.php?g=125807&p=823482

# CHAPTER 8

# Health Policy and Social Program Evaluation

Anne Derouin

## KEY TERMS

**Agency:** An administrative division of the government that provides a particular service. The majority of federal agencies are classified as executive branch agencies. A small number of agencies are not considered part of the executive branch, such as the Library of Congress and the Congressional Budget Office; they are administered directly by Congress and are considered legislative branch agencies. Agencies are largely responsible for policy and program evaluation.

**Evaluation report:** A compilation of the data-driven findings of a program evaluation. Reports are presented in a variety of formats depending on the needs of those requesting the evaluation. Common formats include written reports, oral presentations with multimedia enhancements, films, and videos.

**Health-in-all-policies (HiAP):** Recognizing and evaluating the health effects of non-health policies. A focus of implementation of a culture of health that prioritizes health as a key outcome of policymaking across all levels of government and in the private sector.

**Policy evaluation:** An activity that uses principles and methods to examine the content, implementation, or impact to understand the merit, worth, and utility of a policy.

**Program evaluation design:** A subset of policy design that is often left up to the responsible agency. It is the method selected to collect unbiased data for analysis to determine the extent to which a social program is meeting its designated goals, objectives, and outcomes and to assess the program's merit and worth. Evaluation methods may be qualitative or quantitative.

**Program outcomes evaluation:** Analysis of social programs using a set of guidelines to gain an understanding of how well the policy, program, or intervention is meeting the objectives and goals set forth in the policy's design.

**Chapter 8** Health Policy and Social Program Evaluation

**Quadruple aim:** A framework initially developed by the Institute for Healthcare Improvement for improvements in health system performance that was enhanced in 2014 to highlight four aims of healthcare quality reform efforts: improve quality of patient care, reduce healthcare costs, improve population health status, and maintain or improve job satisfaction among healthcare workers (Bodenheimer & Sinsky, 2014).

**Unintended consequences:** Outcomes of a policy revealed by the evaluation that are not the ones foreseen. These effects can be viewed as either positive ("luck" or a "windfall") or negative ("drawback" or "backfire").

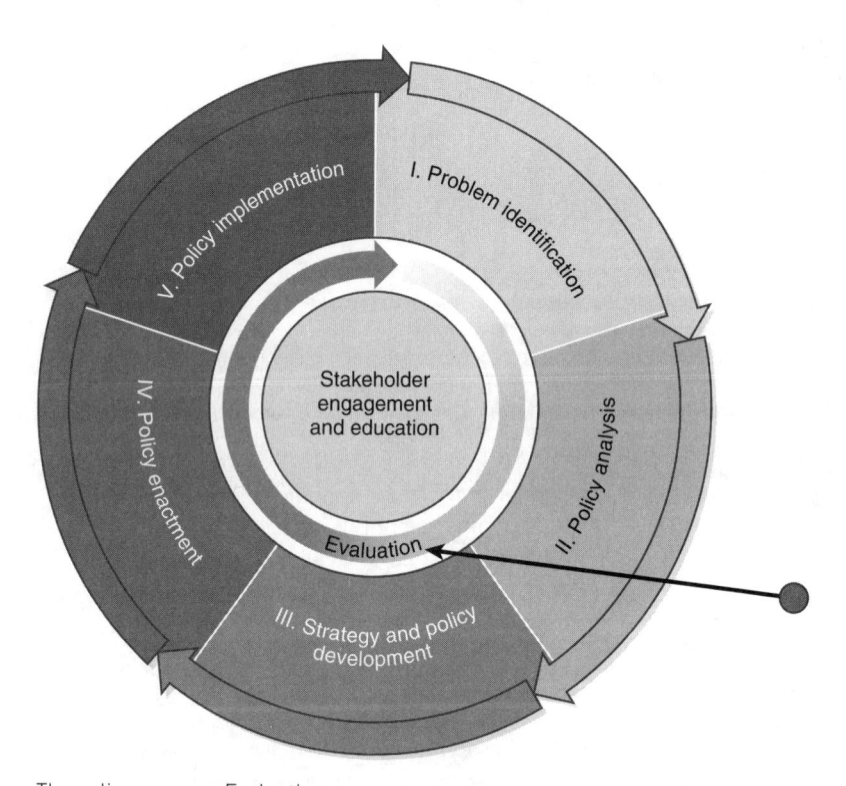

The policy process: Evaluation.

# Introduction

This chapter highlights the process of *evaluation*, a critical step in the effective policy process. Evaluation provides an informed means of feedback, improvement, and justification of expending resources for all health and social programming. Policy or **program outcomes evaluation** systematically investigates social intervention or program effectiveness adapted to the political and organizational environments seeking to inform social action to improve social conditions. Program evaluation can identify ways to improve the quality of the program or innovation, structure it more effectively, and make it more responsive to the needs of its users. Evaluation is important because it informs decision makers about the effectiveness of an intervention (i.e., whether a program is successful), monitors sustainability, and guides future improvements. Evaluation is an invaluable learning tool, with the outcome data often serving as a catalyst for innovation. The James Irvine Foundation notes that evaluation processes are most effective when seen as a complement to a policy's or program's ongoing planning, design, and implementation rather than an external process. Evaluation is a learning process, enabling a creative means of documenting progress, successes, and challenges (Racial Equity Tools [RET], n.d.).

The role of evaluation has become increasingly valuable as federal, state, and local policymakers recognize that nearly every decision and program ultimately affects the health and well-being of populations (Rigby & Hatch, 2016). There is recognition that the physical environments in which people live, work, learn, and play have a tremendous impact on their health outcomes. Reshaping people's economic, physical, social, and service environments can help promote healthy lifestyles and enhance behaviors that reduce risks. Unfortunately, healthcare providers and public health agencies rarely have the mandate, authority, or organizational capacity to make these social and environmental changes. **Health-in-all policies (HiAP)**, an approach to policymaking, acknowledges that social programs such as income, urban development, housing, food distribution, education, water, air quality, energy management, and communication and transportation resources are ultimately linked to the health outcomes of a population. HiAP is a collaborative approach to improving the health of all people by incorporating health considerations into decision making across all sectors and all policy considerations. A HiAP approach to social program evaluation may well be an effective tool to identify gaps and provide evidence that ultimately promotes health equity among historically marginalized populations (Centers for Disease Control and Prevention [CDC], 2016).

Regardless of practice setting, expertise, and level of education, nurses are exceptionally poised to participate in or lead program evaluation. One of the foundations of providing safe and effective professional care is nurses' ongoing *outcome evaluation* based on their assessment, planning, and application of clinical interventions, procedures, or clinical practices. Just as patient-outcome evaluation is essential to effective clinical care, programs rely on outcome evaluation to determine effectiveness, efficiency, and quality. Similar to the nursing process, a systematic evaluation process is useful for program outcomes evaluation (also referred to as simply **policy evaluation** in this chapter) on a larger, more complex scale. Evaluation assesses outcomes, value, and quality and helps to identify potential future investments or innovations that may establish and sustain optimal population outcomes (CDC, 2012). Social policy and program evaluation relies on collecting continuous measurements and data points in a cyclical manner (similar to the nursing process) to ensure ongoing qualitative and quantitative programming, to consider innovation, and to engage key stakeholders.

Two themes of policy design/planning, implementation, and evaluation have been evident over the past decade: (1) a call for professional nurses to practice at their full scope while demonstrating leadership among interprofessional healthcare delivery teams and (2) actively pursuing practices that demonstrate high quality, improved efficiency, and positive patient and organizational outcomes while holding costs steady. A notable theme is remedying health and healthcare disparities as well as inequitable health outcomes among populations. Disparity in health outcomes among different U.S. populations and the implications of historic social policies have been illuminated through evidence-based evaluation. Data show disparities in access to health care; disproportional rates of chronic diseases, such as heart disease and diabetes; higher infant mortality rates; and lower life expectancy among various populations across the nation, within states, and even between neighborhoods, ZIP codes, or even Metro stops. Two examples of evaluation that reveal disparate health are the CDC's health statistics for people living in the 500 most populated U.S. cities between 2016 and 2019 based on age, race, and location (CDC, December 2020) and *Healthy People 2030*, which highlights health disparities based on gender, race or ethnicity, sexual identity, age, disability, socioeconomic status, and geographic locations (HealthyPeople.gov, 2020). By demonstrating disparities present in metropolitan locations like Washington, DC, and New York City through the use of geo-mapping tools, electronic medical records, and community-focused databases, nurses, researchers, policymakers, and other stakeholders can consider social programming and outcome evaluation when constructing health system and community-based programs. Professional nurses have a vital role in addressing each of these themes.

Nurses also have an ethical role in the evaluation of social program outcomes. The American Nurses Association (ANA) updated its *Code of Ethics* in 2015, emphasizing that the professional nurse is "responsible for . . . shaping and reshaping health care in our nation, specifically in areas of health care policy and legislation that affect accessibility, quality, and the cost of health care" (Fowler, 2015). Thoughtful evaluation is a critical step for reshaping the U.S. healthcare system, helping all stakeholders understand the true impact of each effort for improvement while helping direct and define their goals for the future. Nurses have a key role in social policy development and evaluation as the "most trusted" and the largest segment of the healthcare workforce (ANA, 2020). Evaluation is critical to assessing the impact of emerging innovations, social policies, and emerging scientific discovery (Polit & Beck, 2020).

## Evaluation Processes

The process of evaluating health policy and programs may be instituted informally or formally. In small clinical settings such as private practices and rural health centers with limited resources, internal policies and programming occasionally will be evaluated informally through word of mouth, in conversation among a small group, by sharing opinions and experiences through social media, or during in-person team meetings or debriefings. As one might imagine, informal evaluation may actually be gossip or hearsay: the data can be skewed, disjointed, and inaccurate, making any improvement process effort ineffective.

In contrast, formal evaluation processes, termed **program evaluation design**, rely on standardized strategic evaluation processes that ensure that all stakeholders are involved in planning for evaluation prior to implementation of a policy change or programming. Andersen et al. (2009) note that formal evaluation is the appropriate stage after policy implementation to assess effectiveness in terms of accomplishing goals and objectives. They recommend designing evaluation of both short- and long-term outcomes of implementation, including an explanation of how the data relative to healthcare policy will be collected, and providing clear plans for how the results will be disseminated to stakeholders.

Evaluation processes are considered either formative or summative in nature. *Formative evaluations* assist program developers and stakeholders in understanding the progress throughout the development of a program, addressing **unintended consequences** and providing opportunities for improvements or enhancements in the program or policy. Summative evaluation occurs at the end of a program (summing up the data) and seeks to determine the extent to which goals of the project, program, or policy were achieved. Both types of evaluation are critical in assessing healthcare policies, providing invaluable data for nurses to understand the outcomes and implications and to consider future actions.

The evaluation process systematically reveals resource utilization, the achievement of predetermined goals and objectives of a program, and assists in determining how human services policies and programs are solving the social problems that they were designed to alleviate (Westat, 2010). Following a standard set of guidelines or a framework, program evaluation aims to provide critical information that assists in making accurate and well-informed judgments about a program, service, policy, organization, or practice (CDC, 2011). **Table 8-1** highlights the overarching benefits of evaluation.

To promote a national standardized framework for evaluation of healthcare policies, the CDC (2012) designed a theoretical model, or "map," for evaluating the effectiveness of healthcare policies and programs. **Figure 8-1** provides a five-step framework that nurses, healthcare team members, economists, politicians, scientists, and administrators can use in strategically planning processes for collecting and utilizing evaluation data throughout the entire policy or program development process in an effort to ensure that new policies are feasible, useful, accurate, and effective.

This CDC framework offers practical guidelines for planning, implementing, and disseminating evaluation results. It highlights the value of evaluation in the context of the entire policy process as a means to promote effective changes

**Table 8-1** Benefits of Policy and Program Evaluation

| Assess effectiveness (short- and long-term performance measurements). | Assess achievement of goals/aims (accountability measures). | Assess efficiency (cost–benefit relationship). | Determine impact (unintended consequences). | Establish future improvements and goals. |
|---|---|---|---|---|

**Figure 8-1** CDC framework for evaluation in public health.

Centers for Disease Control and Prevention. (2017). A framework for program evaluation. https://www.cdc.gov/eval/framework/

and improvements to health care and society. Within the framework, three main types of evaluation can be systematically performed: (1) policy content (clearly articulated goals, implementation, and evaluation plans of the policy), (2) the implementation of the policy (was the policy implemented as planned?), and (3) the outcome of the policy (did the policy produce the intended outcomes or impact?).

## Steps in the Evaluation Framework

The first step of the evaluation framework begins as the program or policy is being planned. During this step, discussions are held with key stakeholders to determine their interest and degree of buy-in on the development of the proposed policy. Program/policy planners also establish goals and preliminary objectives, build momentum, and set implementation and evaluation timelines.

Step 2 of the framework is the development of a formalized process that involves identifying the person(s) responsible for each part of the process, choosing which qualitative and quantitative data will be collected (and by whom), and selecting the increments of time for collecting information. In step 3, the data are gathered using the determined format and analyzed to reach a conclusion. In step 4, the evaluator considers, often through statistical analyses, the extent of the success of the policy or programs in attaining the objectives and goals.

Step 5 involves formally sharing the evaluation results, conclusions from the findings, and "lessons learned" with stakeholders via an **evaluation report**, a formalized document that highlights the evaluation methods and results. The dissemination of this report is the last step in the CDC framework, and it leads to planning for the next consequential cycle of policy/program evaluation. Typically, an evaluation report provides results based on the data collected, highlights the key finding following implementation of the project, and calls attention to the objectives of the healthcare policy or program that were achieved (if the policy reached its outcomes) and next steps for improvement and sustainability.

The CDC framework for evaluation in public health is an example of a process evaluation cycle that can be continually repeated to analyze outcomes, assess program/policy effectiveness, and plan for improvement and adaptations. At the federal level, oversight and evaluation of policies/programs occurs in the executive agencies and in the General Accounting Office, which has mandated reporting guidelines.

The process evaluation framework will reveal problems or unintended effects of a policy or program. When evaluating an untoward effect, such as an unplanned budget deficit or lack of engagement with the intended population, a rapid-cycle quality improvement (RCQI) evaluation process can be employed. Rather than occurring at planned intervals of evaluation, such as a semi-annual or annual report, the RCQI is useful at the time of a problem's discovery, to evaluate and plan resolution of an untoward outcome or unintended consequence. The RCQI does not replace the standard outcome evaluation or routine budgetary reporting (summative evaluation), but rather would be completed in addition to the standard cycle to address a specific concern (formative evaluation).

Formal evaluations of accredited agencies help assure the public of the reliability and trustworthiness of an **agency**. These evaluations often occur at predetermined intervals (e.g., quarterly, end of fiscal year, end of calendar year) to help determine achievement and provide evidence of value. RCQI program evaluation helps discover causes of problems and address any "unexpected effects that resulted from politics surrounding a policy or the development and implementation of a policy" (Porche, 2012, p. 3). RCQI can occur at any time during a program and often is used to evaluate progress following the launch of a program or during a pilot period. The process is useful for aligning, or realigning, program resources and reiterating the long-term outcome goals for stakeholders. Both types of evaluation are valuable in building successful social programs that influence health outcomes.

## Implications of Evaluation for Health and Healthcare Improvements

Both formative and summative evaluations have provided valuable data for planning and implementing policies that affect environments and the health outcomes of populations. This has been particularly true during the COVID-19 pandemic when both federal and state policy evaluations included cost–benefit analyses of healthcare delivery systems and policy strategies used to prevent the spread of the novel coronavirus in communities. Monitoring health status on a national scale as well as within each state and county became an important aspect of evaluation and analysis, incorporating the expertise of policy stakeholders; financial experts at the federal, state, and local levels; infectious disease experts; public health officials; healthcare providers; those directing large systems of care; private and public insurers; and members of the general public. Professional nurses engaged in the evaluation process, advocating for healthcare cost transparency, personal protective equipment (PPE) for healthcare providers and the community, patient education regarding enrollment in subsidized health insurance plans, and in the dissemination of accurate results. Many professional nursing organizations, including the American Nurses Association (ANA), the National League of Nursing (NLN), the American Association of Colleges of Nurses (AACN), and the American Association of Nurse Practitioners (AANP), were called upon to provide data relevant to resources, safety and well-being of professional practice, and nursing education. These groups were also asked to assist with ongoing data collection and dissemination of evaluation data through professional communication networks to patients, to interprofessional team members, and to other stakeholders.

Both formal and informal evaluations continued to be part of the national, state, and local jurisdictions as the pandemic unfolded. Program evaluation and policy analysis were integrated into each healthcare innovation and social policy that emerged. An example of innovation was the increased use of telehealth to provide healthcare services to people with chronic conditions; telehealth became a mainstay of clinical care during the pandemic. Federal and state agencies as well as insurers used formative evaluation to evaluate the new approach to healthcare delivery, as well as policy analysis to consider value, benefits, and health outcomes as the rapid change occurred. Due to the unprecedented opportunity to use digital communication during the pandemic, telehealth became a case of clinical practice preceding policy. Because the formative evaluation data of telehealth demonstrates the **quadruple aim** goals of patient and provider satisfaction as well as effective healthcare outcomes and cost-effectiveness, telehealth is likely to continue in the future, especially in mental health settings. Formative evaluation will be appropriate to measure the success of incremental change, such as the changes made to support telehealth, in federal and state policies. Other health outcome data collected during the pandemic, such as immunization rates among children, number of prenatal health visits, birthing class attendance, and delayed recommended cancer screenings will also be analyzed. The evaluation data will be paramount in understanding the implications of the disruption in national preventive guidelines and programs during the pandemic.

Summative evaluation of responses to innovations and social programming that emerged during the pandemic will likely influence future social policies and healthcare delivery efforts. Public health officials and policymakers will utilize data that will emerge following the global pandemic to plan for safeguarding the supply chain for PPE, emergency medical devices, and the distribution of vaccines. Social policies to address public housing and educational resources to meet the needs of young children and families, strategies to address food deserts across the nation, and technology networks designed to ensure that rural communities are digitally connected to emergency healthcare resources will result from summative evaluations in the pandemic aftermath. Additionally, both formative and summative evaluation will provide data to address racial inequities in healthcare among communities at both the state and federal levels.

Health equity among white and nonwhite populations has been brought to the forefront during the pandemic, a result of evaluation data demonstrating higher rates of death and disability among Blacks, immigrants, and people of color compared to Caucasians. As this book went to press, observed health disparities during the pandemic have been attributed to frontline workers' increased COVID positivity, decreased rates of health insurance related to unemployment, and fewer visits to healthcare providers (often due to lack of transportation or resources, among other reasons). Data emerging from health and social outcome evaluation reports suggest that one result may be a more diverse healthcare workforce that is determined to alleviate systemic structures that contributed to the disparate outcomes of this era.

# Challenges to Effective Policy and Program Evaluation

Effective health policy and social program evaluation is a "team sport" that relies on skilled and engaged leadership, and members who collaborate to both deliver and evaluate a program or policy. Having a committed and knowledgeable point person, or champion, who is familiar with the goals, implementation plan, and analysis strategy is vital to ensuring that evaluation is completed and that the results are communicated to stakeholders in a meaningful manner. Nurses are poised to serve as champions of a program/project or policy given their key role as the "hub" among healthcare delivery teams and their "most trusted professional" status among laypeople. A skilled statistician who is committed to ethical and accurate data analysis is also paramount to successful evaluation and a vital member of any project or policy planning team. Troubleshooting effective program evaluation is accomplished by using a thoughtful design that relies on well-established, consistent indicators (i.e., data points) and the provision of resources to support accurate data collection, analysis, and dissemination of results. Evaluation methods and data points should be determined prior to program implementation and include agreed-upon time increments for data collection, analysis, and reporting. Scheduling team meetings, setting target dates for data collection and evaluation, and planning for dissemination of the analysis results ensures that key stakeholders have vital information to direct policy and plan adaptations of resources related to a project.

Conditions of program or policy evaluation that may be beyond the control of the evaluators include the pace (rapid or delayed) of policy changes, executive branch pressure for expedient production of evaluation results, and public scrutiny of the results. Some stakeholders may be dissatisfied with the data collection or analysis methods, believe the results are politically tainted, or request further data collection, analysis, or explanation of the findings. Other external factors influencing evaluation results include economic conditions of the affected communities or systems, public awareness of the policy or program, social media, and political campaigns. Lack of a comparable community, agency, or environmental condition may make specific policy evaluation results difficult to interpret or to plan interventions. Finally, as novel healthcare innovations and policies emerge for evaluation, comparative data results often are lacking, making it difficult to understand the long-term impacts. **Figure 8-2** summarizes the challenges that policy evaluators may face.

- Lack of resources to complete the evaluation
- Lack of a champion
- Lack of stakeholder collaboration/buy-in
- Lack of comparative results
- Rapid pace of policy/program evolution
- Demands for early (preliminary) results
- Request for further evaluation and details
- Social media, public opinion, and campaigning

**Figure 8-2** Challenges for policy evaluation.

## Health-in-All-Policies and Community Engagement

Systematic health program and social policy evaluation has demonstrated health disparities among a number of populations across the United States. The CDC and other national entities have highlighted disparities in disease morbidity, infant mortality, and life expectancy nationally, within states, and even within neighborhoods. Several reports are available that showcase and provide background for decision making. The AHRQ's annual *National Healthcare Quality and Disparities Report* presents trends for measures related to access to care, affordable care, care coordination, effective treatment, healthy living, patient safety, and person-centered care. The annual report presents, in chart form, the latest available findings on quality of and access to health care, as well as disparities related to race and ethnicity, income, and other social determinants of health. Although the report does not provide analysis or evaluation of a single policy or social program, trends can inform policymakers whether goals are being met (AHRQ, n.d.).

Healthy People is a second national effort that sets goals and objectives to improve the health and well-being of people in the United States. *Healthy People 2030* is the fifth edition of the Healthy People program. Using evaluation data from of the past four decades, the nation is challenged to address health disparities based on gender, race or ethnicity, sexual identity, age, disability, socioeconomic status, and geographic locations (HealthyPeople.gov, n.d.).

A third national evaluative program is enumerated in the Affordable Care Act and requires all nonprofit hospitals to complete a community health needs assessment (CHNA) process every 3 years (**Figure 8-3**). Although CHNAs are a recent requirement, community health assessments (CHAs) have long been used by hospitals, public health departments, and other social service agencies to identify key community health concerns. The two terms, CHNA and CHA, are used synonymously. A CHA/CHNA is a systematic process involving the community to identify and analyze community health needs and assets, prioritize those needs, and then implement a plan to address significant unmet needs. Upon completing the assessment, hospitals develop implementation strategies to address the significant community health needs identified in the CHA/CHNA. For an example of a CHA see the Spotlight on Yellowstone County, Montana.

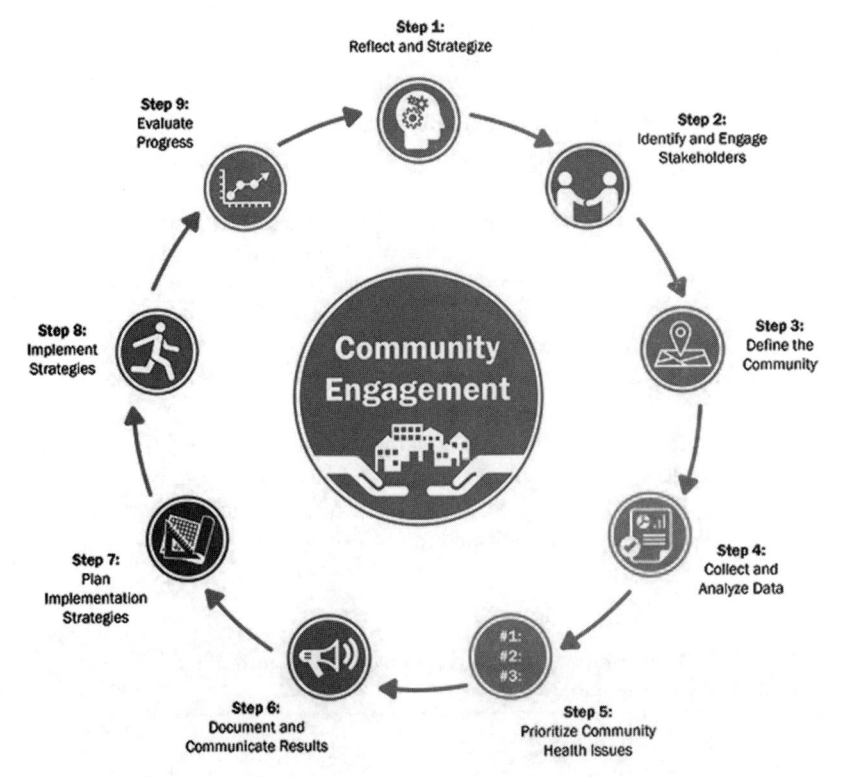

*Challenges to Effective Policy and Program Evaluation* **187**

**Figure 8-3** Community health assessment process (CHAP).
Reproduced from Association for Community Health Improvement. (2017). Community Health Assessment Toolkit. www.healthycommunities.org/assesstoolkit

Having learned from the evaluation of past policies, an example of HiAP planning is the ongoing state and federal legislative discussions around paid parental leave. For the purposes of this book and this example of HiAP, we may use the terms "maternity and paternity leave" as a proxy for "parental leave," because that is the focus of legislators at this time. Evidence shows that paid paternal leave benefits infant growth and development, diminishes harm reduction, promotes parental mental health, and enhances marital and family long-term relationships. The World Health Organization (WHO) recommends a minimum of 16 weeks of leave for new parents; however, most American fathers, both biological and adoptive, take only 10 days or less to bond with newborns before returning to work (Petts et al., 2020). The United States is the only industrialized nation that does not offer paid parental leave (Eichner, 2010).

Despite the evidence supporting parental leave benefits outlined by health professionals, social scientists, and policy experts for federal policy, the Family Medical Leave Act of 1993[1] (unpaid leave) is currently the only mandate

---

1 The FMLA defines "parents" as biological, adoptive, step-, or foster parent who stood in loco parentis (in the place of a parent). The law includes same-sex parents. Parents do not include parents-in-law.

parents may use for protection of a job while taking leave. Maternity leave is regulated by labor and disability laws. The FMLA requires 12 weeks of unpaid leave annually for mothers of newborn or newly adopted children if they work for a company with 50 or more employees. The FMLA requires a physician to signify that the employee meets the eligibility conditions of the Act. Studies show the current laws disproportionately impact minorities and low-income women, who are less likely to take unpaid leave. Many U.S. employers voluntarily offer paid or unpaid maternity leave of varying lengths, which guarantees job protection; however, new parents who work for employers with fewer than 50 employees may not be offered the benefit and are not covered by FMLA. Though several states have adopted laws extending the FMLA requirements to smaller companies, the lack of a national policy supporting paid parental leave means that American fathers and domestic partners are the least likely to take leave from work or receive financial support compared to new fathers globally (Livingston & Thomas, 2019). Legislation that establishes protection for the work release of *both* parents (biological, adoptive, or domestic partners), not just the mother, should be established in the United States.

**Spotlight:** Yellowstone County, Montana, 2020 Community Health Needs Assessment

This 120-page report provides a snapshot of the actual and perceived health of the populations living in Yellowstone County, Montana. Readers are invited to review the report at www.billingsclinic.com/app/files/public/4109/2019-2020-Community-Needs-Health-Assesment-Report.pdf.

The assessment was informed by public focus group input as well as traditional data collection. The Areas of Opportunity determined in the report include consideration of various criteria: standing in comparison with benchmark data (particularly national data); identified trends; the preponderance of significant findings within topic areas; the magnitude of the issue in terms of the number of persons affected; and the potential health impact of a given issue. These also take into account those issues of greatest concern to the community stakeholders (key informants) giving input to this process.

To date, five states (including Washington, DC) have used evaluation data to enact paternity laws (National Conference of State Legislatures, 2017); several large corporations, such as Walmart and Amazon, have adopted paternity/domestic partner leave as company policy to enhance health benefits, establish equity for fathers, and support family well-being. The call for federal legislation regarding paternity leave will likely evolve in the near future as workforce demographics, scientific evidence, and the demographics of political leaders change. It is likely that the evaluation data from states and the analysis of organizations that have adopted paternity leave will provide evaluation data to assist with national policy adoption of paternity leave.

## Using Resources

When designing and implementing policies or programs designed to improve the health of populations and communities, professional nurses must adopt strategies to minimize the challenges to evaluation. Resources are available to guide effective evaluation and offer solutions to common challenges. When reading evaluation results and reports, carefully consider the following questions:

- Were the data strategically collected, analyzed, and disseminated by a reliable research team?
- Is the report complete?
- What bias might be present?
- Is this program or policy achieving the objectives and goals for which it was designed?

## Ethical Considerations

Ethical issues represent another set of challenges relevant to policy and program evaluation. The COVID-19 vaccine distribution plan is an example of an ethical dilemma faced by policymakers, researchers, advocates, and healthcare providers, both during the development process and following vaccine approval. Ethical debates encompassed the questions on who would receive the vaccine first, if it would be required or optional for healthcare providers, and how it would be distributed in the United States and shared globally. The priority of those "next in line" required consideration of equity, beneficence, and autonomy.

Many professional organizations have published ethical guidelines to help avoid conflicts of interest and ethical dilemmas during evaluation processes, including the American Psychological Association (2010), the American Counseling Association (2014), and the American Evaluation Association (2018). The CDC (2020) also offers guidelines to program and policy evaluators that include a brief review of principles and accompanying questions that professional nurses can ask themselves when faced with an ethical challenge. Principles addressed by so many professional organizations highlight both the risks and importance of ethical considerations related to healthcare programming and policy. The overarching themes of each guideline include two key ethical principles: (1) healthcare policy and programming should benefit people while avoiding harm and (2) application and evaluation of programs should be fair and respectful.

These themes of beneficence, safety (nonmaleficence), autonomy, and justice resonate with nursing professionals, as documented in the ANA's *Code of Ethics* (2015). Of the nine provisions in the code, the three highlighted in **Table 8-2** directly relate to the ethical principles of health policy and social program evaluation.

**Table 8-2** ANA Code of Ethics: Provisions and Applications to Policy and Program Evaluation

| Code of Ethics Provision | Application to Policy and Program Evaluation |
|---|---|
| Provision 1: Respect for human dignity | ■ Risks of implementing evaluation methods can include disruption to patients' lives (sacrificing time to answer questions, travel time, lost wages), emotional distress, safety concerns, and social harm.<br>■ Rules for informed consent are adhered to. Participants are clearly and sufficiently informed that an evaluation is taking place; know who will access the data; know how the data will be stored, shared, and safeguarded; know what the evaluation data will be used for; know whether the results will be accessible to them for review; and are offered the option to refuse. |
| Provision 3: Promote and advocate for and protect the rights, health, and safety of patients, individuals, family units, systems, or a community | ■ Identifies standardized nursing policies requiring ongoing evaluation.<br>■ Addresses protection of patients, including sharing data inappropriately, suggesting positive or negative program outcomes without evidence, offering opinions rather than analysis and facts, negating or promoting program outcomes prior to analyzing evaluation results, and failing to protect the identity of all stakeholders. |
| Provision 7: Advancement of the profession through research, scholarly inquiry, professional standards development, and the generation of nursing and health policy | ■ A nurse may be both healthcare provider and program administrator and face an ethical conflict if also serving as the evaluator.<br>■ A policy or program requiring intense personal investment to develop has the risk of evaluation and dissemination of results being skewed, enhanced, or altered.<br>■ Establish clear, but separate, roles for the social program administrator and the evaluator.<br>■ Establish clear evaluation protocols to determine which objective (rather than subjective) data will be collected.<br>■ Complete a standardized evaluation analysis to avoid conflicts. |

ANA Code of Ethics. (2015). Provisions and applications to policy and program evaluation.

Avoiding ethical conflicts that threaten the safe implementation of programs or policies is a paramount concern, highlighting the importance of good policy design, planning, and thoughtful preparation throughout all phases of an evaluation. Strategic efforts to ensure clear delineation of roles (who will be communicating and the key responsibilities of team members) and concrete evaluation objectives (what will be communicated) related to program/policy evaluation enhance teamwork and provide structure for implementation, analysis, and dissemination of the data. Sharing results to various stakeholders using culturally appropriate, nonbiased terminology or medical jargon reduces confusion and enables interdisciplinary professionals, patients, families, and policymakers to readily interpret the data accurately. Straightforward communication also increases the likelihood of accurate and effective information shared via media outlets to community stakeholders.

The U.S. federal, state, and local political environments and the expanse of social programs are complex. Social programs tend to engage stakeholders who range from savvy political and social leaders to healthcare workers, staff, and program recipients—and each of these parties benefits from a clear understanding of how the evaluation plan and resulting data will reflect their efforts and influence the future of a social policy or program.

Clarke (1999) suggested five strategies that can improve communication, enhance engagement, and reduce ethical risks during program evaluation:

1. Identify specific cultural, political, and social environmental factors to address critical aspects of program evaluation.
2. Identify stakeholders and ensure that objectives and goals of the project are established and communicated routinely and consistently to all.
3. Recognize the potential for conflicts among stakeholders and diplomatically address any contentious issues promptly.
4. Involve multiple stakeholders throughout the project planning, design, implementation, and dissemination of results.
5. Routinely communicate the progress of the project as it evolves through the implementation and evaluation cycles.

Professional nurses are familiar with these tenets when collaborating in patient care among intra- and interprofessional team members in clinical or academic environments. These strategies, in combination with the use of healthcare program and policy evaluation theories and the application of professional ethical guidelines, have helped elevate the value and impact of improvement efforts and outcome reporting while also diminishing ethical dilemmas.

## Conclusion

Evaluation is a critical component of all policy and social programs, providing data, commentary, and critical evidence for ongoing improvement, enhancement, and effectiveness. Critical to responsible program development, evaluation assists policymakers, administrators, clinicians, financial stakeholders, and the general public to understand successful outcomes, opportunities for improvement, and potential innovations to promote the health and well-being of individuals, populations, and communities. Participation of nurses in all aspects of healthcare policy and programming evaluation—planning, implementing, collecting data, and disseminating results—is vital. As the largest component of the healthcare workforce, nurses possess critical insights related to application and outcomes of policies and programs. The importance of active engagement among nurses in policy and programming cannot be overemphasized.

When embracing the health-in-all-policies mentality, professional nurses utilize their critical thinking and expert communications skills to consider the benefits of all programs and public policies. Similar to the delivery of effective patient care in clinical settings, nurses engaged in program and policy evaluation use planning, delivery, and assessment skills to determine the effectiveness any new public policy or innovative community health program. As the evidence illuminates the relationship between social programs and policies and the well-being of populations, it is increasingly evident that nurses must be engaged in all aspects of program planning, evaluation, and dissemination of the results. Evaluation is paramount in ongoing health improvement and quality social programming.

Healthcare leaders and innovators use evaluation as a tool to ensure reliability and effectiveness and to generate data for improvement and enhancements. Evaluation is not meant to show weakness, limitations, or vulnerability, but rather to identify areas for improvement. For agencies, it is a team-building exercise, not a daunting or fearsome challenge. Standardized frameworks, theories, and tools are readily available to guide effective quantitative and qualitative program evaluation methods and to ensure that the reported data are reliable and meaningful for all stakeholders. As an essential step in policy and program development, evaluation offers lawmakers, administrators, and program planners a compass for direction in the journey toward a future characterized by improved efficiency, effectiveness, and quality of health outcomes in the United States.

Historically, nurses were underutilized in policy planning and evaluation efforts, but are now increasingly recognized as valuable members of policy and healthcare teams. Poised to participate and lead national, state, and local planning and program evaluations, professional nurses are urged to amplify their voices, expertise, and collective power to influence all levels of healthcare systems and to support a future of positive (and measurable!) change.

## Chapter Discussion Points

1. List the advantages of using a theoretical framework or model to evaluate policy and social or healthcare programs.
2. What does health-in-all-policies imply? What are the implications of health-in-all-policies for professional nurses?

3. Describe the relationship between professional nursing practice and policy evaluation and social programming.
4. Describe the most common challenges to policy and program reporting, and provide strategies to diminish the effects of these challenges.
5. How can ethical conflicts in policy and program evaluation and reporting be avoided or addressed?
6. Describe specific ways in which professional nurses can engage in program and policy evaluation efforts.
7. Identify useful resources available to professional nurses who are planning a healthcare program or innovation.

## CASE STUDY 8-1: Evaluating Clinical Services

A school-based health clinic (SBHC) located in an isolated region of the county has been serving high school students from the school and surrounding community for more than 15 years through financial support from a federal grant, a philanthropic donor, and a regional healthcare system. The advanced practice registered nurse (APRN) working in the clinic has provided services to more than 5,000 clients over the past few years and has collaborated with a number of key stakeholders in the community and education and health professional organizations to promote the benefits of the SBHC. Because of the mandate to use distance-based learning during the COVID-19 pandemic, the donor stopped funding the SBHC. The healthcare system has requested that the APRN "relocate" to another clinical site and provide care via telehealth and has proposed closing the SBHC permanently. Knowing that the students and the local community have ongoing healthcare needs, the school administrative team and parent association president have requested a meeting to discuss the implications of the closure of the clinic.

### Case Study Discussion Questions
1. Who are the key stakeholders the APRN should engage to discuss strategies for program planning?
2. Which evaluation methods and data should the APRN consider sharing with the administrative team at the health system and with policymakers?
3. What ethical considerations and role conflicts might the APRN face?
4. Which communication strategies might the APRN utilize to ensure that an effective message is shared with the stakeholders?
5. Describe the possible unintended consequences (positive and negative) of the evaluation effort.
6. How could the APRNs leverage trustworthiness, influence in the community, and established partnerships to disseminate evaluation data to influence the state policymakers to reinstitute funding for school clinics?

## CASE STUDY 8-2: Walk-in Versus Scheduled Appointments

A state-funded teen clinic has routinely used appointment-only visits for annual health checks and for acute visits involving contraception counseling and treatment and screening for sexually transmitted infections (STIs). The clinic, led by an APRN, serves as a clinical teaching site for health professional students and receives reimbursement for precepting students. Recently, the medical school threatened to withdraw its learners from the clinic because of low patient volume, which has limited the learning experiences of the students. This threat prompted the clinic administrators to evaluate clinic usage. The evaluation led to the discovery that more than half of the appointments scheduled resulted in "no shows." The administrators have decided to change the clinic to a walk-in–only scheduling format and have suggested using social media to promote the clinic's availability.

### Case Study Discussion Questions

1. As the APRN working in the teen clinic, do you agree with this evaluation plan and the analysis to support the decision? Why or why not?
2. Describe a proposal to evaluate the change in scheduling at the clinic. What type of data would it be important to collect as part of the evaluation?
3. Who are the stakeholders in this scenario, and who would be essential to include in the evaluation process?
4. What unintended consequences might arise from the policy change in patient scheduling?
5. Discuss ethical considerations anticipated when changing the clinic's scheduling format and use of social media to promote enrollment.
6. Who would be most appropriate to evaluate the clinic policy, and who would pay for the evaluation?

## References

Agency for Healthcare Research and Quality. (n.d.). *National healthcare quality and disparities reports.* https://www.ahrq.gov/research/findings/nhqrdr/index.html

American Counseling Association. (2014). *ACA code of ethics.* http://www.counseling.org/Resources/aca-code-of-ethics.pdf

American Evaluation Association. (2018). *Guiding principles for evaluators.* https://www.eval.org/About/Guiding-Principles

American Nurses Association. (n.d.). *Code of ethics.* https://www.nursingworld.org/practice-policy/nursing-excellence/ethics/code-of-ethics-for-nurses/

American Nurses Association. (2020, January 6). *ANA president proud of nurses for maintaining #1 spot in Gallup's 2019 most honest and ethical professions poll* [News release]. https://www.nursingworld.org/news/news-releases/2020/american-nurses-association-president-proud-of-nurses-for-maintaining-1-spot--in-gallups-2019-most-honest-and-ethical-professions-poll/

American Psychology Association. (2017). *Ethical principles of psychology and code of conduct.* http://www.apa.org/ethics/code/index.aspx

Andersen, B., Fagerhaug, T., & Beltz, M. (2009). *Root cause analysis and improvement in the healthcare sector: A step-by-step guide.* ASQ Quality Press.

Bodenheimer, T., & Sinsky, C. (2014). From triple to quadruple aim: Care of patient requires care of the providers. *Annals of Family Medicine, 12*(6), 573–476. https://doi.org/10.1270/afm.1713

Centers for Disease Control and Prevention. (2012). *Introduction to program evaluation for public health programs: A self-study guide.* http://www.cdc.gov/eval/guide/CDCEvalManual.pdf

Centers for Disease Control and Prevention. (2016). *Health in all policies.* https://www.cdc.gov/policy/hiap/index.html

Centers for Disease Control and Prevention. (2020). *Evaluation.* https://www.cdc.gov/workplacehealthpromotion/model/evaluation/index.html

Centers for Disease Control and Prevention. (2020, December). *500 Cities Project: 2016-2019.* https://www.cdc.gov/places/about/500-cities-2016-2019/

Clarke, A. (1999). *Evaluation research.* SAGE Publications Ltd. https://www.doi.org/10.4135/9781849209113

Eichner, M. (June 1, 2010). Families, human dignity, and state support for caretaking: Why the United States' failure to ameliorate the work-family conflict is a dereliction of the government's basic responsibilities. *North Carolina Law Review, 88,* 1593–1626.

Folwer, M. (2015). *Guide to the code of ethics for nurses with interpretive statements.* American Nurses Association.

Hasenfeld, Y., Hill, K., & Weaver, D. (n.d.). *A participatory model for evaluating social programs.* The James Irvine Foundation, Los Angeles, CA. https://www.racialequitytools.org/resourcefiles/Eval_Social.pdf

HealthyPeople.gov. (2020). *Disparities.* https://www.healthypeople.gov/2020/about/foundation-health-measures/Disparities

Institute of Medicine. (2010). *Future of nursing: Leading change, advancing health.* https://campaignforaction.org/resource/future-nursing-iom-report/

Livingston, G., & Thomas, D. (2019). *Among 41 countries, only U.S. lacks paid paternal leave.* Pew Research Center. https://www.pewresearch.org/fact-tank/2019/12/16/u-s-lacks-mandated-paid-parental-leave/

National Conference of State Legislatures. (2017). *Paid family leave in the states.* https://www.ncsl.org/research/labor-and-employment/paid-family-leave-in-the-states.aspx

Petts, R. J., Knoester, C., & Waldfogel, J. (2020). Fathers' paternity leave-taking and children's perceptions of father–child relationships in the United States. *Sex Roles, 82,* 173–188. https://doi.org/10.1007/s11199-019-01050-y

Polit, D., & Beck, C. (2020). *Essentials of nursing research: Appraising evidence for nursing practice* (9th ed.). Wolters Kluwer.

Porche, D. (2012). *Health policy: Application for nurses and other healthcare professionals.* Jones & Bartlett Learning.

Racial Equity Tools. (n.d.). *Evaluate.* https://www.racialequitytools.org/resources/evaluate

Rigby, E., & Hatch, M. (2016). Incorporating economic policies into a health-in-all-policies agenda. *Health Affairs, 35*(11), 2044–2052.

Westat, J. F. (2010). *The 2010 user-friendly handbook for project evaluation.* National Science Foundation Directorate for Education & Human Resources, Division of Research, Evaluation, and Communication. National Science Foundation.

# Online Resources

**Academy Health** (www.academyhealth.org): Provides links to health services researchers in health policy and practice and fosters networking among a diverse membership.

**Agency for Healthcare Research and Quality** (www.ahrq.gov): Provides links to multiple resources. The AHRQ's mission is to improve the quality, safety, efficiency, and effectiveness of health care for all Americans.

**American Evaluation Association** (www.eval.org): Free resources for program evaluation and social research methods.

**ANA Code of Ethics** (http://nursingworld.org/DocumentVault/Ethics-1/Code-of-Ethics-for-Nurses.html): The American Nurses Association's code of ethics for nursing practice, including interpretative statements.

**Centers for Disease Control and Prevention, Program Performance and Evaluation Office** (www.cdc.gov/eval/resources/index.htm): Provides links to multiple resources for information or assistance in conducting an evaluation project.

***EducationWeek*** (www.edweek.org/ew/index.html?intc=main-topnav): An online weekly resource that provides commentary on evaluation results and unintended consequences related to federal policy. This resource may be useful to view when considering health-in-all-policies for children, education, and communities.

**Free Management Library** (www.managementhelp.org): Developed by Authenticity Consulting, this site provides extensive online resources for program evaluation and personal, professional, and organization development, including many detailed guidelines, worksheets, and more.

**National Registry of Evidence-Based Programs and Practices** (https://peerta.acf.hhs.gov/content/national-registry-evidence-based-programs-and-practices-nrepp-0): The NREPP is a database that focuses on mental health and substance abuse interventions. It offers a module on how to develop and evaluate a program that is well organized, concise, and easy to read.

**National Science Foundation** (www.nsf.gov/): The NSF is an independent government agency that is responsible for advancing science and engineering. In this role, the NSF has developed multiple tools to use in the evaluation of programs that are applicable to a variety of programs.

**Organisation for Economic Co-operation and Development (OECD)** (www.oe.cd/fdb): An international organization based in France with international partnerships with policy makers, governmental agencies and citizens, that aims to implement, evaluate, and promote evidence-based solutions to a range of social, economic, and environmental challenges that affect health. This site offers global data on employment and health-related policies, healthcare delivery innovations, and economic policies.

**The Practical Playbook** (www.debeaumont.org/programs/practical-playbook/): An evolving library of resources to assist program planning and evaluation for health improvement projects. The site features tools, partnerships, and policies to assist healthcare professionals and the public health workforce. Nurse-led programs are featured on the site, which is updated routinely with emerging programs, evaluation data, and tools.

**Racial Equity Tools** (www.racialequitytools.org): A virtual toolkit that features multiple resources, publications, and tools to address racial equity in health, social, political, and economic programming. Includes a growing library of resources to plan and implement effective evaluation strategies for social programs.

**United Nations World Food Programme** (www.wfp.org): Focuses on the United Nations' food program. The site presents links to 14 modules, providing step-by-step advice on monitoring and evaluation guidelines. A useful resource to review.

# CHAPTER 9

# The Influence of Patient Health Data on Health Policy

Toni Hebda

## KEY TERMS

**Big data:** Very large data sets beyond human capability to analyze or manage without the aid of technology; used to reveal patterns and discover new learning.

**Comparative effectiveness research:** Research that examines the benefits and harms of various methods used to prevent, diagnose, treat, or monitor a health condition or to improve care.

**Crowdsourcing:** A process in which a problem is posed, help solicited, and help offered by an unofficial group of geographically dispersed people.

**Database:** A collection of information organized and used for ease of access, management, and updates.

**Data governance:** A system of policies, people, procedures, and technology for the purpose of data management to ensure that data can be accessed, processed, stored, or transmitted by authorized persons.

**Data science:** The systematic study of digital data.

**Data scientists:** People who specialize in the analysis and interpretation of complex digital data.

**Data set:** Collection of structured data retrievable via a link or index.

**Information blocking:** An intentional effort on the part of vendors and providers to interfere with the electronic exchange of patient health information in an attempt to maintain a competitive advantage.

**Internet of Things (IoT):** Commonplace objects capable of sending and receiving data over the Internet; health care–related examples include wearable devices, biosensors, or other monitoring devices.

**Interoperability:** The ability for information technology or tools to work together to securely exchange and use data and information while retaining a uniform meaning across organizations and regional and national borders. Sometimes referred to as *harmonization* of systems.

**Meaningful Use:** A federal incentive program implemented in 2009 as part of the Health Information Technology for Economic and Clinical Health (HITECH) Act that established requirements for electronic capture and submission of patient information to the Centers for Medicare and Medicaid Services.

**Nurse informaticist:** A registered nurse specialist who uses nursing and other sciences to manage and communicate data, information, knowledge, and wisdom to support nurses, healthcare professionals, consumers, and other stakeholders in decision making.
**Precision medicine:** Treatment customized for the individual on the basis of his or her genetic makeup, environment, and/or lifestyle.
**Predictive analytics:** A facet of data mining that uses extracted data to forecast trends.
**Real-world data (RWD)/real-world evidence (RWE):** Information derived from sources outside of randomized clinical trials that may include electronic health records, disease registries, claims data, data from personal devices and applications, and the Internet of Things.
**Small data:** Data sets of limited size that allow for full evaluation and understanding by analysts.

# Introduction

Over time, we have seen an increased reliance on data to drive decisions in the nation's healthcare system. West (2019) noted that data-driven decisions provide an organized framework for action that eliminates haphazard responses and subjectivity, fosters predictions, and supports the testing of the efficacy of different strategies. Technological advances permit us to collect, store, manipulate, and analyze huge pools of data that can reveal previously unknown patterns to inform us, provide evidence, guide our decisions, and improve outcomes, surpassing traditional research findings. However, the health policy process (see **Figure 9-1**) is only as good as the information and evidence acquired and used

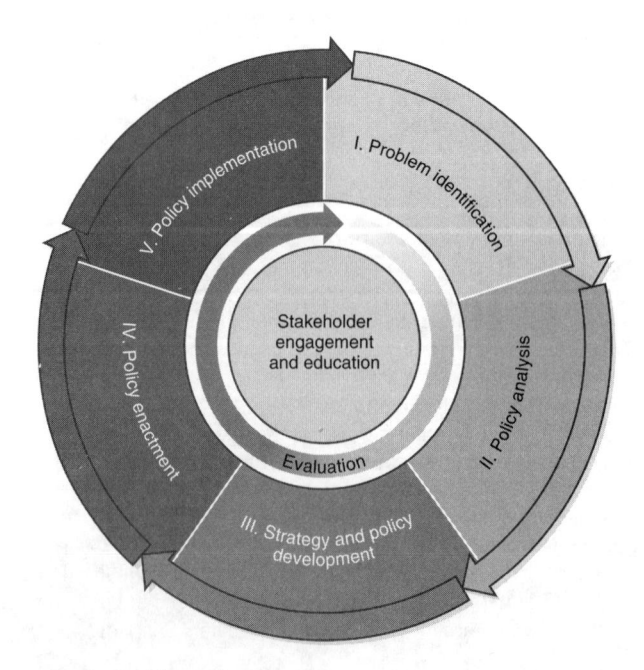

**Figure 9-1** The policy process.

for problem identification, analysis, strategy development, and evaluation. Data capture and usage are equally important in public/community health as they are in acute or other patient-care settings.

Businesses leverage technology daily to collect information on shopper preferences with each use of a customer's preferred-shopper card, completion of a survey, or product registration. This information is then used to improve services, target specific populations, and improve efficiencies. If you can access your bank account through any ATM in the world, why is obtaining, managing, and using health- and healthcare-related data seemingly so hard? For a variety of reasons, the healthcare sector has lagged behind the business world in its collection and use of data to drive decisions. Some of these include, but are not limited to, a resistant culture among health professionals, resource constraints, difficulties in identifying and quantifying measures of success, failure to adequately invest in and make use of the technology, and the cost-prohibitive infrastructure required to support data-driven decisions (see **Figure 9-2**). The healthcare delivery system has begun to embrace some of the same types of tools used by big business in an effort to achieve the same types of benefits. This transformation is being propelled by federal policies and regulations that seek to contain skyrocketing healthcare costs, moving away from the historic fee-for-service model to reimbursement models based on the patient experience and outcomes.

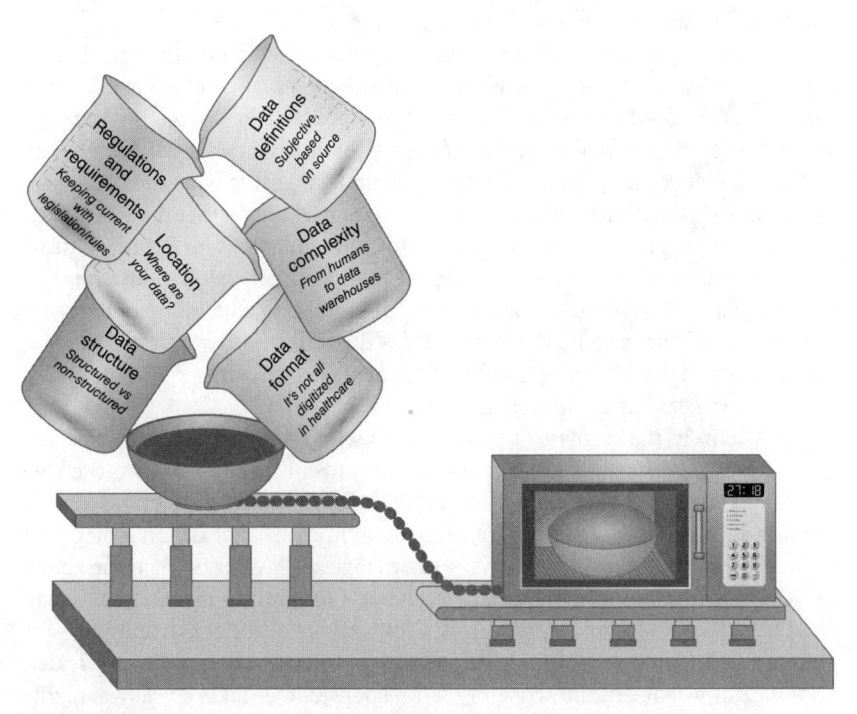

**Figure 9-2** Why healthcare data is difficult.

Strategic management thrives on data, data, and more data to measure progress toward identified goals (Dash et al., 2019; Mennella & Pravikoff, 2018). Given the data-intensive nature of the healthcare industry, Lai et al. (2019) indicate that an increased emphasis on data to support decisions has great potential to effect change. Many sources of data can support the operation of a healthcare delivery system (both the nation's System and smaller hospital/clinic systems) and inform the delivery of patient services. Measuring processes, results, and performance is crucial to an organization's success.

Electronic health records (EHRs) and the data contained within those records represent an important data source. Aggregate data collected through the federal **Meaningful Use** program represents one data set that can be used to drive strategic decisions. The term **data set** refers to structured data that can be retrieved via a link or index (Zhao et al., 2018). Other sources of data include study findings, pharmaceutical "events," clinical databases, diagnostic results, insurance claims data, and data from a growing number of telehealth and point-of-care consumer devices used for health tracking and disease management. In some instances, social media can also be considered a source of data.

However, despite such rich resources, there are many issues that must be resolved, such as standardization of data tools and methods, equal access to EHRs, a hierarchical culture surrounding medical records, the cost of switching from paper to EHRs, guaranteeing privacy, data security, and the human resources needed to fulfill the promise of all that data. Because nurses at the point of care generate and use patient, institutional, and other data for evidence-based practice (EBP), they must be part of those teams that define who, what, where, and how data are collected and used.

Just as healthcare providers have recognized the importance of data to support decisions at a local level, it has also become apparent that data and evidence are needed to inform state and federal policymakers, because data support each step in the policymaking process (Gutenberg et al., 2018; Jose et al., 2017). Challenges for policymakers include understanding what the data mean and how their decisions will affect caregivers, as well as whether their decisions are cost effective and prevention oriented, improve outcomes, detect new threats earlier, better manage chronic disease, move toward **precision medicine**, and improve care across borders (Mählmann, 2017). Having data is key, but it is not the end-all: it must also be the right data, at the right time, where it is needed, and in a format that can be acted upon to support decision makers (Shahmoradi et al., 2017; Thakkar & Gordon, 2019).

Collectively, the vastness of available data sets dwarfs the results from a single study or even a meta-analysis. This capability to collect large data sets (i.e., big data), and to manipulate and analyze those data to discover new knowledge, is exciting and consistent with our transformation from an information society to a knowledge society (Ricaurte, 2016). A knowledge society exists when the ability to create new meanings from data exists, allowing for improvement of the human condition. Nurses are considered knowledge workers. Although definitions vary, one popular definition of *knowledge worker* is a worker who possesses, creates, and uses knowledge in the scope of their responsibilities and typically is highly skilled and heavily reliant upon critical-thinking skills (Surawski, 2019).

The transition to a knowledge society holds great potential to improve health care, but it also requires the development of new skills and responsibilities to realize those advances (Lai et al., 2019). Many leaders in nursing education feel that big data influences how students learn, analyze, and research problems and how policy is or is not developed. In the healthcare realm, nurses can play a pivotal role in developing and using tools and methods associated with big data, and the subsequent knowledge generated, so as to influence health policies that provide for the best use of resources to improve health. This role is consistent with the American Nurses Association's (2015) Social Policy Statement, which informs other health professionals, legislators, other regulators, funding bodies, and the public about nursing's responsibility, accountability, and contribution to health care. Nurse involvement is imperative to ensure that discoveries are useful for nursing.

In an effort to prepare nurses for this role, throughout this chapter we explore issues that have health policy implications and address the following five questions:

1. What is the relationship between data and electronic resources and health care?
2. What is big data, and how does it impact policy and health care?
3. What is the relationship between data and evidence-informed practice?
4. What initiatives have been implemented to support big data?
5. What are the implications of policies related to health information technology for registered nurses, advanced practice registered nurses, and other healthcare professionals?

## Data and Electronic Resources: Their Relationship to Health Care

Healthcare professionals and consumers alike have ready access to a wide variety of electronic resources that serve to expedite access to information and services. **Table 9-1** provides an overview of some types of available resources. A critical consideration for both healthcare professionals and consumers is whether sources provide truly reliable and valid information. Government, academic, and professional organization websites are considered to be good sources, although they are not entirely free of bias. Scrutinizing a website for the sponsoring organization's mission statement, funding sources, and background information on who sits on the board of directors can sometimes reveal political bias. Information with no clear authorship, date of publication or review, or evidence of subject-matter expertise for posted content should be avoided.

## Big Data: Its Significance for Healthcare Delivery and Policy

At the forefront of health information technology, the vision is for high-quality care, lower costs, a healthy population, and engaged people. Health care is a highly political endeavor, and so is health information and the associated

**Table 9-1** Types of Electronic Resources With Some Exemplars

| Type | Exemplar |
|---|---|
| Websites | Professional organizations:<br>　American Nurses Association (www.nursingworld.org)<br>　American Association of Nurse Practitioners (www.aanp.org)<br>　American Medical Association (www.ama-assn.org)<br>　American Association of Medical Colleges (www.aamc.org)<br>　American Association of Colleges of Nursing (www.aacnnursing.org)<br>Government agencies:<br>　U.S. Department of Health and Human Services (www.hhs.gov)<br>　Library of Congress (www.loc.gov)<br>Healthcare-focused organizations and accrediting bodies:<br>　World Health Organization (www.who.int)<br>　American Diabetes Association (www.diabetes.org) (and other disease-specific organizations)<br>　The Joint Commission (www.jointcommission.org) |
| Social media | Social networking: Facebook (www.facebook.com), LinkedIn (www.linkedin.com)<br>Photo sharing: Pinterest (www.pinterest.com), Snapchat (www.snapchat.com), Flickr (www.flickr.com), Instagram (www.instagram.com)<br>Video sharing: YouTube (www.youtube.com), Vimeo (www.vimeo.com), TikTok (www.tiktok.com), Yahoo Video (www.yahoo.com/video), Shutterfly (www.shutterfly.com)<br>Microblogging: Twitter (www.twitter.com), tumblr (www.tumblr.com)<br>Blogging: Network Solutions (www.networksolutions.com, WordPress (www.wordpress,.com), GoDaddy (www.godaddy.com), SquareSpace (www.squarespace.com),<br>Crowdsourcing: CrowdFunding (www.crowdfunding.com), GoFundMe (www.gofundme.com), Indiegogo (www.go.indiegogo.com), Kickstarter Live streaming (www.kickstarter.com): Twitch (www.Twitch.tv), FacebookLive (www.facebook.com/live), Periscope (www.periscope.com), YouTube Live (www.youtube.com/live), Wowza (www.wowza.com) |
| Search engines (in order of volume of users) | Google (www.google.com)<br>Bing (www.bing.com)<br>Yahoo (www.yahoo.com)<br>Baidu (www.baidu.com)<br>Yandex (www.yandex.com)<br>DuckDuckGo (www.duckduckgo.com)<br>Sogou (www.sogou.com)<br>Ecosia (www.ecosia.org) |

# Big Data: Its Significance for Healthcare Delivery and Policy

| Type | Exemplar |
|---|---|
| Electronic databases (select examples) | Google Scholar (www.scholar.google.com)<br>Science Direct (www.sciencedirect.com)<br>Scopus (www.scopus.com)<br>PubMed (www.pubmed.ncbi.nlm.nih.gov)<br>Medline (www.nlm.nih.gov/medline/medline_overview.html)<br>CINAHL (www.ebsco.com/products/research-databases/cinahl-database)<br>Ovid (www.ovid.com)<br>U.S. National Library of Medicine: electronic databases and directories by alphabetical listing (www.nlm.nih.gov/services/databases_abc.html) |
| Information systems | Electronic health records (vendors): Epic (www.epic.com/software#PatientEngagement), Cerner (www.cerner.com), CareCloud (www.carecloud.com), NextGen (www.nextgen.com), Athena Health (www.athenahealth.com), GECentricity (www.gehealthcare.com)<br>Clinical support systems<br>Administrative systems |

big data. The literature indicates little agreement on a definition for *big data*, although the National Institute of Standards and Technology (NIST), an entity within the U.S. Department of Commerce, has been working to develop agreement on key concepts associated with big data (NIST, 2019). The term **big data** has been used to refer to very large data sets (Bassan & Harel, 2018; Favaretto et al., 2020; Ienca et al., 2018). Big data comprises different types of data of varying levels of complexity and in different formats (structured and unstructured). It may include processed and unprocessed items from several sources that can be analyzed to reveal patterns, trends, and associations. The healthcare industry defines big data by its size, the ability to make sense of the data, its complexity, and the degree to which the data flow into the organization. Oftentimes, big data is characterized in the literature by the "five Vs": volume, veracity, velocity, variety, and value (NIST, 2019; Witjas-Paalberends et al., 2018):

1. *Volume*: The amount of data or size of the data set.
2. *Veracity*: The accuracy of the data.
3. *Velocity*: The rate of data flow.
4. *Variety*: Data from multiple sources, domains, and types.
5. *Value*: The economic and social wealth that is inherent to any data set.

Big data is beyond human capability to comprehend or manage without the aid of computers. In many cases, it endeavors to encompass entire complex processes. Healthcare professionals and health services researchers manipulate and analyze big data to provide policymakers and thought leaders with vital information.

Examination of big data enables an organization to identify effective processes, eliminate wasteful processes, improve products and services, enhance the customer experience, and establish a competitive advantage. In the healthcare arena, big data provides a tool to benchmark performance against other organizations, improve patient outcomes, and measure innovation, and may point to significant cost-saving opportunities. In this way, big data complements traditional sources of data, such as the data obtained from the trending of vital signs for a single patient or the findings of a study; the latter data are sometimes referred to as **small data** because they can be evaluated and understood by an individual (NIST, 2019).

The ability to use big data as a tool requires an understanding of what it is, what its background and sources are, which surrounding issues are relevant, and how it can be applied to healthcare delivery and policy. Nurse informaticists, health services researchers, and data scientists have special expertise in these areas and can facilitate the collection, analysis, and application of knowledge gleaned from big data. A **nurse informaticist** is a specialist who integrates nursing and additional sciences to "support nurses and healthcare consumers, patients, and other stakeholders in their decision making to achieve desired outcomes through the identification, management, and communication of data, information, knowledge, and wisdom via the use of information structures, processes, and technologies" (American Nurses Association [ANA], 2020). **Data scientists** specialize in the analysis and interpretation of complex digital data; their skill sets include statistics, mastery of data analytics software, knowledge of machine learning, the ability to translate findings into actionable results, and programming and database skills (Meyer, 2019).

Big data has the potential to create value, which may be economic or social, extending beyond healthcare providers and consumers to include businesses, governments, and professional organizations (Vayena et al., 2018). Big data has the potential to support the development of precision medicine, disease prevention, and expand health promotion efforts (Kyriazis et al., 2017). Bush et al. (2019) noted that gaps between research and the application of precision medicine exist; policymakers often determine the value of such applications of new knowledge. Big data also supports tools for improved fraud detection and prevention.

Traditional data sets are collected with an express purpose or objective in mind. This purpose provides direction for which data are collected and in what format and what methods are used to safeguard integrity and security. Traditional data sets can also be used as sources for big data. EHRs and databases are two examples of traditional sources of big data.

EHRs represent one of the best sources of big data in health care today. Organizations commonly use data found in EHRs to track/report metrics such as patient outcomes, length of stay, number of sentinel incidents, nurse hours per patient day, and costs to support research. EHRs may also offer users the opportunity to customize views of patient data for individuals or populations, access clinical decision support (tools that guide healthcare providers' judgments) suggest evidence-based practice guidelines and literature, provide treatment reminders, and use lockout features and alarms. Integration with monitoring devices and point-of-care devices, such as glucometers or urine output, provides additional data streams for EHRs while eliminating the need to manually enter measurements such as vital signs, thereby simultaneously streamlining workflow and improving *data quality*, a term that refers to data attributes of completeness, accuracy, consistency, credibility, timelessness, and consistency. Nurses engaging with the devices that create a flow of data about the patient are positioned to provide strong, useful information and stories to policymakers. Nonclinician thought leaders and policymakers may misunderstand or simply not know the implications of legislation regarding health information technology; they rely upon clinicians to inform them so as to avoid unintentional consequences.

Data may be transmitted in a real-time manner from EHRs directly into databases, saving time, money, and labor and reducing errors in the process. One such example is an electronic disease reporting process called the Digital Bridge Initiative. Local health departments are well-positioned to monitor community health data, flag potential public health threats, and intervene to prevent endemics, pandemics, and epidemics—but the data must be high quality. However, case reporting methods vary significantly across local health jurisdictions, ranging from paper-based to electronic-based reporting from clinicians and hospitals. The Digital Bridge Initiative is a collaboration among the largest healthcare providers, EHR vendors, and public health practice associations in the United States. The initiative's vision is to improve the health of our nation by creating a bidirectional information exchange between health care and public health. Issues for the initiative include privacy and data security (Black et al., 2019). As its first project, the Digital Bridge designed a nationally scalable, multi-jurisdictional approach to electronic case reporting, or eCR, that automated the generation and transmission of case reports from EHRs to public health agencies for review and action.

The realization of large-scale data collection on a real-time basis requires resolution of issues that include, but are not limited to, the ability to exchange and use data and information across different vendor platforms, organizations, and borders while retaining a uniform meaning—a concept known as **interoperability** (Healthcare Information and Management Systems Society [HIMSS], 2020).

A **database** is a collection of information organized and used to provide ease of access, management, and updates to its contents. EHRs fit this basic definition because of their reliance upon database technology to house information, but EHRs' emphasis on their content rather than overall functionality leads most individuals to consider databases to be a separate entity from EHRs. A staggering amount of health-related information now exists in different databases across various settings. One example that is familiar to U.S. healthcare providers and consumers is the Hospital Consumer Assessment of Healthcare Providers and Systems (HCAHPS) survey. HCAHPS collects data on hospitalized patients' perspectives on their care experience (Centers for Medicare and Medicaid Services [CMS], 2020). It has created a national standard that enables comparison across all participating hospitals. HCAHPS scores provide financial incentives in the form of increased or decreased Medicare reimbursement for hospitals to improve the quality of care provided, and the results are available to the public. Notably, hospital reimbursement from the Centers for Medicare and Medicaid Services (CMS) is determined by HCAHPS ranking.

Public and private stakeholders need to do more than just address policies and technical approaches to achieve real, meaningful, seamless interoperability—our culture also needs to change. If the goal of using big data in health care is to improve health (prevent illness), the culture must support and incentivize consumers/patients to easily and securely access their own electronic health information when and where they need it most. Our common goal and culture should be to enable individual health information to be shared with all providers without information blocking. Health professionals must embrace federally recognized, national interoperability standards and policies, so that we are no longer engaged with competing standards, but are instead innovating on a set of core standards.

Other databases collect information about specific diseases, encounter information, and clinical data. Disease registries enable tracking of clinical care and outcomes for specific patient populations, such as those impacted by cancer, heart disease, trauma, infectious diseases, diabetes, asthma, and more recently, the novel human coronavirus and the resulting COVID-19 pandemic (Garavand et al., 2020; Walkey et al., 2020). Input is accepted from multiple sources. The underlying intention in creating such a registry is to minimize fragmentation of care, identify at-risk populations, and improve care through evidence-based practices. Chronic disease registries also support evaluation of providers to ensure that they use current evidence; however, this evaluation may not include data that reflect patient choice and provider judgment.

The Healthcare Cost and Utilization Project (HCUP) maintains encounter-level information on inpatient hospital stays, emergency department visits, and ambulatory surgery in U.S. hospitals. The HCUP databases

**Spotlight:** RN Uses Data to Influence Health Policy

Elizabeth Fildes, EdD, RN, CNE, CARN-AP, PHNA-BC, FIAAN, FAAN, is an internationally known tobacco-control expert. She served 14 years as a director and principal investigator at the University of Nevada School of Medicine, where she developed the Nevada Tobacco Users Helpline and other programs to support nicotine addiction intervention. This comprehensive tobacco-control program led to a nearly 9% decrease in the prevalence of tobacco use between 1997 and 2015. Evidence from similar, successful programs in Massachusetts and California was used to secure more than $4 million to support agencies providing tobacco-control programs. Agencies were also asked to provide data in funding requests. Fildes also worked with the Philippine Secretary of Health in 2012 to start a national quit-line in the Philippines.

In 2015, Fildes began working with U.S. nursing programs to emphasize the role of nurses in comprehensive tobacco control programs at the local, state, national, and international levels. She advocated for the integration of tobacco cessation in the nursing school curriculum and assisted faculty in integrating the content into their courses. As a result of this work, smoking cessation is now included in the health, wellness, and prevention course in undergraduate nursing programs on 21 campuses in as many states and in a large RN-to-BSN program.

are created by the U.S. Department of Health and Human Services' Agency for Healthcare Research and Quality (AHRQ) through a federal–state–industry partnership. An excellent resource of databases and repositories is Health Services Research Information Central, which can be accessed through the HCUP website (www.ahrq.gov/data/hcup/index.html).

The National Patient-Centered Clinical Research Network (PCORnet) supports a repository of clinical data gathered in a variety of healthcare settings, including hospitals, physician offices, and community clinics; health plans; registries; and patient-reported outcomes, for the purpose of conducting **comparative effectiveness research**, a type of research that examines the benefits and harms of various methods used to prevent, diagnose, treat, or monitor a health condition or to improve care. PCORnet collects and stores data in standardized, interoperable formats to facilitate secure sharing designed to ensure confidentiality of the data (Patient-Centered Outcomes Research Institute, n.d.).

Although global digitization makes it easier for healthcare professionals and the public to create, post, and transmit information, currently no mechanism is in place to ensure the accuracy of information available on the Internet. Healthcare professionals recognize the potential to study data gleaned from a variety of electronic resources, including Internet searches, social media, crowdsourcing, mobile applications (apps), and body sensors, and these data may serve as a valuable source of research and knowledge and learning through big data exploration.

The Internet facilitates the creation, collection, sharing, and use of information, but it can also be used to collect research information and big data. An estimated 7.5 billion people will be connected to the Internet by 2030, representing 90% of the global population (Morgan, 2019). Internet searches to find health information to aid healthcare decision making are one common use of this resource by healthcare consumers. Researchers continue to work to determine how consumers choose these websites, how many searches are performed, and which websites are visited (Zhang et al., 2017).

For those who are not connected to a high-speed bandwidth, the digital divide is enormous. Access to personal health records is a daunting issue in the United States, given that the average reading level is at the eighth grade. The Program for the International Assessment of Adult Competencies (PIAAC) was developed by the Organisation for Economic Cooperation and Development (OECD) to determine the ability of adults to successfully participate in 21st-century society and the global economy. One part of the PIAAC measures an adult's ability to use computer technology in solving problems. Nurses must recognize that adults who are not digitally literate are, on average, less educated, older, and more likely to be Black, Hispanic, or foreign born, compared to digitally literate adults. Compared to digitally literate adults, adults who are not digitally literate have a lower rate of labor force participation and tend to work in lower-skilled jobs. Compared to adults internationally, a smaller proportion of U.S. adults are not digitally literate; about 16% of U.S. adults are not digitally literate, compared to 23% of adults internationally (Mamedova, 2018).

In excess of 325,000 mobile apps now exist to track health-related information (Wagner, 2020). Real-time data streams from fitness tracking apps and sensors, particularly when combined with Twitter data, might be mined to provide early warnings of emergency situations, adverse drug reactions or drug misuse, disease outbreaks, and the development of chronic disease issues. These kinds of apps may allow public health officials, healthcare delivery systems, and individual nurses to better prepare for these events, assuming that someone is analyzing data for trends and that agency policy supports this approach.

**Crowdsourcing** is a process in which a task or problem is posed and solutions solicited, resulting in the formation of an unofficial group of geographically dispersed individuals who offer their help (Bandaragoda et al., 2018; Magnassen & Stensgaard, 2019; Zhao et al., 2020). In some instances, the public are actively involved in research activities, which is referred to as *citizen science*. Another research approach that has been used is text mining of shared experiences from online support groups. Crowdsourcing and related activities can provide insights for healthcare professionals into the patient experience. As with other forms of social media, there is no assurance of the accuracy of all posted information. Along with its potential benefits, this form of publicly available medical data presents concerns related to privacy and the possibility of discrimination, erroneous research findings, and even litigation.

Big data can be derived from many sources, and thus researchers are no longer dependent on research findings as the primary source of evidence (Bhatt, 2019; Swift et al., 2018). This has given rise to the terms **real-world data (RWD)** and **real-world evidence (RWE)**, which are often used interchangeably to refer to information derived from sources outside of randomized clinical trial findings that may include, but are not limited to, EHRs, disease registries, claims data, data from personal devices and applications, and the **Internet of Things (IoT)**. RWD or RWE complement clinical trials, with each having limitations in design necessitating the application of the most appropriate methods for collection and analysis to extract relevant information to meet its potential to support healthcare

---

**Spotlight:** Disease Tracking via Social Media

Social media data have been mined to detect early signs of disease outbreaks, to recruit research subjects, to provide interventions, and to monitor population health and behavior (Sinnenberg et al., 2017; Zhang et al., 2020). One specific social networking site that has been explored is Twitter, where users interact via messages limited to 280 characters. The advantages of Twitter for disease detection and management include:

- Real-time data
- Global reach
- High volume of posts
- Ability to search posts for content, frequency of discussion, or response by topic
- Analysis of content to predict demand for services or patient outcomes

decision making (Katkade et al., 2018; Suvarna, 2018). The 21st Century Cures Act served to provide greater attention to RWE when Congress directed the Department of Health and Human Services to consider RWE for FDA drug approval (Krause & Saver, 2018).

## Issues With Big Data

Issues associated with big data include, but are not limited to, data quality, different data types and formats that complicate the ability to exchange data, data governance, barriers to sharing data, a lack of understanding of results, limits of the available tools and human resources, uneven production of learning, possible misinterpretation or misuse, and its sheer volume. Quality data are accurate, complete, consistent, clear, precise, and useful (Charnock, 2019). One concern related to data quality is that not all groups are represented equally online, because minority groups, the poor, and the elderly often have limited access (Benke & Benke, 2018; Goldkind et al., 2018). Poor data quality can occur when, for example, fields are left blank, a wrong choice is entered, or a typing or spelling error is made. Organizations can improve poor quality data through machine methods (computer applications or software) that scrub or clean data, but correct entry from the beginning is always the best option (Cheng et al., 2018). Poor-quality data negatively impacts decision making, raises information management costs, and compromises big data findings (Bassan & Harel, 2018; Benke & Benke, 2018; Hoffman, 2018).

Data may be structured or unstructured, as well as raw or processed. *Structured data* are typically organized into a repository or database for effective processing. *Unstructured data* may exhibit internal organization but not reside in databases. Examples of unstructured data include documents, emails, and multimedia resources.

**Data governance** refers to the policies, standards, processes, and controls applied to the organization's data to ensure that it is available when, where, and to whom it is needed; is usable; and is appropriately secured (NIST, 2019). At present, the growth in new information is outpacing the ability to develop policies and technology, thereby exposing organizations to legal, financial, and organizational risks. Data governance needs to reflect knowledgeable and appropriate use of data both within and beyond the walls of any one organization. One proposed solution is the creation of data collaboratives where participants have a say on issues related to the use of their data (Evans & Krumholz, 2019).

Barriers to sharing data have included a lack of interoperability, **information blocking** by healthcare software vendors and delivery systems in an attempt to maintain a competitive advantage, and an inconsistent slate of state and federal privacy laws (Black et al., 2018; Fan et al., 2018; Perlin et al., 2016; Powell & Alexander, 2019). Concerns have also been raised about the ethics of the process of collecting and storing data that may be about or from vulnerable populations in the event that those data may prove useful at a future date (Rosen et al., 2020; Rothstein et al., 2020). The single largest barrier to the ability to share data, however, has been the lack of interoperability.

Big data benefits cannot be realized unless the vast amounts of diverse data are amassed, accessible, shared, and analyzed (Mählmann, 2017; Thakkar & Gordon, 2019). Conventional strategies do not support big data analysis. A knowledge strategy and infrastructure, expertise, and tools are required to discover new learning and knowledge in big data. The late arrival of healthcare organizations to the big data phenomenon and the shortage of skilled personnel capable of dealing with this resource have placed health care at a disadvantage for turning data first into knowledge and then into actionable results.

The sheer volume of data produced from myriad sources leads to delays in processing, extraction, and turning it into knowledge; activities that are further exacerbated by the current shortage of data scientists (Song & Zhu, 2016). Consideration must also be given to whether the data is actually relevant for the problem or question being asked (Rizk & Elragal, 2020).

Another issue that all nurses will need to consider is how artificial intelligence models are created and whether they need further evaluation over time (Carroll, 2019; Wang, Kaushal, et al., 2019). Nurses can do this through clear communication of the intent of the model and review for whether models demonstrate transparency.

Nurses in practice settings need to have a grasp of big data and data science within the context of evidence-informed practice (Proctor & Wilson, 2018). Although the concept of evidence gleaned from big data is not difficult to understand, the ability to discern patterns in big data requires expertise provided through data science. **Data science** is a methodology for deriving useful knowledge directly from data through discovery, hypothesis formation, and hypothesis testing (NIST, 2019). It is an emerging discipline that incorporates techniques and theories from many areas, including **predictive analytics**, a facet of data mining that uses extracted data to forecast trends.

One example of a use of predictive analytics is in the field of workforce planning. Health workforce planning is critical. The formulation of national human resources for health policies and strategies requires evidence-based planning to rationalize decisions. A range of tools and resources exists to assist countries in developing a national health workforce strategic plan. Such plans normally include short- and long-term targets and cost estimates for scaling up education and training for health workers, reducing workforce imbalances, strengthening the performance of staff, improving staff retention, and adapting to any major health sector reforms, while also being harmonized with broader strategies for social and economic development.

There is a shortage of data scientists in all fields at present, and the shortage is especially acute in health care. There is also a lag in the inclusion of data science into course content in formal academic programs. As with other emerging areas of competencies, all healthcare professionals must make an effort to keep abreast of ongoing developments. Moving forward, it is essential that all nursing education programs include content on understanding data and different methods of analysis so nurses are empowered to use data for planning, setting policy, and evaluating outcomes. Nurse leaders must possess data literacy, the ability to use analytic tools, and be able to use big data to benefit their staff, patients, and organizations. This ability starts with an understanding of what data needs to be collected and why. Informatics nurse specialists are ideally suited to support these efforts as they understand both the information technology and healthcare domains, setting them up for roles as data scientists (Boicey, 2020).

# The Relationship Between Evidence-Informed Practice and Big Data

The terms *evidence-informed practice* (EIP) and *evidence-based practice* (EBP) are sometimes used interchangeably but actually refer to different concepts (Florczak, 2017). EBP is an approach that takes the best evidence, evidence-based theories, clinician expertise, and patient preferences and values to make decisions about patient care using a five-step process. EIP requires practitioners to be familiar with the levels of research evidence and clinical insights and to use them creatively without introducing nonscientific bias or the need to go through the five-step process of EBP. EIP extends beyond evidence to incorporate other factors that influence the nurse's care decisions—namely, context and patient values.

The demand for the best evidence leads healthcare professionals to consider options that include combining data from separate studies for a greater impact of research findings as well as analyzing big data. Combining data from separate studies requires input from experts, because data collected from different sources are not easily compared (Riddle et al., 2018). Increasingly, big data is seen as a form of evidence either on its own or as a supplement to clinical trials and is being used to inform policy and practice decisions (Guttenberg et al., 2018). A learning health system captures and delivers the best available evidence to guide and support decision making (Bindman, 2017).

# Initiatives That Support Big Data

Effective big data use requires a combination of policy, legislation, a knowledge strategy, infrastructure, and skills (Wang, Kung, et al., 2019). Health policies need clear objectives if they are to be effective. Vaynea et al. (2018) noted that a natural starting place for governments is to link national data sets to analyze performance and utilization of services and that EHRs provide a great starting point at the organizational level.

The following questions, among others, should be considered when formulating policies for big data use:

- Which aspects of big data are relevant for health care?
- What is the intent of the policy/data use?
- What barriers exist to achieving the objectives of the policy?
- What are the incentives to share information?

Examination of these questions will determine whether data are classified as personal, proprietary, or government-held, leading to strategies for how to link or share the appropriate types of data. Intent speaks to the ways that the data may be used. In health care, improvement of patient outcomes and reform of payments to providers constitute examples of intent. Barriers include concerns over how data will be used, privacy, loss of competitive advantage, technology issues, and user fatigue with technology, among others. Incentives revolve around building a case for data sharing as well as providing financial incentives for this practice.

The paradox is that although health policy helps to establish a framework for big data, big data also serves to inform policy. Legislation establishes requirements and incentives so that policies can be carried out. Some important exemplars of U.S. legislation and initiatives that helped to provide a framework for use of big data in health care are provided in **Table 9-2**. As big data use increases, legislation and professional practices will need to keep pace to ensure that data are always used appropriately and mistakes are avoided.

Work has been in progress for a number of years among healthcare and informatics professionals to lay the groundwork for evidence-based practices. Bakken (as cited in Remus & Donelle, 2019) noted five building blocks for informatics infrastructures: the adoption of standardized nomenclatures or languages, evidence in electronic format, standards for data exchange, processes that support attainment and acquisition of evidence to a situation, and the presence of informatics knowledge and skills. The adoption of Meaningful Use–certified EHRs moved health data into an electronic format while using the ANA-recognized language SNOMED (Systematized Nomenclature of Medicine Clinical Terms). The Cures Act contained further provisions to enable interoperability across different healthcare vendor software products to enable widespread sharing of health information.

One example of ongoing efforts to lay the groundwork for big data may be seen in North Carolina, where government, private-sector actors, payers, providers, administrators, and patients came together in 2020 to devise a long-term statewide data strategy to facilitate the achievement of better health, at lower costs, while improving the patient experience. A summary of this effort concluded that vision, focused leadership, trust, and cooperation among all stakeholders were needed to transform healthcare (McKethan & DuBard, 2020).

# Implications for RNs, APRNs, and Other Healthcare Professionals

More than at any previous point in history, RNs, APRNs, and other healthcare professionals now have the power of knowledge gleaned from large pools of information within reach, primarily through EHRs, various databases, and increasingly via additional data streams from mobile technology, wearable sensors, social media, and tracking apps. The ability to harness and use this

**Table 9-2** Important Legislation and Initiatives for Health Information Technology

| Public Law, Executive Order, or Initiative | Year Enacted | Major Content Related to Data |
|---|---|---|
| Health Insurance Portability and Accountability Act (HIPAA) | 1996 | ■ Impacts healthcare data availability.<br>■ Ensures a bridge for health insurance coverage for persons who have a change in employment.<br>■ Requires national electronic standards for claim submission.<br>■ Provisions protect the privacy of personal health information. |
| Medicare Improvements for Patients and Providers Act | 2008 | ■ Provides financial incentives for electronic prescribing (e-prescribing), which creates digital data for analysis. |
| American Recovery and Reinvestment Act | 2009 | ■ Provided an economic stimulus package.<br>■ Allocated funds to create jobs, boost economic growth, and increase accountability and transparency in government spending.<br>■ Funded comparative effectiveness research.<br>■ Created a nationwide health information network.<br>■ Provided financial incentives for hospitals and physicians who adopted and began using EHRs.<br>■ Strengthened HIPAA privacy and security requirements.<br>■ Included Title VIII Health Information Technology for Economic and Clinical Health Act. |
| Health Information Technology for Economic and Clinical Health Act | 2009 | ■ Offers financial incentives to providers participating in Medicare and Medicaid for adoption of certified EHRs; ushered in widespread adoption of EHRs in the United States.<br>■ Goals included improvements in care and reduced disparities.<br>■ Increased digital data for big data purposes. |
| Patient Protection and Affordable Care Act with its amendment, the Health Care and Education Reconciliation Act | 2010 | ■ Provided incentives for reporting provider performance; established public reporting of quality and cost metrics.<br>■ Increased hospital data collection and analysis.<br>■ Increased the ability to share data across settings. |

*(continues)*

**Table 9-2** Important Legislation and Initiatives for Health Information Technology *(continued)*

| Public Law, Executive Order, or Initiative | Year Enacted | Major Content Related to Data |
|---|---|---|
| Genetic Information Nondiscrimination Act | 2008 | ■ Protects individuals from discrimination by insurers and employers based on the results of genetic information and test results, encouraging data collection and use. |
| President Obama's Executive Order 13642: Making "Open and Machine Readable" the New Default for Government Information | 2013 | ■ Federal government requirement to make information easy to find, access, and use.<br>■ Adds to the amount of digital data available for exploration and to support decision making. |
| Medicare Access and CHIP Reauthorization Act of 2015 | 2015 | ■ Reforms Medicare payments to physicians, other providers, and suppliers to reflect a value-based payment model, effective 2019.<br>■ Monitors program effectiveness and reports on Medicare-eligible provider performance. |
| Precision Medicine Initiative | 2015 | ■ Research initiative that considers individual differences in genetic makeup, environments, and lifestyles.<br>■ Seeks to improve treatments for cancer, expand research, create new public–private partnerships, and infrastructure needed to expand cancer genomics. |
| 21st Century Cures Act | 2016 | ■ Among its many provisions, the most important for data sharing is the requirement for technical criteria for certified EHRs that will improve interoperability, paving the way for greater sharing and use of data.<br>■ Also provides funding for several federal agencies and programs that include the National Institutes of Health Innovation Projects, including the Precision Medicine Initiative, Food and Drug Administration (FDA) activities required by the bill, and grants to states to address the opioid abuse crisis. |

knowledge requires awareness of the potential of big data as a new form of evidence, a plan for how it may be used, skills to understand the significance of findings, and the ability to apply the evidence and learning in practice settings. Working to obtain this level of awareness and learning will necessitate the combination of personal and professional strategies, professional accountability, and advocacy.

Nurses have experience in the traditional uses of EHRs, claims data, and public health data, and they have knowledge of how health care works, which uniquely qualifies them to use big data. RNs, APRNs, and other healthcare professionals need to consider which data and information they would like to be able to retrieve from EHRs as evidence to better support their work and improve patient outcomes. As an example, it would be logical for patients rated as being at a high risk of falling to require more staff attention, but the current fall risk assessments may not provide the real-time aggregate information on increased acuity levels that is needed for safe staffing on a unit-by-unit basis or throughout the organization. This type of information would support safe staffing levels, enhance patient safety, and demonstrate the need for increased staffing (and costs) when greater numbers of at-risk patients are receiving care. APRNs concerned about the possibility of position cuts could request data that would demonstrate a link between level of staff preparation and patient outcomes. There are an infinite number of ways to apply big data from EHRs, public databases, and other data streams so as to further contribute to learning, patient safety, patient satisfaction, and lower costs. These goals are shared by thought leaders and policymakers: nurses can combine their firsthand patient narratives with such data analyses to inform better health policies.

Entry-level data science knowledge and skills for nurses include (Topaz & Pruinelli, 2017):

- Identifying big data characteristics and uses
- Understanding the sources and types of data captured by EHRs and other information systems
- Appreciating the relevance of big data for health care and patient outcomes
- Using data for clinical decision making
- Communicating effectively with other members of the healthcare delivery team to use data for improved decision making

Advanced data science knowledge and skills for nurses build upon entry-level skills to include collaboration with other disciplines to use data sets for research, to master analytic tools to aid their work with big data, and to use data quality validation to merge different data types together to support clinical decision-making (Topaz & Pruinelli, 2017).

As nurses at all levels are exposed to data science content, both baccalaureate-level and advanced practice nurses will become able to evaluate and use findings generated through data science methods. Nurses, however, must do even more. As knowledge workers, nurses must be involved in knowledge management. Starting at the point of data entry, all nurses have a legal and ethical obligation to ensure data quality. Input of accurate data and clear, unambiguous entries provide a solid foundation for usable data later. A concrete example in which information quality is critical is family history documentation that, when well done, can predict health risks and contribute to a targeted treatment approach referred to as precision medicine, which considers a patient's genetic background, environment, and lifestyle (Hickey et al., 2017; Lee et al., 2019), Nurses can provide feedback on electronic systems design and adoption of data standards to ensure that important information is collected, stored in a usable format, and available for reuse.

## Health Policy Implications

The nation needs an interoperable health system that empowers individuals to use their electronic health information to the fullest extent; enables providers and communities to deliver smarter, safer, and more efficient care; and promotes innovation at all levels (see **Figure 9-3**). According to the Office of the National Coordinator for Health Information Technology (2015):

> The vision is a learning health system where individuals are at the center of their care; where providers have a seamless ability to securely access and use health information from different sources; where an individual's health information is not limited to what is stored in electronic health records (EHRs), but includes information from many different sources (including technologies that individuals use) and portrays a longitudinal picture of their health, not just episodes of care; where diagnostic tests are only repeated when necessary, because

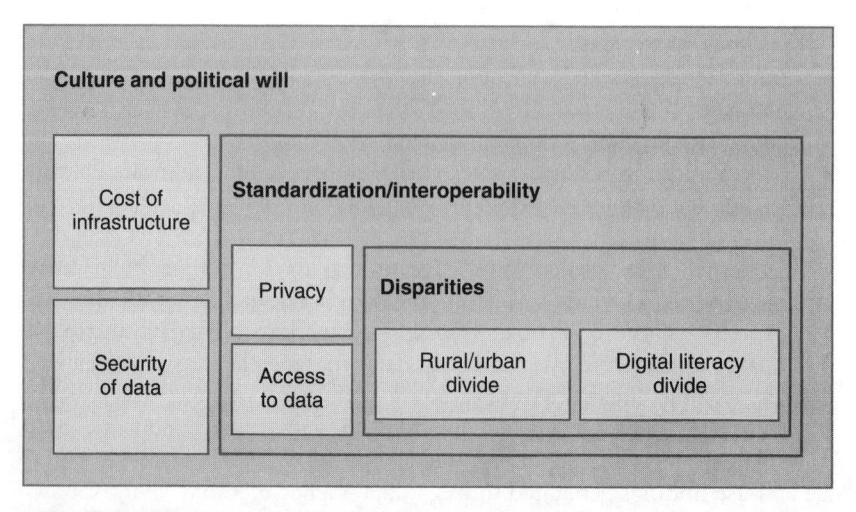

**Figure 9-3** Policy issues within healthcare data management.

the information is readily available; and where public health agencies and researchers can rapidly learn, develop, and deliver cutting edge treatments.

The Office of the National Coordinator for Health Information Technology (called ONC) is under the auspices of the executive branch of the federal government, with the national coordinator reporting to the secretary of Health and Human Services. The position of national coordinator (and the attending support workers) was created in 2004 via an executive order and was legislatively mandated in the Health Information Technology for Economic and Clinical Health Act of 2009. The purpose of ONC is to be a resource to the nation's health System to support the adoption of health information technology and the promotion of nationwide health information exchange to improve health care. At present, a quick look at the ONC's leadership shows no nurses on the staff. Nurses generate and are well-equipped to analyze and use health data; nurses must be engaged at all levels of government and policy.

Nurses should craft and implement data policies and integrate findings from big data at the point of care. The nurse with advanced data science knowledge and skills should use data science methods to research nursing phenomena. This can include formal research as well as using small data downloaded from EHRs within an organization to discover relationships and support decisions. Even nurses who lack access to analytic software can use advanced features of spreadsheets, create pivot tables, and use graphics to visualize data (Parker & Nelson, 2020). All nurses, and advanced practice nurses in particular, have an obligation to shape health policy to support big data and to use big data findings to influence policy and resource allocation.

## Conclusion

A variety of sources, platforms, and settings generating electronic health information can inform health goals, behaviors, and policy. The secure and seamless flow of this information is foundational to achieving the national priorities listed in **Table 9-3**.

Changing the healthcare delivery culture, providing feedback from the point of care, performing research, and translating research into practice are nursing's present and future roles toward achieving these national priorities. Nurses have been engaged in discharge planning, home care, and readmission reduction long before the COVID-19 pandemic in 2020 placed an emphasis on remote care and telehealth. As technology is used to reduce costs through remote care, the future includes nurses delegating tasks to artificial intelligence (AI). It has been suggested that AI has the potential to do 40% of the tasks now completed by nonclinical staff and 30% of the tasks done by clinical staff (Ahuja, 2019). Learning how data collected through smart devices and merged with AI can help healthcare organizations respond faster and improve the patient experience.

**Table 9-3** Health Information Technology (IT) and Health Policy Priorities

| Program/Initiative | Description |
| --- | --- |
| Healthcare delivery system reform | The availability of electronic health information is essential for advancing the broader strategy to improve the healthcare system by paying healthcare providers for what works, unlocking healthcare data, and finding new ways to coordinate and integrate care to improve quality. |
| Precision Medicine Initiative | Make usable electronic health information readily available and easily transferable for patients, healthcare providers, and researchers. |
| Cancer Moonshot (Genomics Data Commons) | The flow of electronic health information using the latest technology is critical to accelerating efforts to cure cancer by, for example, providing access to millions of cancer pathologies, genomic sequences, family histories, and treatment outcomes at once. Includes collaboration with Amazon and Microsoft to build a sustainable model for maintaining cancer genomic data in the cloud. |
| Prescription drug monitoring programs | Use of state and municipal databases by clinicians and pharmacists to track controlled substances issued to their patients. |
| Public health | Modernizing public health practice to emphasize actions across sectors—environmental, policy, and systems—that directly affect all of the determinants of health. It is also instrumental for detecting, tracking, managing, and preventing communicable diseases. |
| Research and innovation | Interoperability is critical to creating an effective learning healthcare system in which the latest research and clinical trials inform clinical care and patient encounters; in turn, the results of clinical care and patient encounters inform subsequent research and scientific inquiry as well as the future of health and patient care. |
| Improve health IT disparities | Eliminate the digital divide and digital illiteracy by building a strong foundation of health IT in our healthcare system, equipping every person with a long-term, digital picture of their health over their lifespan. |

Office of the National Coordinator for Health Information Technology (ONC), Office of the Secretary, United States Department of Health and Human Services (HHS). (2016). Report to Congress on Health Information Technology Progress at https://dashboard.healthit.gov/report-to-congress/2016-report-congress-examining-hitech-era-future-health-information-technology.php

# CASE STUDY 9-1: Research Evidence Versus Big Data

Your hospital's evidence-based practice council has looked at levels of traditional research and ways to incorporate evidence into care, with an emphasis on building evidence into clinical pathways used to guide care and documentation. As the APRN leading the council, you believe that the members now demonstrate a good grasp of different levels of research findings and are making excellent progress with their work to integrate evidence into practice. Your chief nursing officer, however, states that this is not enough; he expects to see the integration of findings from big data at the point of care. Council members have expressed great anxiety relative to the push to use big data findings, protesting that they have limited knowledge about big data, let alone how to make the best use of its related findings.

### Case Study Discussion Questions

1. As the APRN leading the council, do you agree with this decision by the chief nursing officer? Defend your position.
2. Write a one-page explanation for the council outlining the differences between data and big data.
3. Compare the use of research outcomes for a specific patient problem and the use of big data in addressing population-based health problems.
4. What resources (e.g., people, technology) would your hospital need in order to use big data appropriately?
5. Describe how population-based data (e.g., pre- and postintervention data) can be used to create community-level health policy.
6. Which implications does the integration of big data findings at your facility and elsewhere have for healthcare policy development at the local, state, and national levels?

# CASE STUDY 9-2: Implications of Using Various Data Sources

The technology committee at your medical center has been asked to look at current applications within the facility that generate data streams to determine which applications should feed into patient records. Some devices, such as glucometers and other point-of-care testing devices, automatically feed results into the patient's EHR. Other devices that track fitness, for example, are heavily used outside of the medical center but have not been linked with health records. As the APRN representative on the committee, you have been asked to provide your expert opinion on the integration of these additional data streams.

### Case Study Discussion Questions

1. Which types of body sensors, tracking devices, and applications would provide valuable information to nurses and other healthcare professionals when providing care to a patient? Discuss the pros and cons of the value of each item vis-à-vis EHRs.

2. What relationships do you see between these types of data streams and the ability to inform and shape healthcare policy in your medical center?
3. Describe the relationship between the policy at your organization and the inclusion of additional data streams into EHRs. How do individual hospitals stream their EHR data into big data sets? How does national healthcare policy support, or not support, the inclusion of additional data streams into EHRs? Into big data findings?
4. Discuss how nurse-sensitive data can be used to create health policy at the state or national level.
5. Describe ethical and security issues involved in including patients' personal information in EHRs (Hint: think about the patient who has an implanted electronic medical device such as an ICD/pacemaker).
6. Create a framework or model that illustrates how the integration of multiple data streams collected from point-of-service devices can be used to inform healthcare policy.

# CASE STUDY 9-3: Magnet Status and Big Data

Your 600-bed medical center is a Magnet facility and was one of the first healthcare delivery systems in the nation to attain Magnet recognition. Maintaining Magnet recognition is a goal for the organization that requires planning and resources. You recently joined a committee that is responsible for overseeing the process to apply for Magnet recognition.

### Case Study Discussion Questions

1. How can aggregate data collected from this facility be used to demonstrate the value of nursing (e.g., a correlation between nurse credentials and patient outcomes)?
2. Analyze how data obtained from all Magnet facilities in the United States can be used to influence national healthcare policy relative to the following issues:
    a. The value of nursing care
    b. Allocation of resources for specific populations
    c. Funding for further education for nurses

## Suggested Activity

Watch the 116th Congress Senate HELP Committee's hearings on implementing the 21st Century Cures Act (March 26 and May 7 of 2019):

   Part 1 (March 26): www.help.senate.gov/hearings/implementing-the-21st-century-cures-act-making-electronic-health-information-available-to-patients-and-providers

   Part 2 (May 7): www.help.senate.gov/hearings/implementing-the-21st-century-cures-act-making-electronic-health-information-available-to-patients-and-providers-part-ii

## Suggested Activity Discussion Questions

1. After watching the hearing(s), list three things that you learned about the act.
2. List three new questions that you have. Attempt to find answers to these questions.
3. List three ways in which you will apply what you have learned from watching this hearing to your personal or professional life.
4. Who were the witnesses, and how were the witnesses chosen?
5. Which senator was in charge of this hearing? Why? What actions did the senator take during the hearing?
6. What is the Pew Charitable Trust, and why would a project director from Pew be invited to give testimony to a senate committee? Is the Pew Charitable Trust a politically biased source of information (support your answer)?
7. What is the Healthcare Leadership Council? Why is testimony from this group pertinent? Does this group include nurses?
8. After viewing these hearings, do you have a better understanding of the 21st Century Cures Act (or perhaps of one part of the act)?

## Chapter Discussion Points

1. How do electronic resources support healthcare policy?
2. How would you prioritize sources of health information to inform policy (Hint: think about the biggest versus the best?)
3. What is your role, as a registered nurse or APRN, to transform data to evidence to inform practice? To inform health policy?
4. Name one health policy initiative that has supported the transition to big data, and provide your rationale.

## References

Ahuja A. S. (2019). The impact of artificial intelligence in medicine on the future role of the physician. *PeerJ*, 7, e7702. https://doi.org/10.7717/peerj.7702

American Nurses Association. (2015). *Nursing's social policy statement: The essence of the profession* (3rd ed). Author. https://www.nursingworld.org/nurses-books/guide-to-nursings-social-policy-statement-understanding-the-profession-fr/

American Nurses Association. (2020). *Nursing informatics: Scope and standards of practice* (3rd ed.). Author.

Anderson, A. (2019, January 31). *A flawless model for achieving your goals* [Video]. TEDxZagreb. YouTube. https://www.youtube.com/watch?v=jQeUkvz2OjA

Bandaragoda, T. R., De Silva, D., Alahakoon, D., Ranasinghe, W., & Bolton, D. (2018). Text mining for personalized knowledge extraction from online support groups. *Journal of the Association for Information Science and Technology*, 69(12), 1446–1459.

Bassan, S., & Harel, O. (2018). The ethics in synthetics: Statistics in the service of ethics and law in health-related research in big data from multiple sources. *Journal of Law and Health*, 31(1), 87–117.

Benke, K., & Benke, G. (2018). Artificial intelligence and big data in public health. *International Journal of Environmental Research and Public Health*, 15(12), 2796. https://doi.org/10.3390/ijerph15122796

Bhatt, A. (2019). Conducting real-world evidence studies in India. *Perspectives in Clinical Research*, 10(2), 51. https://doi.org/10.4103/picr.PICR_8_19

Bindman, A. B. (2017). The Agency for Healthcare Research and Quality and the development of a learning health care system. *JAMA Internal Medicine, 177*(7), 909–910. https://doi.org/10.1001/jamainternmed.2017.2589

Black, J., Hulkower, R., & Ramanathan, T. (2018). Health information blocking: Responses under the 21st Century Cures Act. *Public Health Reports, 133*(5), 610–613.

Black, J., Hulkower, R., Suarez, W., Patel, S., & Elliott, B. (2019). Public health surveillance: Electronic reporting as a point of reference. *Journal of Law, Medicine & Ethics, 47*(Suppl. 2), 19–22. https://doi.org/10.1177/1073110519857309

Boicey, C. M. (2020, August 20). *Welcome and opening keynote: The value of nursing data ... in times of a pandemic.* American Nursing Informatics Association Virtual Conference.

Bush, W. S., Cooke Bailey, J. N., Beno, M. F., & Crawford, D. C. (2019). Bridging the gaps in personalized medicine value assessment: A review of the need for outcome metrics across stakeholders and scientific disciplines. *Public Health Genomics, 22*(1–2), 16–24. https://doi.org/10.1159/000501974

Carroll, W. 2019. Nursing informaticists safeguarding the use of emerging technologies. *Online Journal of Nursing Informatics, 23*(3).

Centers for Medicare and Medicaid Services (CMS). (2020). *HCAHPS: Patients' perspectives of care survey.* https://www.cms.gov/Medicare/Quality-Initiatives-Patient-Assessment-Instruments/HospitalQualityInits/HospitalHCAHPS

Charnock, V. (2019). Electronic healthcare records and data quality. *Health Information & Libraries Journal, 36*(1), 91–95. https://doi.org/10.1111/hir.12249

Cheng, H., Feng, D., Shi, X., & Chen, C. (2018). Data quality analysis and cleaning strategy for wireless sensor networks. *EURASIP Journal on Wireless Communications and Networking, 2018*(1), 61. https://doi.org/10.1186/s13638-018-1069-6

Dash, S., Shakyawar, S. K., Sharma, M., & Kaushik, S. (2019). Big data in healthcare: Management, analysis and future prospects. *Journal of Big Data, 6*(1), 54. https://doi.org/10.1186/s40537-019-0217-0

Evans, B. J., & Krumholz, H. M. (2019). People-powered data collaboratives: Fueling data science with the health-related experiences of individuals. *Journal of the American Medical Informatics Association, 26*(2), 159–161. https://doi.org/10.1093/jamia/ocy159

Fan, L., Gil-Garcia, J. R., Song, Y., Cronemberger, F., Hua, G., Werthmuller, D., Burke, G., Costello, J., Meyers, B. R., & Hong, X. (2019). Sharing big data using blockchain technologies in local governments: Some technical, organizational and policy considerations. *Information Polity, 24*(4), 419–435. https://doi.org/10.3233/IP-190156

Favaretto, M., Clercq, E. D., Schneble, C. O., & Elger, B. S. (2020). What is your definition of big data? Researchers' understanding of the phenomenon of the decade. *PLOS One, 15*(2), e0228987. https://doi.org/10.1371/journal.pone.0228987

Florczak, K. L. (2017). Evidence or clinicians or the person. *Nursing Science Quarterly, 30*(1), 17–20.

Garavand, A., Emami, H., Rabiei, R., Pishgahi, M., & Vahidi-Asl, M. (2020). Designing the Coronary Artery Disease Registry with data management processes approach: A comparative systematic review in selected registries. *International Cardiovascular Research Journal, 14*(1), 1–6.

Goldkind, L., Thinyane, M., & Choi, M. (2018). Small data, big justice: The intersection of data science, social good, and social services. *Journal of Technology in Human Services, 36*(4), 175–178. https://doi.org/10.1080/15228835.2018.1539369

Gutenberg, J., Katrakazas, P., Trenkova, L., Murdin, L., Brdarić, D., Koloutsou, N., Ploumidou, K., Pontoppidan, N. H., & Laplante-Lévesque, A. (2018). Big data for sound policies: Toward evidence-informed hearing health policies. *American Journal of Audiology, 27*(3S), 493–502. https://doi.org/10.1044/2018_AJA-IMIA3-18-0003

Healthcare Information and Management Systems Society. (2020). *Interoperability in the healthcare.* https://www.himss.org/resources/interoperability-healthcare

Hickey, K. T., Katapodi, M. C., Coleman, B., Reuter-Rice, K., & Starkweather, A. R. (2017). Improving utilization of the family history in the electronic health record. *Journal of Nursing Scholarship, 49*(1), 80–86.

Hoffman, S. (2018). Big data analytics. *Indiana Health Law Review, 15*(2), 227–246. https://doi.org/10.18060/3911.0048

# References

Ienca, M., Ferretti, A., Hurst, S., Puhan, M., Lovis, C., & Vayena, E. (2018). Considerations for ethics review of big data health research: A scoping review. *PLOS One, 13*(10), e0204937. https://doi.org/10.1371/journal.pone.0204937

Jose, K., Venn, A., Jarman, L., Seal, J., Teale, B., Scott, J., & Sanderson, K. (2017). Partnering Healthy@Work: An Australian university–government partnership facilitating policy-relevant research. *Health Promotion International, 32*(6), 964–976. https://doi.org/10.1093/heapro/daw033

Katkade, V. B., Sanders, K. N., & Zou, K. H. (2018). Real world data: An opportunity to supplement existing evidence for the use of long-established medicines in health care decision making. *Journal of Multidisciplinary Healthcare, 11*, 295–304. https://doi.org/10.2147/JMDH.S160029

Krause, J. H., & Saver, R. S. (2018). Real-world evidence in the real world: Beyond the FDA. *American Journal of Law & Medicine, 44*(2–3), 161–179. https://doi.org/10.1177/0098858818789423

Kyriazis, D., Autexier, S., Brondino, I., Boniface, M., Donat, L., Engen, V., Fernandez, R., Jimenez-Peris, R., Jordan, B., Jurak, G., Kiourtis, A., Kosmidis, T., Lustrek, M., Maglogiannis, I., Mantas, J., Martinez, A., Mavrogiorgou, A., Menychtas, A., Montandon, L., . . . Wajid, U. (2017). CrowdHEALTH: Holistic health records and big data analytics for health policy making and personalized health. *Studies in Health Technology and Informatics, 238*, 19–23. https://doi.org/10.3233/978-1-61499-781-8-19

Lai, P. K., Mai, C. W., Sulaiman, L. H., & Limm, P. K. C. (2019). Healthcare big data analytics: Re-engineering healthcare delivery through innovation. *International E-Journal of Science, Medicine & Education, 13*(3), 10–13.

Lee, J., Hamideh, D., & Nebeker, C. (2019). Qualifying and quantifying the precision medicine rhetoric. *BMC Genomics, 20*(1), 868. https://doi.org/10.1186/s12864-019-6242-8

Magnussen, R., & Stensgaard, A. G. (2019). Knowledge collaboration between professionals and nonprofessionals: A systematic mapping review of citizen science, crowd sourcing and community-driven research. *Proceedings of the European Conference on Games Based Learning*, 470–477.

Måhlmann, L. (2017). Big data for public health policy-making: Policy empowerment. *Public Health Genomics, 20*(6), 312–320.

Mamedova, S., & Pawlowski, E. (2018, 1 May). *A description of US adults who are not digitally literate*. American Institutes for Research. https://www.air.org/resource/description-u-s-adults-who-are-not-digitally-literate

McKethan, A., & DuBard, A. (2020). Toward a health data strategy for North Carolina. *North Carolina Medical Journal, 81*(3), 181–184. https://doi.org/10.18043/ncm.81.3.181

Mennella, H., & Pravikoff, D. (2018, December 7). *Evidence-based care. CINAHL nursing guide*. EBSCO.

Meyer, M. A. (2019). Healthcare data scientist qualifications, skills, and job focus: A content analysis of job postings. *Journal of the American Medical Informatics Association: JAMIA, 26*(5), 383–391. https://doi.org/10.1093/jamia/ocy181

Morgan, S. (2019, July 18). Humans on the Internet will triple from 2015 to 2022 and hit 6 billion. *Cybercrime Magazine*. https://cybersecurityventures.com/how-many-internet-users-will-the-world-have-in-2022-and-in-2030/

NIST Big Data Public Working Group, Definitions and Taxonomies Subgroup. (2019). *NIST Big Data Interoperability Framework: volume 1, definitions version 3*. No. NIST SP 1500-1r2 (p. NIST SP 1500-1r2). National Institute of Standards and Technology. https://doi.org/10.6028/NIST.SP.1500-1r2

Office of the National Coordinator for Health Information Technology. (n.d.). *ONC's Cures Act final rule: Major changes from the proposed rule to the final rule*. https://www.healthit.gov/curesrule/overview/major-changes-proposed-rule-final-rule

Office of the National Coordinator for Health Information Technology. (2015). *Connecting health and care for the nation*. https://www.healthit.gov/sites/default/files/hie-interoperability/nationwide-interoperability-roadmap-final-version-1.0.pdf

Parker, C., & Nelson, T. (2020, August 22). Data analytics using Excel—Part 3. American Nursing Informatics Association Virtual Conference.

Patient-Centered Outcomes Research Institute. (n.d.). *PCORnet: The National Patient-Centered Clinical Research Network*. https://pcornet.org/about/

Perlin, J. B., Baker, D. B., Brailer, D. J., Fridsma, D. B., Frisse, M. E., Halamka, J. D., Levi, J., Mandl, K. D., Marchibroda, J. M., Platt, R., & Tang, P. C. (2016). *Information technology

# CHAPTER 10

# Financing Health Care

Nancy M. Short

## KEY TERMS

**Adverse selection:** A market situation in which a person buying insurance (a buyer) has more information than the insurer (a seller). A form of information asymmetry.

**Alternative payment model (APM):** A payment approach that gives added incentive payments to providers to practice high-quality and cost-efficient care. APMs can apply to a specific clinical condition, a care episode, or a population. APMs are administered by the Centers for Medicare and Medicaid Services.

**Coinsurance:** Coinsurance is the percentage of costs the consumer pays after they have met their deductible.

**Comparative effectiveness research (CER):** Research performed to determine the effectiveness of clinical interventions by comparing different treatments for the same condition or for different patient subgroups. The Patient-Centered Outcomes Research Institute (PCORI) is charged with identifying priorities and carrying out this type of research.

**Copay (copayment):** A fixed dollar amount for a covered service (rather than a percentage of the bill) paid by a patient to the provider of the service before receiving the service. It may be defined in an insurance policy and paid by an insured person each time a medical service is accessed. Copays typically vary for different services within the same plan, particularly when they involve services that are considered essential or routine versus those that are considered to be less routine or in the domain of a specialist.

**Essential health benefits:** A set of healthcare service categories that, starting in 2014, have to be covered by certain insurance policies. Insurance policies must cover these benefits in order to be certified and offered in the health insurance marketplace. States expanding their Medicaid programs must provide these benefits to people newly eligible for Medicaid.

**Healthcare disparities:** Typically refers to differences between groups/populations in health insurance coverage, access to and use of care, and quality of care. Health and healthcare disparities often refer to differences that are not explained by variations in health needs, patient preferences, or treatment recommendations and are closely linked to socio-economic, environmental, and/or systemic disadvantages. The terms *health inequality* and *inequity* also are used to refer to disparities (Artiga et al., 2020).

**227**

**Table 10-1** Direct Pay Compared to Traditional Healthcare Finance Methods

| Health Insurance | Self-Funded Employer Health Insurance | Medicare and Medicaid | Out of Pocket $$$ |
|---|---|---|---|
| **Traditional:** Insurers negotiate discounted rates with the medical providers in their network. Providers charge different amounts to different insurers for the same procedure, but these rates are not publicly available. | **Traditional:** Employers hire a preferred provider organization (PPO), which negotiates discounted rates with medical providers on the employer's behalf. Employers pay claims out of their operating budgets. | **Traditional:** Government determines how much to reimburse medical providers for all procedures on the basis of recommendations from the American Medical Association. Rates are often modest, leading some physicians to refuse to accept or limit such coverage. | **Traditional:** Patients pay medical providers directly. In the past, uninsured patients' bills were based on the artificially inflated prices providers used to begin negotiations with insurers. Some traditional providers are offering cash-only prices that are lower than insurers' negotiated rates. |
| **With direct pay:** The idea is that health insurance begins to look more like auto insurance: insurers estimate the cost of a procedure and send a check to the patient, who compares prices and chooses a provider. | **With direct pay:** Employers partner with medical providers on the basis of their publicly available prices and then pay them directly. Employers pay medical bills out of their operating budget. | **With direct pay:** If most medical providers posted their prices, the government could potentially set reimbursement rates based on the average regional price of a procedure. | **With direct pay:** Patients still pay providers directly, but because price lists are posted publicly, regional providers compete on price, quality, and reputation. |

approved by that state. A state-based marketplace is a government agency offering subsidized "Obamacare" plans (i.e., plans designed within the ACA) for the state, similar to **Healthcare.gov** but created and maintained by the individual state. Private plans, outside of the HIXs, continue to be available; however, private plans are now more likely to be available for purchase only in designated "open enrollment" periods that coincide with those of the HIXs' open enrollment periods. It is worth noting that the correct use of the term, "Obamacare," is limited to these health insurance exchanges and not to the entire Affordable Care Act.

As of 2021 only a handful of states maintained their own HIX; all others depend on the federal government (Healthcare.gov) to provide the infrastructure for the exchange. The following states have their own HIX:

- California: Covered California
- Colorado: Connect for Health Colorado
- Connecticut: Access Health CT
- District of Columbia: DC Health Link
- Idaho: Your Health Idaho
- Maryland: Maryland Health Connection
- Massachusetts: Health Connector
- Minnesota: MNsure
- New Jersey: Get Covered NJ
- New York: New York State of Health
- Pennsylvania: Pennie
- Rhode Island: HealthSource RI
- Vermont: Vermont Health Connect
- Washington: Washington Healthplanfinder

Insurance plans in the HIX marketplace are primarily separated into four categories—Bronze, Silver, Gold, or Platinum—based on the percentage the plan pays of the average overall cost of providing **essential health benefits** to members. The plan category a person chooses affects the total amount that individual will spend for essential health benefits during the year. The percentages the plans will pay, on average, are 60% (Bronze), 70% (Silver), 80% (Gold), and 90% (Platinum). Let's pretend that you purchase a Bronze plan and receive covered health services that cost $100: insurance will (on average) pay $60 and you will be responsible to pay $40 (see **Figure 10-4**).

The average premium for a Bronze plan in 2020 was $1,041 per month for an individual. Bronze plans have the least expensive premiums, but the highest **copay** and **coinsurance** costs in the HIX marketplace. See **Figure 10-5** regarding the difference between copayments and coinsurance and refer to the Key Terms for definitions of these two very different (and confusing) terms.

The ACA requires the following 10 essential health benefits to be included in every **qualified health insurance plan (QHP)**:[1]

1. Well-baby and well-child care for children younger than age 21
2. Oral health and vision services for children

---

[1] Some health plans without these 10 benefits were grandfathered into the QHP program. Under Trump administration rules, states choose from 50 essential benefit benchmark plans, instead of 10. Additionally, states may pick and choose which benefits are included in their essential health benefit benchmark plan by drawing from plans used in other states.

further than the Cruz Amendment to the Senate's Better Care Reconciliation Act or the Graham-Cassidy-Heller-Johnson bill, which would have allowed coverage that is not legal under the ACA and funneled money directly to the states to spend on their own health coverage priorities. Like those bills, the 1332 guidance promises to further exacerbate differences in coverage between red and blue states. (Jost, 2018)

The small business health insurance options program (SHOP) was also created within the ACA and is available to employers with up to 100 Full Time Equivalents.[3] If a business wants to use SHOP, it must offer coverage to all of its full-time employees (generally those working 30 or more hours per week on average) *and* at least 70% of full-time employees must enroll in the business/SHOP plan (as opposed to being covered by a spouse's insurance or as an individual on the HIX). More information on SHOP can be obtained from the Center for Consumer Information and Insurance Oversight.

# The Individual Mandate and Penalties

The individual mandate within the ACA was the requirement that all U.S. residents either have health insurance or pay a penalty. The mandate was intended to help keep the premiums for ACA-defined insurance policies low by ensuring that more healthy people entered the health insurance market and balanced the risk pool. In 2017, the penalty/responsibility for not having a QHP—that is, the "individual shared responsibility payment"—was set to be $695 per adult and $347 per child younger than 18. The maximum penalty was set at $2,085 or 2.5% of household taxable income (whichever was greater). In December 2017, Republican-backed tax overhaul legislation reduced the penalty for not having insurance to $0 and made it retrospective for that tax year. The ACA's federal individual mandate penalty has been $0 since the start of 2017.

Prior to the reduction of the penalty to $0, any penalties were paid when income tax forms were filed with the Internal Revenue Service the following year. If a person obtained insurance outside of the marketplace, they had to report that insurance coverage to the IRS every year when filing the tax return. The insurer and the employer (if applicable) provided the necessary proof of coverage to include in the tax return. There were no liens, levies, or criminal penalties for failing to pay the fee.

President Joe Biden has proposed what has been labelled as the Affordable Care Act 2.0. The Biden plan would bring back the individual mandate along with the penalties. According to Sotomayor and Memoli (2020), reporting for NBC News:

> Americans would have the option of buying into a "Medicare-like" plan or keeping their private insurance under the Biden plan. People

---

[3] An FTE for a 40-hour workweek equals 2080 hours. Employees may work partial FTEs. In this example, 50 employees does not always equal 50 FTEs.

living in states that failed to expand Medicaid would be given premium free Medicaid. Biden's plan also calls for the end of the Hyde Amendment, a provision that prevents federal funding for abortions unless a child is conceived through rape or incest or the mother's health is in jeopardy.

A discussion of the individual mandate to have health insurance is not complete without mentioning the exemptions from paying penalties (as originally written in the ACA), although these are now moot in light of the change to the $0 penalty. The 117th Congress and administration sworn in in 2021 may or may not reinstitute the penalties. In general, exemptions are income related, hardship related, group-membership related, and health-coverage related:

- People who have to pay more than 8% of their income for the lowest-cost premium
- People who do not pay taxes because their income is too low
- People with certain religious exemptions
- Prisoners, while incarcerated
- People experiencing a hardship (e.g., victims of domestic violence, persons being evicted from their place of residence)
- Native Americans and Alaska Natives
- People who would have been covered had their state of residence elected to expand Medicaid
- Mixed-status families (documented and undocumented immigrants within one nuclear family)

So, what happened as a result of eliminating the penalty for not having health insurance? The short answer is, not much. Democrats predicted that up to 23 million people would drop or lose coverage as a result of the Republican-led efforts. However, the Congressional Budget Office estimates that only 2.5 million people chose to drop their insurance as a result of the elimination of the penalty and other changes to the ACA. It is believed that, under the threat of the penalty, many people discovered that they were eligible for lower-cost or subsidized health insurance from the HIXs and decided to maintain their insurance coverage (Kessler, 2019). Some economists predicted that the U.S. health insurance market for individual insurance would fail if forced to include those with preexisting conditions while healthy people chose to remain out of the risk pool. This also didn't happen; the individual insurance market continued to make a profit (Fehr, 2020).

# Healthcare Entitlement Programs

Medicare and Medicaid are publicly funded social entitlement programs and are the "third rail" (i.e., electrified and deadly) of healthcare politics. Anyone meeting the eligibility requirements for Medicare Part A or Medicaid is *entitled* to all the promised benefits, no matter the condition of the government's (state or federal) finances. As an analogy, think of your personal budget. You plan for of $144.60 for Part B. In 2021, Part D premiums ranged from $0 to $77.10 per month and were adjusted for income.

## Medicaid

Medicaid was enacted under the Social Security Act in 1965 as a companion to Medicare. It entitles states to federal matching funds on an open-ended basis and eligible individuals to a set of specific benefits. The program is means tested, and it allows states to choose to provide broader coverage. In addition to providing health insurance coverage, Medicaid provides assistance to low-income Medicare beneficiaries (called *dual-eligibles*), long-term care assistance (nursing home and in-home community-based services), and support for the safety-net system of health care. The largest source of federal funding to the states, Medicaid is the largest health insurance program in the United States.

Medicaid fills large gaps in the U.S. health insurance market, finances the lion's share of long-term care, and provides core support for the health centers and safety-net hospitals that serve the nation's uninsured population and millions of others. Within broad federal guidelines, states design their own Medicaid programs. Medicaid reimburses private providers to provide services to beneficiaries. In 2018, 25% of the U.S. population received health insurance from Medicaid. Disabled and elderly adults make up only 25% of enrollees, but they account for approximately 50% of Medicaid expenditures. Medicaid provides coverage for 60% of all long-term care residents, making Medicaid the major program paying for long-term care. Children account for more than two-fifths of Medicaid enrollees but only one-fifth of Medicaid spending (Center on Budget and Policy Priorities, 2020).

In March 2021, 39 states had expanded Medicaid: for those 11 states that opted out of the ACA Medicaid expansion plan, Medicaid coverage requires that beneficiaries have low incomes (defined by each state using the federal poverty guidelines) *and* meet one of these categories of need:

- Pregnant or recent postpartum
- Younger than age 18 years
- Older than age 65 years and blind or disabled

These restrictions were in place across the majority of Medicaid programs[6] prior to the implementation of the ACA.

Medically needy persons whose incomes are too high to be eligible for Medicaid may also be covered (each state determines eligibility). In addition, states may define optional eligibility groups. In 2020, the federal poverty level was $12,760 for an individual and $26,200 for a family of four in the continental United States and a little higher in Alaska and Hawaii (U.S. Department of Health and Human Services, 2020).

One of the arguments against expanding Medicaid is a fear of increasing the overall health expenditures for the United States (Rosenbaum et al., 2017).

---

[6] Some states had CMS waivers that changed these criteria, and some states had already expanded coverage beyond these criteria.

**National Health Expenditures as a Percentage of Gross Domestic Product, 1960–2020**

| Year | Percent |
|---|---|
| 1960 | 5.2 |
| 1965 | 5.9 |
| 1970 | 7.2 |
| 1975 | 8.1 |
| 1980 | 9.1 |
| 1985 | 10.4 |
| 1990 | 12.3 |
| 1995 | 13.7 |
| 2000 | 13.8 |
| 2005 | 15.9 |
| 2010 | 17.7 |
| 2015 | 18.9 |
| 2020 | 21.3 (Projected) |

Data: Centers for Medicare and Medicaid Services, The Lewin Group

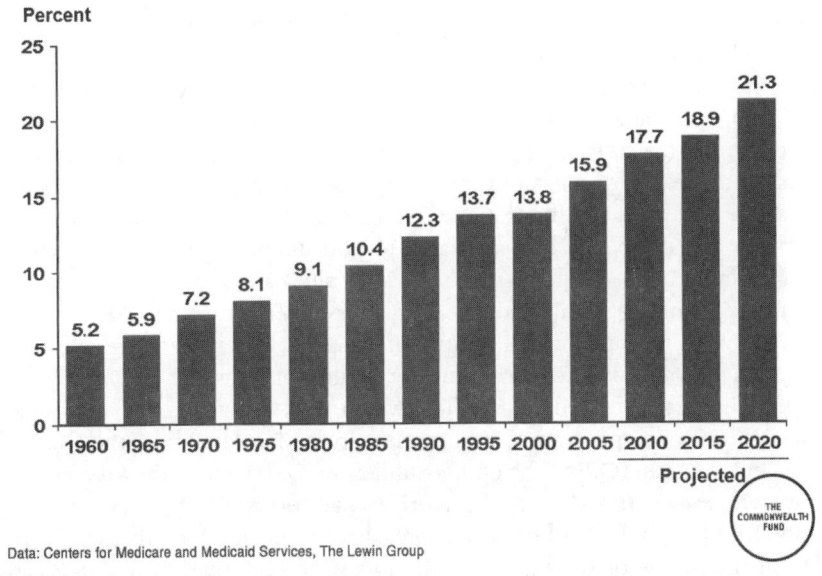

**Figure 10-6** National health expenditures as percentage of gross domestic product (GDP).
https://www.commonwealthfund.org/chart/national-health-expenditures-percentage-gross-domestic-product-1960-2020

See **Figure 10-6**. Historically, fraud, waste and abuse in Medicaid is also cited as a reason not to expand the program. The John Locke Foundation (an organization with conservative ideology) reported that after expanding Medicaid, some states found that the newly enrolled beneficiaries were much more expensive to cover than estimated by the federal government. Other arguments include: (1) expansion of Medicaid does not fix the basic problem of high prices and high costs for health care, (2) expansion is a sort of one-size-fits-all approach to helping the uninsured, (3) oversight and accountability of the current Medicaid program is problematic so why make it even bigger, and (4) Medicaid reimburses providers at substantially lower rates than private insurance and may lead to providers refusing Medicaid patients (Roberts, 2019).

## Provider Payment Models

The long-term goal of the federal government is to move providers (physicians, APRNs, hospitals, and all other health professionals who are reimbursed by federal programs) from a payment system rewarding volume of care to a model based on the quality of management of the health of populations. The term *population management* is applied to diverse groups: the populations living within the boundaries of a ZIP code, a population of patients with diabetes being treated within a specific practice, or the population of patients undergoing hip replacement in a hospital. Health care is currently in the middle of a transition from a system of payment based on the volume of services provided (fee-for-service) to payment based on the value of those services (value-based care and alternative payment models). The Centers for Medicare and Medicaid Services (CMS) has set a goal of increasingly tying Medicare payment to value.

The Medicare Access and CHIP Reauthorization Act (MACRA) of 2015 is a complex federal law that ended the physician and APRN reimbursement model under the *sustainable growth rate* (SGR). The SGR proved to be unsustainable in the face of constantly increasing Medicare expenses. The Center for Medicare and Medicaid Innovation (CMMI) has wide authority to design and test new and promising models geared toward improving healthcare quality and lowering costs. While most of the CMMI alternative payment models are currently being tested in Medicare, engaging payers outside of Medicare is imperative to improve overall health outcomes; however, Medicare will lead the path for other insurers. Payment for quality of outcomes is at the heart of the changes instituted by MACRA, which took effect in 2017; providers must choose one option for reimbursement from Medicare under the Quality Payment Program (QPP). The options under the QPP include the **alternative payment model (APM)** and the **Merit-based Incentive Payment System (MIPS)**. Although there is no single approach to payment reform that will work for all physicians or their patients, the following objectives of the QPP can serve as a starting point toward understanding alternative payment and service delivery models (QPP, n.d.):

1. To improve beneficiary population health
2. To improve the care received by Medicare beneficiaries
3. To lower costs to the Medicare program through improvement of care and health
4. To advance the use of healthcare information between allied providers and patients
5. To educate, engage, and empower patients as members of their care team
6. To maximize QPP participation with a flexible and transparent design, and easy-to-use program tools
7. To maximize QPP participation through education, outreach, and support tailored to the needs of practices, especially those that are small, rural, and in underserved areas
8. To expand APM participation
9. To provide accurate, timely, and actionable performance data to clinicians, patients and other stakeholders
10. To continuously improve QPP, based on participant feedback and collaboration

Types of payment models include fee-for-service, bundled care, accountable care, shared decision making, and the direct decision support model. Physicians and APRNs must choose whether to participate in APMs or in the MIPS. **Figure 10-7** depicts the overall trajectory of the payment framework models. A more in-depth discussion of payment and reimbursement options for providers is beyond the scope of this chapter.

## Hospitals and Outpatient Reimbursement

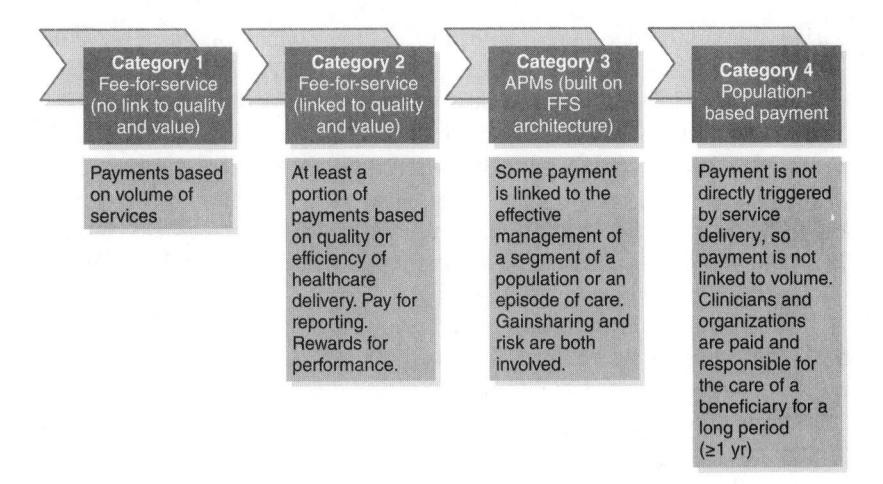

| Category 1 Fee-for-service (no link to quality and value) | Category 2 Fee-for-service (linked to quality and value) | Category 3 APMs (built on FFS architecture) | Category 4 Population-based payment |
|---|---|---|---|
| Payments based on volume of services | At least a portion of payments based on quality or efficiency of healthcare delivery. Pay for reporting. Rewards for performance. | Some payment is linked to the effective management of a segment of a population or an episode of care. Gainsharing and risk are both involved. | Payment is not directly triggered by service delivery, so payment is not linked to volume. Clinicians and organizations are paid and responsible for the care of a beneficiary for a long period (≥1 yr) |

**Figure 10-7** Centers for Medicare and Medicaid Services' payment framework trajectory.

# Hospitals and Outpatient Reimbursement

Medicare uses a prospective payment system (PPS) method of reimbursement whereby payment is made based on a predetermined, fixed amount. The Social Security Act established a system of payment for the operating costs of acute care hospital inpatient stays under Medicare Part A based on set rates. This payment system is referred to as the Inpatient Prospective Payment System (IPPS). Under the IPPS, each case is categorized into a diagnosis-related group (DRG). Each DRG has a payment weight assigned to it, based on the average resources used to treat Medicare patients in that DRG. The general DRG system was created collaboratively with Yale University's Schools of Management and Public Health in order to classify the care that hospitals provide by separating all of the potential human disease diagnoses into more than 20 body systems, and then subdividing those systems into more than 450 groups. Fees are assessed by factoring the body system and groups affected, with the amount of hospital resources required to treat the condition. The result is a fixed rate for patient services known as the DRG. The CMS adopted DRGs as a reimbursement system in 1983 (Value Health Care Services, n.d.).

In 1987, the DRG system was split into the All-Patient DRG (AP-DRG) system, which incorporates billing for non-Medicare patients, and the MS-DRG system, which sets billing for Medicare patients. The MS-DRG is the most widely used system today because of the growing number of Medicare patients. Payments are calculated using wage variations, geographic locations, and the percentage of Medicare patients that a hospital treats.

If the hospital treats a high percentage of low-income patients, it receives an add-on payment known as the *disproportionate share hospital* (often written as

*DSH* and pronounced as "dish") adjustment. This provides for a percentage increase in Medicare payments for hospitals that qualify. The base DRG payment rate is divided into a labor-related and nonlabor shares. The labor-related share is adjusted by the wage index applicable to average wages in the geographic region where the hospital is located. Thus, hospitals in areas with high costs of living receive a higher Medicare reimbursement. If a hospital is an approved teaching hospital, it receives an add-on payment for each case paid through IPPS. This add-on is known as the *indirect medical education adjustment*, and the amount varies based on the ratio of residents to beds.

The Outpatient Prospective Payment System (OPPS) was launched in August 2002 and is the system through which Medicare decides how much money a hospital or community mental health center will get for providing outpatient care to patients with Medicare. Again, the rate of reimbursement varies with the geographic location of the hospital or clinic. The Ambulatory Payment Classification (APC) divides all outpatient services into groups based on clinical and cost similarities. With a few exceptions, all services within an APC have the same payment rate. Expensive drugs and biologicals also have separate APCs. In 2008, CMS implemented an OPPS to pay for facility services such as nursing, recovery care, anesthesia, drugs, and other supplies. Physician services are reimbursed separately under the resource-based relative value scale (RBRVS[7]) schedule.

As discussed earlier, traditionally, health goods and services were billed for and paid based on a single illness or visit. There was no incentive to coordinate patient care across providers or disciplines, and the result was fragmentation of care. The Bundled Payments for Care Improvements initiative was launched in 2018 as part of the alternative payments program. Originally, 29 patient "episodes of care" were listed as eligible for bundled payment. The Bundled Payment initiative tested whether linking payments for all providers (e.g., hospital + physicians + rehabilitation center+ labs) that furnish Medicare-covered goods and services during an inpatient hospitalization could reduce Medicare expenditures while maintaining or improving the quality of care. The theory was that bundling payments would provide the incentive necessary for these groups to work together. The idea was that the providers would share any financial gains or losses associated with the care of the patient, leading to reduced complications from a hospitalization and lower costs. It was thought that providers would be more likely to adhere to best practices, be more judicious in their prescribing practices to decrease use of drugs or procedures that have potentially adverse effects, and take steps to reduce avoidable readmissions, all of which would affect the profit potential from the bundled payment. However, studies have shown mixed results from this initiative. A new bundled payment program for hospitals is expected to be launched in 2023.

The Medicare Payment Advisory Committee (MedPAC) oversees attempts to innovate Medicare. Recall that whatever Medicare pays for is usually followed

---

[7] Payments under the RBRVS are based on the principle that payments for various services should reflect their relative resource use. A formula is used to calculate the resources used in providing medical services. This value is multiplied by a conversion factor that determines the final dollar payment.

and adopted by nongovernment insurers. Medicare's payment practices also have a strong impact on provider behavior. For example, after MedPAC approved Medicare reimbursement for bariatric surgery (as a treatment for morbid obesity) in 2006, bariatric centers popped up all over the country. When setting payment rates, it is important for MedPAC members to consider the incentives that they create and ensure that the program is not unintentionally incentivizing poor care. At times, Medicare's payment systems have encouraged undesirable provider behavior, including furnishing unnecessary services and avoiding certain patients.

# Access to Care

Health policy analysts commonly refer to an "Iron Triangle of Health Care," which consists of cost of care, quality of care, and access to care (see **Figure 10-8**). The conceptual model provides a framework for the relationships among cost, quality, and access in all sorts of institutions, including policymaking, health care, and businesses. Basically, a change in one side of the triangle will affect the other sides, demonstrating various tradeoffs. For example, if access to care increases because of improved reimbursement or insurance coverage, both the cost of care and the quality of care should be monitored for unintended consequences. The goal of government reimbursement law, rules, and regulations is to lower costs while maintaining or improving quality and access to care. The Iron Triangle of Health Policy was introduced by William Kissick (1994) in his book *Medicine's Dilemmas: Infinite Needs Versus Finite Resources*.

The concept of access is too often described as individuals getting to and from health services and having the ability to pay for the services either by a third party or from their own pocket. Nurses know that access to healthcare services refers to much more: the ability of a person to be able to get to and from health services, to obtain the most effective services in a timely manner, to receive care from the correct provider for the identified need, to receive care at an affordable price, and to have care delivered with satisfactory dignity/compassion.

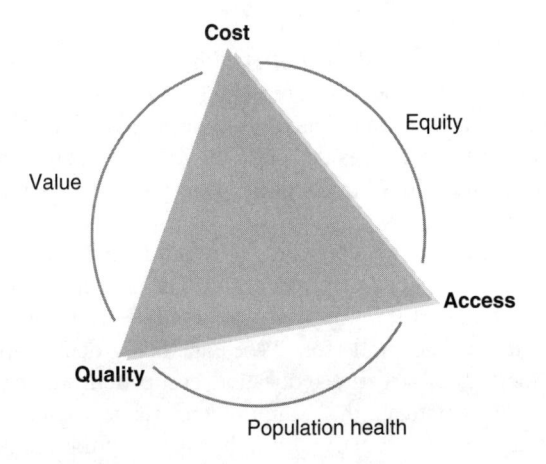

**Figure 10-8** Iron Triangle of Health Policy.

A number of models have been developed that describe access to care, including the Health Care Access Barriers model, Andersen's Behavioral Model of Health Services Utilization, and the Eight Factor Model:

- **Health Care Access Barriers Model.** This model facilitates the design of community health interventions by targeting measurable and modifiable determinants of health status (Carillo et al., 2011).

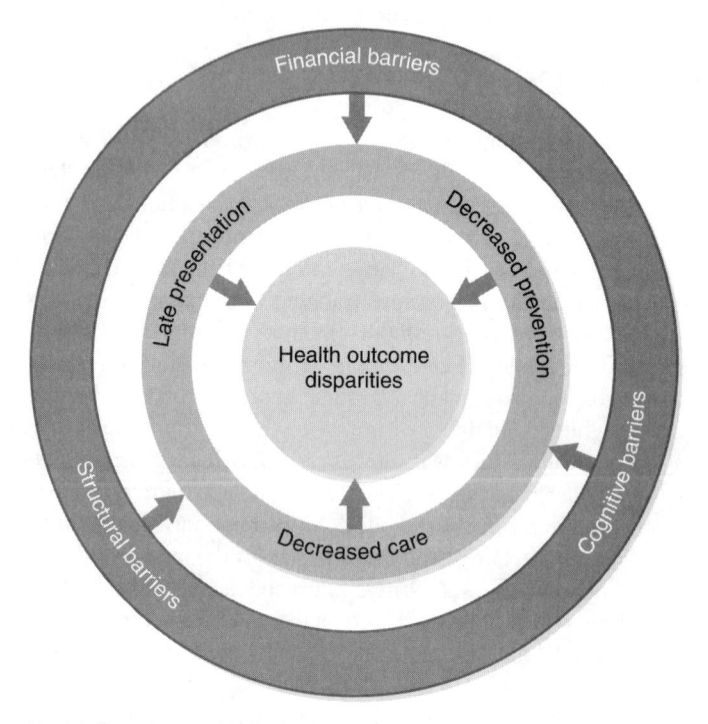

Health Care Access Behavior Model

Data from Carrillo, JE, Carrillo, VA, Perez, HR, Salas-Lopez, D, Natale-Pereira, A, Byron, AT (2011). Defining and targeting healthcare access barriers. *Journal of Health Care for the Poor and Underserved.* 22, 2:562-575.

- **Andersen's Behavioral Model of Health Services Utilization.** This model was proposed by Andersen in the 1960s, and since then it has undergone multiple revisions. A Web search of "Andersen's model of health utilization" will generate many images depicting the model and attempts to modernize it. Andersen introduced many of the concepts we now think of as intuitive when discussing access to care, such as consumer satisfaction with services. However, he and other researchers were primarily interested in how a consumer makes decisions with regard to utilizing health services. The model serves as a tool for the study of a broad set of determinants, both modifiable and not modifiable (Anderson, 1968), including demographic factors (age and gender), social structure (education, occupation, ethnicity, and other factors measuring status in the community, as well as coping and the health of the physical environment), and health beliefs (attitudes, values, and knowledge that might influence perceptions of need and use of health services).

Access to Care 249

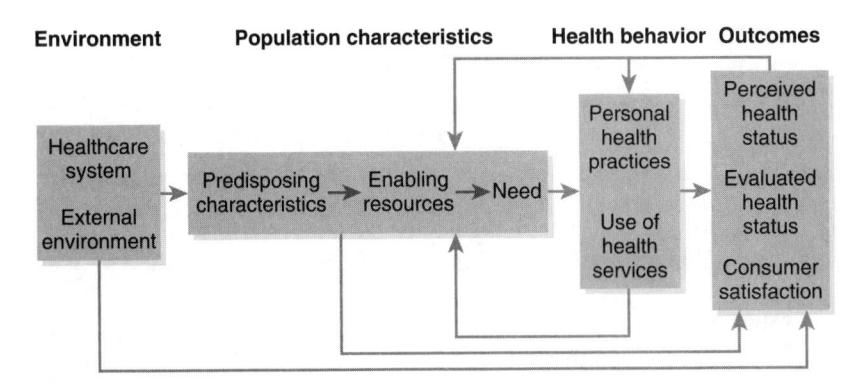

Andersen's Behavioral Model of Health Services Utilization

Data from Andersen, R. M. (2008). National health surveys and the behavioral model of health services use. *Medical Care*, 647–653.

- ***Eight Factor Model.*** The Eight Factor Model was proposed by Margie Lovett-Scott, EdD, RN, and Faith Prather, PhD (2012) as a way to compare access to services from one nation to the next. They refer to their model as measuring "true access." The eight factors depicted by the model are: (1) historical, (2) structure, (3) financing, (4) interventional, (5) preventive, (6) resources, (7) major health issues, and (8) health disparities.

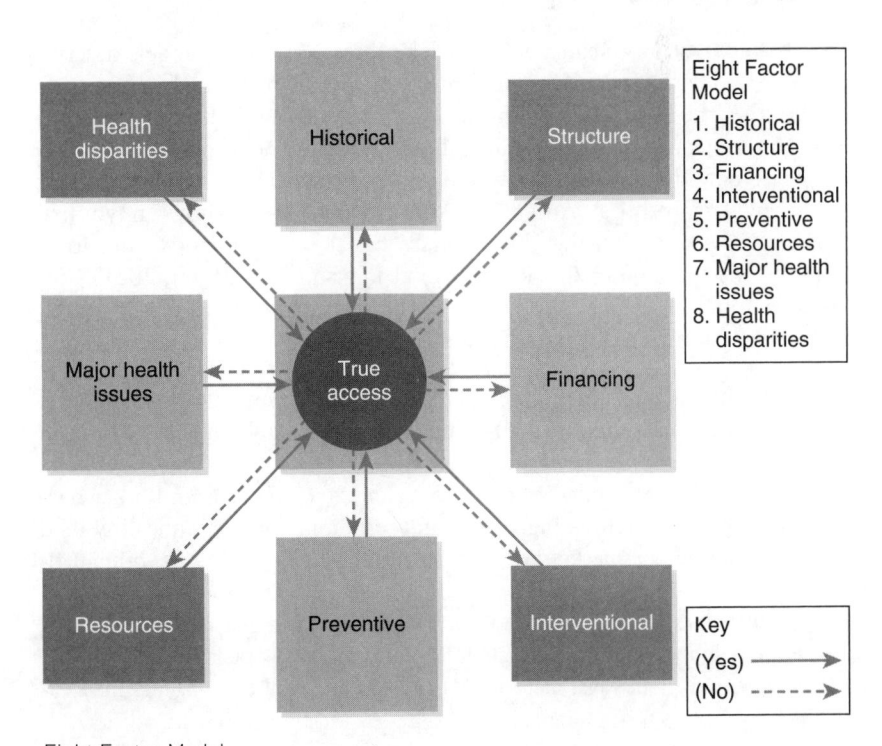

Eight Factor Model

A widely used and direct approach to measuring access is population-based surveys. Population-based surveys use a broad set of measures that capture dimensions of access, including aspects of primary care, the process of care seeking (e.g., the ease and convenience of getting to a doctor), barriers to care (e.g., language and transportation problems), and unmet health needs. With these surveys, researchers can make inferences about who is at greatest risk for lack of access to care by comparing vulnerable populations, such as the uninsured, people with low incomes, and those with poor health, to the rest of the population.

Population-based surveys, however, are not the best instruments to capture health outcomes as they relate to access. For example, surveys cannot tell researchers whether individuals are receiving good-quality care in the most appropriate setting and at the lowest possible cost. To examine these issues, researchers use hospital discharge data to determine rates of avoidable hospitalizations. *Avoidable hospitalizations* refers to a set of conditions, such as asthma and diabetes, that are considered treatable in ambulatory settings and for which hospitalization indicates a lack of access to high-quality primary care. Interest in this type of outcome-based measure is likely to increase. Barriers to healthcare access play an important role in understanding the causes of health and healthcare disparities.

## Disparities

**Health disparity** is a category in two of the three conceptual models describing access to care. An often quoted saying is that "our ZIP code determines our health." The Robert Wood Johnson Foundation (RWJF), the largest philanthropy in the United States focused solely on health, provides an interactive map exploring how the Census tract where you live predicts your life expectancy (www.rwjf.org/en/library/interactives/whereyouliveaffectshowlongyoulive.html). Not everyone in the United States has the same opportunities for a healthy, long life. The RWJF (Robert Wood Johnson Foundation, 2021) supports an approach called the "Culture of Health" to reduce the gaps in health across neighborhoods that stem from multiple factors:

- *Education and income* are directly linked to health. Communities with weak tax bases cannot support high-quality schools, and jobs are often scarce in neighborhoods with struggling economies.
- *Unsafe or unhealthy housing* exposes residents to allergens and other hazards such as overcrowding. Stores and restaurants selling unhealthy food may outnumber markets with fresh produce or restaurants with nutritious food.
- *Opportunities for residents to exercise*, walk, or cycle may be limited, and some neighborhoods are unsafe for children to play outside.
- *Proximity* to highways, factories, or other sources of toxic agents may expose residents to pollutants.

- *Access to primary care* providers and good hospitals may be limited.
- *Unreliable or expensive public transit* can isolate residents from good jobs, health and child care, and social services.
- *Residential segregation* and features that isolate communities (e.g., highways) can limit social cohesion, stifle economic growth, and perpetuate cycles of poverty.

The scope of this topic exceeds this discussion of healthcare finance. Readers are urged to pursue this topic as a part of understanding structural racism and the barriers set up at all levels of our socie+.5ty for some populations. Our goal as nurses who are interested in policy is to promote and achieve **health equity**. The pandemic and social unrest of 2020 raised greater awareness of health disparities, **healthcare disparities**, the social determinants of health, and the **political determinants of health (PDoH)**.

# Information Asymmetry in Health Care

**Information asymmetry** is the term used by economists to point out that healthcare consumption differs from purchasing other goods and services because of the inability of patients, providers, or payers to possess all the information needed for completely informed decision making. Optimal rational decision making requires "perfect information"—that is, the situation in which consumers are just as knowledgeable as sellers.

As an example, imagine you want to buy a car. You gather all the information that you can to eliminate any advantage the car seller may have in terms of the worth of this particular car. Being newly informed, you may choose to go to several dealerships before you find a seller that meets your expectations (or utility).

Now think about the typical healthcare experience. You go to your primary care provider (PCP) for your annual physical examination, and the PCP finds an abnormality and refers you to a specialist. Depending on your level of information, you will blindly trust the specialist or you may shop around. You may be very hard-pressed to learn about the quality or performance of either your primary care provider or the specialist. If you are referred to a hospital, you are probably unable to learn the nurse-to-patient ratio even though evidence shows that this factor is critical to your well-being. Clearly, information asymmetry is present at many points in this scenario.

Healthcare professionals might argue that they generally know what is "best" for patients. The problem of asymmetric information differs from a simple information problem in that one party possesses knowledge needed to enable rational decision making that the other party lacks. However, the healthcare professional and the insurer have a potential conflict of interest because of the exchange of money. The potential for benefiting monetarily from a decision may affect the decision-making process. In health care, the patient delegates much decision making to the healthcare professional (and sometimes even to the insurer).

Asymmetric information also affects healthcare professionals when patients conceal lifestyle information or state that they are in compliance with a treatment when they are not. In addition, a patient's caregiver may withhold or distort information that would be helpful to the provider. Insurers face information asymmetry as well—clients (consumers who are the buyers of insurance) know much more about the state of their health and their future plans than an insurer knows.

## Adverse Selection and Moral Hazard

Two specific types of information asymmetry are adverse selection and moral hazard. Economists use the terms **adverse selection** and **moral hazard** to describe the situations insurers face when consumers have greater information about their health than the insurers or payers do. Adverse selection occurs when a person participates in a health plan based *solely* on the likelihood that he or she will have higher than usual health expenses (e.g., planning to get pregnant). Moral hazard occurs when a health plan member uses more health services than that person ordinarily would simply because they are insured (e.g., a person with orthodontic coverage gets braces on his teeth for cosmetic purposes only). Insurers and payers may also lack sufficient information regarding the choices and decisions of providers and may be unable to ascertain if a procedure is truly medically necessary.

The patient, who does not pay the bill, demands as much care as possible. In contrast, the "insurance company maximizes profits by paying for as little as possible; . . . it is very costly for either the patient or the insurance company to prove the 'right' course of treatment. In short, information asymmetry makes health care different from the rest of the economy" (Wheelan, 2002, p. 86).

Imagine that you have consciously chosen not to purchase health insurance because you are young and enjoy good health; you decide it is cheaper to pay the annual penalty. Recall that insurers may no longer deny health insurance to those who have preexisting health conditions. Within a few months, you unexpectedly become pregnant and decide that you do not want to pay the full cost of prenatal care, delivery, and postpartum care, so you seek a private insurer such as Blue Cross and Blue Shield (BCBS) to purchase insurance. After the baby is born, and BCBS has paid for the costs of your pregnancy and delivery, you decide that you no longer need insurance and drop your coverage. This is an example of adverse selection.

If millions of people made this kind of choice, it would have dire effects on the insurance market. Insurance markets rely upon having a mix of customers who will not require payouts for healthcare episodes and customers who will. In other words, in the health insurance market, the healthy subsidize the sick. If only the old, the sick, or the disabled purchased health insurance, the market would collapse under the weight of their expenses. The scenario in health insurance is similar to that for other types of insurance, such as fire, life, and automobile—those customers who do not use the benefits subsidize those who do. Mandating the purchase of health insurance is an economic strategy designed to create a sustainable risk pool of beneficiaries.

# Comparative Effectiveness Research and Quality-Adjusted Life-Years

Imagine a system of research in which new discoveries or approaches to reduce or eliminate disease are tested for effectiveness against doing nothing at all. The current gold standard for research in the United States is the randomized control trial in which a group of subjects receives a treatment while another group receives no treatment. Effectiveness is decided by whether the disease or condition responded to the new approach, but the new approach is not compared to any other approach.

As a result of the 2009 American Recovery and Reinvestment Act (ARRA) and the 2010 ACA, the federal government made major investments in **comparative effectiveness research (CER)**. CER compares the overall benefits of one therapeutic approach with those of another for the majority of patients. These investments are yielding new information about which treatments work best for which population of patients. But how will this research be used beyond informing provider decisions?

Here is an example of a current dilemma: Solvadi is a drug developed to treat hepatitis C, a life-threatening disease that often goes unrecognized until it reaches its final stages. Solvadi costs $1,000 per 400 mg tablet/dose, and a full treatment regimen costs $84,000. In March 2014, the high price of this medication led to street protests in San Francisco. Health experts say that treating every person with advanced liver disease (from hepatitis C) in California would cost $6.3 billion if Solvadi was given to all those patients. With a success rate of about 90%, Solvadi is an improvement over older drugs, for which regimens cost only $25,000 (U.S. Senate Committee on Finance, 2015). In July 2020, the high costs of cancer drugs led 118 oncologists to rebuke the pharmaceutical industry. Dr. Ayalew Tefferi, a hematologist at the Mayo Clinic in Rochester, Minnesota, said in a news release, "The average gross household income in the U.S. is about $52,000 per year. For an insured patient with cancer who needs a drug that costs $120,000 per year, the out-of-pocket expenses could be as much as $25,000 to $30,000—more than half their average household income" (Healthcare Global, 2020).

Should public insurance (i.e., Medicare and Medicaid) pay for Solvadi or for high-priced cancer drugs? Does a regimen of Solvadi have cost benefits when compared to a liver transplant and lifelong immunotherapy? Is avoiding chronic disease "worth" the cost? How many productive years of life are gained? If California's Medicaid program typically spends $3,500 per beneficiary per year, how many new beneficiaries could be covered for the $6.3 billion? Economists and health services researchers tackle these types of questions by conducting CER and using a concept called **quality-adjusted life-years (QALYs)**.

QALY is an economic concept developed in the 1960s to facilitate cost-effectiveness analysis. Economists have attempted to include personal preferences regarding age and health conditions and have created a catalog known as the EQ-5D Index. For instance, if you have colon cancer and you are a 65-year-old White female, your EQ-5D index for QALYs is 0.93; that is, if you live 1 year with colon cancer, it is only worth 93% of a year with full health and no diseases. If you have two conditions at the same time (e.g., colon cancer and neurotic disorder), your EQ-5D index is 0.79. Once economists know how many QALYs a treatment is worth, they can figure out its cost per QALY—the broadest measure of the cost-effectiveness of health care.

In general, a QALY carries an economic value of between $70,000 and $150,000 per quality life-year gained by applying a treatment or approach (Anderson et al., 2014). Will CER be used to determine not only a treatment's effectiveness but also the cost-effectiveness, and ultimately, payment decisions? CER findings can be translated into practice in a variety of ways, some of which may be more acceptable to the public than others. QALYs have been linked to CER in the United Kingdom by the National Institute for Clinical Excellence and have led to debates about *rationing* care. This "R" word represents a slippery slope for opponents of government funding for CER.

The Patient-Centered Outcomes Research Institute (PCORI) was created under the ACA to coordinate government activity around CER. The ACA does not include cost-effectiveness determinations among the guidelines for PCORI. PCORI conducts research to provide information about the best available evidence to help patients and their healthcare providers make more informed decisions. PCORI's research is intended to give patients a better understanding of the prevention, treatment, and care options available and the science that supports those options.

# Bending the Healthcare Cost Curve Downward

Historically, prior to the 1990s, physicians and hospitals were paid for each procedure, test, visit, and consultation; that is, they received more pay for doing "more," whether or not "more" resulted in good patient outcomes. This kind of practice drives up healthcare costs. One of the ways more recent health policies seek to reduce healthcare costs in the United States is by encouraging providers and hospitals to form networks to provide good-quality care to Medicare beneficiaries while holding costs down. In such a system, providers get paid more if they keep their patients well. One of the challenges for hospitals and providers is that the incentives seek to reduce hospital stays, emergency room visits, and use of expensive specialist and testing services—all the ways that hospitals and physicians make money in the fee-for-service system.

Unlike in other industries, prices for health care vary dramatically depending on who is paying and on geography. The U.S. system is a bit like shopping in a department store where there are no prices marked on the goods. You check out, and a few weeks later, you receive a bill that reads, "Pay this." Growing movements toward price transparency in health care hope to empower patients to overcome information asymmetry, make wise choices, and foment competition that may lower prices. Physicians and hospitals that rarely competed on cost have been cushioned by third-party payers who pay the bulk of the bills. Some argue that true price transparency will destabilize the healthcare industry. Others think that transparency may confuse consumers (Beck, 2014).

# Policies to Watch

## Price Transparency

Congress wants to stop "surprise billing." This has bipartisan support, and there is enough political will to get something done. In November 2019, President Trump issued the Price and Quality Transparency in American Healthcare executive order, directing the CMS to take steps to increase price transparency to empower patients and increase competition among hospitals, group health plans, and health insurance issuers in the individual and group markets. As a result, two rules were issued: (1) the 2020 Outpatient Prospective Payment System and Ambulatory Surgical Center price transparency requirements for hospitals to make standard charges public and (2) the transparency in coverage rule (*Federal Register*, 2019).

Together, it is hoped that these two rules will give consumers real-time, personalized access to cost-sharing information, including an estimate of their cost-sharing liability for all covered healthcare items and services through an online tool that most group health plans and health insurance issuers would be required to make available to all of their members and in paper form at the consumer's request. The rules should also force insurers to disclose on a public website their negotiated rates for in-network providers and allowed amounts paid for out-of-network providers. Making this information available to the public is intended to drive innovation; support informed, price-conscious decision making; and promote competition in the healthcare industry.

From January 1, 2021, each hospital operating in the United States is required to provide clear, accessible pricing information online about the items and services they provide in two ways: (1) as a comprehensive machine-readable file with all items and services and (2) in a display of shoppable services in a consumer-friendly format.

Will these actions really empower consumers? Does the typical American healthcare consumer have the health and digital literacy required to utilize these tools? Is health care truly "shoppable," as these rules imply? A new industry seems to be blooming, with many companies advertising that they have electronic tools and apps to aid hospitals, providers, and insurers in accomplishing this task.

## COVID-19 Pandemic

Some federal regulations were relaxed to facilitate efficient care during the pandemic, such as those around telehealth use, availability, and reimbursement. Thought leaders and healthcare executives will be watching closely to see whether any of these changes become permanent. The focus on the patient is also increasing, particularly as competition from disruptive, more consumer-focused industries such as retail and tech emerges. Disruptions by the pandemic may cause health systems to hold off on spending on building and expansion. Health care is moving toward a consumer-centered model where people can shop for care and share data with an endless array of apps and services.

## Implications of Eliminating the Essential Benefits

No individual can consistently and accurately predict their medical needs for the coming year. Thus, expecting people to purchase insurance coverage each year only for the services they anticipate needing is illogical and, in fact, conceptually inconsistent with the principle of insuring against uncertain events. Presumably, if consumers choose to purchase cheaper health insurance with fewer benefits, then they will pay for uncovered and unexpected needs out of pocket. This was the situation before the ACA. This seems to be a chicken-and-egg situation: consumers need affordable insurance, but consumers cannot anticipate their health needs. Will uncovered health needs lead to consumers avoiding getting care due to costs?

## Provider Fee and Practice Changes

Provider groups are concerned that some proposals in the Medicare Physician Fee Schedule rule for 2021 would exacerbate the financial challenges physicians already faced during the COVID-19 pandemic, including lack of adequate telehealth reimbursement and sustainable practice revenue. A rule released by CMS in August 2020 proposed several changes to the Medicare Physician Fee Schedule for 2021, including steep payment cuts for some specialties, changes to the telehealth coverage list, and new quality reporting requirements. Provider groups called on CMS to reconsider the payment changes in order to support providers who saw practice revenue decrease by an average of 50% (Robeznieks, 2020).

CMS is proposing workforce changes to ensure healthcare professionals can practice at the top of their professional training. The CMS proposal would continue allowing nurse practitioners, clinical nurse specialists, physician assistants, and certified nurse-midwives (instead of only physicians) to supervise other providers performing diagnostic tests as long as it is consistent with state law and licensure and they maintain the required relationships with supervising/collaborating physicians. The proposed rule would also clarify that pharmacists can provide services as part of the professional services of a practitioner who bills Medicare.

According to the proposed rule, physical and occupational therapy assistants (instead of only physical and occupational therapists) would also be able to provide maintenance therapy in outpatient settings and physical or occupational therapists, speech-language pathologists, and other clinicians who directly bill Medicare would be able to review and verify, versus redocument, information already entered by other members of the clinical team into a patient's medical record.

## Landmark Legislation (COVID-19 Relief Package) Costs $1.9 Trillion

The American Rescue Plan Act of 2021 (ARPA) became a law in March 2021 and is the biggest change to the Affordable Care Act in over a decade. The reforms, which are in effect until March 2023, expand subsidies to purchase health insurance and make insurance available to people of all incomes for the first time. Specifically, the Rescue Plan addresses the sky-high premiums for people who (previously) did not qualify for federal tax credits to help pay for them. For the next 2 years, the Rescue Plan will expand tax credits to higher earners and cap the maximum premium anyone is expected to pay at 8.5% of their income. The Congressional Budget Office estimates that 1.3 million more people will be insured in 2022. Fiscal conservatives warn that the predicted cost of $34 billion for these changes will significantly add to the national debt. ARPA is a large and complex law and among many other things, it does the following (Public Law 117-2, 2021):

- Boosts tax credits at lower incomes so people making less than 150% of the FPL are expected to pay $0 in premiums for a benchmark plan on a HIX
- Provides free health insurance on the HIX for those receiving unemployment benefits
- Boosts incentives for states to expand Medicaid by having the federal government pick pay for new recipients
- Provides $8.5 billion to reimburse rural healthcare providers for healthcare-related expenses and lost revenues attributable to COVID–19
- Allocates $10 billion for the purposes of carrying out activities under the Defense Production Act. The funding can be used for the manufacturing and procurement of medical supplies and equipment related to combating the COVID-19 pandemic.
- Boosts the entire healthcare System without asking insurers, hospitals, or providers to cut costs or Americans to pay new taxes
- Cuts child poverty by about one-half via the child tax credit. Low and moderate-income families will receive $3,000 annually per child, or $3,600 per child under 6, in monthly installments. This holds for families who pay $0 in taxes (who have not previously received child tax credits).
- Boosts childcare facilities with additional funding

## Conclusion

During the election campaigns of 2020, candidates frequently spoke for and against schemes to improve healthcare safety, quality, and access while lowering costs . . . or at least holding costs steady. Providing high quality, affordable care with equal access for all is the unicorn that politicians chase; at least, they want us to believe they are chasing that goal. Healthcare finance and the economic principles that drive those finances are important to you as a practicing nurse. The concepts and proposed policies are important to you as an informed citizen.

The Democrats are expected to try to make the changes to the ACA within ARPA permanent. Will there be unintended consequences to this broad reaching (and expensive) law? As more Americans move to government-sponsored health insurance, will incomes for physicians, APRNs, and hospitals decline?

There is a great deal of policy for nurses to be informed about. The U.S. election cycle provides you with continuing opportunities to make your informed choice for representation in government in 2022, 2024, and onward. Remember that patient care is a highly political endeavor.

## Chapter Discussion Points

1. Discuss the role of economists in the healthcare policy process. Read about the work of current health economists (e.g., Joseph Antos, James Capretta, Jeffrey Sachs, and Gail Wilensky) to understand their role.
2. Access the blog created by the journal *Health Affairs* (www.healthaffairs.org/blog/) and use the keyword "economics" to search for the latest articles about healthcare economics.
3. Discuss the gross national product (GNP) in terms of healthcare expenditures. Which sorts of programs will not receive funding when health care consumes a large percentage of federal expenditures?
4. Research some articles on cost shifting in health care. Identify policies that use this method. Argue the benefits and losses of cost shifting. Also, research cross-subsidization in health care. How does this differ from cost shifting?
5. Who finances most long-term care in the United States? Take a poll of your peers prior to researching this question to see what they think is the answer. Are nurses well informed about this economic issue, and does this meet your expectation?
6. How does QALY analysis benefit the young over the old?
7. Discover and discuss examples of health and healthcare equity issues in your community by finding and reading the most recent *Community Assessment* (from your local public health department).

# CASE STUDY 10-1: Economic Value of BSN Education for RNs

Retrieve and read the following study from the March 2014 issue of *The Lancet*: "Nurse Staffing and Education and Hospital Mortality in Nine European Countries: A Retrospective Observational Study" by Linda Aiken, PhD, and colleagues of the Center for Health Outcomes and Policy Research at the University of Pennsylvania School of Nursing. This study shows that increasing a nurse's workload by one patient increases the likelihood of an inpatient dying within 30 days of admission by 7% (odds ratio [OR], 1.068; 95% confidence interval [CI], 1.031–1.106), and every 10% increase in bachelor's degree nurses is associated with a 7% decrease in this likelihood (OR, 0.929; 95% CI, 0.886–0.973). These associations imply that patients in hospitals in which 60% of nurses have bachelor's degrees and where nurses care for an average of six patients will have almost 30% lower mortality than patients in hospitals in which only 30% of nurses have bachelor's degrees and nurses care for an average of eight patients.

### Case Study Discussion Questions

1. State your interpretation of these data. Using these conclusions, discuss the implications for hospital leaders when making staffing decisions.
2. Discover the percentage of BSN-prepared nurses licensed in your state. If possible, discover the percentage of BSN-prepared nurses in a hospital or facility in your area.
3. How easily can an average person find out the RN:patient and BSN RN:patient ratio in hospitals? Why do you think this situation exists? What does it mean to you and your family? Who or which entities can change this situation?

## CASE STUDY 10-2: Economic Impact of States Declining Medicaid Expansion

Recall that Medicaid is a joint federal and state entitlement health insurance program. The ACA of 2010 required all states to eliminate the use of categories to determine eligibility and expand the Medicaid program to all persons younger than age 65 with incomes at or below 138% of the federal poverty level. However, in June 2012, the U.S. Supreme Court ruled that requiring states to expand their Medicaid programs was unconstitutional. Per the ruling, each state can make its own decision on whether to expand the program. By 2016, 32 states and Washington, D.C. had opted to expand their Medicaid programs. Declining expansion means that Medicaid continues as it was prior to the ACA's implementation, with category-based eligibility.

### Case Study Discussion Questions

1. Determine whether your state has expanded its Medicaid program.
2. Explain why a very poor person (income below FPL) younger than 65 years living in one of the states that declined Medicaid expansion may be ineligible to participate in the health insurance exchanges.
3. What is the economic effect on the state (and on the hospital or site where you work or are being trained) of having a large population of uninsured people?
4. Why would a state choose not to participate in Medicaid expansion despite the federal promise of paying for the additional beneficiaries?
5. The U.S. Constitution does not include a "right" to health care. Debate the pros and cons of a universal Medicare-for-all healthcare finance program for the United States. Refer to the ANA Code of Ethics to inform your debate.

## References

Anderson, J. L., Heidenreich, P. A., Barnett, P. G., Creager, M. A., Fonarow, G. C., Gibbons, R. J., Halperin, J. L., Hlatky, M. A., Jacobs, A. K., Mark, D. B., Masoudi, F. A., Peterson, E. D., & Shaw, L. J. (2014). ACC/AHA statement on cost/value methodology in clinical practice guidelines and performance measures: A report of the American College of Cardiology/American Heart Association Task Force on Performance Measures and Task Force on Practice Guidelines. *Circulation*, 129, 2329–2345. http://doi.org/10.1161/CIR.0000000000000042

Andersen, R. M. (1968). *Behavioral model of families' use of health service* (Research Series No. 25). Center for Health Administration Studies, University of Chicago.

Andersen, R. M. (2008). National health surveys and the behavioral model of health services use. *Medical Care*, 46(7), 647–653.

Artiga, S., Orgera, K., & Pham, O. (2020, March 4). *Disparities in health and healthcare: Five key questions and answers*. Kaiser Family Foundation. https://www.kff.org/racial-equity-and-health-policy/issue-brief/disparities-in-health-and-health-care-five-key-questions-and-answers/

Assistant Secretary of Planning and Evaluation. (2016, October 24). *Health plan choice and premiums in the 2017 health insurance marketplace*. Research brief. U.S. Department of Health and Human Services. https://aspe.hhs.gov/system/files/pdf/212721/2017MarketplaceLandscapeBrief.pdf

Beck, M. (2014, February 23). How to bring the price of health care into the open. *Wall Street Journal*. http://online.wsj.com/news/articles/SB10001424052702303650204579375242842086688

Bureau of Labor Statistics. (2019a). *Consumer expenditures—2018* [Press release]. https://www.bls.gov/opub/reports/consumer-expenditures/2018/home.htm

Bureau of Labor Statistics. (2019b, December 18). *Employer costs for employee compensation*. [Press release]. https://www.bls.gov/bls/news-release/ecec.htm

Carrillo, J. E., Carrillo, V. A., Perez, H. R., Salas-Lopez, D., Natale-Pereira, A., & Byron, A. T. (2011). Defining and targeting healthcare access barriers. *Journal of Health Care for the Poor and Underserved, 22*(2), 562–575.
Center on Budget and Policy Priorities. (2020, April 14). *Policy basics: Introduction to Medicaid.* https://www.cbpp.org/research/health/policy-basics-introduction-to-medicaid
Centers for Medicare and Medicaid Services. (2017). National health expenditure data. https://www.cms.gov/research-statistics-data-and-systems/statistics-trends-and-reports/nationalhealth expenddata/nationalhealthaccountshistorical.html
Einav, L., Finkelstein, A., Mullainathan, S., & Obermeyer, Z. (2018). Predictive modeling of U.S. healthcare spending in late life. *Science, 29,* 1462–1465.
*Federal Register.* (2020, November 27). *Medicare and Medicaid programs: CY 2020 hospital outpatient PPS policy changes and payment rates and ambulatory surgical center payment system policy changes and payment rates. Price transparency requirements for hospitals to make standard charges public.* https://www.federalregister.gov/documents/2019/11/27/2019-24931/medicare-and-medicaid-programs-cy-2020-hospital-outpatient-pps-policy-changes-and-payment-rates-and
Fehr, R., McDermott, D., & Cox, C. (2020). *Individual insurance market performance in 2019.* Kaiser Family Foundation. https://www.kff.org/private-insurance/issue-brief/individual-insurance-market-performance-in-2019/
Getzen, T. (2010). *Health economics and financing* (4th ed.). John Wiley & Sons.
Healthcare Global. (2020, July 27). *Rising cancer drug costs lead to doctor protests against Big Pharma.* https://www.healthcareglobal.com/hospitals/rising-cancer-drug-costs-lead-doctor-protests-against-big-pharma
Hussey, P. S., Wertheimer, S., & Mehrota, A. (2013). The association between health care quality and cost: A systematic review. *Annals of Internal Medicine, 158*(1), 27–34.
Jost, T. (2018, October 30). *Using the 1332 state waiver program to undermines the Affordable Care Act state by state.* Commonwealth Fund. https://www.commonwealthfund.org/blog/2018/using-1332-state-waiver-program-undermine-affordable-care-act-state-state
Kaiser Family Foundation. (2020a). *A dozen facts about Medicare Advantage in 2020.* https://www.kff.org/medicare/issue-brief/a-dozen-facts-about-medicare-advantage-in-2020/
Kaiser Family Foundation. (2020b). *Average family premiums rose 4%, to $21,342 in 2020, benchmark KFF employer health benefit survey finds.* https://www.kff.org/health-costs/press-release/average-family-premiums-rose-4-to-21342-in-2020-benchmark-kff-employer-health-benefit-survey-finds/on November 17, 2020.
Kaiser Family Foundation. (2020c). *Total number of Medicare beneficiaries.* https://www.kff.org/medicare/state-indicator/total-medicare-beneficiaries/?currentTimeframe=0&selectedDistributions=total&sortModel=%7B%22colId%22:%22Location%22,%22sort%22:%22asc%22%7D
Kessler, G. (2019, February 26). The CBOs shifting view on the impact of the Obamacare individual mandate. *Washington Post.* https://www.washingtonpost.com/politics/2019/02/26/cbos-shifting-view-impact-obamacare-individual-mandate/
Kissick, W. L.(1994). *Medicine's dilemmas: Infinite needs versus finite resources.* Yale University Press.
Lovett-Scott, M., & Prather, F. (2012). *Global health systems: Comparing strategies for delivering health systems.* Jones & Bartlett Learning.
National Conference of State Legislatures. (2020, August 31). *Health finance issues.* https://www.ncsl.org/research/health/health-finance-issues.aspx
Nunn, R., Parsons, J., & Shambaugh, J. (2020, March 10). *A dozen facts about the economics of the US health-care system.* Brookings Institute Report. https://www.brookings.edu/wp-content/uploads/2020/03/HealthCare_Facts_WEB_FINAL.pdf
Patient Protection and Affordable Care Act of 2010. Pub. L. No. 111–148, § 3022.
Public Law 117-2. (March 11, 2021). The American Rescue Plan Act of 2021. https://www.congress.gov/bill/117th-congress/house-bill/1319/text
QPP. (n.d.) *Objectives of the program.* https://qpp.cms.gov/about/qpp-overview
Robert Wood Johnson Foundation. (March 18, 2021). *Building a culture of health.* https://www.rwjf.org/en/how-we-work/building-a-culture-of-health.html
Roberts, J. (January 24, 2019). *The case against Medicaid expansion.* The John Locke Foundation. https://www.johnlocke.org/update/the-case-against-medicaid-expansion/

Robeznieks, A. (October 28, 2020). *Physician survey details depth of pandemic's financial impact.* https://www.ama-assn.org/practice-management/sustainability/physician-survey-details-depth-pandemic-s-financial-impact

Rosenbaum, S., Rothenberg, S., Gunsalus, R., & Schmucker, R. (2017, January 12). *Medicaid's future: What might ACA repeal mean?* Commonwealth Fund. http://www.commonwealthfund.org/publications/issue-briefs/2017/jan/medicaids-future-aca-repeal

Sotomayor, M., & Memoli, M. (2020). *Biden health care plan would build on Obamacare.* https://www.nbcnews.com/card/biden-health-care-plan-would-build-obamacare-n1029811

Statista. (n.d.). *National per capita health expenditure in the United States from 1960 to 2020 (in U.S. dollars).* https://www.statista.com/statistics/184955/us-national-health-expenditures-per-capita-since-1960/

Stein, H. (1986). *Washington bedtime stories: The politics of money and jobs.* The Free Press.

U.S. Department of Health and Human Services. (n.d.). *Poverty guidelines.* https://aspe.hhs.gov/poverty-guidelines

U.S. Senate Committee of Finance. (December,2015). *The price of Solvadi and its impact on the U.S. health care system.* Senate Prints 114-20 Part 1. https://www.govinfo.gov/content/pkg/CPRT-114SPRT97329/html/CPRT-114SPRT97329-Part1.htm

Value Health Care Services. (n.d.). *What is a Medicare severity diagnosis-related group?* https://valuehealthcareservices.com/education/what-is-a-medicare-severity-diagnosis-related-group-ms-drg/

Wheelan, C. (2002). *Naked economics: Undressing the dismal science.* W. W. Norton.

# Online Resources

**Alliance for Health Policy (www.allhealthpolicy.org):** Nonpartisan, well-respected organization providing analytical materials and webcasts by health economists and other health experts.

**America's Health Insurance Plan (www.ahip.org):** The national association for insurance companies providing coverage for health care and related services.

**California HealthCare Foundation (www.chcf.org):** This organization's annual chartbook provides a wealth of data and graphics.

**Centers for Medicare and Medicaid Services (www.cms.gov/NationalHealthExpendData/):** National health expenditure data.

**Centers for Medicare and Medicaid Services (CMS) Data Navigator (www.cms.gov/home/rsds.asp):** The Data Navigator introduces healthcare data users to the Medicare and Medicaid program data maintained by CMS. Intended for use by researchers and analysts.

**Commonwealth Fund (www.commonwealthfund.org):** Supports independent research on healthcare issues and makes grants to improve healthcare practice and policy. Not to be confused with the Commonwealth Foundation.

**Consumer Expenditure Survey, Bureau of Labor Statistics (www.bls.gov/cex/):** Details of consumer healthcare expenditures.

**Consumer Price Indexes, Bureau of Labor Statistics (www.bls.gov/cpi/):** Monthly data on changes in the prices paid by urban consumers for a representative basket of goods and services.

**Current Population Survey, U.S. Census Bureau (www.census.gov):** Everything you want to know about the U.S. Census and the U.S. population.

**Dartmouth Atlas of Health Care (www.dartmouthatlas.org):** Brings together researchers in diverse disciplines—including epidemiology, economics, and statistics—to generate an accurate description of how medical resources are distributed and used in the United States.

**HealthCare.gov (www.healthcare.gov):** Federal government website maintained by the U.S. Department of Health and Human Services. Provides information about the federal health insurance exchange.

**Kaiser Family Foundation (www.kff.org):** Nonpartisan, nongovernmental organization that provides data, facts, and analysis of healthcare issues and health policy.

**MedPAC (www.medpac.gov/)**: A nonpartisan legislative branch agency that provides the U.S. Congress with analysis and policy advice on the Medicare program. It is required to report to Congress twice per year and is responsible to alert Congress of impending funding shortages.

**Organisation for Economic Co-operation and Development (www.oecd.org/)**: An organization of 35 member countries with the mission to promote policies that will improve the economic and social well-being of people around the world. It works with governments to understand what drives economic, social, and environmental change.

# CHAPTER 11

# The Impact of Nurse Influence on Global Health Policy

Jeri A. Milstead

## KEY TERMS

**Alliance for Ethical International Recruitment Practices (Alliance):** An independent subsidiary of CGFNS that certifies international recruiters who agree to abide by a code of fair and ethical practice, educates nurses about their rights, and conducts research through surveys of foreign nurses about their experience of working in the U.S. (Alliance, n.d.).

**Commission on Graduates of Foreign Nursing Schools International (CGFNS):** A non-governmental organization that authenticates academic records and professional licenses of nurses and other healthcare professionals who are educated or who work outside the U.S. and seek employment in this country (CGFNS, 2020).

**Globalization:** Process that describes the movement of capital (human and social), individuals, and private or governmental organizations across geographic boundaries in which human health effects, and is affected by social, economic, and political systems (Globalization 101, 2020).

**International Council of Nurses (ICN):** A federation of national nurses' associations that support competent and quality practice, intellectual knowledge, and global health policy toward a professional nurse workforce (ICN, n.d.).

**Migration of human capital:** The movement of people, with their stock of knowledge, habits, and social and personality attributes, including creativity, along with the ability to perform labor so as to produce economic value across international borders.

**Nongovernmental organization (NGO):** A nonprofit, voluntary citizens group that is organized on a local, national, or international level to address issues in support of the public good.

**Public Health Emergency of International Concern (PHEIC):** A designation by the World Health Organization (WHO) of large-scale health issues. A problem does not have to reach pandemic status to be identified as a PHEIC.

**Push–pull factors:** Factors that either forcefully push people into migration or attract them. A push factor is generally some problem that results in people wanting to migrate.

**2020 Triad Statement:** A joint agreement between the International Council of Nurses, the International Confederation of Midwives, and the World Health Organization in response to nurse leadership during the COVID-19 pandemic.
**World Health Organization (WHO):** An agency of the United Nations established in 1948 in Geneva, Switzerland. The WHO is concerned with international public health. It monitors and combats infectious and noncommunicable diseases and seeks to ensure the safety of air, food, water, medicines, and vaccines for all. This ambitious mission is funded by donations from its 194 member nations.

# Introduction

*Global health = local health.* This statement posits that health issues affecting people in a large geographic area have implications for diagnosis, treatment, and preventive measures at the local level as well. Conversely, emerging diseases may not grow to epidemic or pandemic proportions if they are noticed, reported, and addressed at a local/tribal/regional level. The juxtaposition of policies at the international, national/federal, state/provincial, and local levels is important from the standpoint of the impact of recognizing health issues and addressing them by designing, implementing, and evaluating effective policies and programs. Policies allocate and direct resources, but they also reflect the values and perspectives of those who write them. Legal, economic, social, religious, political, and cultural perspectives frame how health issues are perceived—and, perhaps more important, how they shape the range of solutions considered.

A health-based nursing model includes social and humane considerations. For example, when confronted with a population that resists a vaccination policy for mumps, a nursing model might interject the implications of potential sterility of unvaccinated males and the resultant social cost to the population as a means to increase adherence. Professional nurses have long recognized their potential for influencing health policy around the world. From faith-based missions to more formalized organizations, nurses want a voice in decisions that affect the health of people locally and globally. The nurse role extends beyond the bedside to advocacy through political action. The concepts and competencies of the policy process of decision making have not been major components of nurse education programs in many countries, despite the early example of Florence Nightingale and the current emphasis of the International Council of Nurses (ICN) on health policy and programs. Nurses make up half of the global health workforce (Drennan & Ross, 2019) and have power, not just in numbers, but in the depth of clinical knowledge they can bring to policymakers (**Figure 11-1**).

In this chapter, globalization, as related to health care, is examined through the lens of the migration of human capital. The chapter culminates with six examples of nurses whose work has had significant impact on policymaking in their countries and highlights the importance of the role of the nurse in the policy arena. These examples describe a variety of opportunities in which nurses can influence health policies and social programs.

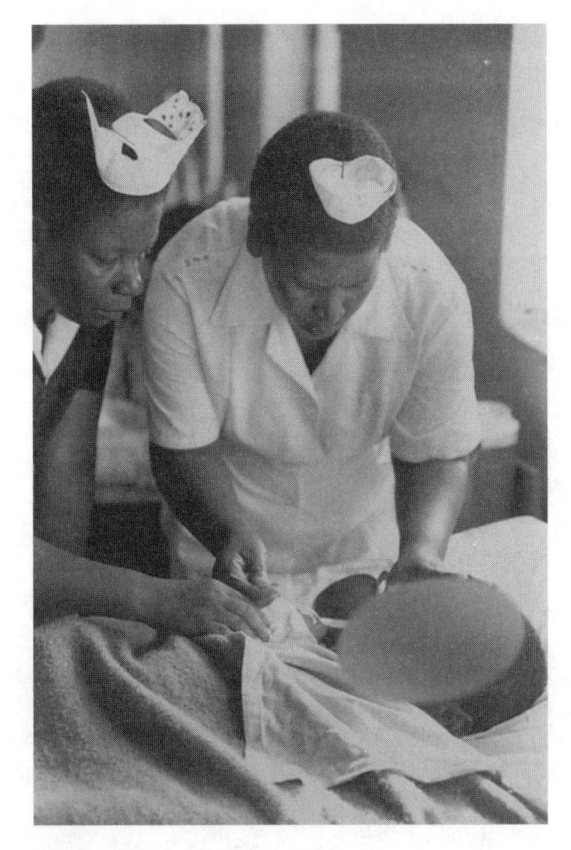

**Figure 11-1** A nurse in Tanzania.
© World Health Organization/Louise Gubb, 1990.

## International Organizations

Three international organizations focus on health issues and nurses in countries and territories around the globe: the United Nations, the World Health Organization, and the International Council of Nurses. The United Nations (UN) is an organization comprising 193 member states. The UN takes action on a wide range of issues that confront humanity, including peace and security, climate change, human rights, terrorism, health emergencies, gender equality, sustainable development, and more (United Nations, n.d.a). In 2015, building on *The Millennium Goals*, the UN developed the *2030 Agenda for Sustainable Development*, a "universal call to action to end poverty, protect the planet and improve the lives and prospects of everyone, everywhere" (United Nations, n.d.b). The Agenda consists of 17 Sustainable Development Goals (SDGs) that address social, economic, and environmental determinants of health and 169 associated targets focused on five themes: people, planet, peace, prosperity, and partnership (Rosa & Hassmiller, 2020) (see **Figure 11-2**). All 17 goals were adopted in 2015 and accompanied by a

**Figure 11-2** The UN Sustainable Development Goals.
Reproduced from United Nations. (n.d.). Sustainable development goals: 17 goals to transform our world. https://www.uhcpartnership.net/country-profile/tanzania/

15-year plan of strategies for achievement. The Agenda recognizes for the first time the contribution of human migration on sustainable development. The Agenda's core principle is to "leave no one behind." The central reference to migration is Target 10.7: "to facilitate orderly, safe, regular and responsible migration and mobility of people, including through the implementation of planned and well-managed migration policies." However, migration is a "cross-cutting issue which is relevant to all 17 SDGs and most of the 169 Targets" (Migration Data Portal, n.d.). In 2020, the COVID-19 pandemic put on hold many programs that were addressing the SDGs by reallocating funds and personnel to pandemic-related activities.

Health is a part of most of the SDGs. Nurses are involved in many programs that deal with the goals and often are a significant part of the leadership team.

The **World Health Organization (WHO)** is the UN agency charged with coordinating international public health policy. It has no legal authority to mandate policy or actions in member states. It is funded by member states that voluntarily pay assessed and donated contributions from member states and other partners. Primary activities include developing partnerships with other global health initiatives, conducting research, setting norms, providing technical support, and monitoring health trends around the world. Since 1948, the guiding principle has been that all people should enjoy the highest standard of health, regardless of race, religion, political belief, and economic or social conditions. Over the years, people have come together to reiterate and reinforce this principle—for example, the Declaration of Alma-Ata in 1978 set the aspirational goal of health for all. The WHO monitors international health trends and coordinates activities such as childhood vaccination projects.

Some member states have criticized WHO for budget constraints and slow response. Some countries have not paid their allotted amounts, and some programs cost more than was originally budgeted. These two factors result in budget deficits that ultimately limit the types and extent of programs available. Criticism of the general philosophy, lack of legal authority, and alleged inefficient internal operations has led some national heads to voice their concerns and to threaten to or actually withhold funds and services. The WHO can declare a **Public Health Emergency of International Concern** (**PHEIC**, pronounced "fake"), such as the COVID-19 pandemic in 2020, during which the WHO offered guidance to health officials, provided technical support, and recommended trade policies to try to slow transmission of communicable disease (Council on Foreign Relations, n.d.; WHO, n.d.).

More than 600 government chief nursing and midwifery officers, leaders and representatives of national nursing associations and midwifery associations, together with the International Council of Nurses, the International Confederation of Midwives, the World Health Organization, key partners, (including WHO Collaborating Centers for Nursing and Midwifery) and regulators from over 145 countries gathered virtually for the 8th ICN-ICM-WHO Triad Meeting on June 16–18, 2020. The meeting occurred during a time of "unparalleled significance" due to convergence of the International Year of the Nurse and the Midwife with the COVID-19 pandemic. The dual spotlight served to acknowledge that midwives and nurses put their lives at risk to respond to the pandemic and provide essential health services. The meeting focused on how midwives and nurses can be protected, their leadership maintained and supported, and their contributions to emergency response, universal health coverage, and the health and well-being of global populations sustained currently and into the future. As a result, the participants committed to the **2020 Triad Statement** that supports WHO member states in the development and implementation of actions to improve working conditions and practice standards, eliminate discrimination, maximize the role, and leverage data to outline a roadmap for future policy dialogue (WHO, 2020). **Table 11-1** briefly describes the 10 areas of support in the 2020 Triad Statement.

The **International Council of Nurses (ICN)** is a **nongovernmental organization (NGO)** headquartered in Geneva, Switzerland, that is committed to ensuring that nurses have a voice in the development and implementation of health policy and ensuring that these policies are effective and meet the real needs of patients, families, and communities around the world. Participation in health policy is a core component of the ICN definition of "nurse." ICN has an official relationship with the WHO (ICN, n.d.).

# Globalization, Immigration, and Migration

**Globalization** of health and health care generally takes the form of two disparate approaches. First, business and industry in a country may solicit and hire human capital (e.g., RNs, MDs, scientists) from foreign countries to expand research and development of manufactured products and services such

### Table 11-1  2020 Triad Statement

1. Leverage data and evidence for policy dialogue.
2. Manage human resources.
3. Support nurse and midwife leadership.
4. Match education and training to health system objectives.
5. Enable practice to the full extent of the law.
6. Eliminate all forms of discrimination.
7. Maximize nurse and midwife roles as bridges to communities.
8. Address gaps in data.
9. Increase funding as an investment.
10. Ensure decent working conditions and environments.

Data from 2020 TRIAD STATEMENT, International Council of Nurses – International Confederation of Midwives – World Health Organization, WHO. www.who.int/Publications/m/item/2020-Triad-Statement

---

as health care. **Migration of human capital** can contribute tremendously to the profitability of a company and to local, regional, or national governmental entities through tax and other positive economic incentives and can benefit the individuals who have accepted jobs that improve their lives (**Figure 11-3**). The second force of globalization occurs with migration away from a source country: migration can have devastating effects on the economy, healthcare system, population health, and a wide array of social issues in countries experiencing a loss of health professionals.

When the human capital being attracted away from a home country is health professionals, the stability of the health workforce of the home country is often ruined. **Push-pull factors** come into play. Push factors in a home country that drive nurses to seek employment in other countries include low wages, poor nurse reputation, political upheaval, and poor quality of life. Pull factors that attract nurses to other countries include better wages, positive reputation as a nurse, political stability, and a better quality of life.

Immigration has to do with those who migrate *into* a foreign country. Laws in every nation establish the process for seeking visitor, resident, or citizen status. Legal documents are required when seeking work in a foreign country. Obtaining a visa can be a time-consuming, perplexing process that also takes time. Wading through the myriad types of visas can be puzzling. A complete list of categories available for visas in the United States is available at www.travel.state.gov/content/travel/en/404.html.

Other approvals may be required. For example, all nurses who are interested in working in the United States must have their nursing education and practice credentials evaluated and verified by the **Commission on Graduates of Foreign Nursing Schools International (CGFNS)**. According to CGFNS: "The

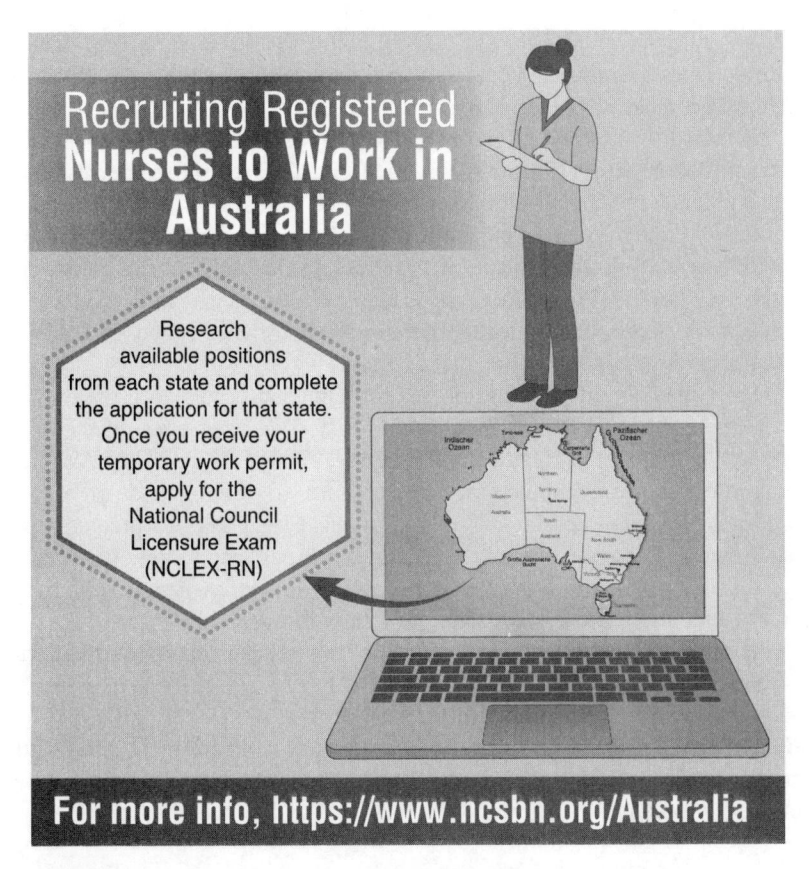

**FIGURE 11-3** Poster recruiting registered nurses to work in Australia.

Credentials Evaluation Service (CES) Professional Report provides a detailed analysis of credentials earned at multiple levels of nursing education received outside the United States. CES includes a statement of comparability of a healthcare worker's education when assessed against U.S. standards" (CGFNS, n.d.). CGFNS also provides evaluation of written and oral English language that is required by some U.S. states prior to issuing a nurse license.

Migration of nurses across political or geographic borders creates opportunity for the nurse but may have unintended consequences. For example, multiple and complex electronic and technological equipment may be so formidable that the nurse does not function at the full scope of practice of a nurse in the United States. Language accents, unfamiliarity with idioms, racial discrimination, and difficulty with written and spoken English may lead to social isolation. Even small, close-knit groups of nurses who live together may not have enough emotional, physical, or financial support to be content and productive; they may choose to return to their original countries.

Not all opportunities for foreign employment are legitimate or ethical; some are shams that lure nurses either to jobs that are nonexistent or jobs with questionable conditions. Alleged unethical recruitment companies entice nurses to relocate with promises of fanciful lifestyles and large salaries. In reality, these types of companies deal in human trafficking. Recruiters can mislead, lie, and trap nurses by severely restricting or totally controlling wages, manipulating their lives, and even forcing illegal drug use. CGFNS has become alert to nefarious companies (Shaffer et al., 2020). In 2008, a group of nurses, nurse organizations, unions, and employers convened to discuss reports of negative employment practices that were surfacing. This group became the **Alliance for Ethical International Recruitment Practices (Alliance)** and was subsumed within CGFNS in 2014. The Alliance helps foreign nurses understand their employment rights and assures that employment agencies adhere to a code of ethical and fair practices.

Concerned about the ethics of "brain drain" that occurs with the outflow of a workforce, the WHO established a Global Code of Practice on the International Recruitment of Health Care Personnel (Global Code, 2011). Although nonbinding, the code encourages member states to honor human rights and appropriate working conditions and to establish legal rules to protect workers. The code also urges the development of policies that address the original causes of the problem of losing an experienced workforce—aging, retirement, and out-migration due to low wages or other working and living conditions.

Aging and retirement present a double challenge. Countries with fast-growing aging populations (e.g., Japan, Italy, Cuba, and China) seek nurses from other countries to combat the erosion of their retirement-age workforces (**Figure 11-4**). Aggressive recruitment campaigns by some hospitals and healthcare agencies offer relocation bonuses and other perks (i.e., pull factors) to lure younger nurses to fill vacancies. Work visas are good for a limited period, often

**FIGURE 11-4** Recruiting foreign nurses.

2 years with a possible extension of 2 more years. Usually, these nurses must return to their own countries for a specified time before they can reapply for another tour. Strategic policies rather than temporary or stop-gap measures are needed to address the long-term impact of the aging workforce.

Many of the same factors that cause migration (e.g., search for a better quality of life or different culture) spur immigration. However, persons may emigrate (i.e., exit or leave a country) because of nefarious or odious governments or corrupt officials. Policies in the receiving country may make immigration difficult. For example, some immigrants seek political asylum, but regulations in the receiving country may place severe restrictions on the process to request asylum or apply for citizenship. Courts that review these applications may be understaffed or staffed with people who do not understand the language of the seeker. Some policies may require proof of harassment, torment, or persecution. In dire instances, families are separated—children from parents, spouse from spouse—and may not (or ever) be reunited. Immigration of large numbers of people from different countries can create situations in which communicable diseases run rampant and chronic health problems are exacerbated. Such situations can foment epidemics. Local public health policies may not have access to detention centers or are ignored by those in charge.

## Conclusion

What does all of this mean for nurses? If the role of the nurse goes beyond direct care of patients and families to communities and society, then a nurse's ability to effect change, often through policymaking, is as important as the technical ability to deliver safe, quality care. Nurses use "exquisite problem-solving skills" (Disch, 2017, p. 5), are experts in therapeutic communication, and know how to maneuver through organizations. Nurses use concepts such as social justice, moral resilience, and critical thinking to frame moral and ethical questions (Woodward et al., 2016). Participation in policymaking is a logical extension and expression of professional values; however, nurses are not often included in policy discussions, even at the institutional level. Strategic plans for potential disasters usually are made at the board of directors/trustee level, and there is a dearth of nurse members on institutional boards.

Allison Squires, PhD, RN, FAAN, is associate professor and director of the Florence S. Downs PhD Program in Nursing Research and Theory Development at New York University's Rory Meyers College of Nursing and a 2019–2020 distinguished nurse scholar in residence at the National Academy of Medicine. Squires has worked on research projects that have shaped policy in 36 countries. She notes:

> Nurses creating the evidence that shapes policy, no matter what their country, is critical for advancing the profession across the globe. We need more capacity to conduct the research that shapes policy. With COVID-19, we've learned that we cannot do things the way we have always done them. (See **Figure 11-5**.) Nurses absent from policymaking and decisions is no longer an option anywhere. Nurses not creating

**FIGURE 11-5** Global nurse workforce and COVID-19.
©Christos Georghiou/Shutterstock

the evidence to shape policy is no longer an option. Collectively, we need north-south, east-west collaborations to build the research capacity we need in the profession to influence policy in all our countries. (Personal communication, September 18, 2020)

Academic institutions are recognizing that in order to have the influence nurses seek, education programs must "systematically expand educational opportunities, bolster research capacity, and promote partnership with policymakers" (Gimbel et al., 2017, p. 123; Turale & Kunabiktikul, 2019). Nurse leaders and educators should prepare nurses for policymaking. Further, "employing institutions must top wasting nursing time and skills with poorly designed work roles that diminish the value of nursing" (McDonald, 2019, p. 458). The nurse perspective is critical when decisions are being made that affect nurses, patients, or healthcare organizations. Sophistication evolves from the baccalaureate to master's to doctoral level. Ellenbecker et al. (2017) delineated the policy role and suggested health policy content and teaching activities for all levels of professional nurse education. Postgraduate continuing education programs can focus on issues that call for action and refresh skills. Nurses must learn to leverage knowledge as a power tactic for influence in the policy arena.

Although this text is written from the perspective of the democratic governmental system in the United States, the authors acknowledge that there are political systems in every country through which decisions are made. The extent of nurse involvement in those systems affects policy decisions relating to the health of patients, society, and the profession. The type of governmental structure, the way that nurses are viewed in the dominant culture, and the way nurses are educated all have a bearing on the scope of participation. A primary responsibility of government is the protection of its citizens. Protection assumes safety—safety from physical harm and disease. Safety from disease and disability assumes a condition of well-being and health. The health of the public is important to government officials; nurses are the direct link between citizen safety and health and government goals.

The question becomes: to what extent are nurses involved in creating, designing, implementing, and evaluating health policies in their countries? What follows are six examples of nurses who were or are making a difference in decisions involving patients, healthcare delivery, health-related policies, and the profession. Each example offers occasions in which the reader can consider personal opportunities for political and policy-related engagement.

## References

Alliance for Ethical International Recruitment Practices. (n.d.). *About us.* http://www.cgfnsalliance.org
Commission on Graduates of Foreign Nursing Schools International. (n.d.). *Services.* https://www.cgfns.org/services
Commission on Graduates of Foreign Nursing Schools International. (2020). *About CGFNS.* http://www.cgfns.org/about
Council on Foreign Relations. (n.d.). *What does the World Health Organization do.* https://www.cfr.org/backgrounder/what-does-world-health-organization-do
Disch, J. (2019). Nursing leadership in policy formation. *Nursing Forum, 55,* 4–10.
Drennan, V. M., & Ross, F. (2019). Global nurse shortages—the facts, the impact and action for change. *British Medical Bulletin, 130*(1), 25–37.
Ellenbecker, C. H., Fawcett, J., Jones, E. J., Mahoney, D., Rowlands, B., & Waddell, A. (2017). A staged approach to educating nurses in health policy. *Policy, Politics and Nursing Practice, 18*(1), 44–56.
Gimbel, S., Kohler, P., Mitchell, P., & Emani, A. (2017). Creating academic structures to promote nursing's role in global health policy. *International Nursing Review, 64*(1), 117–125.
Global Code of Practice on the International Recruitment of Health Care Personnel. (2011). World Health Organization.
Globalization 101. (2020). *What is globalization?* https://www.globalization101.org/what-is-globalilzation
International Council of Nurses. (n.d.). *Who we are.* https://icn.ch/who-we-are
McDonald, T. (2019). Watching the glass: Policy hurdles for 21st-century nurses. *International Nursing Review, 66*(4), 456–458.
Migration Data Portal. (n.d.). *Migration data and the Sustainable Development Goals (SDGS).* https://www.migrationdataportal.org/sdgs?node.O
Rosa, W. E., & Hassmiller, S. B. (2020). The sustainable development goals and building a culture of health. *American Journal of Nursing, 120*(6), 168–171.
Shaffer, F. A., Bakshi, M. A., Farrell, N., & Alvarez, T. (2020). The recruitment experiences of foreign-educated health professionals to the United States. *American Journal of Nursing, 121*(3), 28–38.

Suphanchaimat, R., Putthasri, W., Prakongsai, P., & Tangcharoensathien, V. (15 April 2017). Evolution and complexity of government policies to protect the health of undocumented/illegal immigrants in Thailand—the unsolved challenges. *Risk Management Health Policy, 10*, 49–62. https://doi:10.2147/RMHP.S130442

Turale, S., & Kunaviktikul, W. (2019). The contribution of nurses to health policy and advocacy requires leaders to provide training and mentorship. *International Nursing Review, 66*(3), 302–304.

United Nations. (n.d.a). *About the UN.* https://un.org/en/about-un/overview/index/html

United Nations. (n.d.b). *The Sustainable Development Agenda.* un.org/sustainabledevelopment/development-agenda/

Woodward, B., Smart, D., & Benavides-Vaello, S. (2016). Modifiable factors that support political participation by nurses. *Journal of Professional Nursing, 32*(1), 54–61.

World Health Organization. (n.d.). *WHO brochure.* https://www.who.int/about/what-we-do/who-brochure)

World Health Organization. (2020). *2020 Triad Statement.* https://who.int.publications/m/item/2020-triad-statement

# Policy Exemplars Around the World

### EXEMPLAR 11-1

### The Impact of Nurses in the Policy Process in Italy

Alessandro Stievano, PhD, MSoc, MEd, FAAN, FFNMRCSI[1]

### Introduction

Policymakers of the most important health organizations in the world met in Astana, Kazakhstan, in 2018 to celebrate the 40th anniversary of the 1978 Alma-Ata declaration and re-recognised the crucial importance of primary health care in the creation of fair and reinforced health systems (OECD, 2020). Strengthened primary healthcare systems have the potential to improve health outcomes across socioeconomic levels, to make health organizations more people-centered, and to improve health system efficiency. The critical role of primary health care has become clear during the COVID-19 pandemic. As countries sought to deal with the surge in of acutely ill patients, while needing to maintain care for chronic patients under difficult circumstances, the outbreak has stimulated many innovative practices at regional and local levels (OECD, 2020).

Populations are ageing and health needs are becoming incredibly complex. Increments of health expenditure in the past have been cushioned by lower public spending in other fields. Keeping up such reallocations is increasingly difficult in the face of competing demands for government resources, especially after the COVID-19 pandemic. In this demanding context, a widespread and serviceable primary healthcare system that can support the challenges of the 21st century is absolutely pivotal, and nurses are key drivers of this system.

The healthcare system in Italy is a public-based national health service known for providing free-of-charge universal coverage at the point of service. The nursing profession is regulated by the National Federation of Orders for the Nursing Professions (FNOPI) that is a national regulatory agency governed by public law. The FNOPI, at a national level, has the representation

---

[1] Research Coordinator, Centre of Excellence for Nursing Scholarship, OPI Rome, Italy (with acknowledgement to colleagues Ausilia Pulimeno, Ippolito Notarnicola, and Gennaro Rocco)

of the nursing professions (general, pediatrics) in the interest of the public and is the only institution recognized by the law to speak on behalf of all Italian nurses.

In Italy, all nurses must be legally registered if they want to practice, and the evaluation of their competencies is accomplished during the final dissertation held in universities. A national test does not exist; verification of requisites takes place during the final thesis in front of a commission attended by, among others, two representatives of the OPI Provincial Orders. The Provincial Orders issues a license after approving each nurse who has passed the final examination (thesis) at the university. To date, a system is not in place to renew a license, as in other countries, and the same tenet is applied to all other health professions. Since 2002, lifelong learning for all health professionals is mandatory to remain on the register, but there are no clear mechanisms to suspend a health professional who has not accomplished their learning credits. This aspect is currently discussed by the various health professional regulatory authorities and will have clearer rules in the next years. Rules for disciplinary action and license renewal are opportunities for nurses to take political action and exert influence.

### Ageing Population and Community Nursing

In 2045, in Italy, with a population of 59.7 million, there will be more people over 74 (about 34.0% of the population) than those under 35 (18.6 million or 31.2%) (Censis, 2019). At a global level, in most low- and middle-income countries, most people can expect to live into their 70s and beyond. The pace of population ageing around the world is increasing constantly (WHO, 2020a). For people to experience these extra years of life in good health, the health system has to buttress better care for communities and families, aligning the health system to the needs of older people (WHO, 2020b). In this framework, the role of community nurse has emerged in the last decades (Martin et al., 2013). This specialized nurse, who, in the early 1990s was already in force in the Italian Public Health Service (set up in 1978), started being considered an important driver in addressing the needs of communities.

The idea to move legislation for mandatory implementation of community nurses all over Italy was initiated, not just by FNOPI with position statements, but also via organized nursing. The professional Italian Association for Community Nursing strongly advocated for recognition of this nurse specialty for years.

Some physician and patient associations were also strong promoters. Opposition and much resistance came from parts of the medical profession, especially some physicians' unions that throughout the years raised many doubts and impediments to accomplish the community nurse project. These unions constitute the most backward part of the medical profession in Italy, and they are always advocating by stoking unmotivated fears regarding "loss of power" for the medical profession. However, nurses and many physicians do not agree on these short-sighted politics. During the COVID-19 pandemic, the legislative process was fast-tracked when political parties became interested. Italy was one of the first European countries to experience the pandemic and suffer the immediate shortage of qualified nurses and equipment to care for so many patients. The elderly were especially at risk. Members of Parliament (MPs) were fully aware of the devastation that occurred in the country. The need for nurses who were competent to work with whole communities that

*(continues)*

included many older citizens became starkly evident. Community nurses could work with people in their homes, thus reducing the burden on hospitals that were overwhelmed with critically ill patients. Nurses began to exert their influence and press MPs for passage of the law to recognize community health nurses.

The Ministry of Health summoned all the different health professions to legislate "urgent measures" to cope with the pandemic. All the health professions were represented by their regulatory authorities and by the official state-recognized professional associations when a regulatory board was not in place (not all health professions have boards at this time). With the political boost from MPs, nurses and the other allied health professions agreed on a final proposal and were instrumental in passing legislation that officially documented community nurses in terms of stronger intercollaborations and workforce ratios.

The new Decreed Law approved in May 2020 is agile and effective. First, the main aim is to give full recognition to the community nurse's role as a central figure to empower territorial services and home care so as to unburden health care in emergency departments and in acute hospitals. The second article of the law establishes that the community nurse is responsible for home care, and this care has to be accomplished independently by nurses in their scope of practice and in integration with other health professionals in the living environments of citizens. In the third article, some organizational functions of the public health district in the territory are introduced. The last article highlights the main care competencies to be accomplished by community nurses (prevention of illnesses, education on dependencies, prevention of in-house accidents, self-care promotion of chronic patients fostering regular checks, rehabilitation nursing for elderly people, wound and ostomies management, relational support with caregivers of patients in chronic conditions, promotion of therapeutic education in families).

## Conclusion

Italian nurses were extremely pleased that after many years the new specialty was officially acknowledged, and they worked with MPs and other stakeholders to develop acceptable legal language. Compromises were made and some issues, such as better nurse-to-patient ratios, will be dealt with in the next few years. Nurses learned that their knowledge and perspective of the ageing population was essential in convincing the policymakers of the value and critical importance of community nurses.

## References

Censis. (2019). *The Italian society in 2019*. https://www.censis.it/sites/default/files/downloads/Sintesi_la%20societ%C3%A0_italiana_2019pdf

Martin, P., Duffy, T., Johnston, B., Banks, P., Harkess-Murphy, E., & Martin, C. R. (2013). Family health nursing: A response to the global health challenges. *Journal of Family Nursing, 19*(1), 99–118. https://doi.org/10.1177/1074840712471810

Organization for Economic Cooperation and Development (OECD). (2020). *Realising the potential of primary health care*. OECD Health Policy Studies. OECD Publishing. https://doi.org/10.1787/a92adee4-en

World Health Organization. (2020a). *Ageing and life course*. https://www.who.int/ageing/en/

World Health Organization. (2020b). *10 priorities for a decade of action on healthy ageing*. https://www.who.int/ageing/10-priorities/en/

## EXEMPLAR 11-2

### Panama: Persistence Pays When You Have a Goal

*Lydia Gordón de Isaacs, PhD, MSN, BSN, RN*[2]

Persistence pays, especially when it is linked to a selfless goal. Most policy goals do not happen in a short period; policy work takes perseverance, tenacity, and resolve. For Dr. Myrna McLaughlin de Anderson, establishing a well-organized system for palliative care took many years of hard work and dedication.

Myrna, a Panamanian nurse, had a goal—she wanted to make sure that patients did not live or die in pain. Her story began in 1990 when she was working as a clinical nurse, administering chemotherapy at the National Institute of Oncology in Panamá. The attention to patients with cancer was not different from the attention to those with other chronic illnesses, but Myrna noticed that cancer patients who received chemotherapy had special needs, especially during their final stages. Pain was a major issue. With the guidance of a Catholic priest who attended to the spiritual needs of these patients, Myrna communicated her thoughts to a group of colleagues who gave her support. She realized that she had to include other professionals, so she made a strategic decision to form a multidisciplinary group of health professionals; the group was called "Hospes" (translates to "Host" in English). At the beginning, the group was small, and all members were volunteers, but it grew as services became widely known.

At about the same time, Myrna received a call from a friend who needed help for a 17-year-old girl with leukemia. This girl lived in very poor conditions; she was depressed, lonely, and in pain. Myrna organized her Hospes organization to help by providing palliative care to the patient. At this point the group received donations from a benefactor, the friend who had called Myrna. The group ensured that the young patient had a peaceful death, not alone but in the company of nurses and friends, and under the best environmental and medical conditions. After some time, Myrna recognized that Panamá did not have a policy for the care of patients with terminal cancer.

Myrna realized a need that was greater than what she could provide, such as prescriptions for medications, which led her to create the Association of Chemotherapy Patients. The mission of this organization is to fight for cancer patients' rights. The organization became very active and many nurses, patients, and their families were involved. They worked in many ways as advocates for patients' rights. They talked to healthcare authorities, to other care providers, and they organized capacitation programs with the help of the School of Nursing of the University of Panamá.

With the leadership of Dr. McLaughlin de Anderson, a third organization, the Association Hospes for Palliative Care, was established as a multidisciplinary nonprofit group to provide palliative care to terminal patients at their homes. Nurses, physicians, a priest, psychologists, pharmacologists, and a physiotherapist integrated this group. Gradually, palliative care was introduced to the health system, and Hospes began to receive not only cancer patients but also other patients with chronic illnesses.

Myrna built relationships with many people in many situations—government, health care, education, and philanthropy. After a change of government by

---

[2] Lydia Gordón de Isaacs is professor and coordinator of the Doctor of Nursing Program within the School of Nursing at the University of Panama in Panama City, Panama.

*(continues)*

election in 2004, the new Minister of Health had worked with Hospes. He called Myrna to work with him. She became an official adviser to the Minister of Health. In this position, and as a nurse with a doctoral degree, she had the knowledge and skills to promote many legislative efforts. She organized palliative care with a multidisciplinary view as part of the health delivery system. Her leadership resulted in a national policy for palliative care in the Republic of Panama. She eventually represented her country internationally at the World Health Assembly in Geneva, Switzerland. Her participation there was important, for together with other member states, work was carried out to make issues of palliative care visible. Dr. McLaughlin de Anderson was the first nurse to represent the government of the Republic of Panamá at the World Health Assembly in Geneva, Switzerland, where after an inspiring speech, resolution 67.19, 2014 was passed that internationally recognizes palliative care as a human right.

Dr. Myrna Laughlin de Anderson pioneered nurse involvement in the process of making public policy in Panamá. She saw a need, envisioned a solution, and worked with officials to design relevant public policies. She developed professional relationships with officials through which they saw her as a person of integrity and credibility. She created three new organizations that focused on providing quality nursing care to those in need. She is a formidable force and a role model for those who want to make a difference.

Dr. Lydia Gordón de Isaacs interviewed Myrna in July 2020 and closes this vignette with Dr. de Anderson's thoughts: "A nurse should use all the tools available for her advocacy. She should also know where she wants to reach, what is her goal ... she should work without pausing with her goal in mind."

### References
Asociación Nacional de Pacientesde Quimioterapia. (2018). *National Association of Chemotherapy Patients.* https://copaairgolf.com/2018/asociacion-nacional-de-pacientes-de-quimioterapia-national-association-of-chemotherapy-patients/

### EXEMPLAR 11-3

## Empowering Women in Rural Villages in Rwanda: A Sustainable Model

*Harriet A. Fields, EdD, RN*[3]

### Introduction and Background
The third and fifth UN Sustainable Development Goals, "Good Health and Well-Being" and "Gender Equity," particularly relate to women, nursing, and primary health care (United Nations Department of Economic and Social Affairs, n.d.). The World Health Organization (WHO), Nursing Now, and the International

---

[3] Dr. Harriet A. Fields, EdD. Community Health Education and Nursing Education; EdM Public Health Nursing Education. While in graduate school at Columbia, she was research assistant to anthropologist Dr. Margaret Mead at the Museum of Natural History in New York. She lives in Washington. DC.

Council of Nurses (ICN) in 2020 are seeking new global models of health care delivery (WHO, 2018). The domain of nursing is health maintenance, promotion, and prevention of disease and disability, framed by a holistic approach to the human condition within a local, regional, national, and global focus. Nursing offers a different perspective from the medical disease–focused model. Presented here is a nursing holistic health model for the 21st century that is forming now in Rwanda, Africa (**Figure 11-6**).

I found myself in Rwanda after travel restrictions detoured my intention to investigate a project in the Democratic Republic of the Congo. Not to be deterred, and as a public health nurse and nurse educator, I decided to stop in Kigali, the capital, and assess the health needs of the country. My research while there confirmed my findings that it is women who have a pulse on any society, neighborhood, village, or community, and they are the key to accessing health needs of children, family, and the communities (UN Women, 2019). I also found a vast network of women who could become community health workers (CHWs) but few nurses who had up-to-date clinical skills or knowledge of how to organize and supervise CHWs.

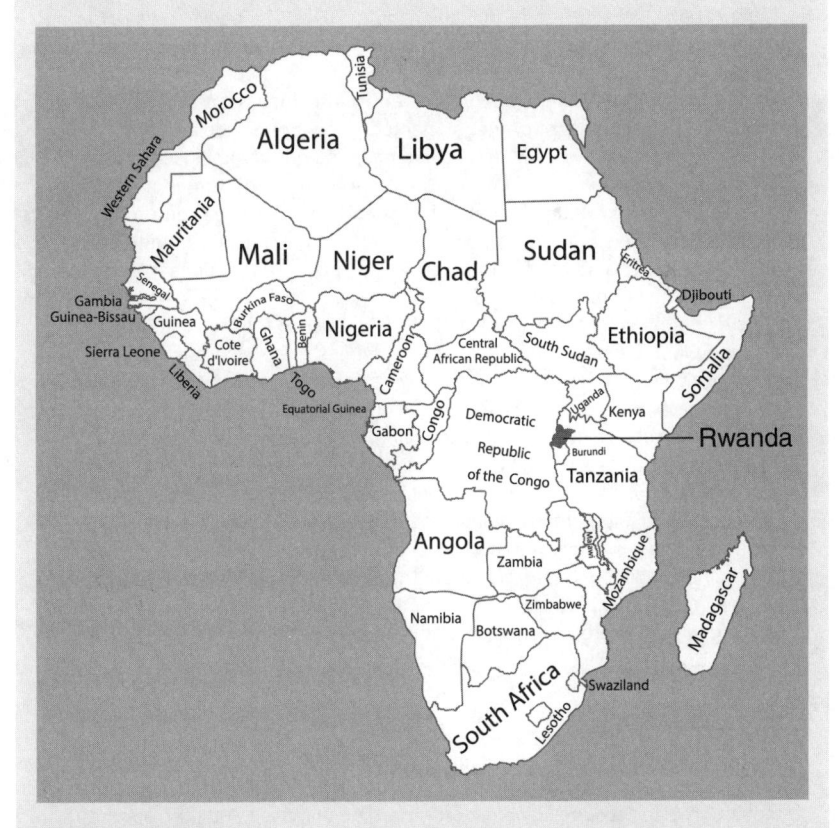

**Figure 11-6** Rwanda.
© Save nature and wildlife/Shutterstock.

*(continues)*

## Making Connections

My plan for developing in-country women as CHWs took nearly 10 years. In August 2012, I met with the minister of health in her offices in Kigali, the capital. I also met with the chief nursing officer of Rwanda in the Ministry of Health. The minister confirmed my assessment saying, "You have uncovered our weakness, Community Health Nursing is a gap. It is a need, we recognize that ... tens of thousands of community health workers lack formal training ... 80% of the population lives in the rural areas, and 80% of the burden of disease is in rural areas" (A. Binagwaho, personal communication, June 2012). At that time the Clinton Health Access Initiative (CHAI) was in Rwanda sponsoring approximately 40 American nurse educators for a year to, as the minister of health said, "staff-up hospital nursing." The minister of health was reinforcing the need I found for a similar program in the rural villages to reach the majority of the population.

I also met with the former head of the nurses and midwives organization in Rwanda, and through ongoing communications the following year, continued to validate the findings: "I think we need well educated people to supervise the real community nursing and midwifery, so getting this programme running would be a stepping stone. I support the idea 100%. I would like to partner in research" (F. Mukakabano, personal communication, June 2013). The network was growing.

In 2013 at a fundraiser in New York City, I met the executive director of a local NGO in Kigali. The vision of this local NGO, Uyisenga ni Imanzi (UNM), since its founding in 2002 has been child- and youth-focused programs addressing special needs of orphans affected by past genocide and/or HIV/AIDS, young girls who were victims of violence, and other vulnerable children. Today, the focus has expanded beyond the original mission: women must be at the center as the knowledge holders of the health needs of the community. My focus has always been empowering women in health in the community, so we joined forces. According to an African proverb, "If you want to go fast, go alone, if you want to go far, go together."

In 2016, with the local NGO and staff of UNM, I visited the initial site for the project in Rwamagana, a rural village about 40 miles east of the capital. Along with the staff of UNM, we interviewed women in their homes, participated in community meetings, met with local authorities, and talked with staff of the Neighborhood Health Center. These discussions led to their identification of health needs of the village/community. A missing link was identified in the process of obtaining health care: lack of communication between local women and regional healthcare professionals and follow-through after health needs are identified. We asked everyone what they wanted from professional nurses. Local nurses noted a lack of continuing education since graduation; they feared their practice was not up to date. This input from nurses identified a direct need for involvement with the local School of Nursing to provide ongoing continuing education to meet local nurses' and community health workers' ongoing village needs.

## A Gap and a Model

Armed with anecdotal data, we began to develop a model of empowerment of women leaders in health. The model is twofold: (1) Train the Trainer programs to teach CHWs to recognize and report emerging diseases and (2) Train the Trainer programs to teach local nurses how to supervise CHWs and provide for continuing education to upgrade CHWs' knowledge and skills. We developed a specific program titled "Grassroots Empowerment of Women as Gatekeepers of the Health of the Community."

Continued validation of needs identified from women in villages came from schools/parents/teachers, community health workers, and local authorities. We now have the new model of global health nursing for the 21st century—nurse-led Train the Trainer programs for CHWs that can be replicated in many countries around the world. This project empowers the most vulnerable in the community, the women, and the voiceless. They are the ones with real knowledge and untapped power to know their own needs and those of the children, families, and overall village/community.

### Expanding the Network Toward Sustainability
In May 2019, I presented this project at the Global Network of Public Health Nursing International Conference 2019 in Nairobi, Kenya. Ministers of Health and Education in both Kenya and Uganda, nurses from the University of Nairobi School of Nursing, and public health nurse educators from Uganda and Kenya told me they have the same need for CHW training; the nurse educators said they would like to be involved as trainers. Nurse leaders in Zambia and Botswana also expressed a need and interest to be involved. From the United States, nurse educators with backgrounds in health projects in Africa and in neighboring countries to Rwanda will also be part of the project. For more information see Profile Media Africa interview https://www.youtube.com/watch?v=BqRMVeD2pSc&feature=em-uploademail.

In Kigali in May 2019, I met with the dean and faculty at the University of Rwanda School of Nursing. Their interest and commitment were reinforced in 2020. The beauty of collaborating with the faculty and graduates of the local school of nursing ensures capacity development and sustainability with local graduates who speak English and the local language of the villages; "The School of Nursing and Midwifery/University of Rwanda is ready to work and collaborate with you ... it is a privilege for the school of Nursing and midwifery to work with you" (Dean M. Mukeshimana and former Dean D. Mukamana, email, June 10, 2020).

In May 2019 the executive director of UNM and I met with the Rwanda Country Director of the U.S. Peace Corps. The Peace Corps has offered us a third-year health volunteer for our project in Rwamagana, a village where the Peace Corps also has a presence (K. Hackett, personal communication, May 20, 2019). (Note that, due to COVID-19, the Peace Corps has suspended most of its programs; the health volunteer position is on hold at present.)

### The Future
We will implement the Train the Trainer programs and develop the evaluation and outcome tools with the University of Rwanda School of Nursing and others. Based on data, training will be revised, and health needs will be reassessed as they change and evolve. After data from evaluations and outcomes are analyzed, this model can be introduced to other villages throughout Rwanda, then to fragile societies in East Africa and other continents.

### Lessons Learned
1. **Advocacy**. This is a grassroots project focusing on the health and education needs that are identified by women in their communities. This is not a program imposed by outsiders who determine the community needs; rather, it is a program that sought initial buy-in from schools/parents/teachers, community health workers, and local authorities.

*(continues)*

2. **Empowerment**. The heart of the project is a focus on women and local community health workers (CHWs). There are not enough nurses and physicians in the country to provide adequate care for the health needs. Teaching CHWs to identify diseases and environmental problems, and to alert professionals to emerging concerns (e.g., epidemics and pandemics) is critical to an effective healthcare system.
3. **Collaboration**. Identifying partners is essential in assuring a successful project. Including the local NGO that has several community sites throughout Rwanda, establishing relationships with government officials, conducting community meetings with women, schools/parents/teachers, community health workers, and local authorities, and connecting with nurse education programs provides insights into what local villages and communities perceive as needs and keeps solutions realistic.

### References
Peace Corps. (n.d.). *Fast facts.* http://peacecorps.gov/news/fast-facts/
Profile Media Africa. (2019, July 9). Interview with Dr. Harriet Fields [video]. https://www.youtube.com/watch?v=BqRMVeD2pSc&feature=em-uploademail
United Nations Department of Economic and Social Affairs, Sustainable Development. (n.d.). *Make the SDGs a reality.* https://sdgs.un.org/#goal_section
UN Women. (2019). *Women and the Sustainable Development Goals (SDGs).* https://www.unwomen.org/en/news/in-focus/women-and-the-sdgs
World Health Organization. (2018). *Nursing Now.* https://www.who.int/hrh/news/2018/nursing_now_campaign/en/

### Suggested Activity
American Association of Colleges of Nursing Webinar, Tues. Jan. 28, 2020. Dr. Fields presents her global health work in Rwanda Empowering Women in Health. The focus is the World Health Organization 2020 Goal for the Year of the Nurse and Midwife and UN Sustainable Development Goals #3 & 5, as Dr. Fields terms it 'Women Empowered Good Health and Well Being.' https://www.aacnnursing.org/Professional-Development/Webinar-Info/sessionaltcd/WF20_01_28

### EXEMPLAR 11-4

### Nurse Involvement in Policy Decisions Affects Public Health in Croatia
*Andreja Šajnić, MSN, RN*[4]

### Introduction
Nurses in Croatia have played a significant role in policy decisions that affect public health, not just because their opinions or voices were heard, but also because Croatian nurses have planned many strategic and thoughtful actions (**Figure 11-7**). One of the best examples is how respiratory oncological nurses

---

[4] Andreja Šajnić, MSN, RN is a clinical respiratory nurse in the Department for Respiratory Diseases at Jordanovac clinic, University Hospital Center Rebro, Zagreb, Croatia.

Policy Exemplars Around the World **283**

**Figure 11-7** Croatia.
©Peter Hermes Furian/Shutterstock

changed healthcare policy and ensured the best treatment for patients with lung cancer and other respiratory diseases.

Lung cancer is one of the most common malignancies and also the leading cause of death among all cancers in women and men in Croatia. Before 2008, patients with lung cancer in Croatia had poor quality of life and survival. In 2008, to provide better care and treatment, respiratory oncological nurses and colleagues from the Department for Respiratory Diseases Jordanovac,[5] University Hospital Centre Rebro,[6] in Zagreb, Croatia, established a nongovernmental organization (NGO) known as Jedra. This association for patients with lung cancer and other respiratory diseases was founded on the initiative of patients, their families, healthcare professionals, and the European Commission,[7] who encounter this disease on a daily basis. The goal was to turn

---

[5] Jordanovac is a respiratory disease clinic located near Rebro.
[6] Rebro is a specific geographic area. The University Hospital Centre in the city of Zagreb, Croatia, is the largest hospital in Croatia. The hospital was established in 1942 as the University Hospital Zagreb, when the main site (Rebro) was first built.
[7] The European Commission is the executive branch of the European Union, responsible for proposing legislation, implementing decisions, upholding the EU treaties, and managing the day-to-day business of the EU.

*(continues)*

lung cancer from a terminal disease into a chronic disease by utilizing better knowledge and new diagnostic and therapeutic possibilities. The NGO was recognized and supported by the media and the public.

Jedra was a national response to a European Commission program to address cancer. Croatia adopted a national program, Fight Against Cancer, to ensure improved efforts for prevention, screening, diagnosis, and treatment with effective, innovative drugs and therapeutics through a multidisciplinary approach. Civil societies do not only manifest the interests and will of citizens, but also offer methods to assess public and government areas in decision making. In this scenario we have two lines—civil society and the nursing profession—that are presenting the interest of the patients. After all, nurses are professional experts and representatives in the field of patients' rights.

### Spotlight

A 3-year global campaign (2016–2018) titled "We Can. I Can." was launched amid World Cancer Day, which Croatia joined with a national-level campaign under the name "Talking Hands." The message of the campaign, "We Can. I Can." is based on the idea that every institution, community, and individual can contribute to reducing morbidity and mortality from cancer. The campaign aims to raise public awareness about cancer, help prevent the disease, facilitate early diagnosis and treatment, and care for patients. The conference highlighted the need to adopt and implement a comprehensive national plan for the fight against cancer, because the incidence and mortality of malignancies in Croatia continues to increase. According to the Croatian Institute for Public Health, each year 21,434 people are diagnosed with cancer in Croatia, and 13,939 die; that is, 38 people die from cancer each day.

From the beginning, nurses organized and coordinated a wide range of campaigns, projects, press conferences, and petitions. Together Against Cancer (a local effort) resulted in a resolution adopted by the Croatian Parliament in 2009 to coordinate research and development from several agencies. Nurse advocacy for the importance of psychological support for lung cancer patients resulted in psychologists becoming part of a multidisciplinary team in 2012. That same year, another project, I Want to Breathe, set a goal for health promotion and awareness of the importance of respiratory health in preschool children and adolescent nonsmokers. Another program, Talking About Lung Cancer, focused on personalized treatment, availability of molecular testing, and targeted therapy, which led to a decision by the Croatian Health Insurance Institute to participate in facilitating therapy for lung cancer patients in 2015. Nurses were leaders in all of these efforts. They wrote letters of support, participated in meetings in which problems and solutions were explored, offered clinical evidence to support decisions, and encouraged inclusion of healthcare professionals and others.

Other European associations of patients and professional experts invited Jedra to participate as a member and active participant. In 2017, an IPF Declaration invited all European Union (EU) member states and the European Commission (EC) to become more actively involved in addressing the key issues of patients with idiopathic pulmonary fibrosis (IPF). A joint European Idiopathic Pulmonary Fibrosis and Related Disorder Federation (EU-IPFF) campaign, Listen for the Sounds of IPF, conducted during IPF World Week, resulted in a petition addressed to the Croatian Ministry of Health to implement the IPF Declaration. Also, in 2017, the EC initiated a Commission for Adoption of a National Cancer Plan. An important outcome was the translation of a manual for patients with lung cancer into several languages. In 2019, nurses were actively involved in a program, Talking about Lung Cancer, on the occasion of Lung Cancer Awareness Month. The goal of that campaign was raising public awareness of lung cancer; promoting education about risk factors; facilitating prevention and treatment; educating health professionals, patients, and their families; and presenting the program of early detection of lung cancer. Nurses volunteered in workshops as part of a Central European Lung Cancer Patient Network and EU-IPFF, completed courses for Train the Trainer IPF program, and actively involved themselves in patient sessions at the International Congress at the European Respiratory Society, the International Association for the Study of Lung Cancer, the World Conference on Lung Cancer, EU-IPFF international meetings, and the Central European Lung Cancer Conference.

Croatian respiratory oncological nurses played the most important role in Jedra as they launched and initiated numerous campaigns and successfully merged the support of professional experts in activities for patients' rights. This is an area where nurses can be independent and successful in carrying out the activities that can contribute to the development of the nursing profession and have an impact on all social spheres.

Statement from Mario Gazić, Chair of the Croatian Chamber of Nurses:

> The Croatian Chamber of Nurses (Chamber) is the only regulatory body for all nurses working in Croatia. The main goal of the Chamber is to protect patients and citizens by ensuring quality, responsible and ethical health care. Since its establishment in 2003, the Chamber has been working on the promotion of nursing as a profession and strengthening the recognition of nurses as highly educated professionals who are key to the functioning of the health system. The influence of the Chamber on health policy-making has grown throughout the years, as nurses, through this regulatory body, have been appointed to commissions, working groups and similar bodies of the Ministry of Health.

*(continues)*

The Chamber issues licenses for nursing practice (a nurse cannot be employed without a license). Every year nurses must collect points per lecture as active or passive participants (something like but not equal to CME). Within 6 years, if a nurse does not collect enough points per year, then the nurse must repeat the initial examination test; if that test is failed, the nurse loses their licence and cannot practice. The Chamber has set criteria for continuing education that is considered acceptable for relicensure. Attendance at courses, professional meetings, and congresses is documented and forms are delivered to the Chamber. Attendance at international events outside Croatia is accepted. Points also are approved for online courses and events.

We believe that much has been achieved when it comes to the visibility and representation of nurses in the Republic of Croatia, but that there is much more to be done with regard to participating in policymaking and decision making crucial to the health system. At the moment, the Croatian Chamber of Nurses is working to increase its influence through media appearances, pointing out problems and offering research-based solutions, so that nurses become a profession that the government of the Republic of Croatia and relevant ministries will recognize as an indispensable collaborator in health decisions.

### EXEMPLAR 11-5

### Nurse Influence in Policy Decisions in Portugal

*Miguel Padilha, PhD, RN, CRRN, PI-Tech4EduSim/CINTESIS[8]*

Dr. Mariana Diniz de Sousa (1929–2013) had a central role in health policy in nursing education and regulation in Portugal. Her journey chronicled that of many nurses who became involved in policy decisions. She studied nursing in Portugal and continued her pedagogy at Yale University. She became an expert in curriculum, faculty promotion, and organizational change. As she progressed in her own development, she crafted a vision for professional nursing in her country of origin, where she became professor and director of a nursing school. Her manager profile and strategic vision of health allowed the establishment of connections with the Minister of Health. Working with him, she learned how governments become aware of problems and how officials shape solutions and measure results. She understood quickly the impact that nurses could have on policy decisions that affect patients, communities, and the profession. Dr. de Sousa became an official advisor to the Minister of Health and, in 1985 was appointed director of Health and Human Resources. In 2008, she was presented the National Health Award, an honor attributed to those who have demonstrated excellence and relevance in the field of health sciences. Dr. de Sousa was especially honored for her unequivocal achievement of better health for citizens of Portugal and for the prestige of organizations within the national health system.

---

[8] José Miguel dos Santos Castro Padilha is the principal investigator of the research group Tech4edusim of CINTESIS and an assistant professor at the Nursing School of Porto (ESEP) since 2007.

For nurses, perhaps the most important role undertaken was in the foundation of the Order of Portuguese Nurses, the institute that regulates nursing practice in the country. She served as president from 1999 to 2003 and played a central role in regulating nursing practice and education. Her leadership drove efforts to require college degrees for nurses (baccalaureate, master's, and PhD), specified the role of specialization, and urged self-regulation as professionals. Her influence and leadership have lasted beyond her lifetime and have benefited thousands of nurses. She has shown how a nurse can influence policies and policymakers. Her concept of professionalism and influence is a beacon for other professions.

The late Dr. Mariana Diniz de Sousa is an exemplar for all nurses worldwide.

## Continuing the Journey

Dr. Miguel Padilha adapted de Sousa's concept of involvement in government to involvement in nursing. His practice in rehabilitation with an interest in respiratory nursing evolved since he worked in a brain trauma injury unit. He was especially attentive to decision-making processes and evidence-based practice. Miguel developed a vision for improving patient care but realized he could not implement his vision alone. He expanded his network to include those outside the profession whose work impacted his practice. He began a collaboration with the hospital health office to be a part of the implementation of electronic health records. As he conducted in-service training for nurses in hospitals and specialty settings, he continued to learn new skills that had relevance to his practice.

In 2003, Miguel moved his career forward when he enrolled in a master's program where he focused on changing clinical practice. He became assistant faculty in the Porto Nursing School where he currently serves as coordinator professor. During his PhD program, he challenged traditional care of patients with chronic obstructive pulmonary disease (COPD) and developed a training program for nurses and a retraining program for COPD patients. His goal, noted in a YouTube video, was to improve the quality of life of COPD patients, contribute to nursing knowledge, and optimize health resources. He taught nurses to take 5 to 10 minutes during their interactions to help patients gain control over their condition, decrease stress, and develop self-care actions. As one nurse (in the video) noted, "I didn't think I had time—it [these few minutes] didn't make nursing easier, it made it better" (www.youtube.com/watch?v=MFMvQT_MkKg). His work was recognized in 2012 by the International Council of Nurses (ICN) with a prestigious award.

In 2016, with advanced experience with electronic technology, he initiated a partnership with a technological enterprise. He began to develop clinical nursing scenarios for a virtual simulator. Two years later he became principal investigator (PI) of a research group to examine technologies for education and simulation (tech4edusim). As PI he is leading a group of researchers from the Center for Health Technology and Services Research (CINTESIS), a research unit from the University of Medicine of Porto, Portugal. He is engaged in changing education and practice by integrating new technologies such as e-learning, massive open online courses, and simulation.

Dr. Padhila's journey reflects how the policy role of nurses exemplified by Dr. de Sousa led to a leadership role in research.

## EXEMPLAR 11-6

### Continuing Nursing Education in Albania: Evolution and Future Prospects for Health Policy

*Ippolito Notarnicola, PhD, RN*[9]

With acknowledgment to my colleagues Blerina Duka and Ina Dedi.

The Republic of Albania, located in southeastern Europe, has a total population of 2,821,977. Albania is composed of the following ethnicities: Albanian (98.1%), Greek (0.9%), and other (1%; includes Vlach, Roma, Macedonian, Montenegrin, and Egyptian). Although the number of people living below the poverty line is falling, Albania remains one of the poorest countries in Europe, with a strong focus on agriculture and (illegal) drug cultivation. The country's weak infrastructure is problematic, with poor roads, regular breakdowns in water and electricity supply in rural areas, and a high unemployment rate. Many people leave the countryside to live in the cities of Tiranë and Durrës. According to the Albanian Constitution, the government and parliamentary bodies determine the educational policy for tertiary education.

Currently in Albania there are six public and six private faculties (education programs) that offer degrees in nursing. Albania has more than 2,500 healthcare facilities (clinics, hospitals). Every year, 2,500 nurses receive academic training as part of a 3-year course of studies. Nevertheless, thousands of nurses are currently unemployed or work for very low wages. On January 7, 2020, data supplied by the Order of the Health Professions (UISH), known as the Order, reported there were about 21,385 nurses. UISH is the single legal regulatory agency for all health professionals in Albania (i.e., nurse, midwife, physical therapy, imaging tech, lab tech, speech therapy, assistant nurse).

Albanian nurses work in complex and dynamic healthcare settings. Their roles and skills are constantly evolving to meet the needs of patients and to incorporate service needs such as labor shortages and skills development problems. The provision of nursing care by nurses has been linked convincingly to improved quality of care, efficiency, and cost reduction (Morrison & Conseil, 2010). There is clear underperformance and underutilization of nurses regarding the services provided by the health system (World Health Organization, 2018). Therefore, redefining the needs and role of nurses in the Albanian health system is needed to create a stimulating and motivating environment for professional teamwork. All this has been magnificently expressed in the draft "Strategy for the Development of Health Care in Albania, 2020–2025" (European Bank for Reconstruction and Development, 2020). New service models will be established to meet the most urgent needs identified at the community level, such as the prevention and control of noncommunicable diseases, home care for the elderly, and models of assistance through digital technology, especially in remote areas. How nurses meet these demanding needs will be pivotal.

Nursing in Albania began a path of development starting in 1992 with "Le Bon Secouers," a Swiss project that opened ecclesiastical high schools in

---

[9] Ippolito Notarnicola, PhD, RN, is a professor of nursing disciplines at the Universities of Rome Tor Vergata, at the University of Rome "La Sapienza" and of the Catholic University "Our Lady of Good Counsel" in Tirana, Italy. He is a nurse research fellow at the Center of Excellence for Culture and Nursing Research of the Order of Nursing Professions in Rome. In honor of his global research in nursing, Professor Notarnicola was awarded the Fellowship by Examination of the Faculty of Nursing and Midwifery in 2020.

Vlorë, Korcë, and Elbasan in collaboration with 2-year schools of nurse training (later 3 and a half years). In 1994 the first university course was established in Tiranë, with the first graduates in nursing in 1998. The Swiss collaboration has strongly influenced the growth of nursing by significantly training the staff and consolidating the Master in health management with the establishment of the Master for Family Nurses (www.eda.admn). This whole process has had many difficulties in its evolution and implementation, but in all of this both church and nurses have worked closely with the government.

## Evolution and Future Prospects of Continuing Education for Nurses in Albania

A gap that starkly appears in health professionals in Albania is the lack of updated competencies due to a lack of planned continuing education (CE). For some years UISH has undertaken initiatives that favored the development of courses on CE. One of the main points of the statute of UISH is the education of nursing professionals in various topics. CE is a key point of priority of state and private health institutions. CE was defined by law and changes and additions were made in 2009 (On Health Care in the Republic of Albania, amended). Representatives of various institutions and the UISH were involved in changing the law. In this regard, the Order has collaborated with the Albanian government and was authorized to make decisions regarding policies and changes in the Albanian nursing education system.

Problems related to CE have been discussed since 2008 within a Swiss project with the Ministry of Health and, in that period, it was decided to create the National Center for Continuing Education (QKEV) for health professionals (On profession regulated, 2009). The QKEV, in collaboration with the Minister of Health, would organize and supervise continuing training for health workers. The QKEV board of directors has always been made up by the Minister of Health and representatives of the Albanian health professional Orders, including UISH. Under the strong insistence of the UISH, nurses were appointed to the board of directors in 2016. At that time, the nurse members of the board began to persuade other members to amend some bills. These actions have facilitated change that was legislated by the Council of Ministers, not through the enactment of a new law, but by modifying the current law on health care (About establishment, 2008) that establishes the obligations of the parties for continuous training would be individual and fulfilled by all actors.

The UISH, in 2016, proposed to the government that nurses should acquire five credits of continuing education every year. This requirement is consistent with European directives (European Commission, 2014). During 2016 the minister of health, Llir Beqja, decided, in agreement with UISH representants, that the credits to be acquired would be 10. In that meeting, the Minister assured that the government would allocate funds to plan the implementation of CE. In addition, the UISH had asked to have an orientation program tailored to the needs of professional nurses and should not leave it to random choice of registrants or turn it into a business for some centers. As it often happens, the UISH was not heard. This is because other health professional Orders, especially the medical one, are still scarce and the allied health professions are not fully visible and recognized at the societal level. The UISH proposed that the credit acquisition program would be managed by UISH itself as it is related to the nursing license.

In this regard, the UISH contacted and worked with Irish experts where the government passed the budget for CE for professional Orders, but this was opposed

*(continues)*

by the Board of Physicians and the proposal was not implemented at the end. Currently the budget allocated by the Albanian government to health centers for carrying out continuous training courses is used only for the training of physicians due to the fact that the Order of Doctors has opposed this, even if the nurses had proposed to the government a different use of the funds intended for CE.

According to the law of March 20, 2009, to improve the quality of health care in Albania (On health care, 2009), nurses must seek lifelong learning through the development and promotion of CE. In light of this legislation, UISH, in the February 2019 board meeting, declared that nurse professionals should know the needs of the health services and their professional development and can maintain high standards for nursing. In this meeting, the regional presidents of the UISH proposed the training courses that the nurses needed. Throughout the COVID pandemic, UISH has organized free training courses for nurses in hospitals and health centers for obtaining the required credits. Nurse involvement influenced UISH to stand strong for a policy in which Albanian nurses determine their own CE needs. Nursing's voice is starting to have a strong impact on policies in this country.

## References

About establishment and functioning of the National Education Center in Continued, of Health Workers Law N° 825, of 14.5.2008 and in addition decision n.306 of 27.6.2002 to the Council of Ministers.

European Bank for Reconstruction and Development. (2020). *DRAFT Albania country strategy*. https://www.ebrd.com/documents/strategy-and-policy-coordination/draft-albania-country-strategy.pdf?blobnocache

European Commission. (2014). Communication from the Commission on Effective, Accessible and Resilient Health Systems. https://ec.europa.eu/health/sites/health/files/systems_performance_assessment/docs/com2014_215_final_en.pdf

Morrison, A., & Conseil. (2010). *Scope of nursing practice and decision-making framework: Toolkit*. International Council of Nurses.

On health care in the Republic of Albania. Law #10 107 (March 30, 2009) (Amended by law n. 51/2013 of 14.2.2013) (Amended by law n. 76/2015 July 16, 2015).

On Professions Regulated in the Republic of Albania. Law #10 171 (October 22, 2009). https://www.eda.admin.ch/deza/it/home/paesi/albania.html/content/dezaprojects/SDC/en/2013/7F08741/phase2?oldPagePath=/content/deza/it/home/laender/albanien.html

World Health Organization. (2018). *Primary health care in Albania: Rapid assessment*. https://www.euro.who.int/en/countries/albania/publications/primary-health-care-in-albania-rapid-assessment-2018

# Chapter Discussion and Summary Activity

Complete the table with brief notes to validate your understanding of the policy process in terms of policy decisions in the exemplar countries discussed in the chapter.

## Applying the Policy Process to Global Nursing Issues

| | Problem Identification | Problem Analysis | Strategy and Policy Development | Policy Enactment | Policy Implementation | Evaluation |
|---|---|---|---|---|---|---|
| Italy | Ageing population | | | | | |
| Croatia | Poor quality of care for respiratory diseases | | | | | |
| Albania | Underutilization of nurses | | | | | |
| Panama | Lack of pain management or palliative care in the country | | | | | |
| Portugal | Lack of professional nursing and its legacy | | | | | |
| Rwanda | Community health workers untrained | | | | | |

## CHAPTER 12

# An Insider's Guide to Engaging in Policy Activities

Nancy M. Short and Jeri A. Milstead

## Introduction

We encourage readers to become seriously involved in the politics of policy-making. This chapter offers ideas and practical steps so that your efforts will be seen by officials as sincere, professional, and focused. If you have not been involved before in the policy process, we have suggestions on how to start; if you have already started, you might enlist colleagues to work with you. It is important that you begin. Your level of sophistication and comfort will increase the more you participate. *You* are the voice of the profession—use it wisely and with knowledge and skill.

## Creating a Fact Sheet

You must be prepared when you visit a congressional or state legislative office. Novices to the world of policy and politics often visit their representative with others as an activity related to a conference or convention. At conferences, you may be handed materials to take with you to a legislative meet-and-greet. These materials are intended to be left with the Member or staff to serve as a reminder or give a nudge to action after you leave the office. This kind of fact sheet (also known as a "leave-behind") is a reasonable way to get introduced to the process, but it is not a highly effective way to share a message. The most effective meeting is one-on-one, that is, face-to-face, with the Member or health staff (legislative aide).

You should prepare a fact sheet that is customized to your message. Criteria for a fact sheet are as follows:

- Keep the document to one page; you may use both the front and the back.
- Use an attractive, easily readable font (at least 12 point).
- Limit the use of multiple fonts, font sizes, bolded words, color, and italics—these make it confusing to read.
- Make sure your fact sheet is free of typos and spelling errors.
- Include a title of your issue at the top of the page. Use plain English; do not use medical jargon. Necessary medical terms must be defined.
- State your "ask" succinctly at the top of the page directly under the title.
- Do not use citations or references. This is not an academic document.
- Bullets, lists, tables, and text boxes must be clearly readable (never use a tiny map or graph).
- List organizations in support of your position (state-level organizations for state issues).
- Know who opposes your "ask," and be ready to address this opposition verbally.
- Provide your full contact information: name, credentials, phone, and email. Unless you have permission to represent your place of work, do not give the impression that you are speaking on your employer's behalf.

For more information about how to construct a fact sheet, visit http://cthealthpolicy.org/wp-content/uploads/2018/04/FACT-SHEETS-AND-ACTION-ALERTS.pdf.

## Contacting Your Legislators

It is crucial that healthcare professionals know how to contact their legislators, agency heads, government staff, and other policymakers. We recommend calling or emailing to avoid security testing and delays imposed on standard mail and packages. Do not send an attachment—no one will open it because it may contain a virus or malware.

A. In general:
 1. Know the correct title and spelling of the Member's (or staff's) name and correct address. If in doubt, call the office and ask (staff are eager to provide this information). If there are credentials, get them right!
 2. Direct your message to the right level: federal issues to U.S. senators and representatives in Washington, D.C.; state messages to state senators and representatives at the state capital.
 3. Be polite. Choose language that is not confrontational or angry.
 4. Avoid healthcare jargon, such as "I'm an APRN working in SICU with GSW patients."
 5. If you use Twitter or other social media, be very careful about what you say—your messages may be read by many others and may be potentially misinterpreted.

6. Do your homework. What is the position of the Member on similar issues? Know whether the Member has sponsored or opposed similar legislation.
B. Via email: Keep your message to three paragraphs.
   *First paragraph:*
   1. Use a salutation: Dear Senator or Dear Representative (or Mr., Ms., Mrs., Dr. if contacting a staff member).
   2. State who you are (e.g., name, constituent, credential such as "Registered Nurse").
   3. Declare your support/opposition to a specific issue; state a bill number if possible. Legislative aides (LAs) keep track of "support" and "do not support" messages.
   *Second paragraph:*
   1. Rationale: Provide one or two reasons to support your position; be brief (limit to one regular page).
   2. Use ordinary language—no medical terminology, no words of three or more syllables, no vague words, no vernacular/local lingo.
   3. Identify any major opposition and include your response to it; include a talking point that the Member may use later.
   4. Include a personal story if you have one—it can be very persuasive evidence. Do not use names or circumstances that are considered privileged or private.
   *Third paragraph:*
   1. Make your "ask." Be specific. Ask the Member to vote for/against a bill or amendment, hold a hearing, or call a press conference (*not* just "support" or "oppose").
   2. Do *not* thank the representative or senator in advance—save this for after he or she has acted.
   3. Offer to be the contact for this issue.
   4. Close with "Sincerely," plus your name/credentials, mailing address, email address and preferred phone number.
C. If you call the Member/staff's office:
   1. You probably will not talk with the Member. Ask for the health LA and write down the name of the person to whom you speak.
   2. Do not expect to talk with the staffer more than 5 minutes, so use notes and talk in a conversational tone—do not read your message, as it will be obvious that you do not know your own words.
D. What *not* to include:
   1. *All* reasons you support or oppose the policy—pick one or two reasons. You should write only one-page emails or letters.
   2. Threats: "If you don't vote for this bill, I will not vote for you."
   3. "Thank you"—save it until you know the Member's action, then be sure to write a thank-you note.
   4. More than one issue—stick to one issue at a time.
E. Follow up:
   1. Within 2 weeks, email or phone the Member's office: Received email? Any questions? Any action on the issue? Anything I can do?

# What to Expect When You Visit Your Policymaker

1. Make an appointment—don't just show up.
2. You may visit in pairs, but if there are many of you, make sure the staff know in advance so that they can arrange a place large enough to accommodate all of you.
3. Dress professionally. Do not show up in jeans or clothing with offensive logos.
4. Do not expect to see the policymaker in person; you probably will talk with a staff member. Staff are very important. Depending on the prestige and length of time in the position, a policymaker may have a small or large staff; each staffer will have one or more specific areas to cover, such as health, agriculture, economic development, or transportation. Staff are responsible for filtering information that is presented to the policymaker. Staff serve as gatekeepers, so it is helpful to build a positive relationship with staff.
5. Research the person you are visiting. If it is a legislator, go to the relevant website—you probably will find information about his or her education, family, interests, and community service, as well as current service on committees. There may be a picture.
6. Know the district or constituency that the policymaker represents. This will give you clues about the person's interests and background. Note any leadership positions the person has held. It is best to visit your own representative, but if you have a particular area of interest, you can choose a person who is the chair or an officer of a relevant committee.
7. Expect your visit to last no more than 5 to 10 minutes—so be focused with your message.
8. Make appropriate greetings (if handshakes are improper, just state a greeting) and look the people you meet in the eye. Speak clearly and with authority.
9. Do not spend much time in "pleasantries"—get to the point of your visit.
10. State why you are there—the specific issue/bill number, your position ("for" or "against"), and why.
11. Be prepared to defend your position. Use evidence-based research (translated into ordinary language), best practice, and other supports.
12. Focus on only one issue per visit. You may be tempted to interject several issues, but you have a very limited amount of time, so do not undercut yourself.
13. Have one- or two-page documents that support your issue ready for the staff to refer to after you leave. For example, you may have "talking points" that summarize your issue. If you are representing an organization, make sure its logo appears on the documents and you have their permission to identify yourself as their agent.
14. Leave your business card so that the staff can contact you.
15. Handwrite a thank-you note within 2 weeks after your visit.

# Preparing to Testify

You may be asked to testify at a hearing about an issue in which you are involved. A hearing is an official meeting of a committee or group of policymakers (i.e., legislators) in which they "hear" arguments for and against an issue. You must follow protocols about who and when and how long you testify.

1. Know where the hearing room is located. Be there before the hearing begins.
2. You may be required to sign in as a witness. You will be called in the order in which you sign in.
3. Know the name of the committee chair and what Members will be attending the hearing.
4. Provide copies of your testimony to each member of the committee. Distribute these copies to their staffs.
5. Have with you a one- to two-page testimony document in a font large enough to read without glasses. If your issue demands a longer response, provide copies to the committee staff and elected Members.
6. Dress as a professional (e.g., no jeans or hoodies). You are representing your organization or issue. Look credible.

## Tips on Testifying

1. Always address the chair first, then any particular members. For example, if a member asks a question, you respond by saying, "Mr. Chairman, Representative (or Senator) XXX, . . ." Do this *every time* you speak. You may want to practice with a colleague.
2. Do not read your testimony. You have provided written copies to each member of the committee, so now is your time to have a "conversation" with them. You may use a few notes—key words large enough for you to read at a glance—to prompt you to make your point and stay on message.
3. Make a single point. Now is *not* the time to bring up all the issues relevant to your case.
4. Provide a personal story that emphasizes your point; state it quickly.
5. You only have a short time to testify (3 to 5 minutes),* but you may be able to extend this window if there are questions from committee members. To make best use of the opportunity, have your rationale in your head so you do not hem and haw and waste time.
6. Speak clearly and loudly. Stand up straight. Dress conservatively and appropriately. Act as a professional. Do not slouch. Do not say "Uh . . ." during your precious speaking time.
7. Do *not* use medical terminology or other confusing language. For example, do not use abbreviations or acronyms (e.g., CABG, IV, MI).
8. If you refer to research or evidence, summarize it without using medical jargon and report results relevant to your issue.

---

* There may be a three-light bulb system used for keeping time. An accepted maxim to keep in mind is, talk when the light is green, talk damned fast when the light is yellow, and sit down when the light is red!

9. Speak positively and with conviction. Use "power" words (e.g., *expertise, overwhelming evidence, significance*).
10. Do *not* equivocate; that is, do not say "kinda," "sorta," "maybe," or "like."
11. Do *not* threaten anyone or become violent. You are a guest.
12. Always close the loop—that is, bring your remarks back to how this issue will affect the constituents of the policymakers and your patients. Otherwise, you are likely to be seen as self-serving.
13. Be prepared to answer any questions from those who oppose part or all of the bill. Again, have a response in your head that you can pull out for a 30-second reply.
14. If you cannot think of a response to a question, go back to your original position and restate your argument. Remember: Just because you are asked a question does not mean you have to answer it. If you get nervous and the question stumps you, keep to your point.
15. If you are asked a question that you cannot answer immediately, tell the questioner that you will get back to him or her with a solid answer promptly.
16. Thank the chair and committee for hearing your testimony. Tell them you are available for comments or questions.

## Providing Testimony for a Regulatory Hearing

When providing comments in writing or as written/oral testimony at a hearing, it is important to follow these guidelines:

- Be transparent about your identity, background, and representation status; that is, be clear about whether comments/testimony represent an organization's position or your own.
- Be specific regarding whether the position you are representing is in support of or in opposition to the regulation. Give examples using brief scenarios or experiences when possible.
- Make sure that there is a body of credible evidence to back up your position. Explain major points using common language; avoid nursing/medical jargon.
- Know the agency's position and respond to those concerns.
- Know the opposition's position and respond to those concerns.
- Convey a willingness to negotiate or compromise toward mutually acceptable resolutions.
- Demonstrate concern for the public good rather than self-interest.
- Be brief and succinct. Limit your remarks to one or two pages. Regulatory agencies may limit the number of minutes for oral testimony; 5 minutes is average.

## Attending an Interested Parties Meeting

Some governmental agencies may invite people or organizations who have a vested interest in an issue within the agency's control to come together to discuss pros and cons of an issue. Rather than appear at an "official" meeting of the agency where specific protocols limit who can speak, an "interested parties" gathering is more informal and encourages open discussion. Time is usually not restricted, and give-and-take is expected. Be alert to notices of these meetings—attendees often work out solutions to problems before legislative or regulatory language is crafted. The agency may require you to sign up or let them know before the meeting if you will be attending and speaking. Your input can be critical.

Regulatory agencies charged with public protection are more likely to address concerns that deal with how the public may be harmed or benefited rather than concerns that give the impression of turf protection and professional jealousy. Demonstrate support for your position by asking colleagues who represent a variety of organizations, professions, and interests to submit comments; interprofessional solidarity projects a powerful message. When a significant number and variety of professionals and organizations form a coalition around a single issue, their collaboration demonstrates an elevated degree of concern and a high level of commitment toward finding a solution. In this way, the volume and breadth of interest expressed in a proposed regulation can serve as the deciding factor in assisting an agency to assess support or nonsupport for the proposed regulation.

## Participating in Public Comment Periods (Influencing Rule Making)

The U.S. federal government requires all agencies to post proposed rules to the *Federal Register* (www.federalregister.gov) and provide for public commentary to be collected for a specific time interval. The agency will summarize all comments and publish the summary in the *Federal Register* prior to adopting a final rule. Professional nurses are extremely well positioned to provide public comments on proposed rules and regulations affecting healthcare delivery, patient care, working conditions for nurses, and many other aspects of the healthcare universe that are subject to regulation.

An excellent site for participation is located at www.regulations.gov. On this site, you may search for regulations by keyword, by date, by agency of origin, and by category.

### Tips for Submitting Effective Comments

A comment can express simple support or dissent for a regulatory action. However, a constructive, information-rich comment that clearly communicates and supports its claims is more likely to have a positive impact on regulatory decision making.

The following tips are meant to help the public submit comments that have an impact and help agency policymakers improve federal regulations:

- Read and understand the regulatory document on which you are commenting.
- Be concise, but support your claims.
- Base your justification on sound reasoning, scientific evidence, and/or how you will be impacted.

- Address tradeoffs and opposing views in your comment.
- There is no minimum or maximum length for an effective comment.
- The comment process is not a vote: One well-supported comment is often more influential than a thousand form letters.
- Attempt to fully understand each issue. If you have questions or do not understand a part of the regulatory document, you may ask for help from the agency contact listed in the document.
- If a rule raises many issues, do not feel obligated to comment on each one. Instead, select those issues that concern and affect you the most and/or you understand the best.
- If you disagree with a proposed action, suggest an alternative (including not regulating the issue at all), and include an explanation and/or analysis of how the alternative might meet the same objective or be more effective.
- Identify your credentials and experience that may distinguish your comments from others. If you are commenting in an area in which you have relevant personal or professional experience (e.g., registered nurse, APRN, scientist, attorney, hospital executive, parent or relative of a person the rule will affect), say so.
- You may provide personal experience in your comment, as may be appropriate. The stories every nurse has to share can be powerful.
- Include examples of how the proposed rule would impact you negatively or positively.
- Keep a copy of your comment in a separate file. This practice helps ensure that you will not lose your comment if you have a problem submitting it using the web form.

## Submitting Form Letters

Organizations often encourage their members to submit form letters designed to address issues common to their membership. Many in the public mistakenly believe that a submitted form letter constitutes a "vote" regarding the issues concerning them. Although public support or opposition may help guide important public policies, agencies make determinations for a proposed action based on sound reasoning and scientific evidence rather than on a majority of votes.

Visit www.regulations.gov/docs/Tips_For_Submitting_Effective_Comments .pdf for more information on submitting effective comments.

## Writing Letters of Support for Legislation/Confirmation

### Courtesy of Catherine Moore

Letters of support should document the appointment candidate's primary area of practice, contributions to professional and community service, and delineate involvement in local, state, and national organizations. A letter from the employer is recommended, as both an indication of the employer's willingness to support time away from work to fulfill the responsibilities of the position during the term of office and as an endorsement of the candidate's professional merit. A personal letter from the appointment candidate should include the rationale for volunteering to serve on the particular board or commission, *evidence of a good match between the individual's expertise and the board or commission purpose*, and expression of clear interest in public service. A specific application form may be required (often found on the governor's website), and a résumé or curriculum vitae should be attached. Appointment decisions include consideration of an individual's potential contributions to the work of the board or commission. This kind of public service requires a substantial time commitment, so it is wise to speak to other board members or the executive director/agency administrator to determine the extent of that commitment.

## How to Write an Op-Ed

A brief history: *Op-ed* is an abbreviation for "opposite the editorial page" (although it is often mistaken for "opinion-editorial"). This sort of newspaper article expresses the informed opinions of a named writer (often an expert) who is usually unaffiliated with the newspaper's editorial board. An op-ed differs from an editorial that is usually unsigned and written by the newspaper's editorial board members. An op-ed is also distinct from a "letter to the editor," in which a reader responds to a previously written article. The first modern op-ed page was created in 1921 by Herbert Swope of *The New York Evening World*; he realized that the page opposite the editorials was "a catchall for book reviews, society boilerplate, and obituaries." Swope explained:

> It occurred to me that nothing is more interesting than opinion when opinion is interesting, so I devised a method of cleaning off the page opposite the editorial, which became the most important in America . . . and thereon I decided to print opinions, ignoring facts. (Meyer, 1990, p. xxxvii).

Beginning in the 1930s, radio began to threaten the primacy of print journalism, a process that later moved even more quickly with the rise of television. To combat this trend, major newspapers such as *The New York Times* and *The Washington Post* began including more openly subjective and opinionated journalism, adding more columns, and growing their op-ed pages. Today, digital blogs and social media threaten print media as the preferred method for obtaining information and forming opinions.

Op-eds are an excellent way for individuals, organizations, businesses, and institutions to articulate a unique position on a particular issue. Think of an op-ed as persuasive writing in its most compelling form. *It is not simply educational—it must offer a solution to an issue that has a political solution.* Unlike a letter to the editor, an op-ed combines an influential opinion with facts, figures, and examples to deliver a thoughtful viewpoint to the thought leaders who often read a newspaper's opinion pages. These articles are also the "bread and butter" of online media outlets, such as *HuffPost*, *Daily Caller*, and *The Health Care Blog*. Critical to the success of an op-ed is to write about a topic that is timely and on the public's radar. Prior to attempting to write an op-ed, you should read op-eds in the newspaper, journal, or digital source to which you plan to submit your own article to get a sense of what opinions already have been expressed.

Newspapers have policies on how to submit articles to their opinion page, and most limit the length to 500 to 750 words. The length limit is also a "suggested" length: Editors have a certain amount of space to fill, so an article that is too short or too long is unacceptable. Digital editors usually require a head shot of the author and a very short biographical sketch, so include this material as an attachment. The email to the editor, with the op-ed attached, should be written as a brief note (in a letter format) pitching your writing. Use an email address that you use frequently and tag the email to give you a receipt notice.

"Striking while the iron is hot" is essential for op-eds. For this reason, writing an op-ed ahead of an event, holding it until you see the right time, and submitting it as an event unfolds may be your best assurance of getting it published. For example, if the Nobel Prize is awarded for research into the physics of brain injury, it is timely to submit your op-ed on why the legislature needs to pass a law regarding tackle football in pee-wee leagues. Your op-ed about violence against nurses in emergency departments is timely if the legislature is debating workplace violence. Right after the president orders a bombing run on a chemical factory in Syria is not the time to try to get your op-ed on legislative funding for diabetes education published; your article will not find space on the op-ed page.

As a professional nurse, you have expertise that nonclinicians (most people) do not have. You have experiences that you can draw on to illustrate problems in the healthcare system and the need for government intervention.

Good sources for more help writing an op-ed can be found at www.umass.edu/pep/sites/default/files/how_to_write_an_oped-duke_2.pdf, the *New York Times* at www.nytimes.com/2004/02/01/opinion/and-now-a-word-from-op-ed.html, and The Op-Ed Project at www.theopedproject.org. Also see **Table 12-1** for steps for writing an effective op-ed.

# Twitter as a Tool to Influence Policy and Politics

"Thinking we're only one signature away from ending the war in Iraq." With this message in April 2007, then-Senator Barack Obama began the very first Twitter campaign for president and, in the process, launched one of the first demonstrations of the power of the social media platform to influence politics and political debate. Obama's first tweet came little more than a year after Twitter founder Jack Dorsey's first tweet on March 21, 2006. Since then, Twitter has grown into a force that bolsters grassroots conversations, disrupts the top-down nature of political leadership and thought, and gives voice to groups usually hidden on the political periphery.

Social media comprise a critical exchange of political mobilization and socialization. Additionally, social media have been shown to be effective in influencing political actions and attitudes of individuals. Twitter is a microblogging site that has become a paramount tool in politics and political campaigns and is considered as the third largest social networking site. Twitter content may consist of news, opinions, daily activity updates, political issues, government policies, and community activities. For instance, politicians often use Twitter to disseminate information, accommodate aspirations, and also interact with the wider community. It is well-acknowledged during a political campaign that

**Table 12-1** Four Steps for Writing an Effective Op-Ed

| | |
|---|---|
| **Step 1:** Identify your topic. | ■ Select an area that you know a lot about, feel passionate about, and have a policy solution for *or* in which the public would benefit from reading your persuasive opinion.<br>■ Timeliness: Is your topic current? Does it have broad appeal to those who will read the blog, newspaper, or journal? |
| **Step 2:** Begin crafting the first draft. | ■ Establish your credibility by stating your credentials and declaring your expertise. Do not forget that you are also a mother/father, daughter/son, sibling, and so on; this role may also add credence to your opinions.<br>■ Use a "grabber": The first paragraph must grab the reader's attention within 10 seconds.<br>■ Use active voice.<br>■ Use a cost–quality–access framework.<br>■ Explain the scope of the problem:<br>　• How it affects the public or a population or community. Use data and statistics, if available.<br>　• Use a poignant, heart-wrenching personal story, if applicable.<br>　• Identify stakeholders who disagree with you; describe why they disagree and inoculate their argument(s).<br>　• Identify ethical dilemmas as appropriate.<br>　• Identify any health or healthcare disparity issues.<br>■ Specify policy-based solutions:<br>　• Include evidence or science on why this policy solution is helpful.<br>　• Be *highly specific* and accurate in describing which sphere of government is involved and which action needs to be taken.<br>　• Offer policy solutions that nongovernment sectors (industry) can adapt to solve the problem.<br>■ Make a call to action: Describe one or more actions that readers can take today to solve this problem. Direct your writing to excite the readers by explaining and clearly linking the policy problems to practical solutions. Make the readers feel compelled to actively support the policy solution.<br>■ Predict what may happen if the problem is not fixed. |
| **Step 3:** Edit your first draft. | ■ Let your first draft rest. After you have walked away from the writing for a few hours, reread it and edit it for clarity and succinctness. Eliminate medical jargon. Perhaps have a nonclinician friend read it for understanding.<br>■ Clarity: Ask yourself, "Is it clear what I'm asking the reader to do?" |
| **Step 4:** Double-check to avoid common errors. | ■ Follow all instructions: Do not go over the word limit established for the targeted publication.<br>■ Permission: Do not mention your employer unless you have permission to do so. If you work where there is a communications or public relations department, check in with it (or read the website) to assure yourself of any rules pertaining to work-related stories. Do not violate Health Insurance Portability and Accountability Act (HIPAA) rules. Even with these restrictions, most nurse stories for a large market can be written and scrubbed of wording that may be a violation of institutional policies. If you meet resistance from your employer but believe your story should be shared, contact the editor of the publication and seek help in writing the piece in such a way that will be acceptable to all parties. |

the image or personality of a candidate takes precedence over jobs, issues, or qualifications in the evaluation of a politician by the public.

Twitter, as a platform, is distinctive due to its collaborative nature and story-changing and story-evolving environment, which leads to more interactive agenda setting for candidates and their followers. Twitter is good for a story (with or without verified sources) on very quick notice, which is quite difficult for conventional media platforms such as newspaper and television. According to social media statistics, in 2019 about 45% of the world's population (3.5 billion people) used social media: 70% of all marketers cited social media as their go-to network for engaging with customers (Mohsin, 2020). Fast-moving and so simple to use, Twitter is arguably the easiest social following to grow from scratch. So, how do *you* gain traction on Twitter to influence policy?

**Amy Anderson**
@AmyAndersonDNP

COVID-19: Lessons Learned and Path Ahead freedomandvalues.com/covid-19- lesso... via freedomandvalues.com

COVID-19: Lessons Learned and Path Ahead | The Heritage Fo...
Foreword Introduction Health Policy COVID-19 Virus: What You Need to Know Saving Lives: Targeted Health Care Policies to ...
🔗 FreedomandValues

12:38 PM · Oct 30, 2020 ·

Reproduced with permission from Amy Anderson.

1. *Tweet frequently*. Three to seven tweets per day maximizes engagement.
2. *Optimize your posting time*. Find out the best times to post on social media. For example, brands typically see the most engagement during weekdays in the early and late afternoons. There are services, such as Sprout, that can help you get your posts sent out at the best time.
3. *Post visual content*. Infographics are shared three times more often than any other type of image on Twitter. If you have some compelling data to share with the world, go for it. Video content is six times more likely to be shared than a typical text-based tweet.
4. *Use hashtags*. Think of hashtags as a way to make your posts searchable. Hashtags are a combination of keywords or phrases preceded by the # symbol, excluding any spaces or punctuations. For example, if you put the # symbol in front of the words "social media," it becomes a hashtag #socialmedia. According to data and best practices on how to use hashtags (Zote, 2020), tweets with at least one hashtag receive 12.6% more engagement than those without them. What does it mean for a Twitter hashtag to become "trending?" Twitter trends are found on the "What's happening" sidebar on desktop, or the search tab on mobile, and show the topics that are currently picking up momentum and

Twitter as a Tool to Influence Policy and Politics **305**

driving the conversation on Twitter. These topics, news stories, and popular hashtags are selected based on global trends, regional ones, or related by Twitter's algorithm to an individual's own interests, depending on user settings.

> **Nancy Short** @ProfShort · Aug 30
> 🏛 Join me and make sure our election runs smoothly!
> 🗳 Prevent voting location closures and long lines at the polls.
> ▶ votevote.org
> #VoteVote
>
> > **VoteVote**
> > America is facing a record shortage of poll workers this year due to the coronavirus. Sign up now to mak...
> > 🔗 votevote.org

5. *Engage with replies, retweets, and tags.* Regularly engaging with other users via tagging, retweeting, and replying immediately lets new followers know that you are human (about 15% of Tweets are by bots) and gets more eyes on your content. You might consider giving someone a Shout Out on Twitter; they might return the favor. Any combination of tagging, retweeting, and replying does not have to take long but is essential to letting those potential followers know you are active.

6. *Create an inviting profile.* Your profile should include a photo, relevant tags, industry keywords, and location information. Your profile should offer an indication of your personality. Giving your followers a sense of who you are is always a plus.

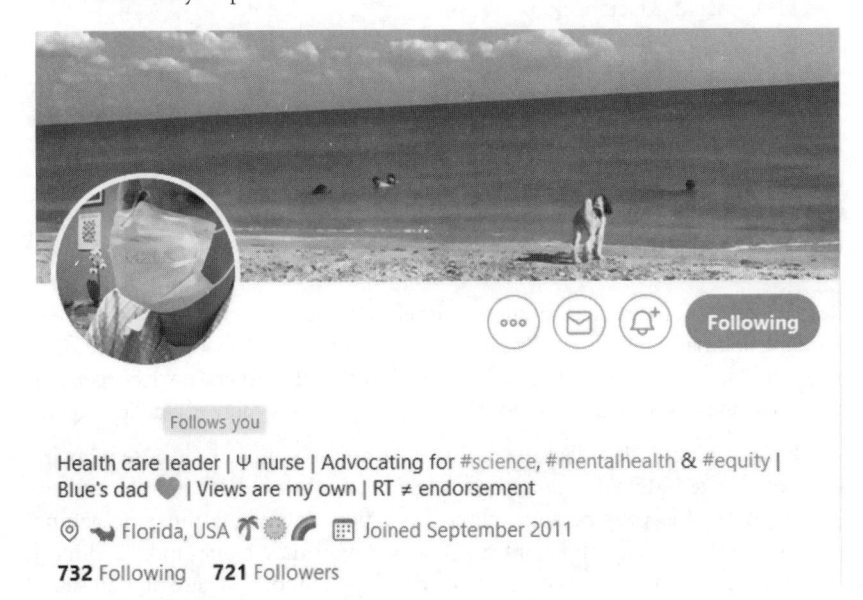

Follows you

Health care leader | Ψ nurse | Advocating for #science, #mentalhealth & #equity | Blue's dad 💙 | Views are my own | RT ≠ endorsement

📍 🐕 Florida, USA 🏖🌊🐾 📅 Joined September 2011

**732** Following    **721** Followers

Reproduced with permission from John Repique.

7. *Identify followers within your network.* Syncing your contact list to Twitter can help you tap into your existing network of people most likely to follow you. If your synced contacts are on Twitter, your account has a higher chance of showing up as a suggestion under the "Who to Follow" section.
8. *Draw in followers outside of Twitter.* Winning more Twitter followers means promoting your profile beyond the platform. Include a link to your social accounts on-site. There are many social button plug-ins via WordPress if you are interested in doing the same. Keep in mind that if you are directing Twitter viewers to your personal social media accounts, these accounts should reflect your political or policy viewpoint and not be littered with cat videos or pictures of your children. For example, the North Carolina Nurses Association attracts followers by advertising four social media accounts.
9. Always know and follow the operational guidelines and policies of your employer. Some employers forbid any posts to social media related to work or working conditions.

Soon, you will be using popular hashtags such as #nurse, #nursing, #nursepractitioner, #aprn, #healthcare, #nursecollab, #nurseproblems, #rnchat, #nurseentrepreneur, #hcr, #ptsafety, and gaining followers.

## Recommended Nonpartisan Twitter Feeds for Fact Checking

Alliance for Health Policy: @AllHealthPolicy

American Nurses Association: @ANA

Commonwealth Fund: @Commonwealthfnd

CSPAN: @CSPAN

Fact Check: @factcheckdotorg

Kaiser Family Foundation Health News: @KHNews

Politifact: @Politifact

RAND Congressional: @RAND_OCR

## Growing From a Novice to an Expert in Policy and Politics

Readers will find themselves at different levels of knowledge and skill with understanding and navigating the political arena. How can you move forward in knowledge and skill to become effective? A modification of Benner's novice-to-expert model (Benner, 1984) can guide your journey to becoming more of a policy expert.

1. **Novice stage.** All of us were at this stage at one point. Even those who are now elected Members of a legislature. You might not have time or interest to go outside your personal clinical practice. You cannot imagine getting involved in policy and politics. However, you may come upon a clinical problem that is just too irritating or riveting to ignore. Where do you start?

Join your professional association, such as the American Nurses Association and the state and local affiliates or a specialty organization. You immediately will begin to receive newsletters, email, publications, notices, and continuing education (CE) offerings that touch on political and policy issues.
2. **(Advanced) Beginner.** You already are a member of a nursing organization, but you have focused on issues other than the policy platform (e.g., bylaws, conventions, nurse awards). Turn your thoughts to issues that may be outside your comfort zone. Are there resources such as brochures or policy briefs available?
    - Is there research that you have never tapped that could expand your knowledge? Rethink your involvement in the organization and make it work for you. Those who staff nursing organizations/associations are helpful for answering questions, directing you to resources, inviting you to meetings, etc. It will not take long before you have a handle on the important issues and nursing's perspective. And—you will be developing a network of colleagues with whom you can discuss, argue, and plan.
    - If just getting started is stopping you, look for 1- to 3-day conferences where you can gain skill and expand your network.
    - Parliamentary procedure is an important skill set that everyone can put to use. It is used by most groups as they conduct their meetings. A basic knowledge of parliamentary procedure can make the group decision process more orderly and can make the meeting run more smoothly. Parliamentary procedure is still used because state laws use it, and most groups still have bylaws that say they will follow a certain parliamentary authority. If your organization's bylaws require adherence to parliamentary procedure, you have to use it. At this step in your development as a policy expert, learn basic parliamentary procedures such a making a main motion or subsidiary motions (tabling, amending, or calling the question) and other important aspects of maintaining order and equity.
3. **Competent.** You are revving up your understanding of policy and politics. You can get involved by participating in a policy project, serving on a policy analysis/research team, and/or serving or chairing the legislative committee of an organization. You might begin visiting with policymakers (at their local offices) and developing relationships. If a policymaker knows you by name, they are more likely to call upon you to answer questions related to nursing and health care. At this stage you are reading widely about policy and politics on a regular basis. You probably find yourself explaining complex issues to your colleagues and family. You are seeking boards, commissions, and other policy-related groups in which to volunteer for service (e.g., local board of public health).
4. **Proficient.** By this stage, you are gaining experience in communicating your issue. This is the time to put yourself out there and make presentations to others about policy issues. You are able to find information about policy and politics easily and you discern bias quickly. You have met with a policymaker to advocate for an issue. You may have provided testimony to a legislative or city council group. You avidly follow political news and are reading policy articles without feeling intimidated. You do not have to know everything about every health issue. The important point is to

become the contact for your policymaker (and staff) so that when an issue emerges, *you* are the person the official turns to for information. You may not be the appropriate person (i.e., the issue may not be in your practice area), but you have a network and can find the appropriate person quickly. The relationship is what counts.
- You have begun writing and submitting/publishing op-eds and articles about policy and politics. You probably donate money to political action groups who support your views and values.
- You may be an elected/appointed leader on the board of a nursing organization or a public commission. This experience includes learning parliamentary procedure, board management issues, financial guidelines for organizations, and establishing yourself as a leader.

5. **Expert.** By the time you have passed through stages 1 through 4, you have become more sophisticated and comfortable. You know your own strengths, can articulate your position, and will have established a relationship with a policymaker. The more you do this, the easier it becomes, and the sharper you will become in making your point and countering opposition. By this time, you also will be part of a team of like-minded health professionals that has a track record of success in bringing problems to the attention of policymakers, in helping them find solutions (often by coming up with reasonable compromises), by helping them design policies, and by helping or actually implementing and evaluating policies and programs. You regularly attend campaign get-togethers to meet your favorite politicians. They know they can count on you for monetary support and expert guidance on specific healthcare issues. You have a strong network of colleagues in policy and politics.

# Wielding Parliamentary Procedures to Influence Policy

Have you ever sat through a meeting that was too long because the guidelines for conducting the meeting were either ignored or not known? How comfortable are you with the rules used to manage meetings? According to the National Association of Parliamentarians (2021):

> Parliamentary procedure, or parliamentary law, refers to the *rules of democracy*—that is, the commonly accepted way a group of people come together, present and discuss possible courses of action, and make decisions. Fundamentally, parliamentary procedure defines how groups of people, no matter how formal or informal, can most effectively meet and make decisions in a fair, consistent manner—and make good use of everyone's time.

Many registered nurses learn basic parliamentary procedure by participating in professional associations, such as the American Nurses Association and its state and district affiliates, or fraternal or civic groups, such as Lions or Kiwanis. Faculty in educational institutions rely on parliamentary procedures, as do government entities.

Most parliamentary procedure is based on *Robert's Rules of Order*, a compendium of rules that direct the conduct of members of a deliberative group. The most recent authoritative version is the newly revised 12th edition (Robert et al., 2020). It is important to be familiar with the current edition. If you are a committee or board chair or just a member (not a chair) of a group, you can move a group through a business session more smoothly if you use the rules.

Where can you learn the rules or become more proficient in their use? Buy the book! However, unless you have a lot of time and concentration, the 714 pages in the 12th edition may be a bit intimidating. YouTube offers dozens of videos, but watch out, most are based on old versions of *Robert's Rules*, or they do not state which version they are using. If the date of the YouTube video is before late 2020, then the content is not current. Participating in a group that uses *Robert's Rules of Order* is an effective way to learn the rules by observing, emulating, asking, and absorbing.

The following are the most frequently used rules that you should be familiar with:

- **Minutes of the preceding meeting.** It is *not* necessary to ask for a motion to approve minutes. It is acceptable to ask if there are any corrections to the minutes and, if there are no corrections, the chair declares that the minutes are approved as read (an actual reading may be dispensed with). If there are changes, they may be accepted by consensus; if there are objections, there must be amendments to change the minutes.
- **Motions.** To put forth an idea to the group, you must make a motion and have it seconded. The motion is debatable, amendable, needs a majority vote to pass, and can be reconsidered. For example, "I move that we adopt a dog as a mascot for our program." Another group member will say "second" to move the motion forward. Note that the proper wording is to "move" an idea, not "to make a motion."
- **Amendments.** To alter a motion, you must amend it. Amendments must be resolved before a main motion can be discussed further. Discussion must be limited to the content of the proposed amendment. For example, "I move to amend the motion by specifying the dog be a dachshund." The amendment must then have a second by another group member. Discussion may then ensue on the amendment, not the original motion. A vote on the amendment must be passed by a simple majority. If there is support for a dachshund being the mascot, a vote will add this particular dog to the original motion. Once an amendment is disposed of (either passed or defeated), the main motion (amended or not) is open for discussion again.
- **Stopping debate.** Debate can be halted by stating, "I call the question." This motion requires a second and a two-thirds vote. This motion immediately closes any further discussion on the motion before the group.
- **Conduct of a meeting (Who can vote?).** In a regular meeting, a quorum is the minimum number of members/attendees necessary to conduct business as stated in an organization's bylaws.

Note that these items are examples and are not exhaustive in their explanations. Always refer to *Robert's Rules of Order* (12th ed.) for the full rule.

If you are deeply interested in becoming an expert, the National Association of Parliamentarians (NAM) offers two credentials: Registered Parliamentarian (RP) and Professional Registered Parliamentarian (PRP) (NAM, n.d.). The American Institute of Parliamentarians (AIP) uses *Robert's Rules* and others, such as *Cannon's Concise Guide to Rules of Order*, and offers the credentials Certified Parliamentarian (CP) and Certified Professional Parliamentarian (CPP), plus an advanced credential for those who are authorized to teach the rules, Certified Professional Parliamentarian–Teacher (CPP-T) (AIP, n.d.).

## Legislative Rules Versus Parliamentary Procedure

Parliamentary procedure should not be confused with other rules that are adopted by legislative bodies. For example, in the U.S. Congress "tabling a motion" results in its permanent removal from discussion. However, "tabling a motion" in most organizations sets the motion aside for the time being. The organization may or may not take the matter back up for discussion or a vote. Congressional power to establish rules derives from Article 1, Section 5 of the U.S. Constitution. Congressional rules may be found online (see Senate Rules & Administration Committee, www.rules.senate.gov/rules-of-the-senate; House of Representatives Committee on Rules, https://rules.house.gov/rules-and-resources. The House of Representative's Committee on Rules offers an online Parliamentary Boot Camp at https://republicans-rules.house.gov/resources/boot-camp.

There is power in knowing how to wield the rules of order for policymaking organizations. It is the difference between being a participant or a spectator. If you have a goal to become an expert policy nurse, you must become comfortable with basic to more complex parliamentary procedures. A good reason for using parliamentary or other formal procedure is to control the direction of the meeting and/or the outcome of a particular matter being discussed. Although this might sound devious, there are times when controversial issues are better simply resolved than expanded.

In addition to reading the new edition of *Robert's Rules of Order*, be sure to check out the following for more information on parliamentary procedure:

- American Institute of Parliamentarians: https://aipparl.org
- National Association of Parliamentarians: www.parliamentarians.org

## Money and Politics

Running for office, supporting health issues, and involvement in the policy arena in general, take time and money. Most professional and business organizations have political action committees (PACs) through which contributions are made to candidates and to support issues that are important to the organization. There are also legal restrictions and processes that the organization must follow, and laws change often. Professional associations will ask you to contribute— perhaps more than once. Political campaigns will do the same. Funds are used for media advertisements, rallies, products (hats, bumper stickers, buttons), staffing offices, and many other activities. Personal and corporate limits specify the amount of money that can be contributed by any one entity at any one time.

Human resources are a huge component of any political campaign. People are needed to staff offices, conduct "lit drops" (distribute brochures and handouts to the public), stuff envelopes, make phone calls, go door-to-door canvassing, arrange for yard signs, and organize projects. Nurses will find myriad opportunities to participate, depending on their available time, availability, interest, and transportation.

Nurses have consolidated their labor force to push for better job security at a time when cash-strapped hospitals are cutting down on costs and personnel. In 2009, three nurses' unions joined to form the National Nurses United, which is outfitted with a PAC and super PAC. Since 1990, the American Association of Nurse Anesthetists has competed with the ANA as the industry's top contributor to federal candidates, committees, and parties. See **Table 12-2**.

**Table 12-2** Top Lobbying Expenses for Nursing Organizations, 2020

| Total for nurses: $5,492,989 Total number of lobbyists reported: 59 ||
| --- | --- |
| Client | Total |
| American Association of Nurse Anesthetists | $310,000 |
| American Association of Nurse Practitioners | $771,764 |
| American College of Nurse-Midwives | $45,000 |
| American Nephrology Nurses Association | $80,000 |
| American Nurses Association | $1,178,925 |
| American Organization for Nursing Leadership | $275,000 |
| AMN Healthcare Services (affiliate: O'Grady Peyton International) | $210,000 |
| Association of Rehabilitation Nurses | $80,000 |
| Emergency Nurses Association | $146,700 |
| International Association of Forensic Nurses | $60,000 |
| National Alliance for Nursing Education | $44,400 |
| National Association of School Nurses | $10,000 |
| National League for Nursing | $53,200 |
| National Association of Pediatric Nurse Associates | $96,000 |
| National Council of State Boards of Nursing | $960,000 |
| Nurse-Family Partnership | $825,000 |
| Oncology Nursing Society | $267,000 |

Data from Open Secrets at https://www.opensecrets.org/industries/lobbying.php?cycle=2020&ind=H1710

According to the Federal Elections Commission, in the 2021–2022 election cycle an individual may give:

- **$2,900** to each candidate or candidate committee per election
- **$5,000** to each political action committee
- A combined total of **$10,000** to state, district, and local party committees per calendar year
- **$36,500** to national party committees per calendar year

## For Serious Thought

- TED Talk by Omar Ahmad, "Political Change with Pen and Paper": www.ted.com/talks/omar_ahmad_political_change_with_pen_and_paper.html
- The Op-Ed Project: www.theopedproject.org
- Read five to eight examples of congressional testimony on the ANA's website: https://p2a.co/ywz5JtS?_ga=2.157587001.2010869788.1604530365-488026692.1604530365
- TED Talk by Bill Davenhall, "Your Health Depends on Where You Live": www.ted.com/talks/bill_davenhall_your_health_depends_on_where_you_live?language=en
- *The Political Determinants of Health* (2020) by Daniel E. Dawes
- Families USA on Health Equity Action for Transformation (HEAT): https://familiesusa.org/join-the-health-equity-action-for-transformation-heat-network/
- Health Resources and Services Administration's Office of Health Equity: www.hrsa.gov/about/organization/bureaus/ohe/
- Campaign for Equity of Care: www.equityofcare.org/
- Congressional Research Service Reports: https://crsreports.congress.gov
- Quadruple Aim (**Figure 12-1**): www.ncbi.nlm.nih.gov/pmc/articles/PMC4226781/

## Recommended E-Subscriptions

- Kaiser Health News updates: Subscribe to this daily email at http://khn.org/email-signup/. Once you enter your email address, you will be given a choice to select the subscriptions you want. Select "First Edition" and KHN Morning Briefing. You also may want to subscribe to Breaking News Alert.
- Track legislation in the current Congress: www.govtrack.us
- Free subscription to Policy Briefs is no longer available; however, an excellent resource is *Health Affairs Health Policy Brief* at www.healthaffairs.org/briefs. The *Health Affairs* podcast is also valuable www.healthaffairs.org/topic/a-health-podyssey?target=topic-multimedia
- Congressional Quarterly (CQ) Roll Call: Sign up for a free trial to track state and federal policy updates at http://cqrollcall.com
- Subscribe to the American Nurses Association's *Daily SmartBrief* at www.smartbrief.com/ana/index.jsp?campaign=story

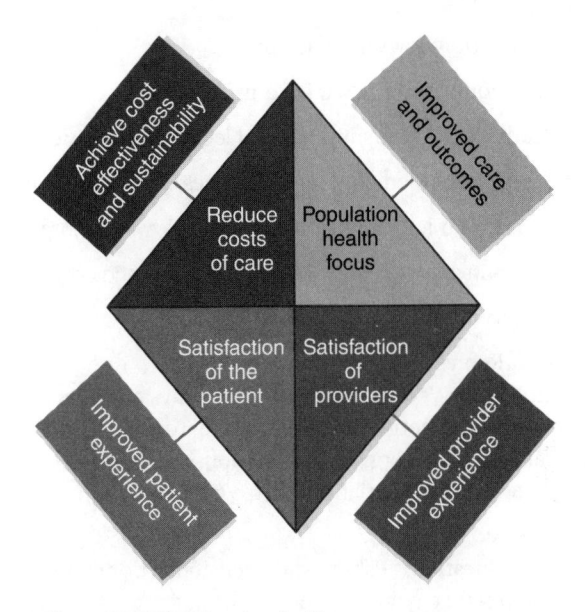

**Figure 12-1** The Quadruple Aim.

- Subscribe to the American Association of Nurse Practitioners' *Daily SmartBrief* at www2.smartbrief.com/signupSystem/subscribe.action?pageSequence=1&briefName=aanp&campaign=in_brief_signup_link&utm_source=brief
- Subscribe to the *New England Journal of Medicine*'s Health Policy and Reform blog at https://cdf.nejm.org/register/reg_multistep_alert.aspx?promo=ONFPAA02&query=lb&utm

# Influential Organizations Affecting Health Policy

American Academy of Applied Science: www.eurekalert.org

American Academy of Nursing: www.aannet.org/home

American Enterprise Institute: www.aei.org

American Nurses Association: www.nursingworld.org

Baldrige National Quality Program: http://baldrigefoundation.org

Cato Institute: www.cato.org

Center for Studying Health System Change: www.hschange.com

Commonwealth Fund: www.commonwealthfund.org

*Federal Register*: www.federalregister.gov

Institute for Healthcare Improvement: www.ihi.org/ihi

Heritage Foundation: www.heritage.org

Kaiser Family Foundation: www.kff.org

Library of Congress for text/summaries of legislation: www.congress.gov

National Academy of Medicine (quality series): https://nam.edu

National Association for Healthcare Quality: www.nahq.org

National Committee for Quality Assurance: www.ncqa.org

National Quality Forum: www.qualityforum.org

U.S. House of Representatives: www.house.gov
- Committee on Ways and Means: http://waysandmeans.house.gov
- Committee of Energy and Commerce (oversees Medicare and Medicaid): http://energycommerce.house.gov
- Committee on Appropriations: http://appropriations.house.gov

U.S. Senate: www.senate.gov
- Health, Education, Labor and Pensions Committee (HELP): http://help.senate.gov
- Finance Committee: http://finance.senate.gov

U.S. Department of Health and Human Services: www.hhs.gov
- Bureau of Health Workforce: https://bhw.hrsa.gov
- Centers for Medicare and Medicaid Services: www.cms.gov
- Medicare Payment Advisory Commission: www.medpac.gov

Urban Institute: www.urban.org/health/index.cfm

White House: www.whitehouse.gov

## References

American Institute of Parliamentarians. (n.d.). *Certified Parliamentarians*. https://aipparl.org/certified

Benner, P. (1984). *From novice to expert: Excellence and power in clinical nursing practice*. Addison-Wesley.

Meyer, K. (1990). *Pundits, poets, and wits*. Oxford University Press.

Mohsin, M. (2020, August 6). *10 social media statistics you need to know* [Blog post]. https://www.oberlo.com/blog/social-media-marketing-statistics

National Association of Parliamentarians. (n.d.). *About*. www.parliamentarians.org/about

Orwell, G. (1946). Politics and the English language. *Horizon, 13*(76), 252–265.

Robert, H. M. III, Honemann, D. H., & Balch, T. J. (2020). *Robert's Rules of Order, newly revised* (12th ed.). Public Affairs.

Zote, J. (2020, August 20). *Twitter hashtags: How to find and use the right trending hashtags*. Sprout Social. https://sproutsocial.com/insights/twitter-hashtags/

# Index

Note: Page numbers followed by b, f and t indicate materials in boxes, figures and tables respectively.

## A

AACN. *See* American Association of Colleges of Nursing
AAG. *See* assistant attorney general
AAN. *See* American Academy of Nursing
AANP. *See* American Association of Nurse Practitioners
access to care, 247–250
activist or cause bias, 34
administrative agencies, 155, 163
administrative procedures act (APA), 147, 155, 158
advanced practice registered nurses (APRNs), 58, 82, 149, 152, 172
   definition of, 1
   history of, 152–154
   policymakers, findings for, 18
   reimbursement for, 163, 165
   scope of practice for, 165
advance premium tax credits, 237
adverse selection, 227, 252
advocacy coalition framework (ACF), 68
Affordable Care Act (ACA), 20, 49, 69, 79, 126, 165, 186, 254
   health insurance market, 235
agency, definition of, 177, 183
Agency for Healthcare Research and Quality (AHRQ), 85–86
agenda setting
   definition, 58
   levels of, 60f
   models and dimensions, 63–71, 64f
AHRQ. *See* Agency for Healthcare Research and Quality
Alliance for Ethical International Recruitment Practices (Alliance), 263, 270
alternative payment models (APMs), 227, 244
American Academy of Nursing (AAN), 115
American Association of Colleges of Nursing (AACN), 184
American Association of Critical Care Nurses, 18
American Association of Nurse Anesthetists, 18
American Association of Nurse Practitioners (AANP), 184
American Counseling Association, 189
American Enterprise Institute (AEI), 48
American Evaluation Association, 189
American Nurses Association (ANA), 18, 115, 117–180, 153, 184
   Code of Ethics, provisions and applications to policy and program evaluation, 190t
American Nurses Credentialing Center (ANCC), 119
American Psychological Association, 189
American Recovery and Reinvestment Act (ARRA), 253
ANA. *See* American Nurses Association
ANCC. *See* American Nurses Credentialing Center
anchoring bias, 38
Andersen's Behavioral Model of Health Services Utilization, 248, 249f
"any willing provider" laws, 163
APA. *See* administrative procedures act, and American Psychological Association
APMs. *See* alternative payment models
APRN Compact, 147, 171
APRNs. *See* advanced practice registered nurses
ARRA. *See* American Recovery and Reinvestment Act
assistant attorney general (AAG), 159
Assistant Secretary of Planning and Evaluation (2016), 233
attribution bias, 38
authority tools, for public policy design, 89

## B

bachelor of science in nursing (BSN), 119
BCBS. *See* Blue Cross and Blue Shield
behavioral dimensions, in public policy design, 92

**315**

belief system, defined, 27, 29
bias
   activist or cause, 34
   anchoring, 38
   attribution, 38
   cognitive, 38
   confirmation, 38
   conservative, 32
   corporate, 34
   defined, 27
   detection of, 35
   framing effect, 39
   gatekeeping, 27, 34–35
   halo effect, 39
   within health care, 40–44
      healthcare provider groups, 40
      health literature, 41–42
      professional conversations, 43–44, 43–44f
      research, 42–43
      scientific studies, 43
   horns effect, 39
   ideological, 27
   liberal, 31–32
   libertarian, 33
   mainstream media, 33
   media, 27
   within media, 28–31
   minimizing, strategies to, 44–45
   within news and media, 28–31, 35–37, 36–37f
   nursing obligations, impact of, 45–49
      fact-checking, 46–47
      influential organizations, 48–49
      political identity, 46
      self-reflection, 45–46
   personal and cognitive, 27, 37–38
   political, 27
   publication, 41
   self-serving, 39
   status quo, 40
big data
   defined, 197, 203
   in healthcare delivery and policy, 201–209
   initiatives, 211–212
   issues, 209–211
   vs. evidence-informed practice, 211
   vs. research evidence, case study, 219
bills becoming laws, process of, 154–155
Blue Cross and Blue Shield (BCBS), 252
board meetings, 158–159
board of nursing (BON), 148. *See also* National Council of State Boards of Nursing; Nurses on Boards Coalition
   board rule-making processes, 161–163, 161t
   definition of, 147
   serving on, 158
BON. *See* board of nursing
bottom-up, defined, 121, 130
Brookings Institution, 48–49
BSN. *See* bachelor of science in nursing
Bush, George W., 165

## C

capacity-building tools, for public policy design, 90
Cato Institute, 49
Caucus, 103–104t
CDC. *See* Centers for Disease Control and Prevention
Centers for Disease Control and Prevention (CDC)
   framework, for evaluation in public health, 181, 182f, 183
Centers for Medicare and Medicaid Services (CMS), 77, 79, 126, 165
   payment framework trajectory, 245f
CER. *See* comparative effectiveness research
certification
   defined, 147
   examinations, 152
   professional, 152
certified nurse midwife, 165
certified registered nurse anesthetist (CRNA), 1, 165
CFR. *See* Code of Federal Regulations
CGFNS. *See* Commission on Graduates of Foreign Nursing Schools International
Children's Health Insurance Program (CHIP), 232
CHIP. *See* Children's Health Insurance Program
Civil Rights Act of 1964, 79
clinical nurse specialist (CNS), 165, 174, 258
CMS. *See* Centers for Medicare and Medicaid Services
CNS. *See* clinical nurse specialist
Code of Ethics
   ANA, provisions and applications to policy and program evaluation, 190t
   for policy and program evaluation, 180
Code of Federal Regulations (CFR), 166
cognitive bias, 38
coinsurance, 227, 235, 236f
Commerce Clause of the U.S. Constitution, 166
Commission on Graduates of Foreign Nursing Schools International (CGFNS), 263
Commonwealth Fund, 48

comparative effectiveness research (CER), 197, 207, 227, 253–254
competency of nurses, monitoring, 159–160
confirmation bias, 38
conservatism, defined, 32
conservative bias, 32
constituents, 97, 112
contextual dimensions, 67
   definition, 57
   examples, 67
   importance of, 67
   list of, 67
copay (copayment), 227, 235, 236f
corporate bias, 34
corporatism, defined, 34
cost sharing, 237
court system, 6
COVID-19 pandemic, 171–172
   finance of health care, 255
   health disparities and, 92
   nurses and, 83, 271, 272f
   personal protective equipment and, 3f
   policy implementation and, 125
   practice waivers during, 173–174
   regulations, 171
   in United States, 92
credentialing, professional, methods of, 150–152
CRNA. *See* certified registered nurse anesthetist
crowdsourcing, 197, 208

## D

data and electronic resources, health care, 201, 202t
database, 197, 205
data governance, 197, 209
data science, 197, 210
data scientists, 197, 204
data set, 197, 200
decision agenda, 59
defense policy, 4
deflection of goals, defined, 121, 129
Department of Defense (DOD), TriCare, 232
dependents target population, 68
design issue, policy, 87–88
deviants target population, 68
DHHS. *See* U.S. Department of Health and Human Services
Digital Bridge Initiative, 205
disproportionate share hospital, 245–246
dissipation of energies, defined, 121, 129
diversion of resources, defined, 121, 129
DOD. *See* Department of Defense

## E

EBP. *See* evidence-based practice
economic costs, 228
economic theory, 229
education policies, 4
EHRs. *See* electronic health records
Eight Factor Model, 249f, 250
EIP. *See* evidence-informed practice
elected officials, relationships with, 22
electronic health records (EHRs)
   APRNs and, 212, 215–216
   registered nurses and, 212, 215–216
Emergency Medical Treatment and Labor Act (EMTALA), 87
Emergency Nurses Association, 18
emergency regulations, federal regulatory process, 163
employer-sponsored health insurance (ESHI), 232, 237
EMTALA. *See* Emergency Medical Treatment and Labor Act
environmental policy, 4
EQ-5D index, 253
ESHI. *See* employer-sponsored health insurance
essential health benefits, 227, 235
e-subscriptions, 312
ethical considerations, during policy and program evaluation, 189–191, 190t
evaluation reports, 177, 182
Evers, Tony, 71
evidence-based practice (EBP), 42, 161, 211
evidence-informed health policy (EIHP) model, 161, 162t
evidence-informed practice (EIP), 211

## F

fact-checking, 46–47
facts, defined, 27
fact sheet, creation of, 293–294
FDA. *See* Food and Drug Administration
federalism, 99
federal poverty level (FPL), 237
*Federal Register*
   public comments and, 299
   purpose of, 166, 167f
federal regulatory process
   emergency regulations, 163
   federal rule making, 166–167, 167f
   healthcare delivery system, regulation in transforming, 167–169
   locating information, 162–163
   need for, 165–173

federal rule making, 166–167, 167f
finance of health care
　adverse selection, 227, 252
　APMs, 244
　CER and, 227, 253–254
　cost for, 254
　COVID-19 pandemic and, 255
　essential health benefits, 227, 235
　healthcare entitlement programs, 239–243, 245f
　health insurance exchanges, 233–235
　health insurance market, 232–238, 233f, 234t
　health outcomes vs. spending, 231, 232f
　information asymmetry, 228, 251–252
　landmark legislation, 256–257
　means testing, 241
　Medicaid expansion, impact of, 259
　Medicare Access and CHIP Reauthorization Act (MACRA) of 2015, 244
　MIPS, 244
　moral hazard, 228, 252
　opportunity costs, 230
　overview, 229–230, 229f
　payment models, 243–244, 245f
　per capita spending, 231
　price transparency, 255
　provider fee and practice changes, 256
　QALYs, 228, 253–254
　spending vs. health outcomes, 231, 232f
　value of BSN education for RNs, 258
527 organizations, 97, 113
Food and Drug Administration (FDA), 230
formal evaluation process, 181, 183
formative evaluations, 181, 183
form letters, public comment periods, 300
FPL. *See* federal poverty level
framing effect, bias, 39
"freedom of choice" laws, 163
*Future of Nursing: Leading Change, Advancing Health, The*, 2, 167

# G

gatekeeping bias, 34–35
　defined, 27, 34
global connectivity of health care
　public policy, nurse involvement in, 274–276
globalization
　definition, 263
　factors affecting out-migration, 270
　and its impact on nursing and health care, 264
　migration of human capital, 268

sustainable development goals, recommendations and actions for, 265–266, 266f
goals, public policy vs., 6
government tools, for public policy design, 89–92
Gross Domestic Product (GDP), 78, 245f

# H

halo effect, bias, 39
HCPs. *See* healthcare provider professionals
health care
　bias and, 40–44
　　healthcare provider groups, 40
　　health literature, 41–42
　　professional conversations, 43–44, 43–44f
　　research, 42–43
　　scientific studies, 43
　data and electronic resources, 201, 202t
Health Care Access Barriers Model, 248, 248f
Health Care and Education Reconciliation Act, 165
healthcare cost curve, 254
healthcare data, difficulty of, 199f
healthcare delivery system, regulation in transforming, 167–169
healthcare disparities, 227, 257
healthcare entitlement programs, 239–243, 245f
healthcare market, 229, 230
healthcare professionals, 251
healthcare provider professionals (HCPs), 1, 4
healthcare reform
　related to clinical practice
　　action taking, 19
　　organizational involvement, 18–19
　　and practice, 9–11, 9f
　　right person to influence, 13–17, 14–16f
healthcare services, electronic access to, 172
health disparities, 77, 92, 228, 250–251
health equity, 228, 251
health finance and health policy intersection, 229f
health-in-all-policies (HiAP), 177
health information technology
　and health policy priorities, 218t
　legislation and initiatives for, 213t
Health Information Technology for Economic and Clinical Health (HITECH) Act, 197
health insurance exchanges (HIXs), 228, 233–235
health insurance market, 232–238, 233f, 234t

health outcomes, healthcare spending and, 231
health policy, 229
 benefits of, 181*t*
 effective, challenges to, 185–191, 186*b*, 190*t*
 for healthcare reform, implications of, 183–185
 and health finance intersection, 229*f*
 influential organizations affecting, 313–314
 nurses' role in, 180
 overview, 181*t*
 processes of, 180–182, 181*t*, 182*f*
 steps in, 182–183
health professions regulation, history of, 152–154
Health Resource Services Administration (HRSA), 115
health services research (HSR), 77, 83, 253
hearings
 providing testimony for, 298
 public rule, 148, 161
Heritage Foundation, 49
HIXs. *See* health insurance exchanges
horns effect, bias, 39
Horoho, Patricia, 82
hortatory tools, for public policy design, 90–91
hospital insurance program, 240
House Nursing Caucus, 22
HRSA. *See* Health Resources and Services Administration
HSR. *See* health services research
human capital, migration of, 263, 268

# I

ICN. *See* International Council of Nurses
ideological bias, defined, 27, 29
ideology, defined, 27, 30
IHS. *See* Indian Health Service
immigration, 267–271
implementation, defined, 121, 123
implementation climate, defined, 121, 127
implementation effectiveness, defined, 121, 124
implementation science, defined, 121, 131
incentive tools, for public policy design, 89–90
Indian Health Service (IHS), 165, 232
infant mortality, 80
informal evaluation, 184
information asymmetry, 228, 251–252
information blocking, 197, 209
information environment, defined, 27, 32

informed consent, 190*t*
infotainment, defined, 27
innovation-values fit, defined, 121, 127
Inpatient Prospective Payment System (IPPS), 245
institutional agenda, 59
interest groups, 97, 113
International Council of Nurses (ICN), 263–264, 265, 267
Internet of Things (IoT), 197, 208
interoperability, 197, 205
interprofessional healthcare workers (IPHCWs), 58, 71
interstate compacts, 172
interstate mobility, 171
IPHCWs. *See* interprofessional healthcare workers
iron triangle, definition, 57, 63, 64*f*, 247*f*

# J

Josiah Macy Jr. Foundation, 169
journalism, defined, 27, 33
journalist, defined, 27, 29
judicial interpretation, 6–7
jurisdiction, 157

# K

Kaiser Family Foundation (KFF), 48, 240
Kingdon model, 64–67, 65*f*, 67
knowledge worker, 200

# L

laws. *See also* legislative process
 implementation of, 154–155
 in policy entity, 4
 public policy vs., 6
learning tools, for public policy design, 91–92
legislation, defined, 97, 106
legislation and politics, policy enactment
 constituents, 111–112
 executive branch, 99–102, 100–102*t*, 101*f*
 funding legislation, 108
 introduction, 98
 judicial branch, 102, 105
 legislative branch, 102, 103–104*t*
 legislative process
  action on bill, 107
  committees, 106–107
  legislation, defined, 106
 legislative staff, 110–111, 111*t*

legislation and politics, policy enactment (*Continued*)
  legislators, 110–111
  nurses, in legislative policy change, 115–116
  power, 108–110, 110*f*
  special interest groups, 112–114
  state and local governments, 105–106
  strategy, political, 114–115
  structure of government, 99
legislation *vs.* regulation, 154–156
legislative language, 77. 84*f*
legislative process. *See also* laws
  action on bill, 107
  committees, 106–107
  legislation, defined, 106
  regulatory process *vs.*, 154–156
legislators, 97, 110
  contacting, 294–295
legislature, 97, 105, 107
liberal bias, 31–32
libertarian bias, 33
licensed practical nurse/licensed vocational nurse (LPN/LVN) educational programs, 149
licensure
  definition and purpose, 147, 150–151
  issues in, 170–172
life expectancy, 80, 180, 186, 231
litigation, 71
lobbyist, 97, 112
LPN/LVN educational programs. *See* licensed practical nurse/licensed vocational nurse educational programs

# M

MACRA. *See* Medicare Access and CHIP Reauthorization Act of 2015
mainstream media bias, 33–34
mandatory reporting, 159–160
meaningful use, definition of, 197, 200
means testing, 228, 241
media
  bias and, 28–31
  defined, 27, 29
  literacy, 27, 29
media bias, defined, 27, 29
media literacy, defined, 27, 29
Medicaid, 78, 242–243
  expansion, economic impact of, 259
  health insurance market and, 232
Medical Expenditure Panel Survey (MEPS), 83
Medicare, 78, 240–242

health insurance market and, 232
reimbursement policies, 163
Medicare Access and CHIP Reauthorization Act (MACRA) of 2015, 244
Medicare Advantage, 165, 240
Medicare Part A, 240
Medicare Part B, 240
Medicare Part C, 240, 241
Medicare Payment Advisory Committee (MedPAC), 246
Medicare Prescription Drug, Improvement, and Modernization Act (MMA), 90, 165
*Medicine's Dilemmas: Infinite Needs Versus Finite Resources*, 247
MEPS. *See* Medical Expenditure Panel Survey
Merit-Based Incentive Payment System (MIPS), 228, 244
Michigan's Department of Licensing and Regulatory Affairs, 148
migration, 267–271
migration of human capital, 263, 268
MIPS. *See* Merit-Based Incentive Payment System
MMA. *See* Medicare Prescription Drug, Improvement, and Modernization Act
model legislation, 77, 82
moral hazard, 228, 252
multistate regulation, 147, 171
mutual recognition model of multistate licensure, 171

# N

National Academy of Medicine, 2, 167
National Conference of State Legislatures, 232
National Council Licensure Examinations (NCLEX), 154
National Council of State Boards of Nursing (NCSBN), 17, 147, 153–154, 171. *See also* board of nursing
National Healthcare Quality and Disparities Reports, 86
national health expenditures in, 243*f*
National League for Nursing (NLN), 18, 153
National Patient-Centered Clinical Research Network (PCORnet), 207
NCLEX. *See* National Council Licensure Examinations
NCSBN. *See* National Council of State Boards of Nursing
news, bias and, 28–31, 35–37, 36–37*f*
New York State Nurses Association (NYSNA), 71

NGO. *See* nongovernmental organization
NLN. *See* National League for Nursing
NMA. *See* Nebraska Medical Association
NoBC. *See* Nurses on Boards Coalition
nongovernmental organization (NGO), 263
North Carolina Association of Nurse Anesthetists, 83
North Carolina General Assembly, 83
North Carolina Nurses Association (NCNA), 83, 116
North Carolina's Nursing Practice Act, 83
notice of proposed rulemaking (NPRM), 166
NP. *See* nurse practitioner
NPAs. *See* nurse practice acts
NPRM. *See* notice of proposed rulemaking
Nurse Aide Registry, 151
nurse informaticist, 198, 204
Nurse Licensure Compact (NLC) model, 171
nurse practice acts (NPAs), 153, 157
nurse practitioner (NP), 1, 165
nurses. *See also* advanced practice registered nurses (APRNs)
  action taking, 19
  bias and, 45–49
    fact-checking, 46–47
    influential organizations, 48–49
    political identity, 46
    self-reflection, 45–46
  education programs, 14
  government regulations, 160–161
  influence health policy, 13–17, 14–16*f*
  involvement in policy decisions, 274–276
  in legislative policy change, 115–116
  in policy implementation, 135
  and policy process, impact in Italy, 274–276
  policy/program evaluation, role in, 180
    for healthcare reform, implications of, 183–185
    processes of, 180–182, 181*t*, 182*f*
    steps in, 182–183
  required skills, 22
  role of, 22
Nurses on Boards Coalition (NoBC), 158–159. *See also* board of nursing
nursing and health care
  factors affecting out-migration, 270
  globalization and its impact on, 264
  migration of human capital, 268
nursing education, to improve involvement in policymaking, 274–276
nursing practice, 3, 9*f*
Nursing Reauthorization Act, 115
Nursing Regulatory Bodies (NRBs), 147, 148
  composition of, 157–158
  rule-making processes, 160–161, 162*t*

## O

objectives, public policy vs., 6
OECD. *See* Organisation for Economic Cooperation and Development
Office of the National Coordinator for Health Information Technology (ONC), 217
Omnibus Budget Reconciliation Act of 1987, 151
Oncology Nurses Society, 18
op-ed (opposite the editorial page), writing, 301–302
opportunity costs, 228, 230
Organisation for Economic Cooperation and Development (OECD), 274
organizational involvement, 18–19
outcome evaluations. *See* program evaluations
out-migration, factors affecting, 270
Outpatient Prospective Payment System (OPPS), 246

## P

PAC. *See* political action committee
path dependency, 68–69
Patient-Centered Outcomes Research Institute (PCORI), 254
Patient Protection and Affordable Care Act. *See* Affordable Care Act
payment models, finance of health care, 243–244, 245*f*
PCORI. *See* Patient-Centered Outcomes Research Institute
PCORnet. *See* National Patient-Centered Clinical Research Network
PCP. *See* primary care provider
personal and cognitive bias, 37–38
  defined, 27
personal values, defined, 27
Pew Health Professions Commission, 150
PICOT, 147, 161
policy
  analysis, 184
  content, 182
  definition, 4
  design, issue, 87–88
  evaluation, definition, 177
  implementation. *See* policy implementation
  implementation of, 182
  instruments, 89–92
  outcome of, 182
  process, 4
    definition, 1
    design, 82–83
    research informing, 83–86

# 322 Index

policy (*Continued*)
    stages of, 79f
    steps in, 8
    as process, 8–9
    stream, 65
    tools, 78, 89
policy enactment, legislation and politics
    constituents, 111–112
    executive branch, 99–102, 100–102t, 101f
    funding legislation, 108
    introduction, 98
    judicial branch, 102, 105
    legislative branch, 102, 103–104t
    legislative process
        action on bill, 107
        committees, 106–107
        legislation, defined, 106
    legislative staff, 110–111, 111t
    legislators, 110–111
    nurses, in legislative policy change, 115–116
    power, 108–110, 110f
    rules and regulations, 112
    special interest groups, 112–114
    state and local governments, 105–106
    strategy, political, 114–115
    structure of government, 99
policy failure, 121, 130. *See also* policy implementation
policy formulation, 78, 124
policy implementation
    conceptual framework, 126–130
    federal and state policy, 124–126
    introduction, 122–124, 123f
    nurses in, 135
    power, 132–135
        dispositional power, 133
        relational power, 133
        structural power, 133
    research *versus* implementation science, 131–132
policy implementation research, 121, 131
policy implications, healthcare data and, 216–217, 216f
policy process, 8–9, 9f, 23–24, 81, 83, 123f, 180f, 198f
    health services research and, 83–86
    impact of nurses in Italy, 274–276
    public opinion and, 86–87
    stages of, 79f
political action committee (PAC), 97, 113
political activism, 19
political agenda, 59, 60f
political bias, defined, 27, 29
political determinants of health (PDoH), 228, 251

political role for nurses, developing, 22
political streams, 65, 66
political system, working with, 22–23
politics
    of clinical practice, 2–4
    defined, 229
    definition, 1, 4
population management, 243
position statements, public policy vs., 6
poverty, 79, 242, 265
power
    political power, 1, 13, 108
        legitmate power, 109
        reward power, 109
        informational power, 109
        coercive power, 109
        referent power, 109
        influences, 110f
    policy implementation and, 132–134
        relational power, 133
        structural power, 133
practice act, 148, 149
practice guidelines, nursing, 153–154, 206
precision medicine, 198, 200
predictive analytics, 198, 210
president pro tempore (U.S. Senate), 98
primary care provider (PCP), 251
problem streams, 65
professional organizations, 18–19
program evaluations
    definition, 177, 179
    design, 177, 181
program outcomes evaluation, defined, 178
progressivism, defined, 31
prospective payment system (PPS), 245
publication bias, 41
public comment periods, 161–162
    form letters, 300
    participating in, 299
    tips for submitting, 299–300
Public Health Emergency of International Concern (PHEIC), 263, 267
public health insurance, 237
Public Health Service Act, 80, 115
public policy
    as an entity, 9–10
    behavioral dimensions in, 92
    bias. *See* bias
    definition, 1, 3
    design
        issues of, 87
        overview, 92–93
        policy instruments (government tools), 89–92
        process, research informing, 83–86

public opinion, research informing, 86–87
global, nurse involvement in, 274–276
political role for nurses, 22–23
process, 8–9, 9f
public rule hearings, 148, 161
punctuated equilibrium theory (PET), 69
push-pull factors, 263, 268

## Q

QALYs. *See* quality adjusted life years
QHP. *See* qualified health insurance plan
quadruple aim, 78, 80, 178
qualified health insurance plan (QHP), 228, 235
qualified health plan, penalties for, 237
quality adjusted life years (QALYs), 228, 253–254
Quality Chasm Series, 167
Quality Payment Program, 244

## R

randomized control trial (RCT), 253
ranking members, 106
rapid cycle quality improvement (RCQI) evaluation, 183
RCQI evaluation. *See* rapid cycle quality improvement evaluation
RCT. *See* randomized control trial
real-world data (RWD), 198, 208
real-world evidence (RWE), 198, 208
recognition, 148, 152
    legislative, 152
    official, 152
registered nurse (RN), 58, 93, 149
    economic value of BSN education for, 258
registration, professional, 148, 151
regulations (rules), 11
    definitions, 2, 6
    and purpose of, 148, 149–150
    implementation of, 155
    issues in, 170–172
    vs. legislation, 154–156
    monitoring, 159–160
    in policy entity, 6
    public policy vs., 6
regulatory process
    health professions, 149–154
    state level, 157
    strengths and weaknesses of, 156
    in transforming healthcare system, 167–169

regulatory responses
    electronic access to healthcare services, 172. *See also* telehealth
    interstate mobility and multistate regulation, 171
    reimbursement, 165
    scope of practice, 165
reimbursement
    for APRNs, 165
    policies, Medicare and Medicaid, 163
    resolutions, public policy *vs.,* 6
risk pool, 228, 232
RN. *See* registered nurse
rule making, influencing, 299–300
rules and regulations. *See* regulations (rules)

## S

scope of practice, for APRNs, 165
self-reflection, 45–46
self-regulation, professional, 153
self-serving bias, 39
Senate Nursing Caucus, 22
SGR. *See* sustainable growth rate
SHOP. *See* small business health insurance options program
sickness insurance, 232
Sigma Theta Tau International, 18
small business health insurance options program (SHOP), 238
small data, 198, 204
SNAP. *See* Supplemental Nutrition Assistance Program
social constructions, 68
social determinants of health (SDoH), 3, 9–10, 186, 251
social media, disease tracking via, 208b
Social Security Act, 79, 245
soft news, 28
speaker of the House (U.S. House of Representatives), 98, 103t
special interest groups, 112–114
SPHM programs. *See* safe patient handling and mobility programs
sponsor/cosponsor, 98, 106
State Bulletin, 162
State Register, 162
state regulatory process, 157
status quo bias, 40
statutes
    definition, 2
    in policy as entity, 4
statutory authority, 148, 149
streams, definition, 58, 64
structural racism, 78, 92

summative evaluation process, 181, 184
"sunshine" laws, 158
Supplemental Nutrition Assistance Program (SNAP), 125
Supremacy Clause of the U.S. Constitution, 166
sustainable growth rate (SGR), 244
symbolic tools, for public policy design, 90–91
systemic agenda, 59

## T

target populations, social construction of, 68
Tavenner, Marilyn, 82
telehealth, 166, 172
testify
 preparing to, 297
 tips on, 297–298
think tank, defined, 48
title, defined, 78
Title VII, 80, 143*t*
Title VIII, 20, 80, 115, 116*f*
top-down, defined, 121, 130
TRICARE, 125
 for Life programs, 232
2020 Triad Statement, 264, 267
Twitter, 35, 208, 302, 304–306

## U

unfunded mandate, 78, 87
unintended consequences, 178, 181
United Nations' Sustainable Development Goals, 265–266, 266*f*
Urban Institute, 48
U.S. Department of Health and Human Services (DHHS), 165
U.S. Department of Veterans Affairs, 170

## V

value, defined, 28
Veterans Health Administration (VHA), 165, 232
VHA. *See* Veterans Health Administration

## W

whistleblowing, 71
WIC program. *See* Women, Infants, and Children program
window of opportunity, definition, 58, 64
workplace safety, case study, 117
World Health Organization (WHO), 264, 266, 267